VOL. 4

ECHOES OF A LIFE LIVED WELL

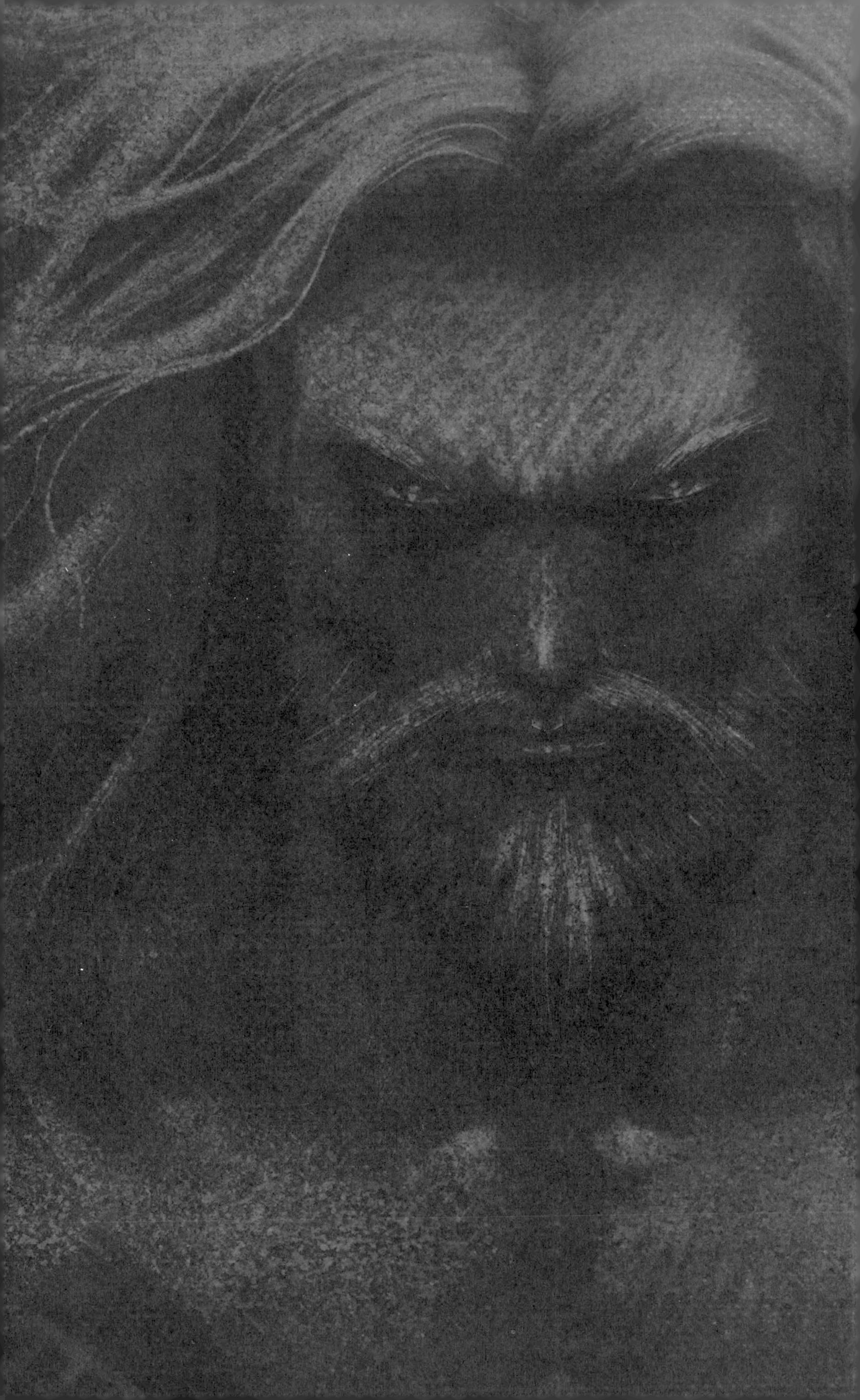

AQUAMAN

ECHOES OF A LIFE LIVED WELL

**KELLY SUE DeCONNICK
JORDAN CLARK**
writers

**MIGUEL MENDONÇA
ROBSON ROCHA
MARCO SANTUCCI**
pencillers

**MIGUEL MENDONÇA
DANIEL HENRIQUES
MARCO SANTUCCI**
inkers

ROMULO FAJARDO JR.
colorist

CLAYTON COWLES
letterer

**ROBSON ROCHA, DANIEL HENRIQUES,
and MARCELO MAIOLO**
collection cover artists

AQUAMAN CREATED BY PAUL NORRIS

SUPERMAN CREATED BY
ND JOE SHUSTER
ARRANGEMENT
Y SIEGEL FAMILY

VOL. 4

ALEX R. CARR ANDREA SHEA Editors – Original Series
JEB WOODARD Group Editor – Collected Editions
REZA LOKMAN Editor – Collected Edition
STEVE COOK Design Director – Books
LOUIS PRANDI Publication Design
SUZANNAH ROWNTREE Publication Production

BOB HARRAS Senior VP – Editor-in-Chief, DC Comics

DANIEL CHERRY III Senior VP – General Manager
JIM LEE Publisher & Chief Creative Officer
BOBBIE CHASE VP – Global Publishing Initiatives & Digital Strategy
DON FALLETTI VP – Manufacturing Operations & Workflow Management
LAWRENCE GANEM VP – Talent Services
ALISON GILL Senior VP – Manufacturing & Operations
HANK KANALZ Senior VP – Publishing Strategy & Support Services
DAN MIRON VP – Publishing Operations
NICK J. NAPOLITANO VP – Manufacturing Administration & Design
NANCY SPEARS VP – Sales
JONAH WEILAND VP – Marketing & Creative Services
MICHELE R. WELLS VP & Executive Editor, Young Reader

AQUAMAN VOL. 4:
ECHOES OF A LIFE LIVED WELL
Published by DC Comics.

DC Comics, 2900 West Alameda Ave.,
Burbank, CA 91505
Printed by LSC Communications,
Owensville, MO, USA. 1/1/21. First Printing.
ISBN: 978-1-77950-588-0

Library of Congress Cataloging-in-Publication Data
is available.

PEFC Certified
This product is from sustainably managed forests and controlled sources
PEFC/29-31-337
www.pefc.org

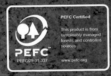

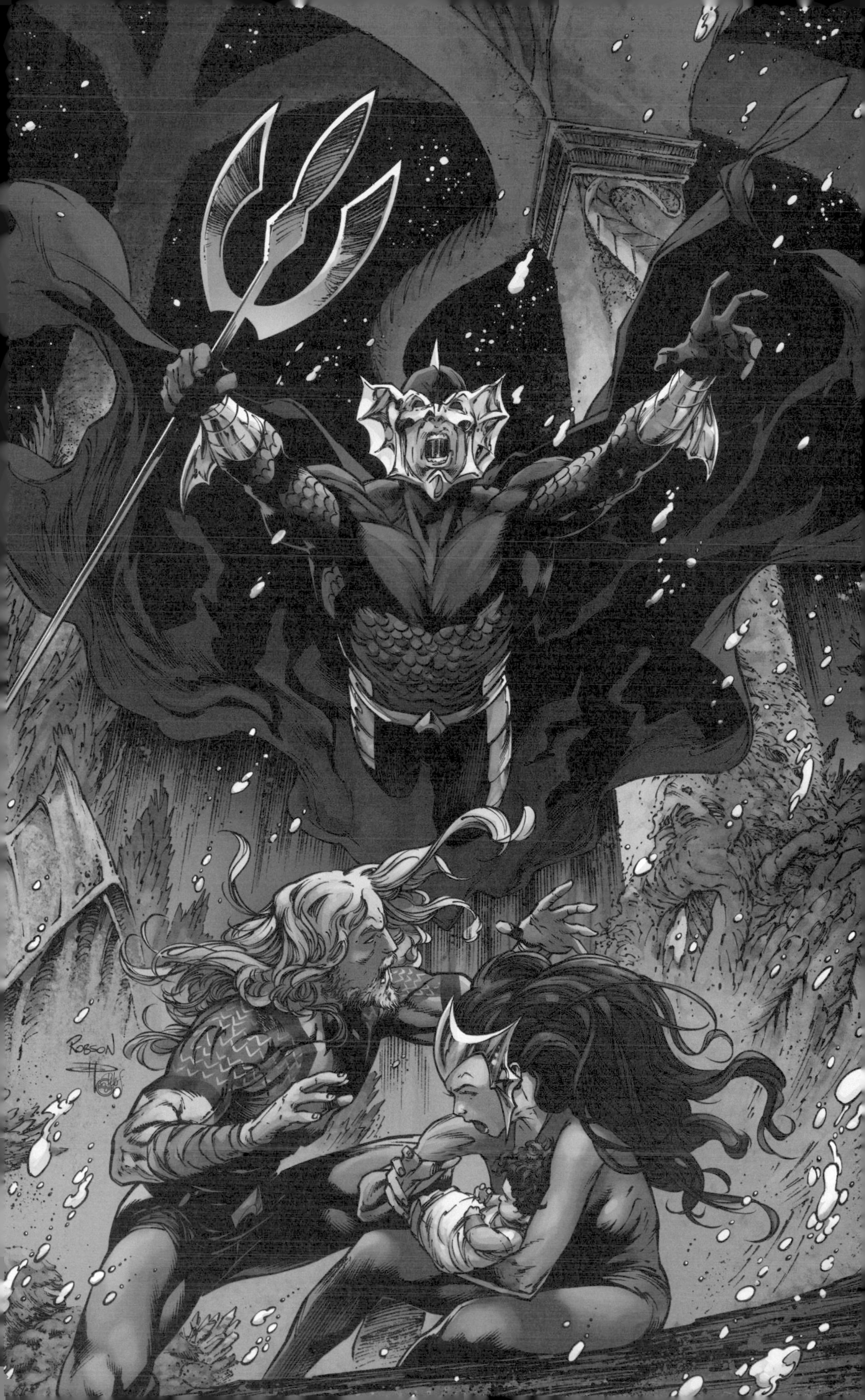
ROBSON

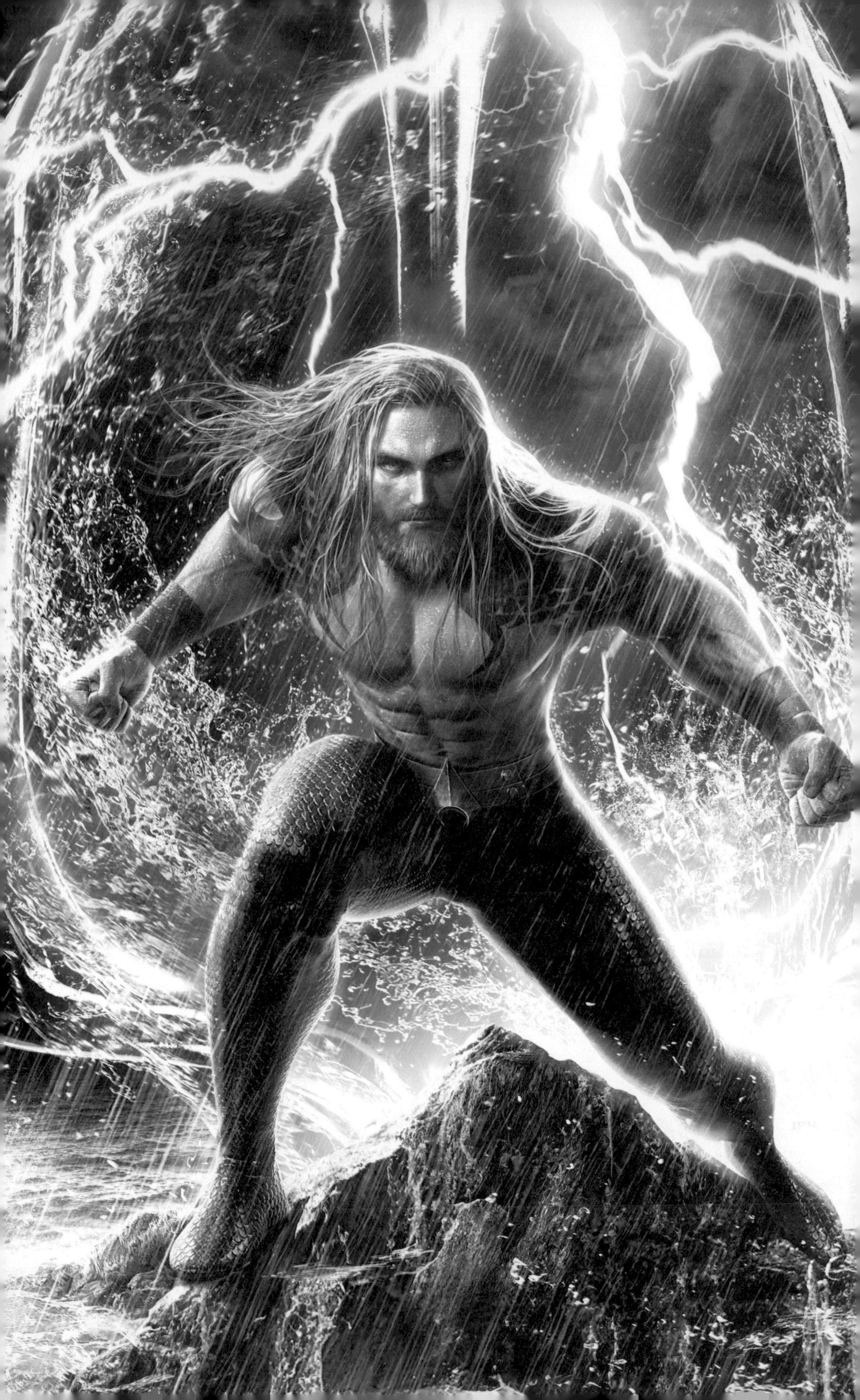

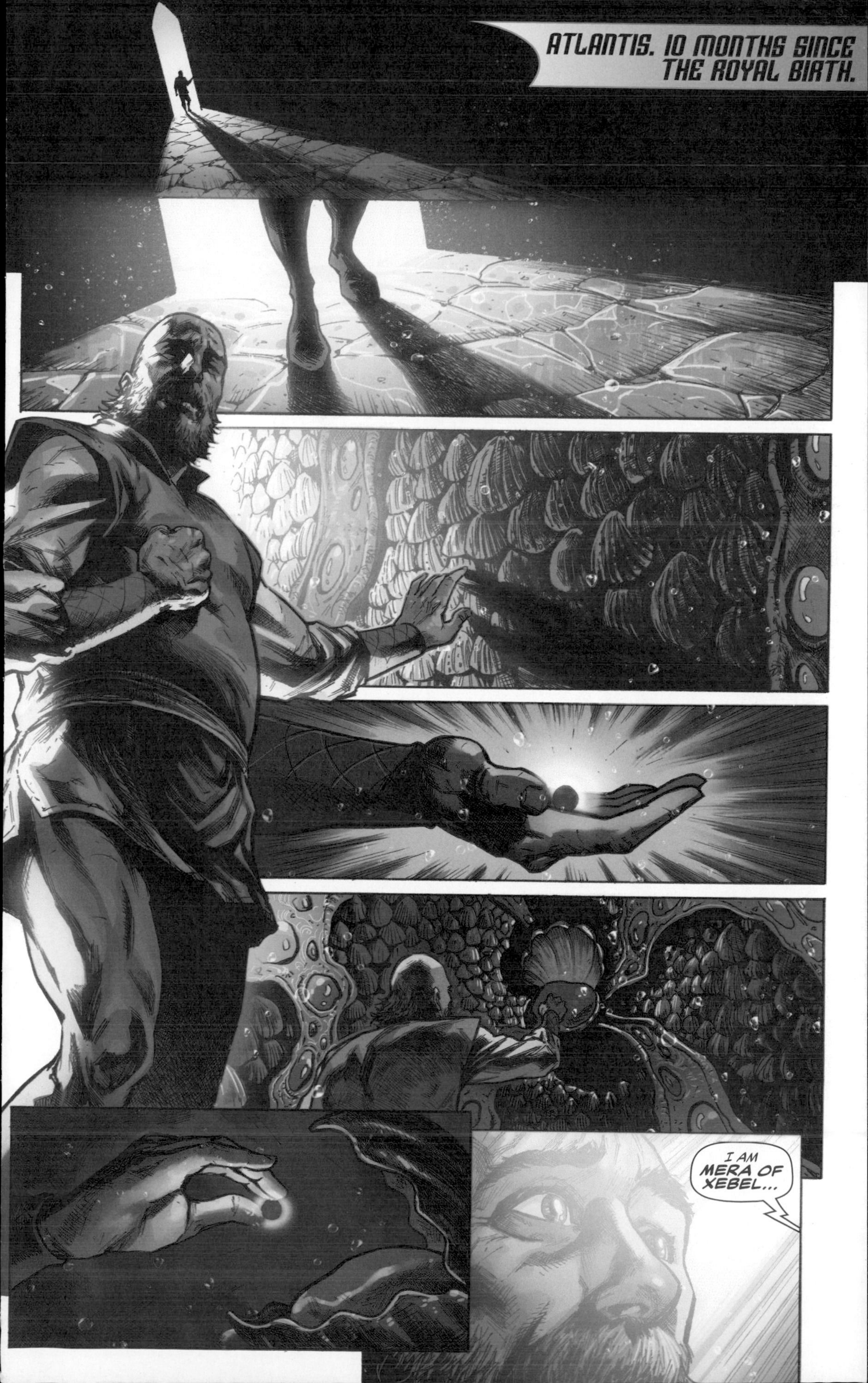
ATLANTIS. 10 MONTHS SINCE THE ROYAL BIRTH.
I AM MERA OF XEBEL...

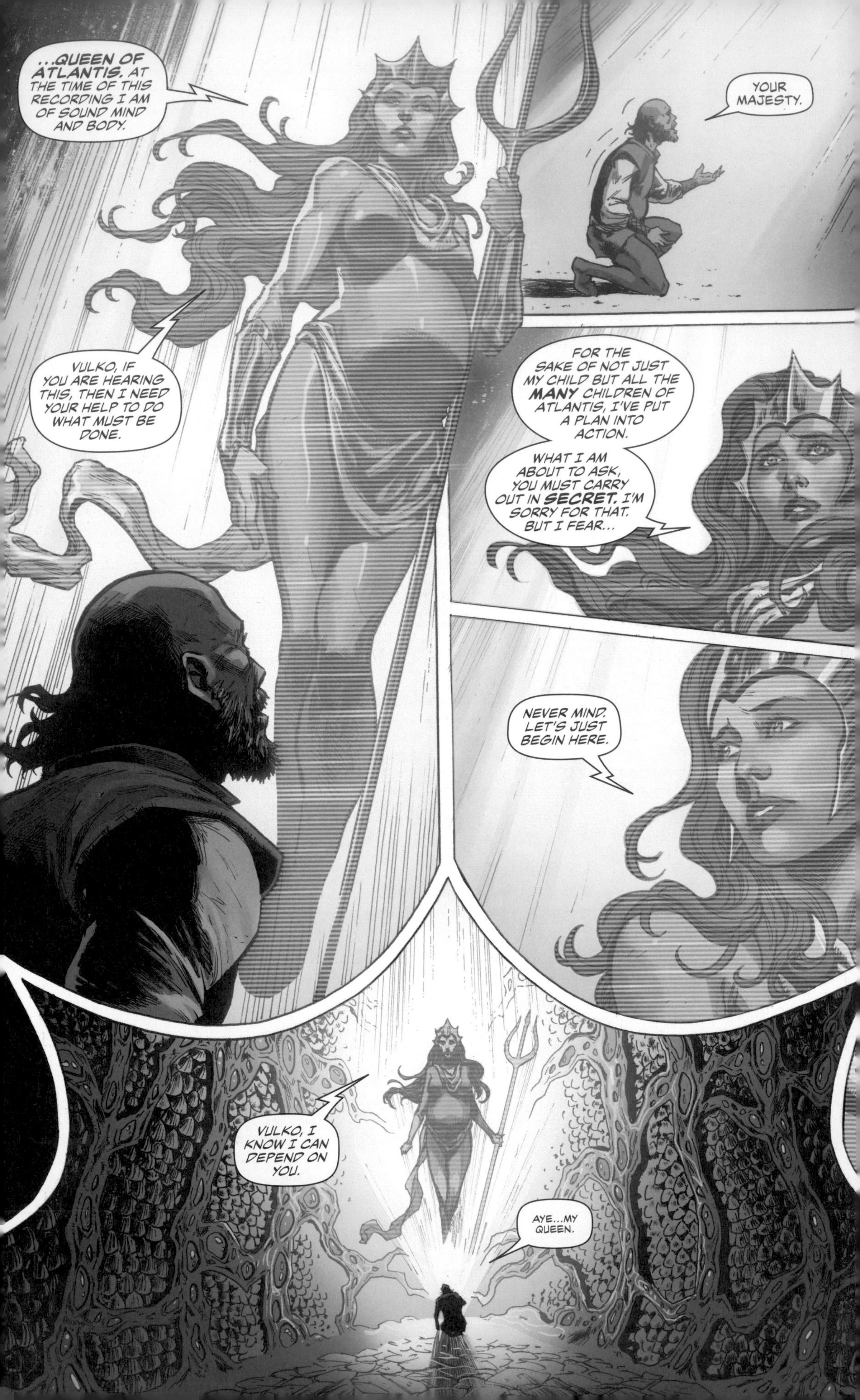
...QUEEN OF ATLANTIS. AT THE TIME OF THIS RECORDING I AM OF SOUND MIND AND BODY.
YOUR MAJESTY.
VULKO, IF YOU ARE HEARING THIS, THEN I NEED YOUR HELP TO DO WHAT MUST BE DONE.
FOR THE SAKE OF NOT JUST MY CHILD BUT ALL THE MANY CHILDREN OF ATLANTIS, I'VE PUT A PLAN INTO ACTION.
WHAT I AM ABOUT TO ASK, YOU MUST CARRY OUT IN SECRET. I'M SORRY FOR THAT. BUT I FEAR...
NEVER MIND. LET'S JUST BEGIN HERE.
VULKO, I KNOW I CAN DEPEND ON YOU.
AYE...MY QUEEN.

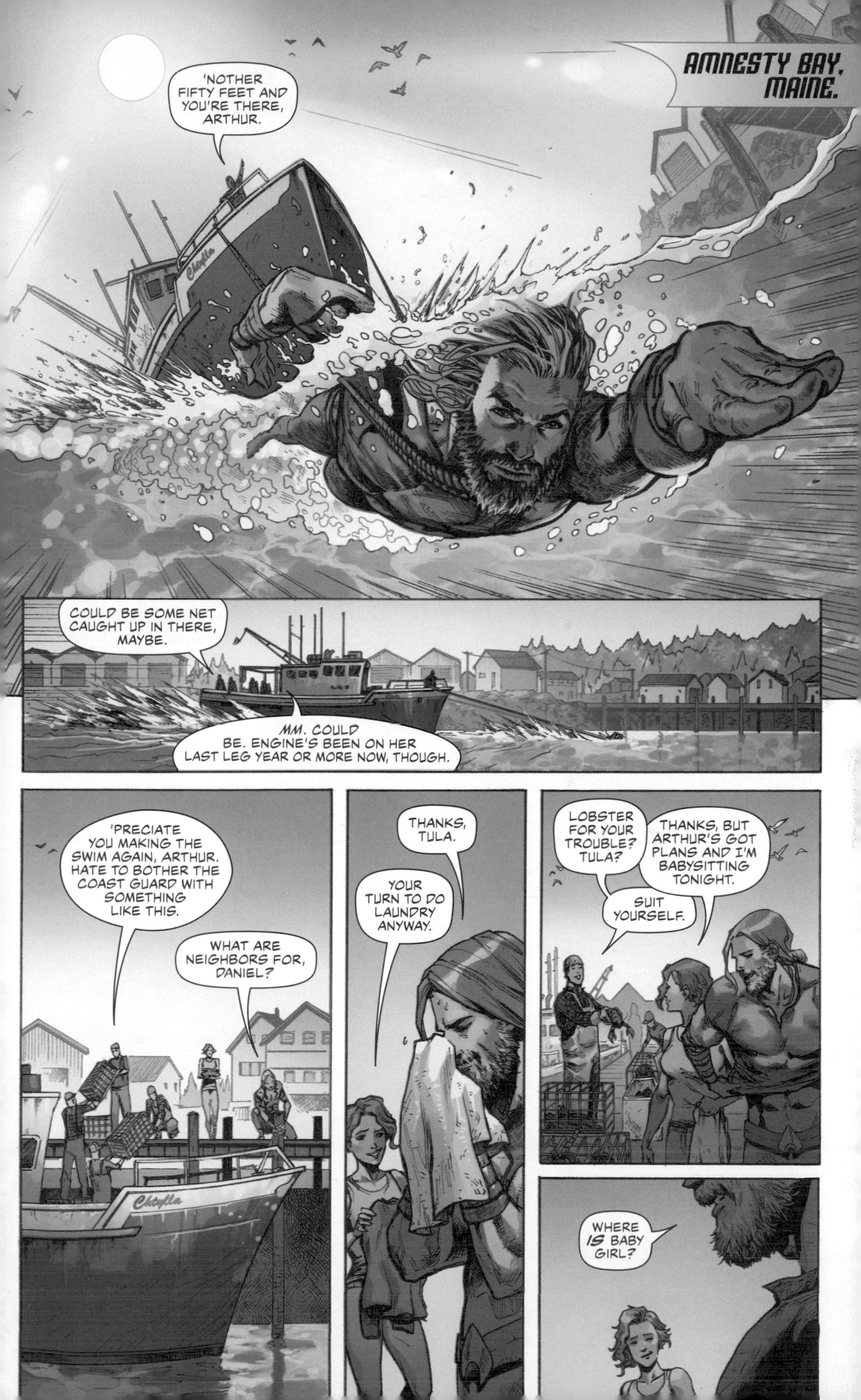
AMNESTY BAY, MAINE.
'NOTHER FIFTY FEET AND YOU'RE THERE, ARTHUR.
COULD BE SOME NET CAUGHT UP IN THERE, MAYBE.
MM. COULD BE. ENGINE'S BEEN ON HER LAST LEG YEAR OR MORE NOW, THOUGH.
'PRECIATE YOU MAKING THE SWIM AGAIN, ARTHUR. HATE TO BOTHER THE COAST GUARD WITH SOMETHING LIKE THIS.
WHAT ARE NEIGHBORS FOR, DANIEL?
THANKS, TULA.
YOUR TURN TO DO LAUNDRY ANYWAY.
LOBSTER FOR YOUR TROUBLE? TULA?
THANKS, BUT ARTHUR'S GOT PLANS AND I'M BABYSITTING TONIGHT.
SUIT YOURSELF.
WHERE IS BABY GIRL?

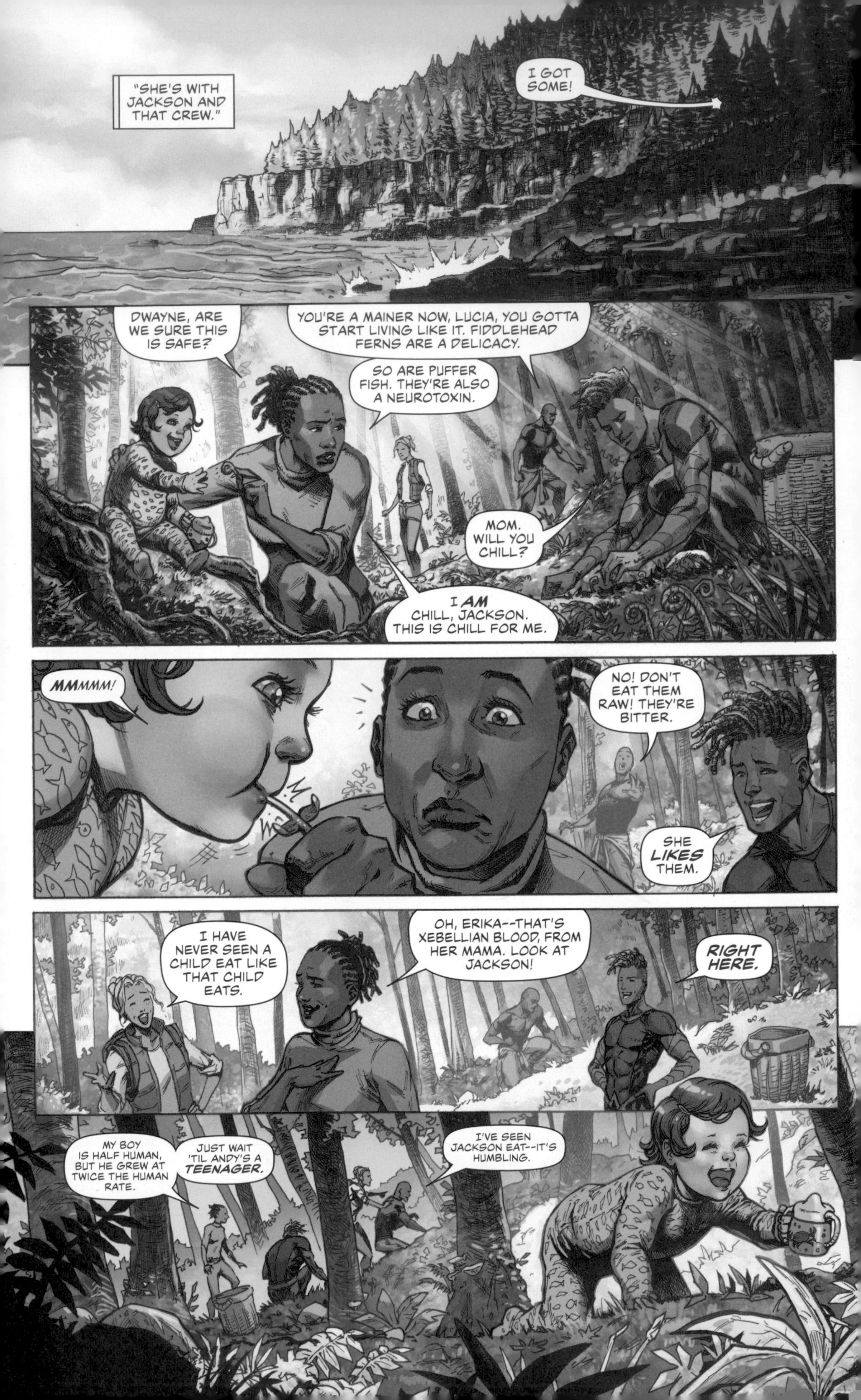
"SHE'S WITH JACKSON AND THAT CREW."
I GOT SOME!
DWAYNE, ARE WE SURE THIS IS SAFE?
YOU'RE A MAINER NOW, LUCIA, YOU GOTTA START LIVING LIKE IT. FIDDLEHEAD FERNS ARE A DELICACY.
SO ARE PUFFER FISH. THEY'RE ALSO A NEUROTOXIN.
MOM. WILL YOU CHILL?
I AM CHILL, JACKSON. THIS IS CHILL FOR ME.
MMMMM!
NO! DON'T EAT THEM RAW! THEY'RE BITTER.
SHE LIKES THEM.
I HAVE NEVER SEEN A CHILD EAT LIKE THAT CHILD EATS.
OH, ERIKA--THAT'S XEBELLIAN BLOOD, FROM HER MAMA. LOOK AT JACKSON!
RIGHT HERE.
MY BOY IS HALF HUMAN, BUT HE GREW AT TWICE THE HUMAN RATE.
JUST WAIT 'TIL ANDY'S A TEENAGER.
I'VE SEEN JACKSON EAT--IT'S HUMBLING.

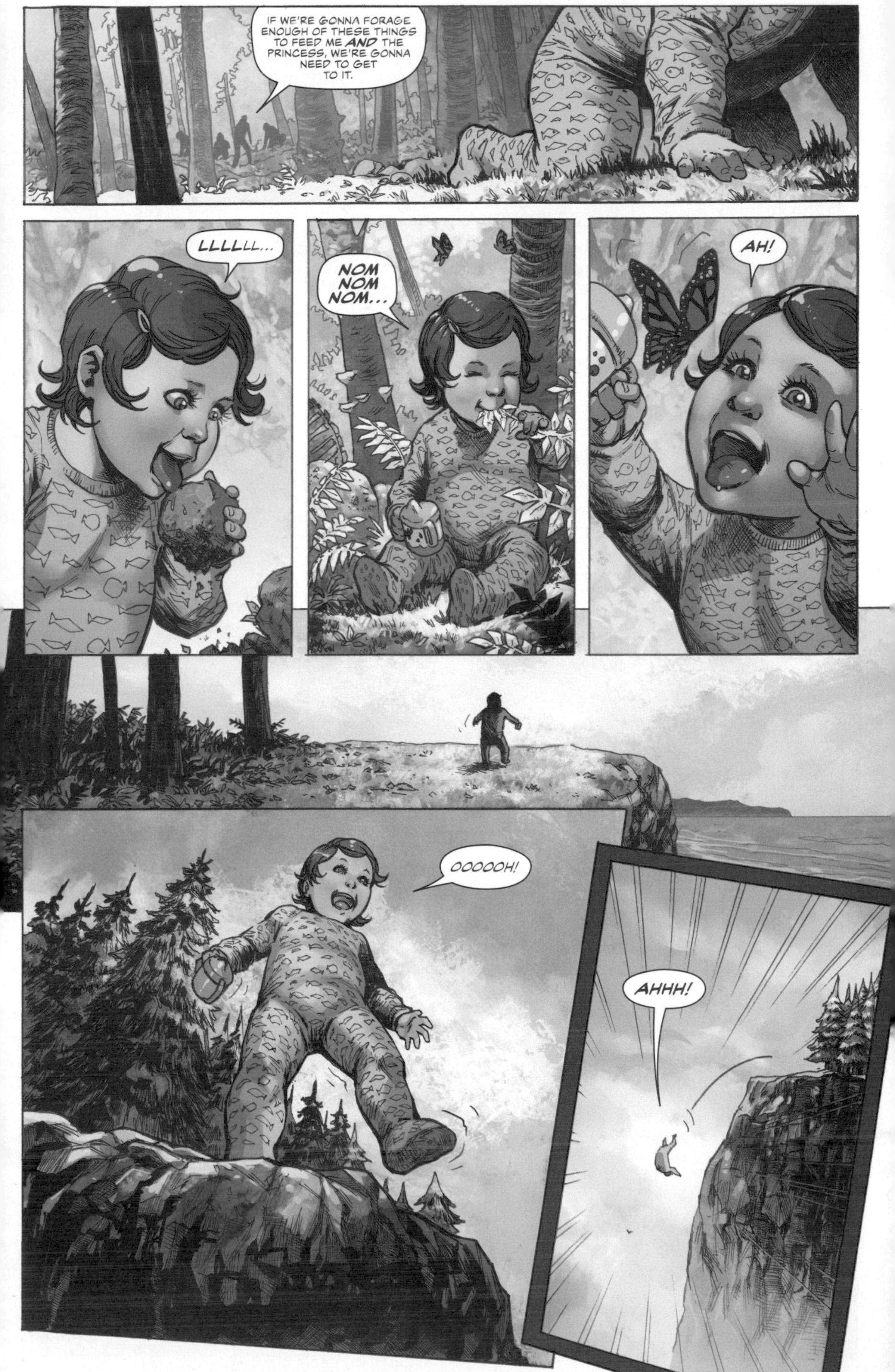
IF WE'RE GONNA FORAGE ENOUGH OF THESE THINGS TO FEED ME AND THE PRINCESS, WE'RE GONNA NEED TO GET TO IT.
LLLLLL...
NOM NOM NOM...
AH!
OOOOOH!
AHHH!

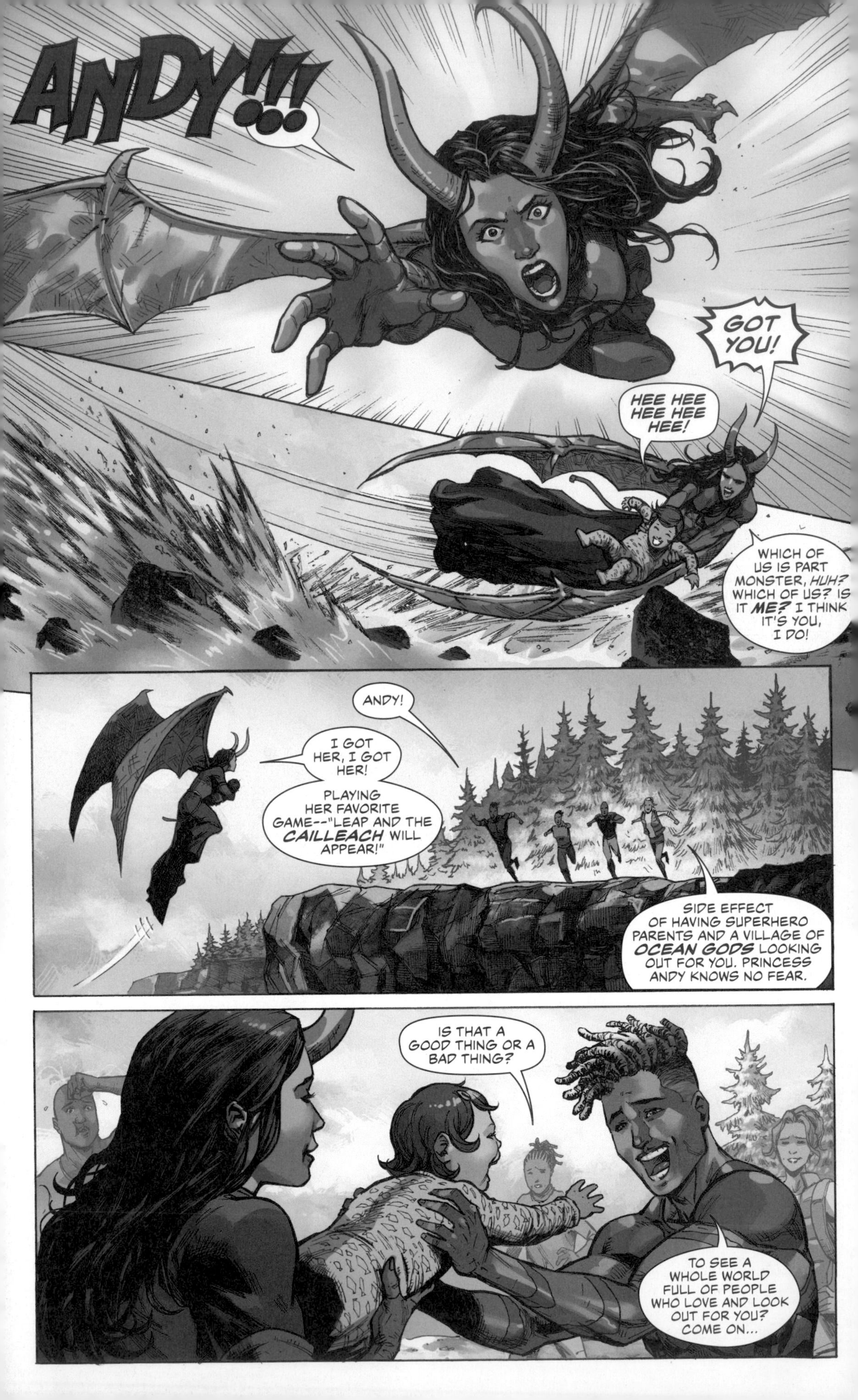
ANDY!!!
GOT YOU!
HEE HEE HEE HEE HEE!
WHICH OF US IS PART MONSTER, HUH? WHICH OF US? IS IT ME? I THINK IT'S YOU, I DO!
ANDY!
I GOT HER, I GOT HER!
PLAYING HER FAVORITE GAME--"LEAP AND THE CAILLEACH WILL APPEAR!"
SIDE EFFECT OF HAVING SUPERHERO PARENTS AND A VILLAGE OF OCEAN GODS LOOKING OUT FOR YOU. PRINCESS ANDY KNOWS NO FEAR.
IS THAT A GOOD THING OR A BAD THING?
TO SEE A WHOLE WORLD FULL OF PEOPLE WHO LOVE AND LOOK OUT FOR YOU? COME ON...

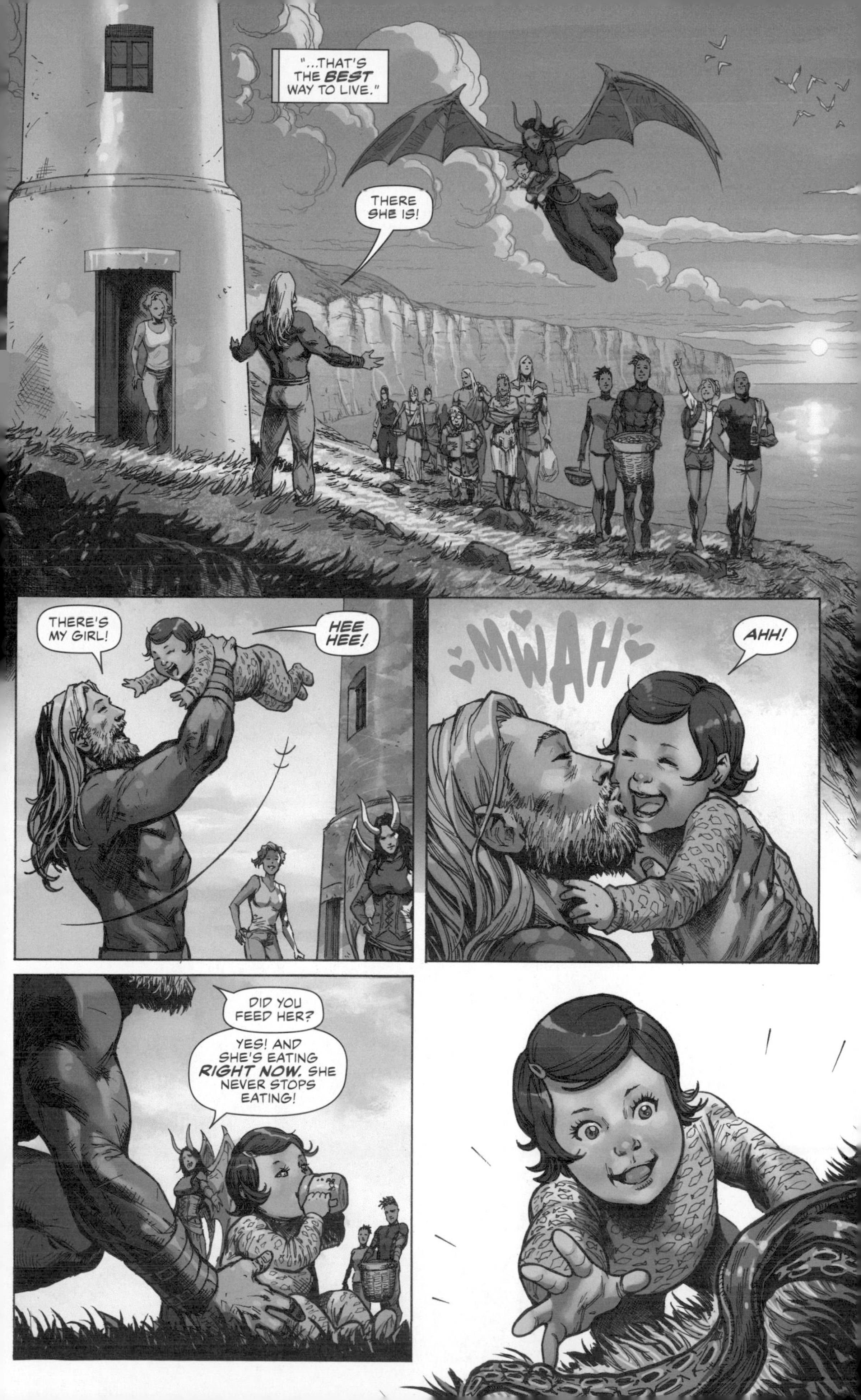
"...THAT'S THE BEST WAY TO LIVE."
THERE SHE IS!
THERE'S MY GIRL!
HEE HEE!
MWAH
AHH!
DID YOU FEED HER?
YES! AND SHE'S EATING RIGHT NOW. SHE NEVER STOPS EATING!

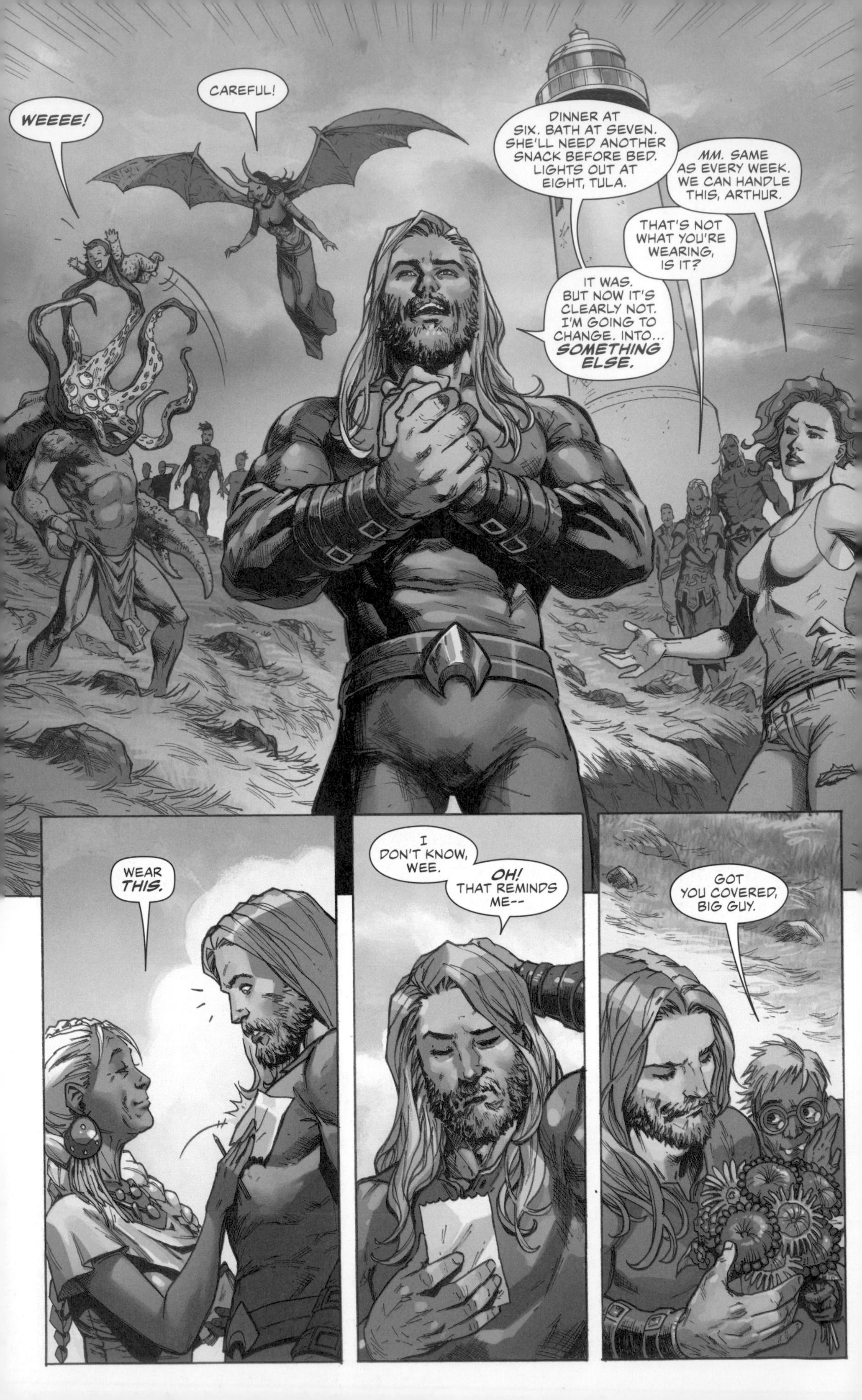

WEEEE!
CAREFUL!
DINNER AT SIX. BATH AT SEVEN. SHE'LL NEED ANOTHER SNACK BEFORE BED. LIGHTS OUT AT EIGHT, TULA.
MM. SAME AS EVERY WEEK. WE CAN HANDLE THIS, ARTHUR.
THAT'S NOT WHAT YOU'RE WEARING, IS IT?
IT WAS. BUT NOW IT'S CLEARLY NOT. I'M GOING TO CHANGE. INTO... SOMETHING ELSE.
WEAR THIS.
I DON'T KNOW, WEE.
OH! THAT REMINDS ME--
GOT YOU COVERED, BIG GUY.

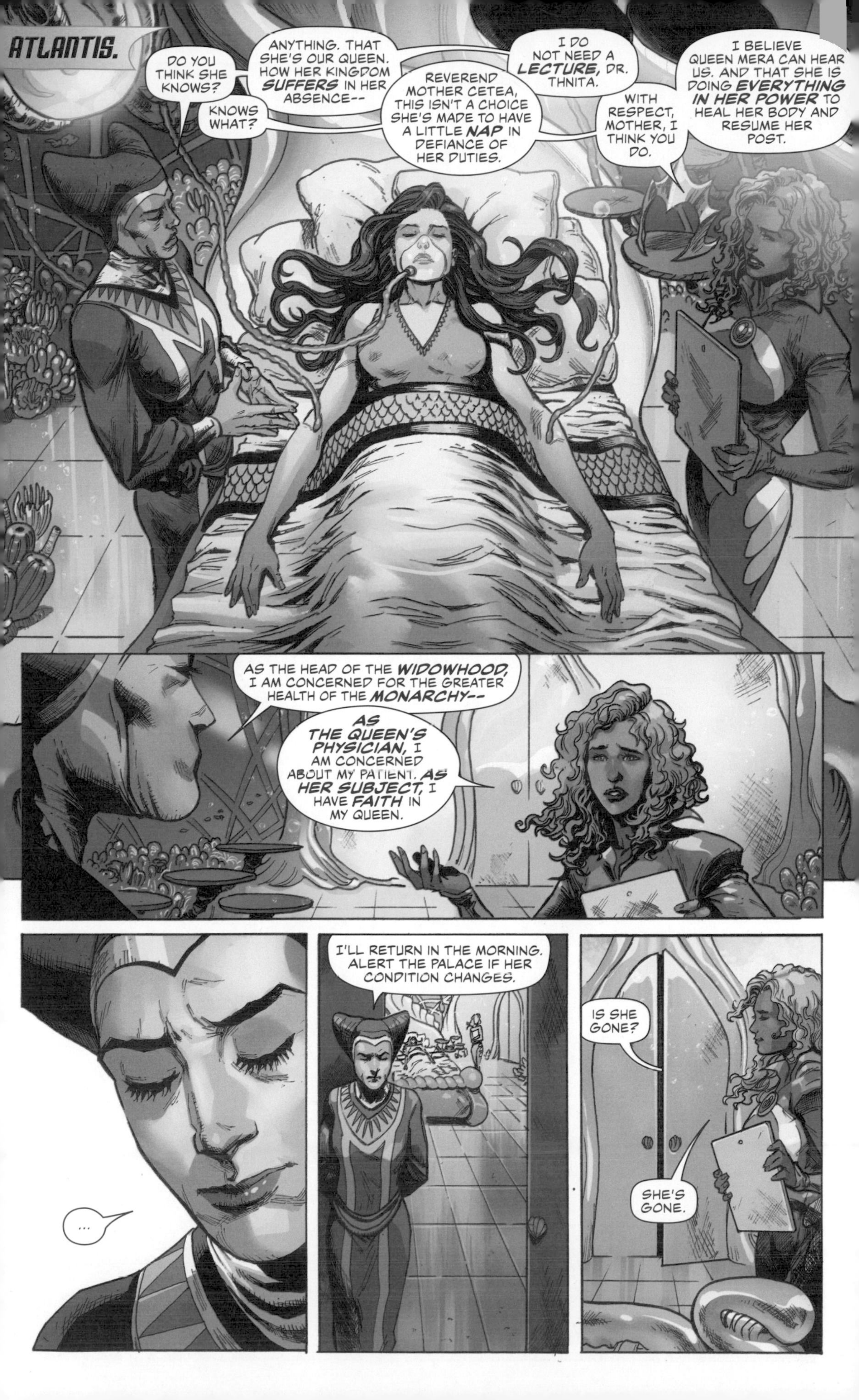
ATLANTIS.
DO YOU THINK SHE KNOWS?
KNOWS WHAT?
ANYTHING. THAT SHE'S OUR QUEEN. HOW HER KINGDOM SUFFERS IN HER ABSENCE--
REVEREND MOTHER CETEA, THIS ISN'T A CHOICE SHE'S MADE TO HAVE A LITTLE NAP IN DEFIANCE OF HER DUTIES.
I DO NOT NEED A LECTURE, DR. THNITA.
WITH RESPECT, MOTHER, I THINK YOU DO.
I BELIEVE QUEEN MERA CAN HEAR US. AND THAT SHE IS DOING EVERYTHING IN HER POWER TO HEAL HER BODY AND RESUME HER POST.
AS THE HEAD OF THE WIDOWHOOD, I AM CONCERNED FOR THE GREATER HEALTH OF THE MONARCHY--
AS THE QUEEN'S PHYSICIAN, I AM CONCERNED ABOUT MY PATIENT. AS HER SUBJECT, I HAVE FAITH IN MY QUEEN.
...
I'LL RETURN IN THE MORNING. ALERT THE PALACE IF HER CONDITION CHANGES.
IS SHE GONE?
SHE'S GONE.

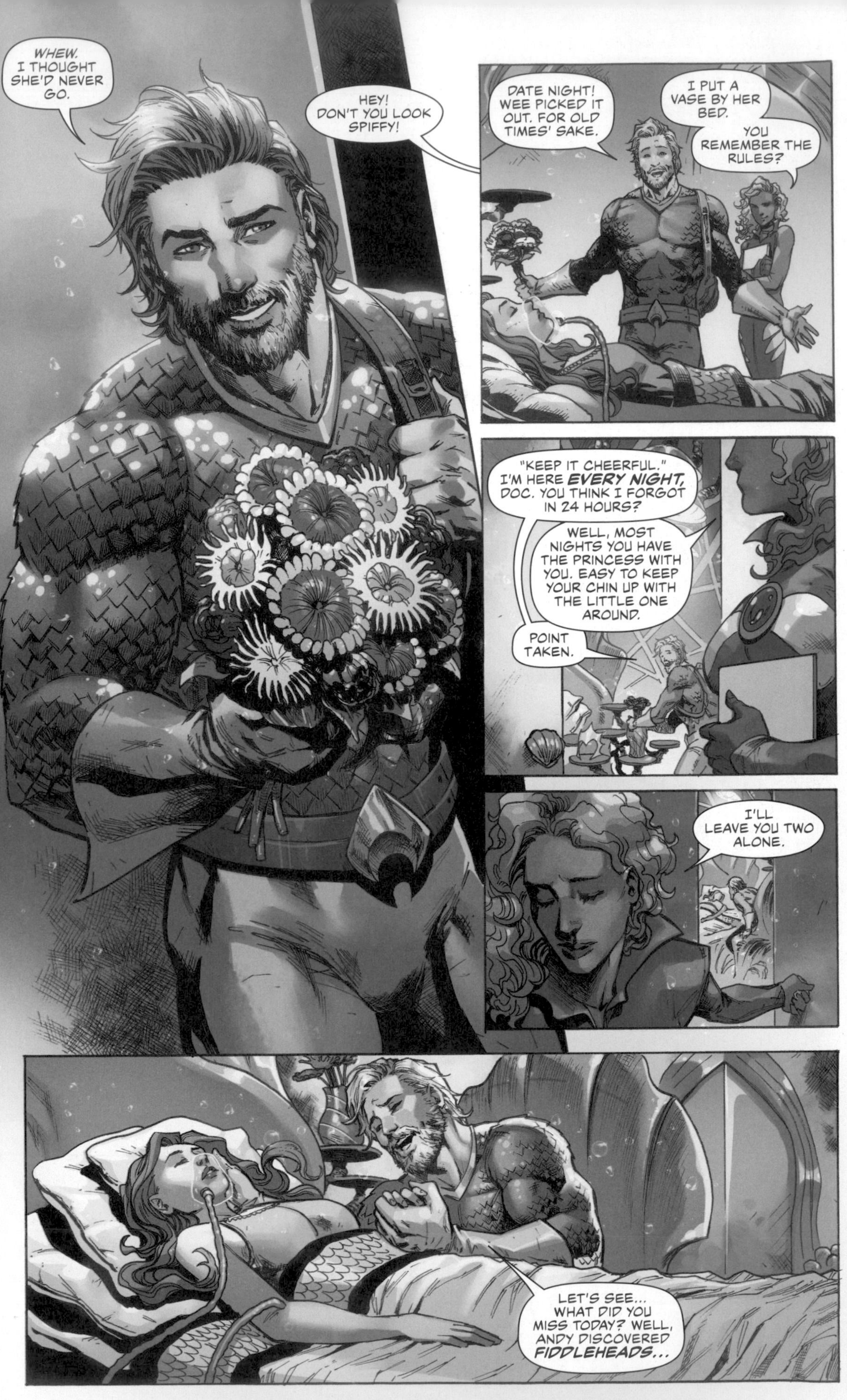
WHEW. I THOUGHT SHE'D NEVER GO.
HEY! DON'T YOU LOOK SPIFFY!
DATE NIGHT! WEE PICKED IT OUT. FOR OLD TIMES' SAKE.
I PUT A VASE BY HER BED.
YOU REMEMBER THE RULES?
"KEEP IT CHEERFUL." I'M HERE EVERY NIGHT, DOC. YOU THINK I FORGOT IN 24 HOURS?
WELL, MOST NIGHTS YOU HAVE THE PRINCESS WITH YOU. EASY TO KEEP YOUR CHIN UP WITH THE LITTLE ONE AROUND.
POINT TAKEN.
I'LL LEAVE YOU TWO ALONE.
LET'S SEE... WHAT DID YOU MISS TODAY? WELL, ANDY DISCOVERED FIDDLEHEADS...

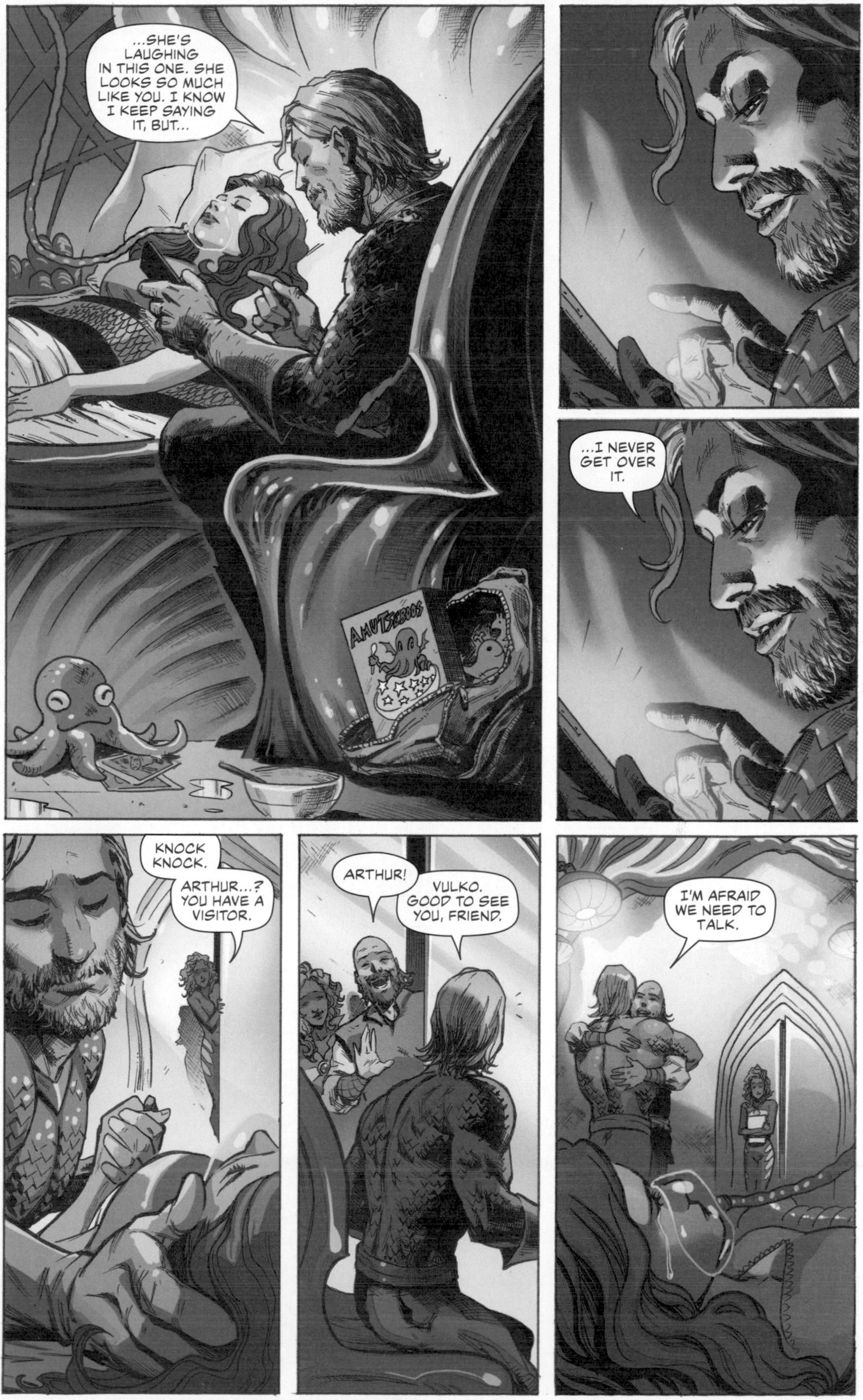

...SHE'S LAUGHING IN THIS ONE. SHE LOOKS SO MUCH LIKE YOU. I KNOW I KEEP SAYING IT, BUT...
AMUTSEBOOS
...I NEVER GET OVER IT.
KNOCK KNOCK.
ARTHUR...? YOU HAVE A VISITOR.
ARTHUR!
VULKO. GOOD TO SEE YOU, FRIEND.
I'M AFRAID WE NEED TO TALK.

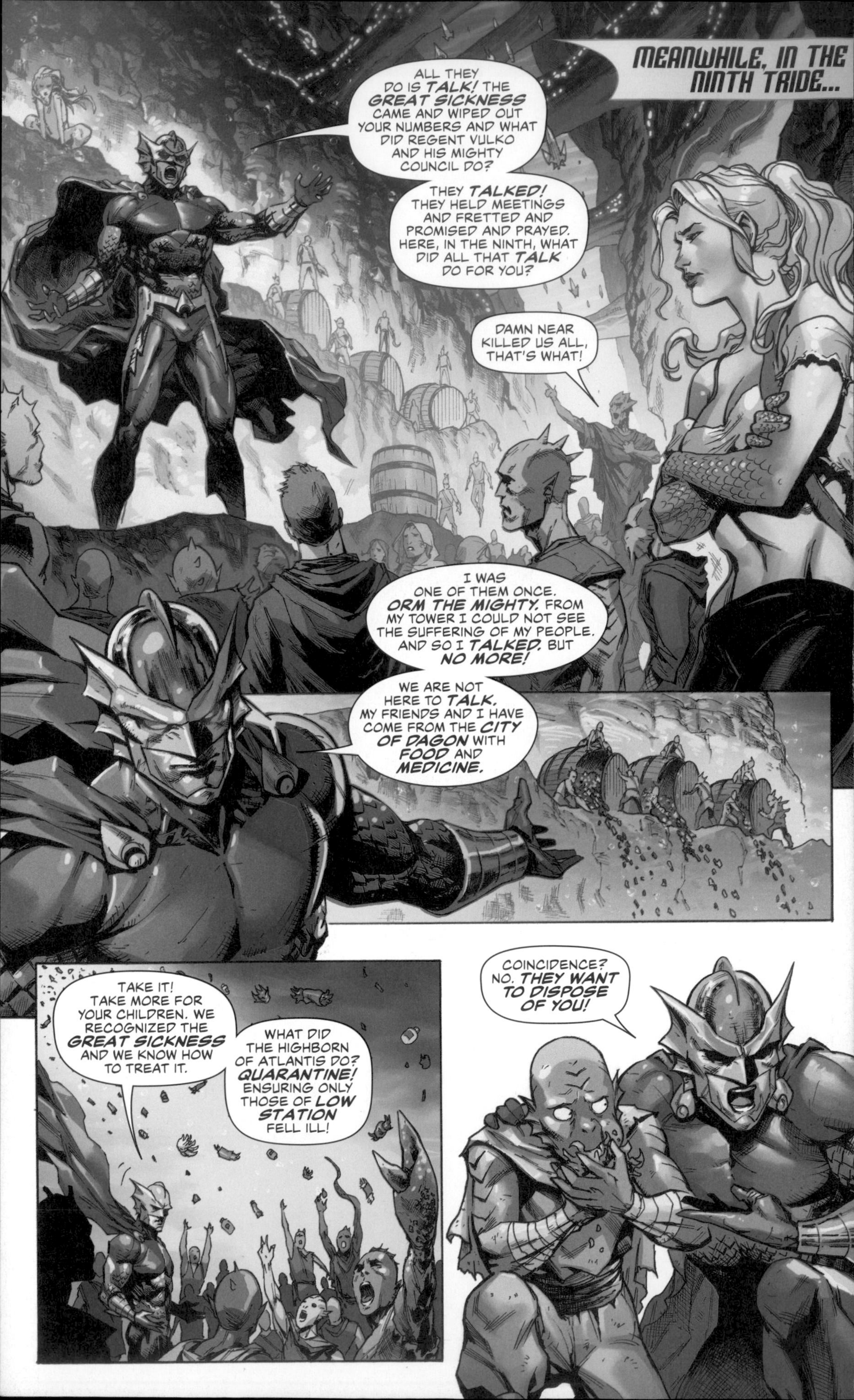
MEANWHILE, IN THE NINTH TRIDE...
ALL THEY DO IS TALK! THE GREAT SICKNESS CAME AND WIPED OUT YOUR NUMBERS AND WHAT DID REGENT VULKO AND HIS MIGHTY COUNCIL DO?
THEY TALKED! THEY HELD MEETINGS AND FRETTED AND PROMISED AND PRAYED. HERE, IN THE NINTH, WHAT DID ALL THAT TALK DO FOR YOU?
DAMN NEAR KILLED US ALL, THAT'S WHAT!
I WAS ONE OF THEM ONCE. ORM THE MIGHTY. FROM MY TOWER I COULD NOT SEE THE SUFFERING OF MY PEOPLE. AND SO I TALKED. BUT NO MORE!
WE ARE NOT HERE TO TALK. MY FRIENDS AND I HAVE COME FROM THE CITY OF DAGON WITH FOOD AND MEDICINE.
TAKE IT! TAKE MORE FOR YOUR CHILDREN. WE RECOGNIZED THE GREAT SICKNESS AND WE KNOW HOW TO TREAT IT.
WHAT DID THE HIGHBORN OF ATLANTIS DO? QUARANTINE! ENSURING ONLY THOSE OF LOW STATION FELL ILL!
COINCIDENCE? NO. THEY WANT TO DISPOSE OF YOU!

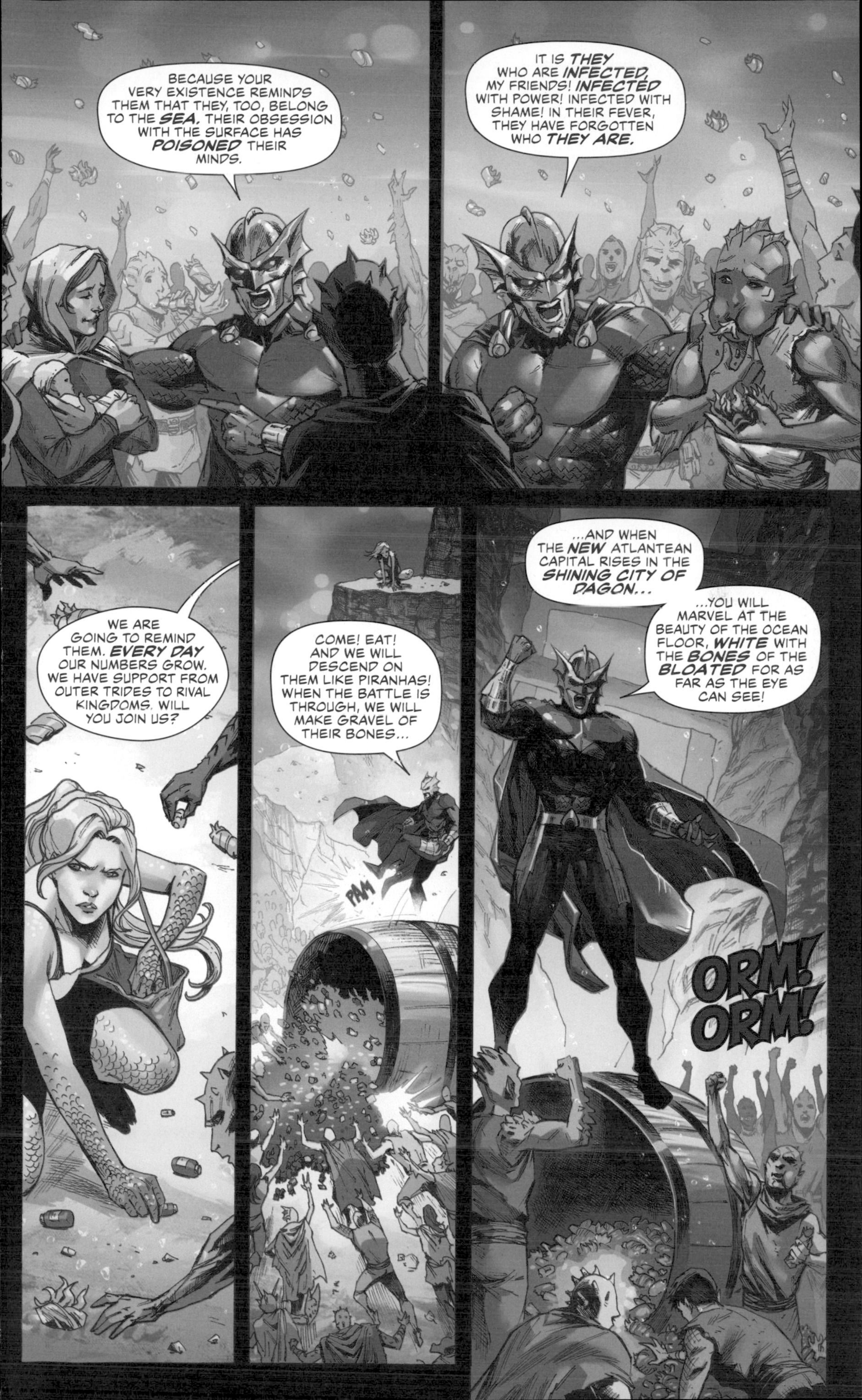
BECAUSE YOUR VERY EXISTENCE REMINDS THEM THAT THEY, TOO, BELONG TO THE SEA. THEIR OBSESSION WITH THE SURFACE HAS POISONED THEIR MINDS.
IT IS THEY WHO ARE INFECTED, MY FRIENDS! INFECTED WITH POWER! INFECTED WITH SHAME! IN THEIR FEVER, THEY HAVE FORGOTTEN WHO THEY ARE.
WE ARE GOING TO REMIND THEM. EVERY DAY OUR NUMBERS GROW. WE HAVE SUPPORT FROM OUTER TRIBES TO RIVAL KINGDOMS. WILL YOU JOIN US?
COME! EAT! AND WE WILL DESCEND ON THEM LIKE PIRANHAS! WHEN THE BATTLE IS THROUGH, WE WILL MAKE GRAVEL OF THEIR BONES...
PAM
...AND WHEN THE NEW ATLANTEAN CAPITAL RISES IN THE SHINING CITY OF DAGON...
...YOU WILL MARVEL AT THE BEAUTY OF THE OCEAN FLOOR, WHITE WITH THE BONES OF THE BLOATED FOR AS FAR AS THE EYE CAN SEE!
ORM! ORM!

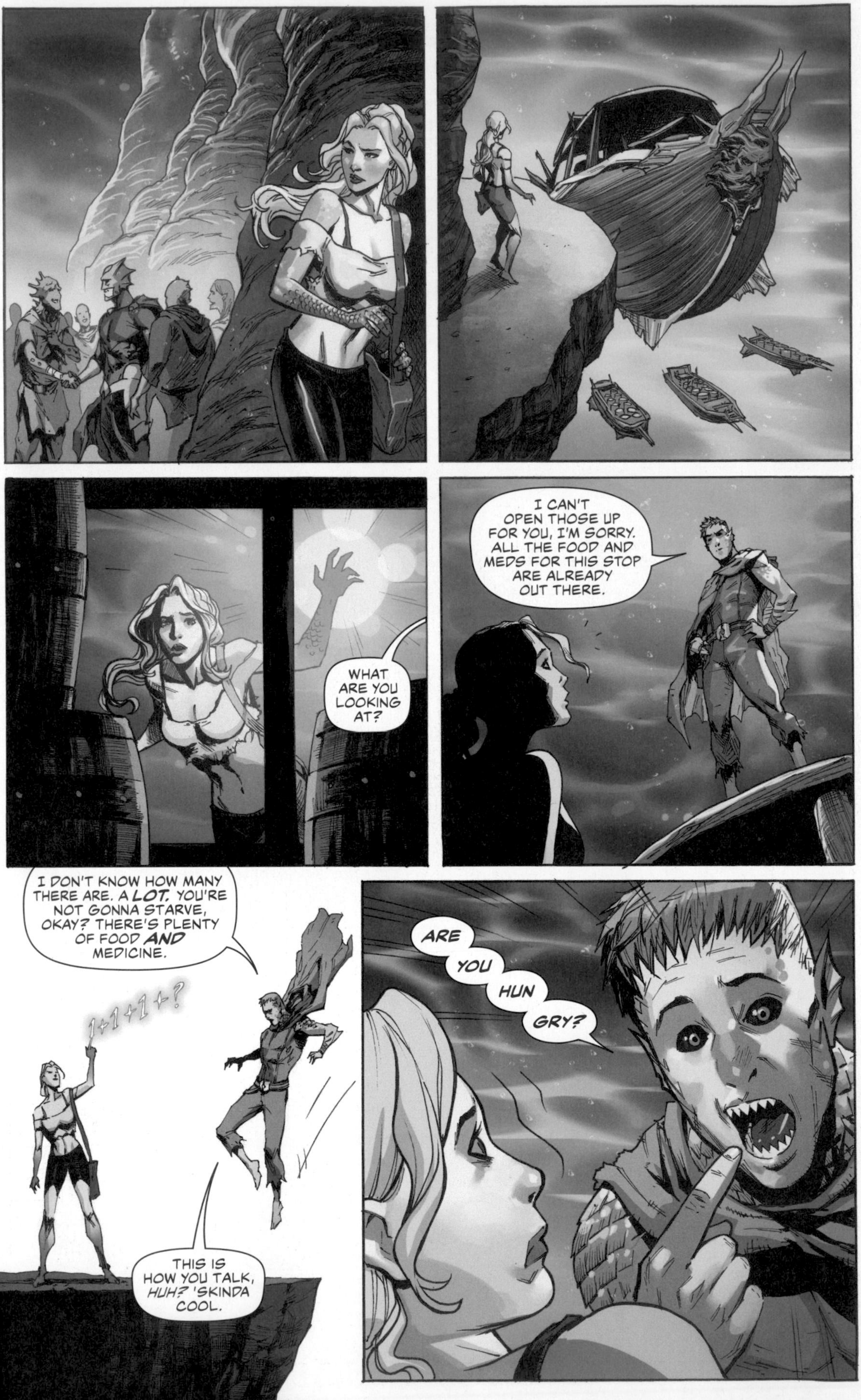
WHAT ARE YOU LOOKING AT?
I CAN'T OPEN THOSE UP FOR YOU, I'M SORRY. ALL THE FOOD AND MEDS FOR THIS STOP ARE ALREADY OUT THERE.
I DON'T KNOW HOW MANY THERE ARE. A LOT. YOU'RE NOT GONNA STARVE, OKAY? THERE'S PLENTY OF FOOD AND MEDICINE.
1+1+1+?
THIS IS HOW YOU TALK, HUH? 'SKINDA COOL.
ARE YOU HUN GRY?

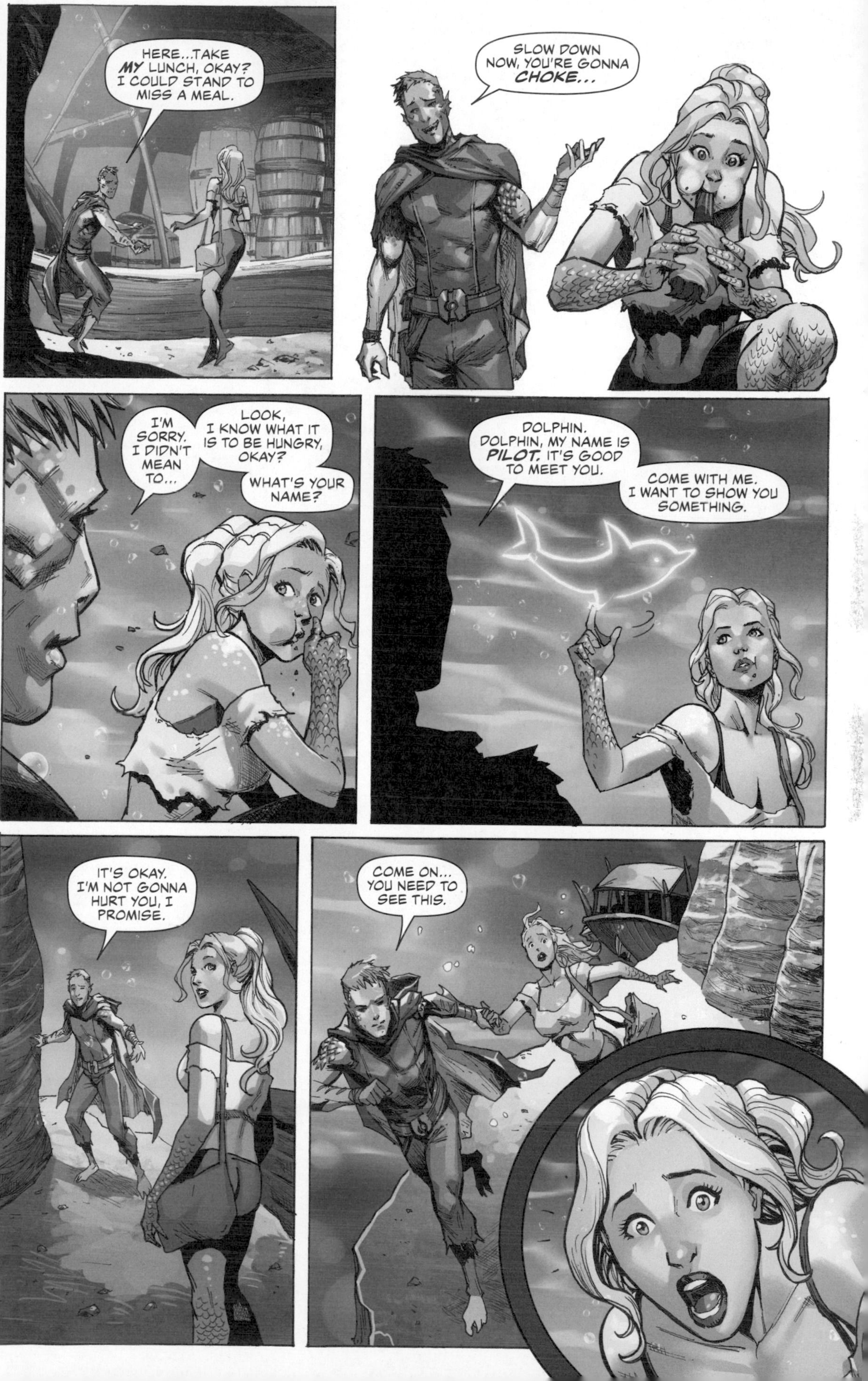
HERE...TAKE *MY* LUNCH, OKAY? I COULD STAND TO MISS A MEAL.
SLOW DOWN NOW, YOU'RE GONNA *CHOKE...*
I'M SORRY. I DIDN'T MEAN TO...
LOOK, I KNOW WHAT IT IS TO BE HUNGRY, OKAY?
WHAT'S YOUR NAME?
DOLPHIN. DOLPHIN, MY NAME IS *PILOT.* IT'S GOOD TO MEET YOU.
COME WITH ME. I WANT TO SHOW YOU SOMETHING.
IT'S OKAY. I'M NOT GONNA HURT YOU, I PROMISE.
COME ON... YOU NEED TO SEE THIS.

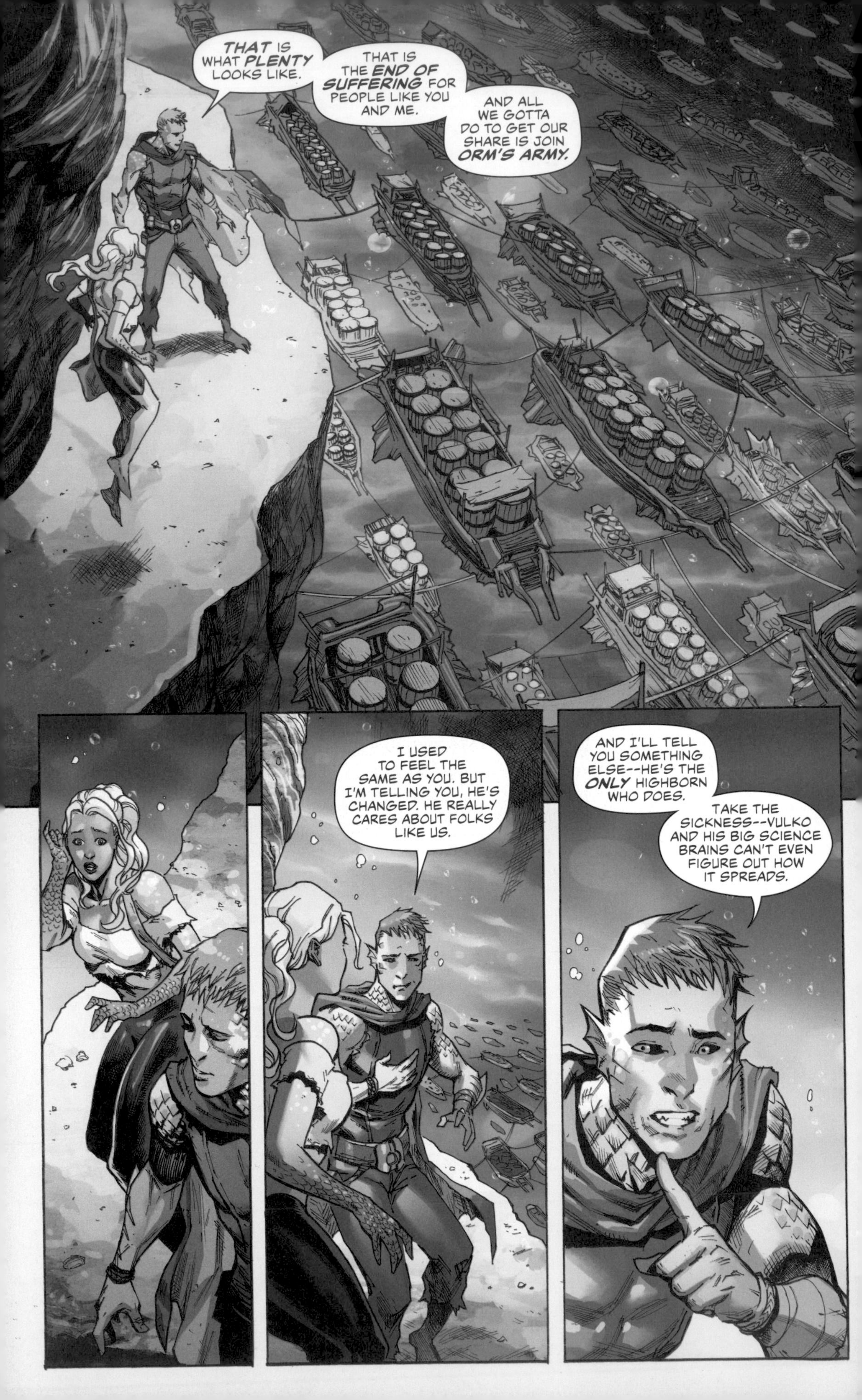
THAT IS WHAT PLENTY LOOKS LIKE.
THAT IS THE END OF SUFFERING FOR PEOPLE LIKE YOU AND ME.
AND ALL WE GOTTA DO TO GET OUR SHARE IS JOIN ORM'S ARMY.
I USED TO FEEL THE SAME AS YOU. BUT I'M TELLING YOU, HE'S CHANGED. HE REALLY CARES ABOUT FOLKS LIKE US.
AND I'LL TELL YOU SOMETHING ELSE--HE'S THE ONLY HIGHBORN WHO DOES.
TAKE THE SICKNESS--VULKO AND HIS BIG SCIENCE BRAINS CAN'T EVEN FIGURE OUT HOW IT SPREADS.

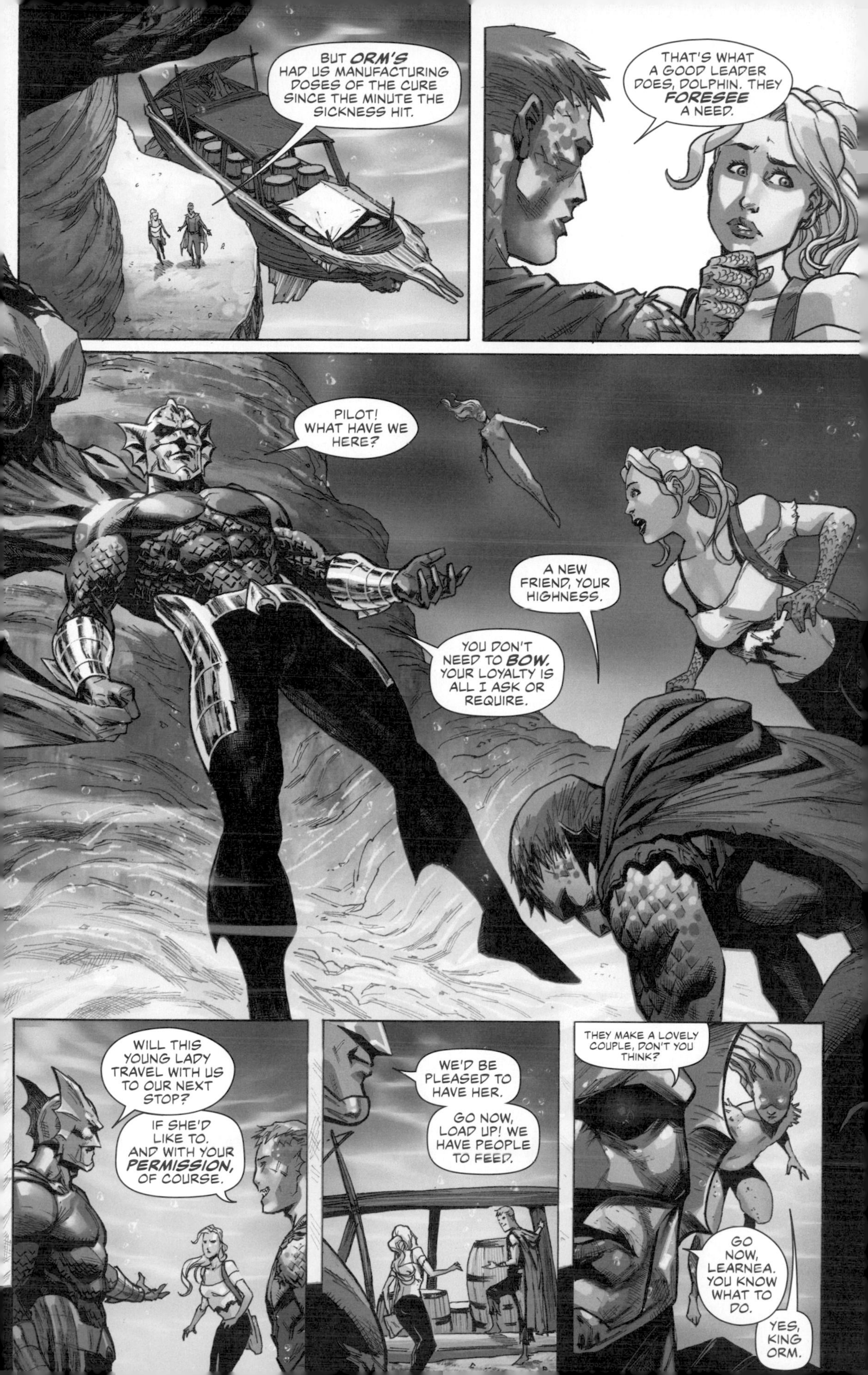
BUT ORM'S HAD US MANUFACTURING DOSES OF THE CURE SINCE THE MINUTE THE SICKNESS HIT.
THAT'S WHAT A GOOD LEADER DOES, DOLPHIN. THEY FORESEE A NEED.
PILOT! WHAT HAVE WE HERE?
A NEW FRIEND, YOUR HIGHNESS.
YOU DON'T NEED TO BOW. YOUR LOYALTY IS ALL I ASK OR REQUIRE.
WILL THIS YOUNG LADY TRAVEL WITH US TO OUR NEXT STOP?
IF SHE'D LIKE TO. AND WITH YOUR PERMISSION, OF COURSE.
WE'D BE PLEASED TO HAVE HER.
GO NOW, LOAD UP! WE HAVE PEOPLE TO FEED.
THEY MAKE A LOVELY COUPLE, DON'T YOU THINK?
GO NOW, LEARNEA. YOU KNOW WHAT TO DO.
YES, KING ORM.

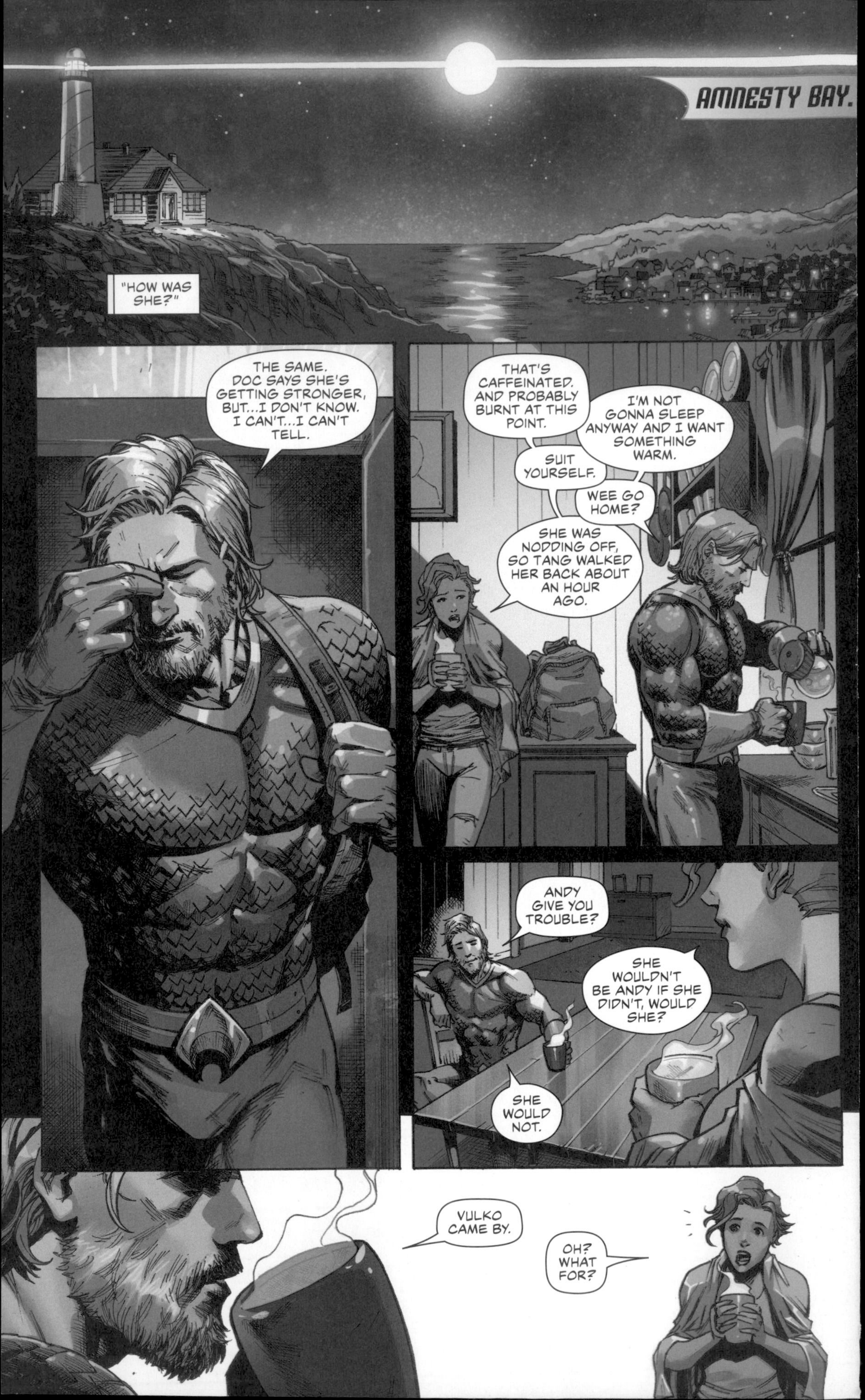
AMNESTY BAY.
"HOW WAS SHE?"
THE SAME. DOC SAYS SHE'S GETTING STRONGER, BUT...I DON'T KNOW. I CAN'T...I CAN'T TELL.
THAT'S CAFFEINATED. AND PROBABLY BURNT AT THIS POINT.
I'M NOT GONNA SLEEP ANYWAY AND I WANT SOMETHING WARM.
SUIT YOURSELF.
WEE GO HOME?
SHE WAS NODDING OFF, SO TANG WALKED HER BACK ABOUT AN HOUR AGO.
ANDY GIVE YOU TROUBLE?
SHE WOULDN'T BE ANDY IF SHE DIDN'T, WOULD SHE?
SHE WOULD NOT.
VULKO CAME BY.
OH? WHAT FOR?

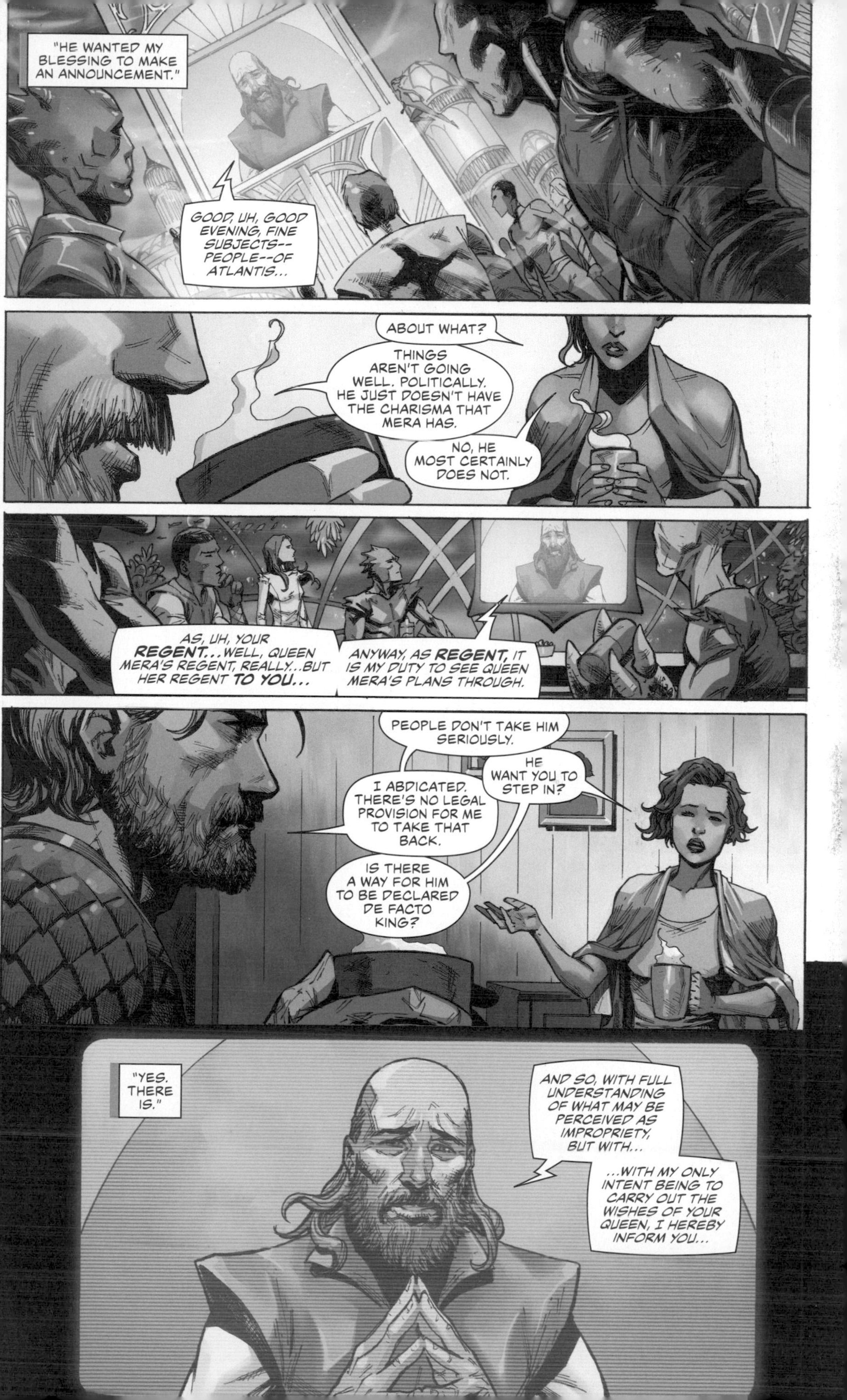
"HE WANTED MY BLESSING TO MAKE AN ANNOUNCEMENT."
GOOD, UH, GOOD EVENING, FINE SUBJECTS-- PEOPLE--OF ATLANTIS...
ABOUT WHAT?
THINGS AREN'T GOING WELL. POLITICALLY. HE JUST DOESN'T HAVE THE CHARISMA THAT MERA HAS.
NO, HE MOST CERTAINLY DOES NOT.
AS, UH, YOUR REGENT...WELL, QUEEN MERA'S REGENT, REALLY...BUT HER REGENT TO YOU...
ANYWAY, AS REGENT, IT IS MY DUTY TO SEE QUEEN MERA'S PLANS THROUGH.
PEOPLE DON'T TAKE HIM SERIOUSLY.
HE WANT YOU TO STEP IN?
I ABDICATED. THERE'S NO LEGAL PROVISION FOR ME TO TAKE THAT BACK.
IS THERE A WAY FOR HIM TO BE DECLARED DE FACTO KING?
"YES. THERE IS."
AND SO, WITH FULL UNDERSTANDING OF WHAT MAY BE PERCEIVED AS IMPROPRIETY, BUT WITH...
...WITH MY ONLY INTENT BEING TO CARRY OUT THE WISHES OF YOUR QUEEN, I HEREBY INFORM YOU...

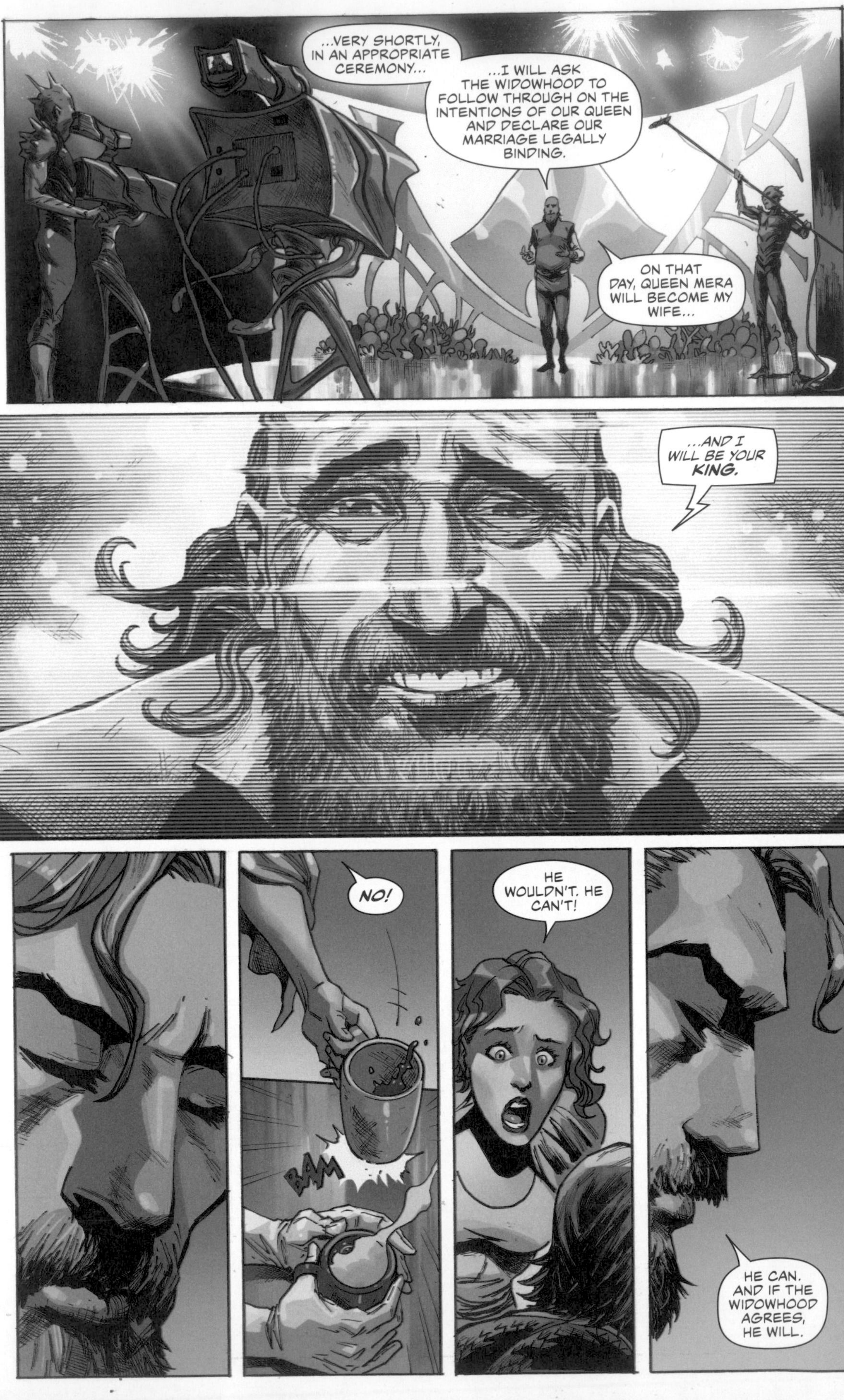
...VERY SHORTLY, IN AN APPROPRIATE CEREMONY...
...I WILL ASK THE WIDOWHOOD TO FOLLOW THROUGH ON THE INTENTIONS OF OUR QUEEN AND DECLARE OUR MARRIAGE LEGALLY BINDING.
ON THAT DAY, QUEEN MERA WILL BECOME MY WIFE...
...AND I WILL BE YOUR KING.
NO!
BAM
HE WOULDN'T. HE CAN'T!
HE CAN. AND IF THE WIDOWHOOD AGREES, HE WILL.

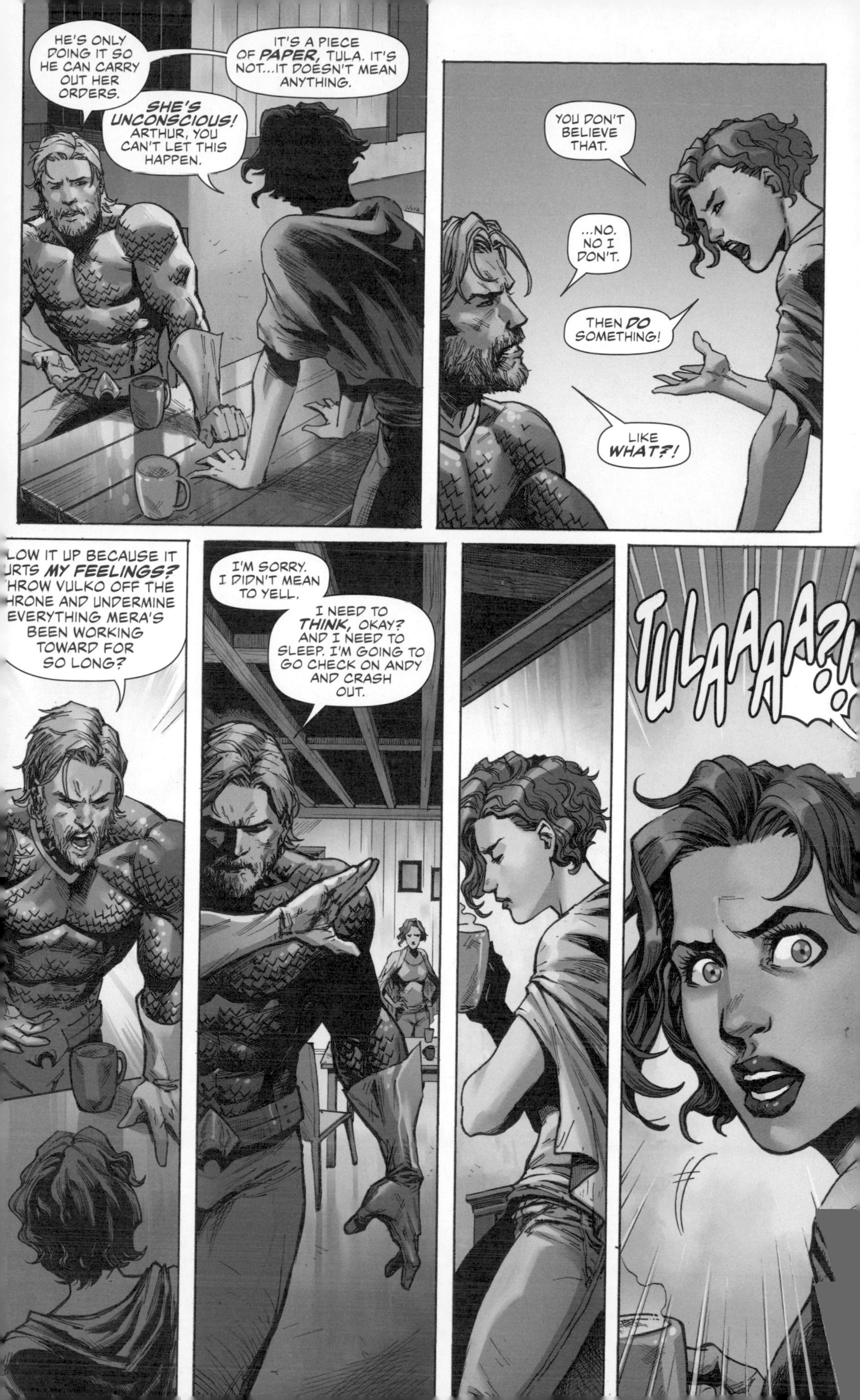

HE'S ONLY DOING IT SO HE CAN CARRY OUT HER ORDERS.
IT'S A PIECE OF PAPER, TULA. IT'S NOT...IT DOESN'T MEAN ANYTHING.
SHE'S UNCONSCIOUS! ARTHUR, YOU CAN'T LET THIS HAPPEN.
YOU DON'T BELIEVE THAT.
...NO. NO I DON'T.
THEN DO SOMETHING!
LIKE WHAT?!
LOW IT UP BECAUSE IT URTS MY FEELINGS? THROW VULKO OFF THE HRONE AND UNDERMINE EVERYTHING MERA'S BEEN WORKING TOWARD FOR SO LONG?
I'M SORRY. I DIDN'T MEAN TO YELL.
I NEED TO THINK, OKAY? AND I NEED TO SLEEP. I'M GOING TO GO CHECK ON ANDY AND CRASH OUT.
TULAAAA?!

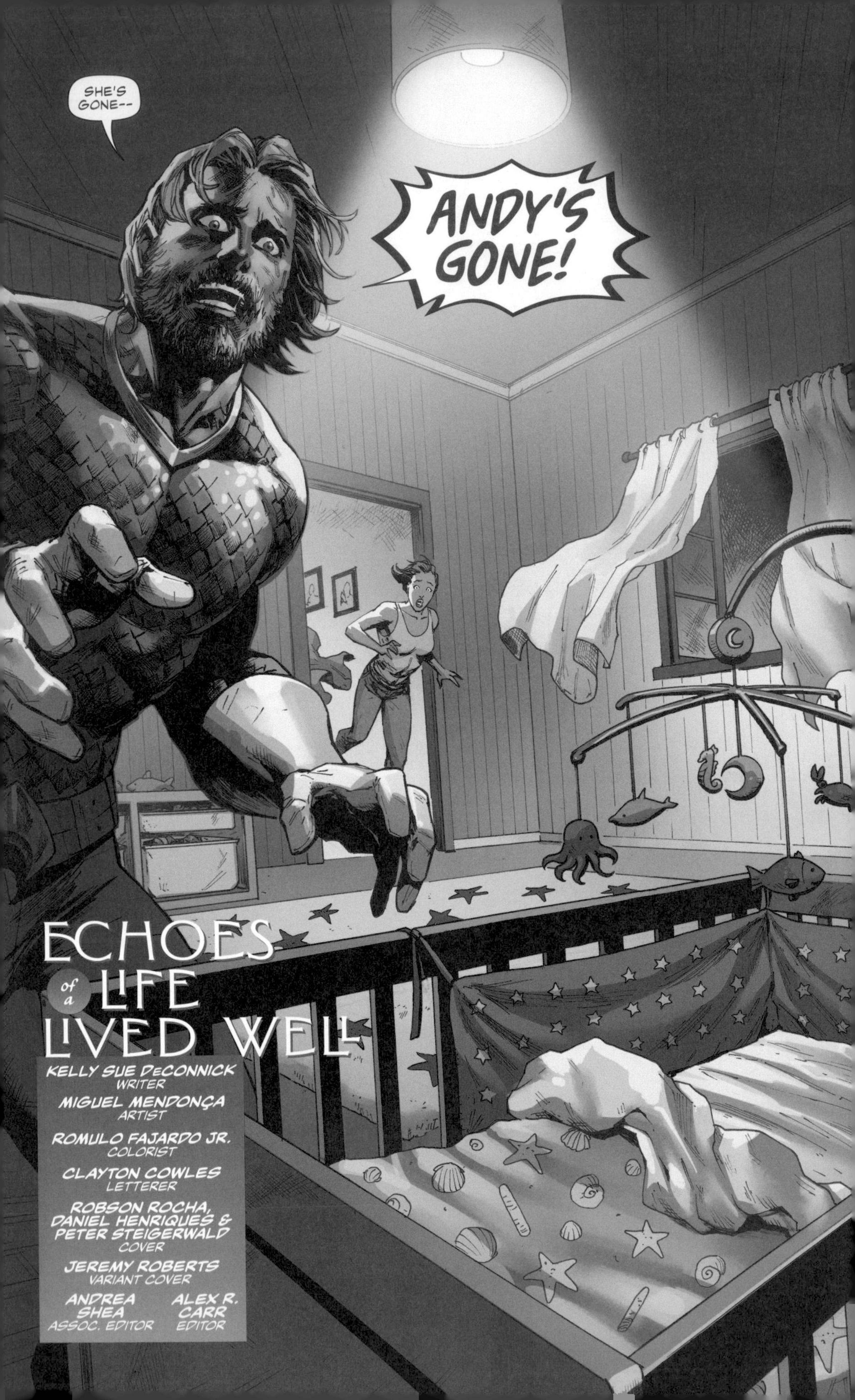
SHE'S GONE--
ANDY'S GONE!
ECHOES of a LIFE LIVED WELL
KELLY SUE DECONNICK WRITER
MIGUEL MENDONÇA ARTIST
ROMULO FAJARDO JR. COLORIST
CLAYTON COWLES LETTERER
ROBSON ROCHA, DANIEL HENRIQUES & PETER STEIGERWALD COVER
JEREMY ROBERTS VARIANT COVER
ANDREA SHEA ASSOC. EDITOR
ALEX R. CARR EDITOR

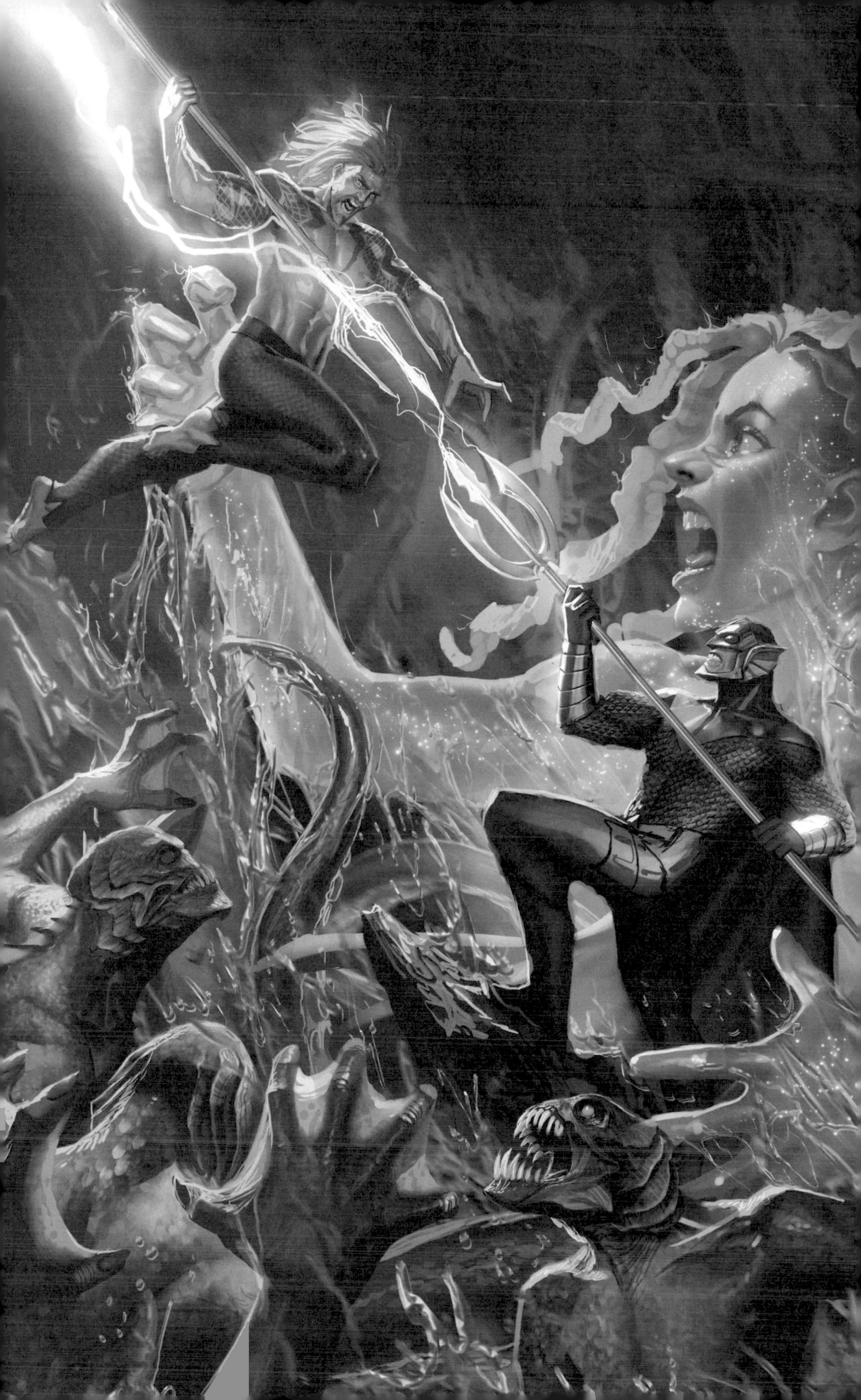

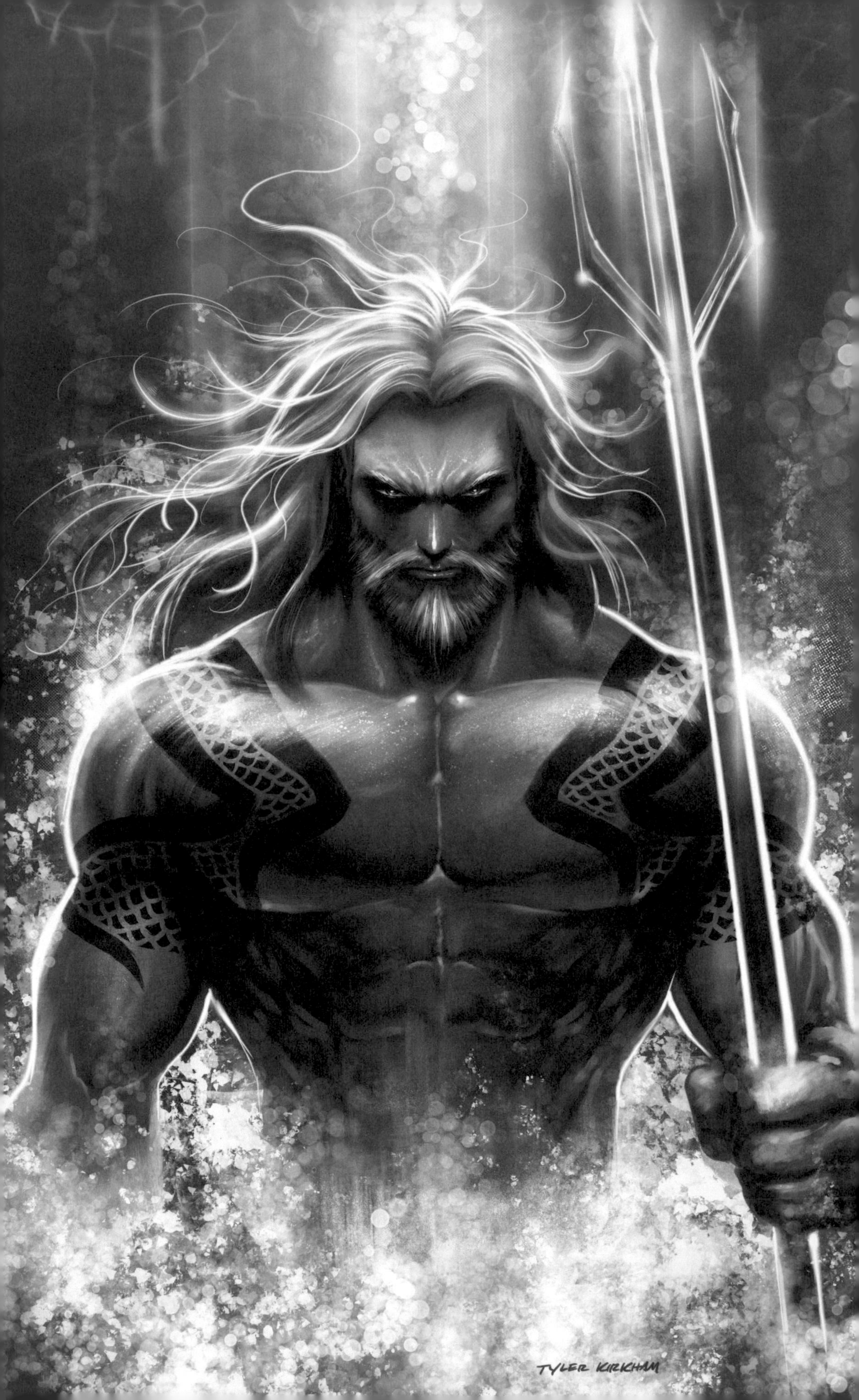
TYLER KIRKHAM

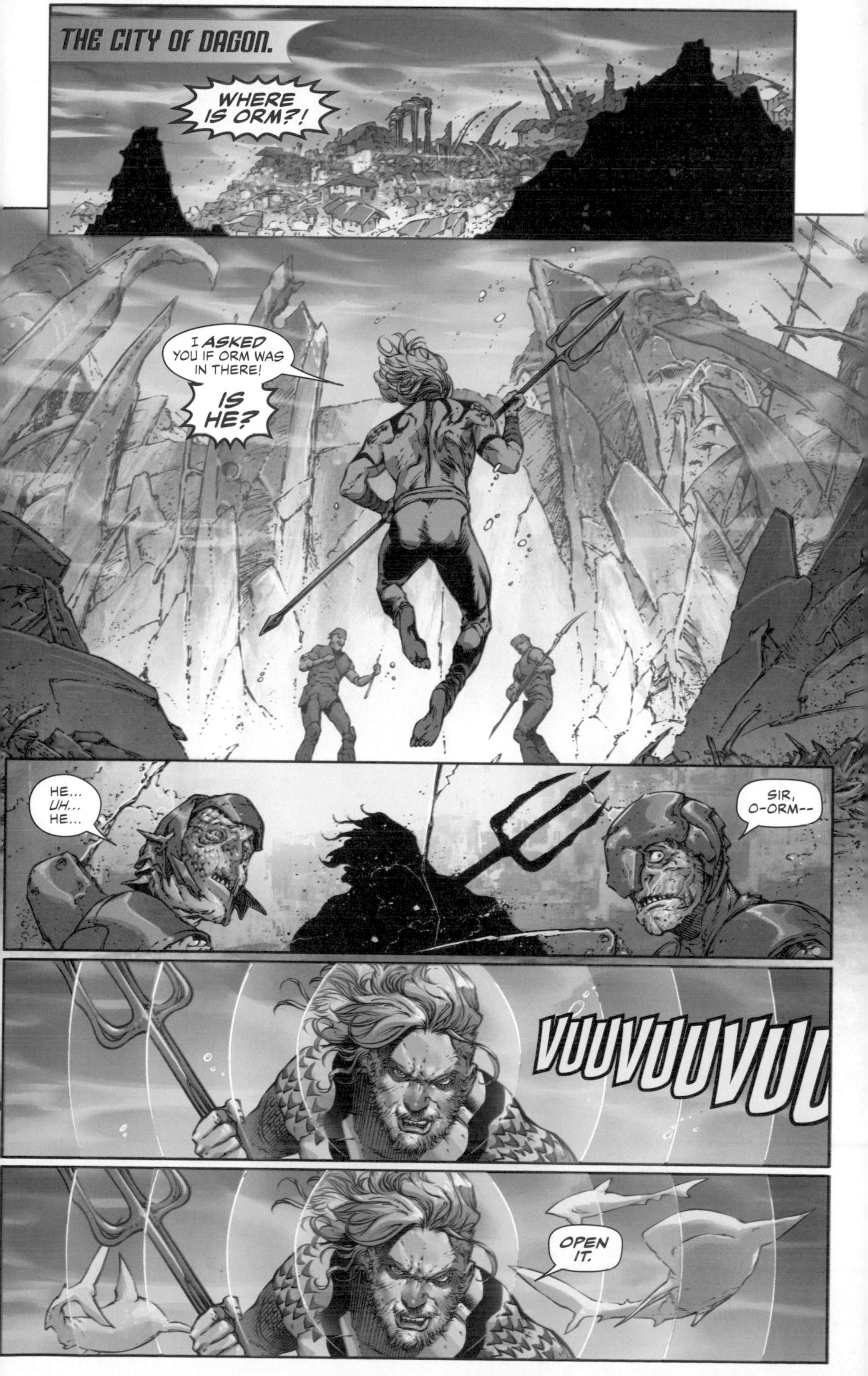
THE CITY OF DAGON.
WHERE IS ORM?!
I ASKED YOU IF ORM WAS IN THERE!
IS HE?
HE... UH... HE...
SIR, O-ORM--
VUUVUUVUU
OPEN IT.

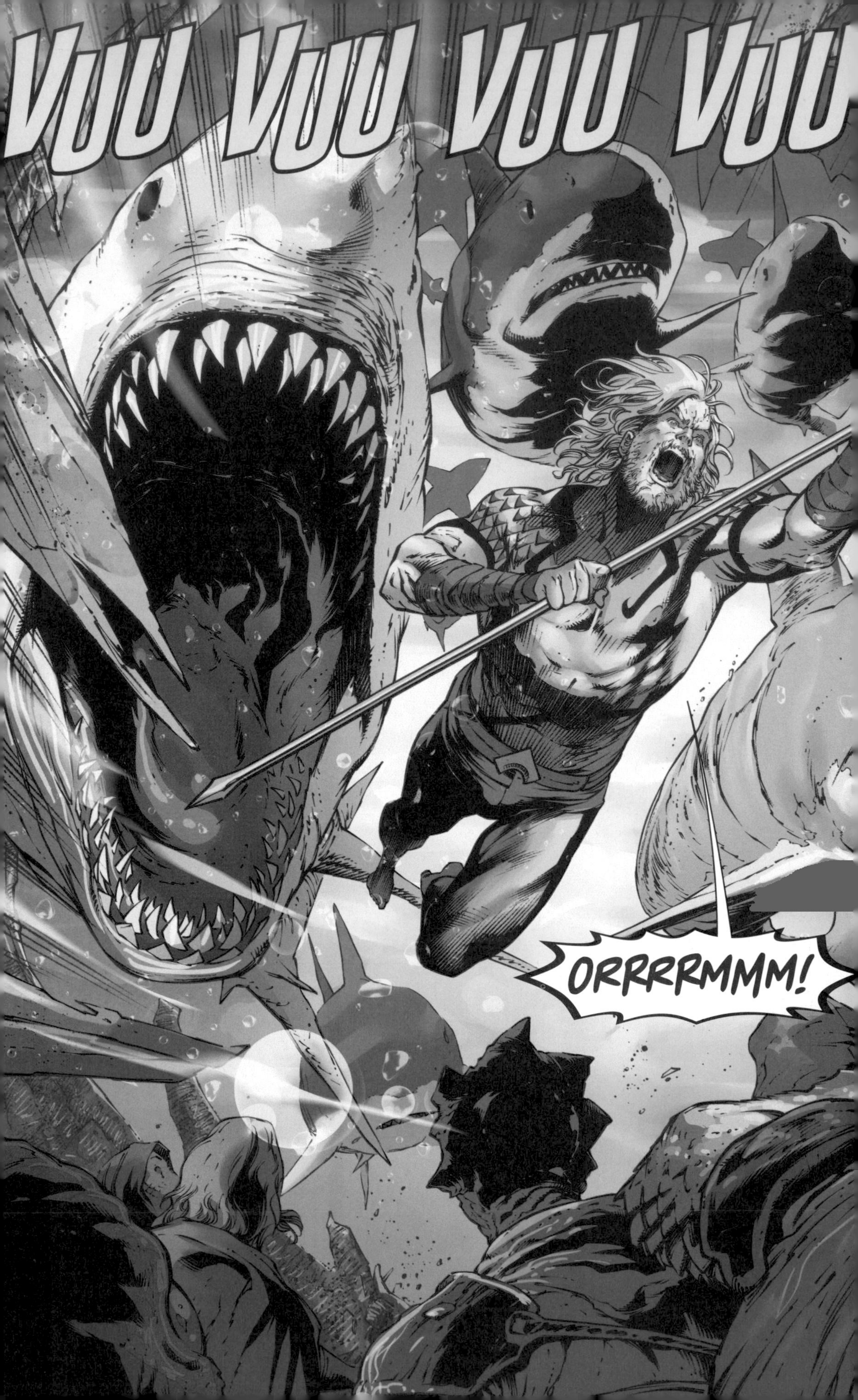
VUU VUU VUU VUU
ORRRRMMM!

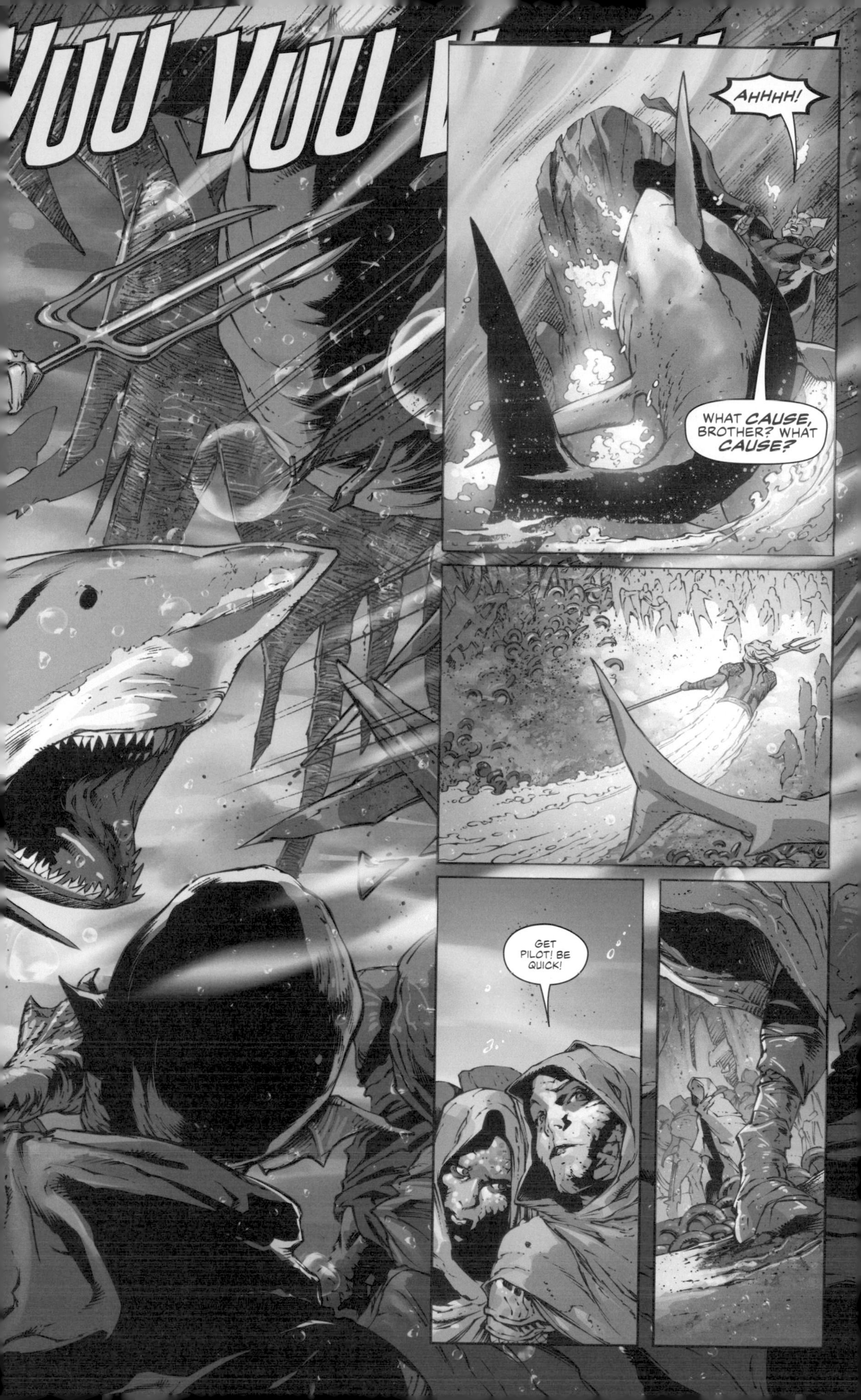
VUU VUU
AHHHH!
WHAT CAUSE, BROTHER? WHAT CAUSE?
GET PILOT! BE QUICK!

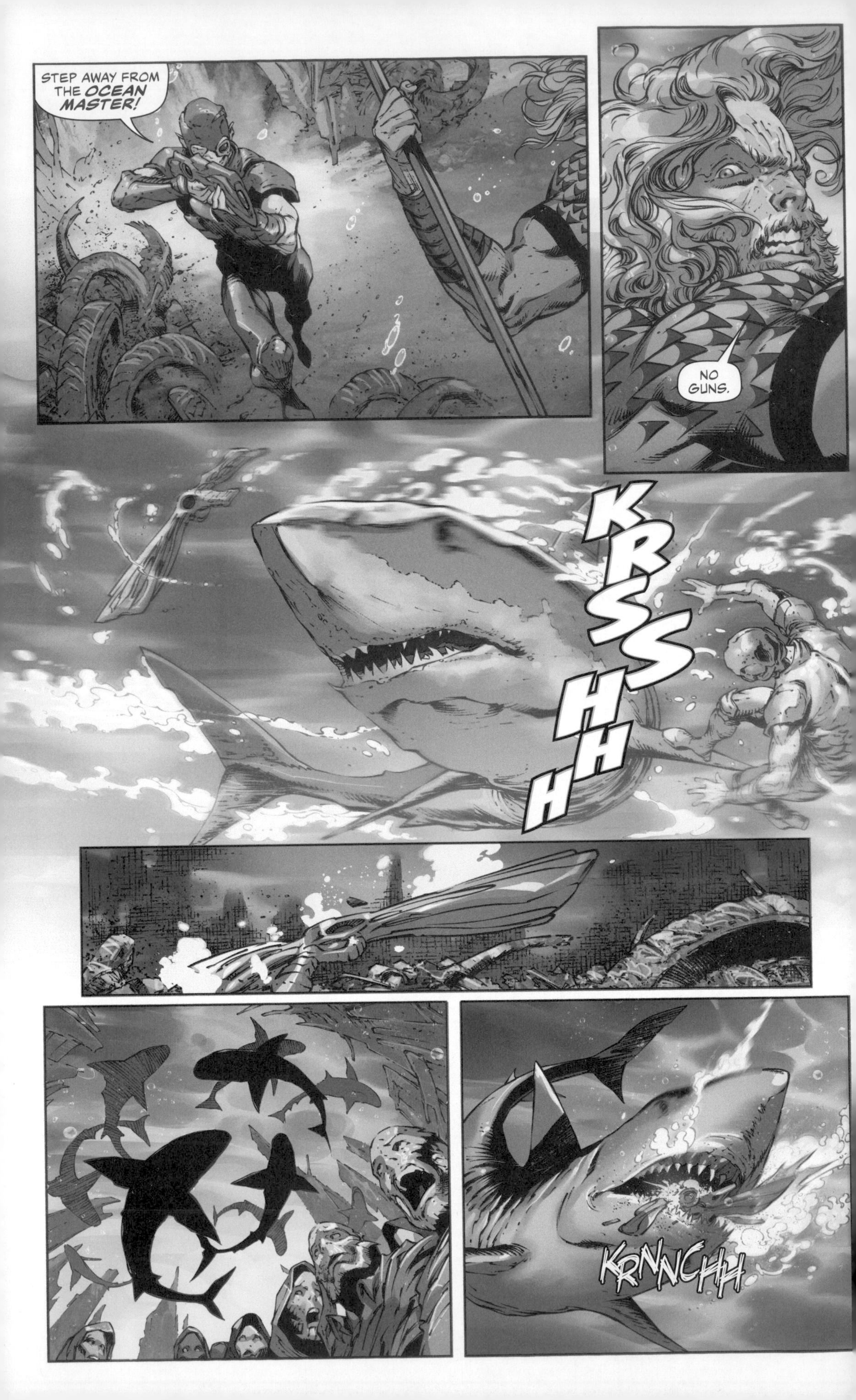
STEP AWAY FROM THE *OCEAN MASTER!*
NO GUNS.
KRSSHHH
KRNNCHH

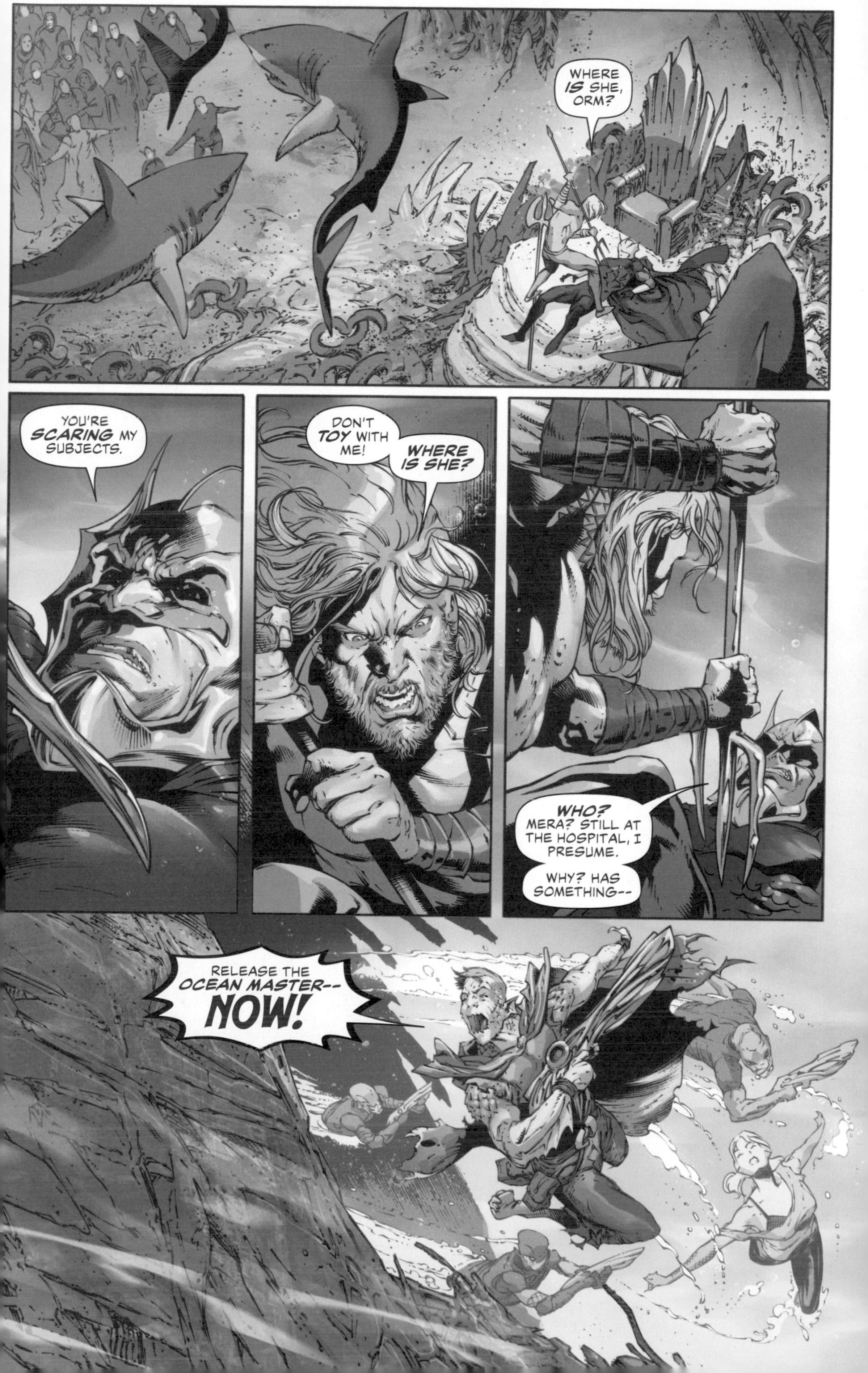
WHERE IS SHE, ORM?
YOU'RE SCARING MY SUBJECTS.
DON'T TOY WITH ME!
WHERE IS SHE?
WHO? MERA? STILL AT THE HOSPITAL, I PRESUME.
WHY? HAS SOMETHING--
RELEASE THE OCEAN MASTER-- NOW!

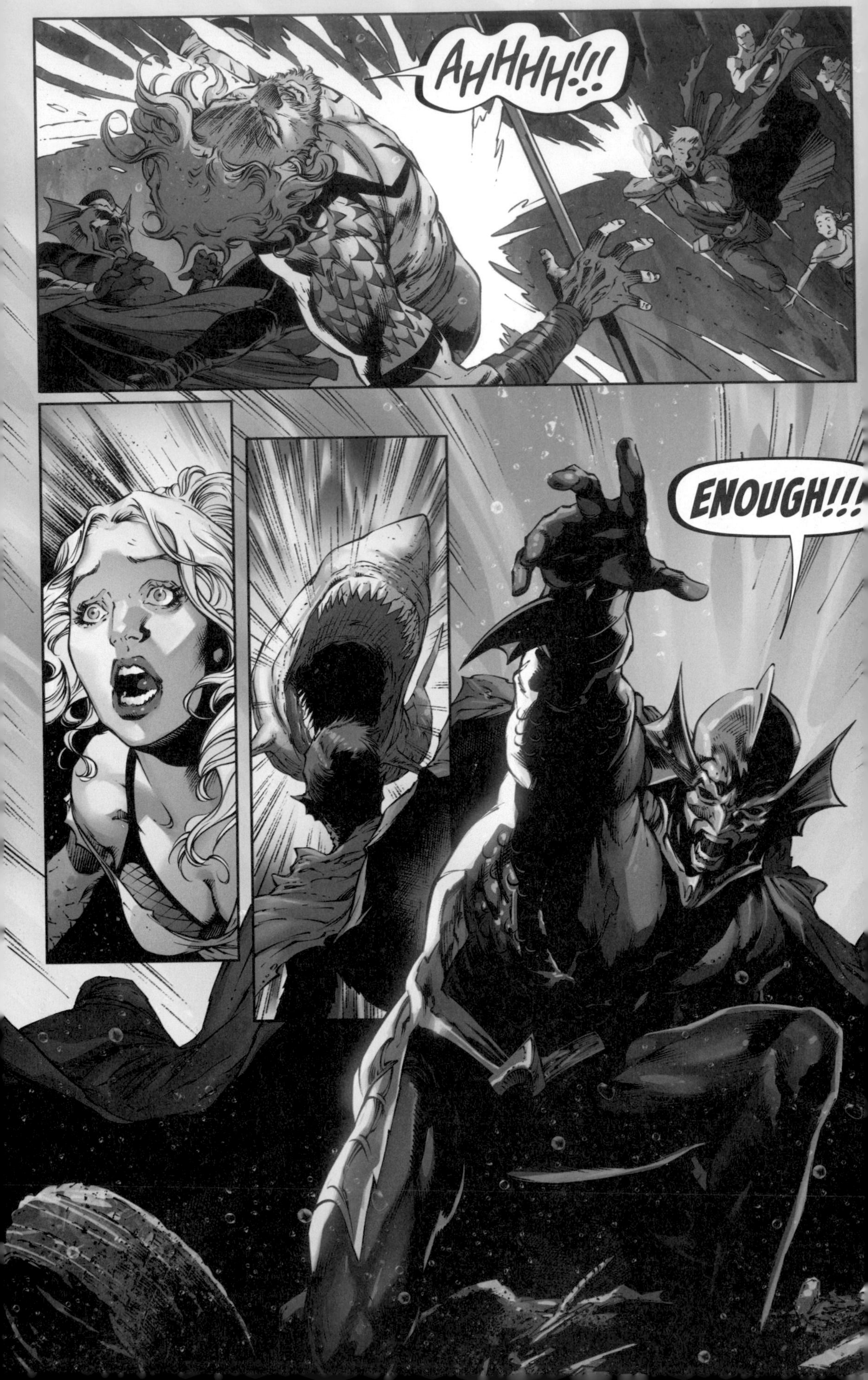
AHHHH!!!
ENOUGH!!!

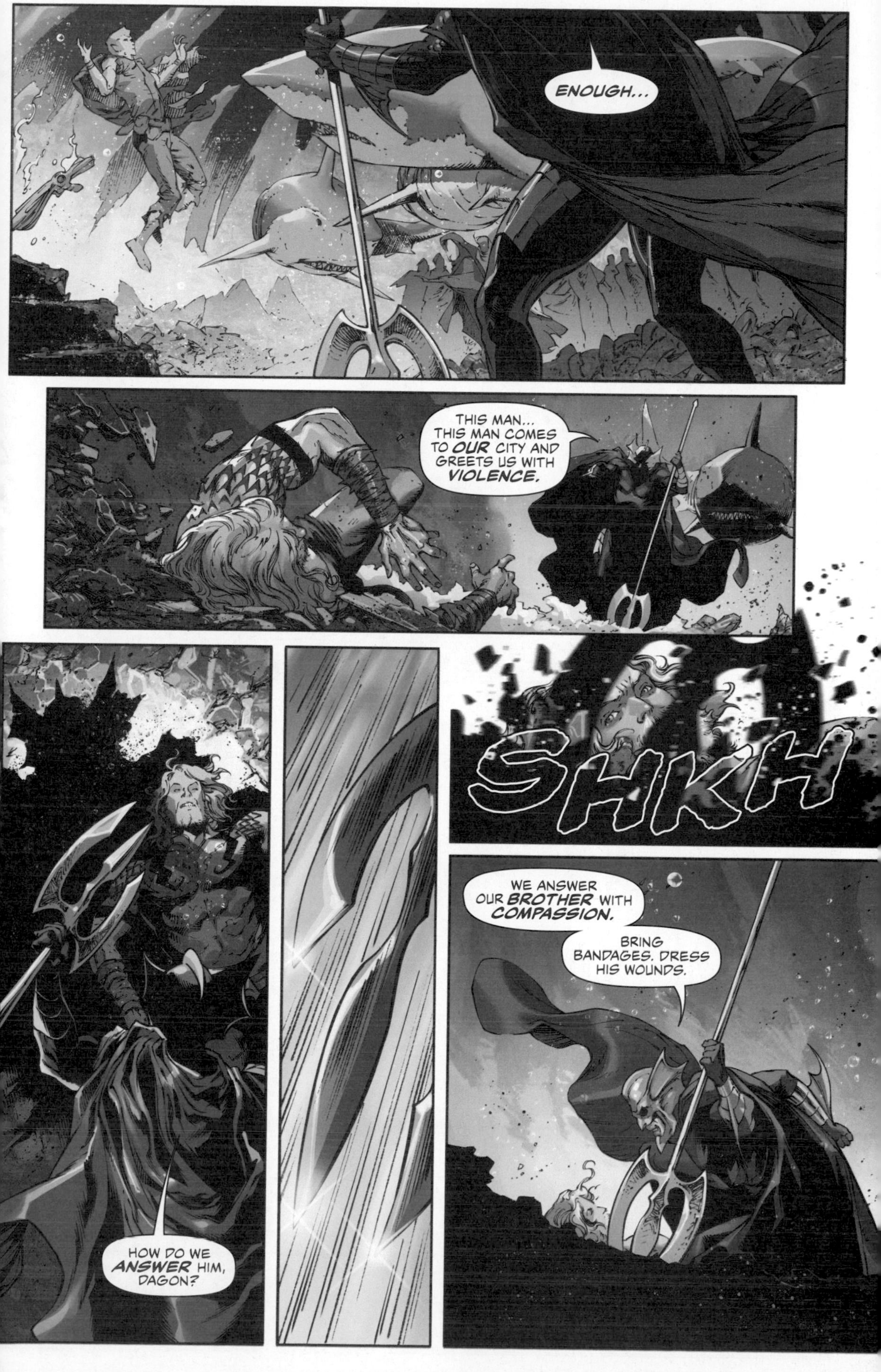
ENOUGH...
THIS MAN... THIS MAN COMES TO OUR CITY AND GREETS US WITH VIOLENCE.
HOW DO WE ANSWER HIM, DAGON?
SHKH
WE ANSWER OUR BROTHER WITH COMPASSION.
BRING BANDAGES. DRESS HIS WOUNDS.

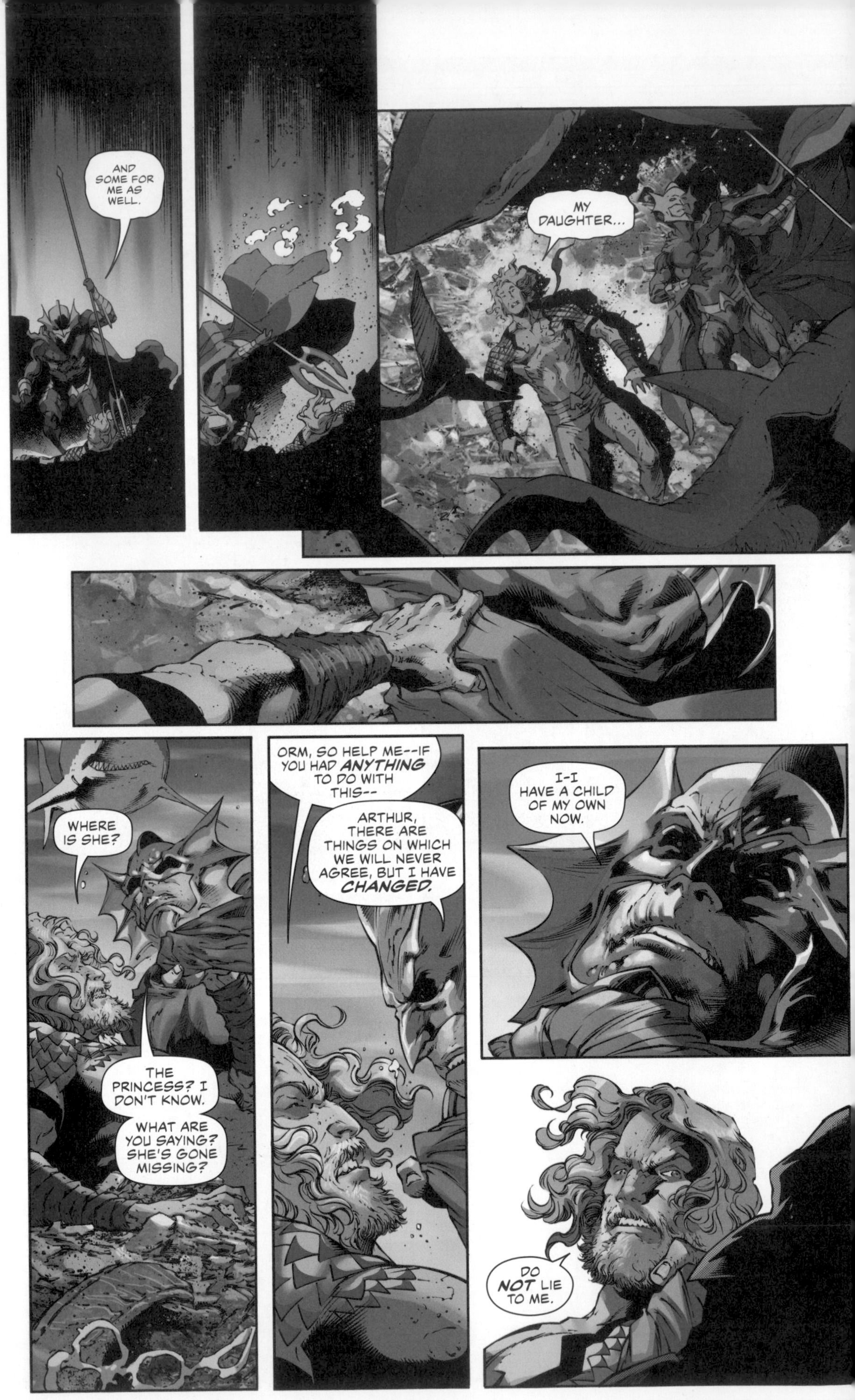
AND SOME FOR ME AS WELL.
MY DAUGHTER...
WHERE IS SHE?
THE PRINCESS? I DON'T KNOW.
WHAT ARE YOU SAYING? SHE'S GONE MISSING?
ORM, SO HELP ME--IF YOU HAD ANYTHING TO DO WITH THIS--
ARTHUR, THERE ARE THINGS ON WHICH WE WILL NEVER AGREE, BUT I HAVE CHANGED.
I-I HAVE A CHILD OF MY OWN NOW.
DO NOT LIE TO ME.

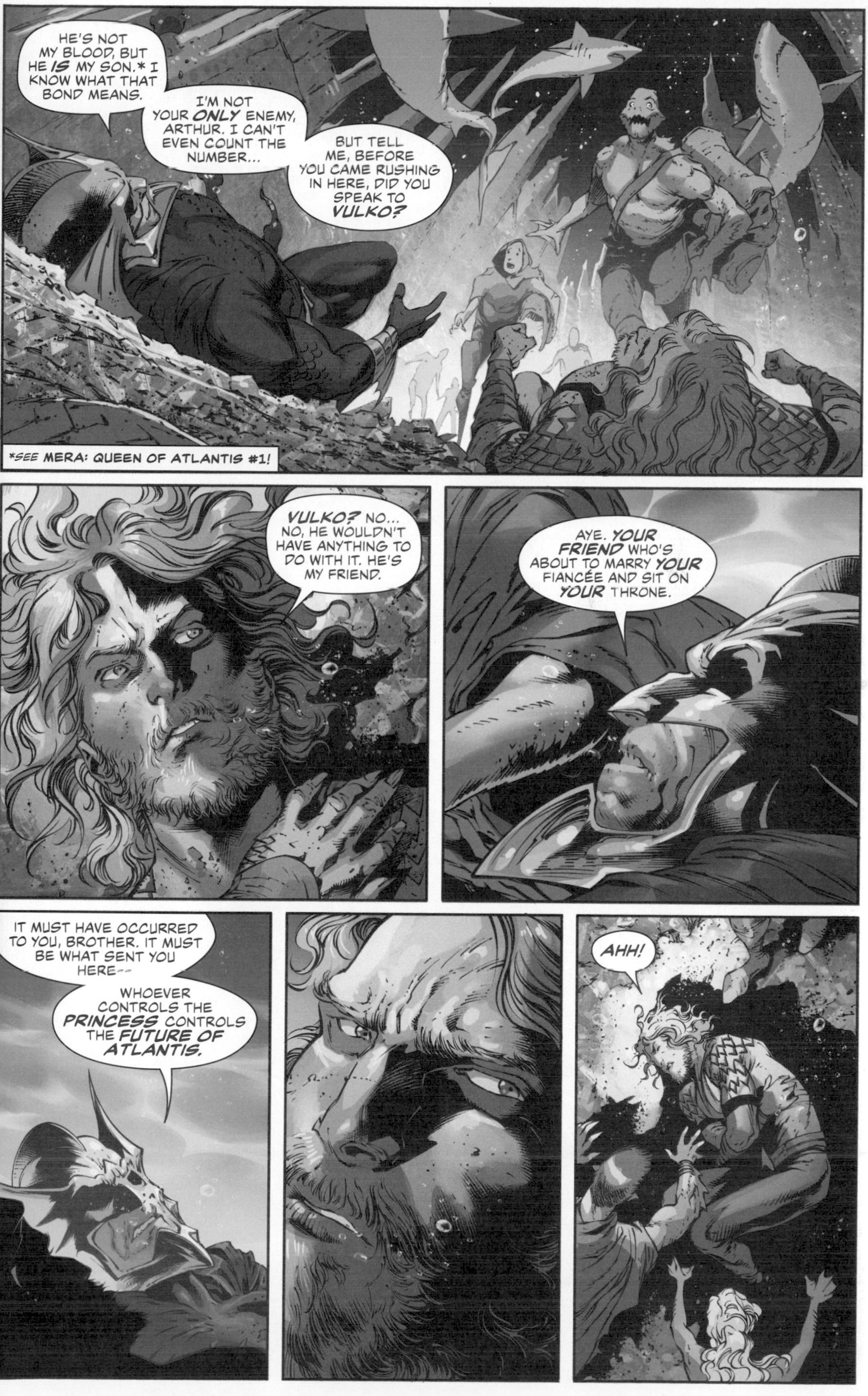
HE'S NOT MY BLOOD, BUT HE IS MY SON.* I KNOW WHAT THAT BOND MEANS.
I'M NOT YOUR ONLY ENEMY, ARTHUR. I CAN'T EVEN COUNT THE NUMBER...
BUT TELL ME, BEFORE YOU CAME RUSHING IN HERE, DID YOU SPEAK TO VULKO?
*SEE MERA: QUEEN OF ATLANTIS #1!
VULKO? NO... NO, HE WOULDN'T HAVE ANYTHING TO DO WITH IT. HE'S MY FRIEND.
AYE. YOUR FRIEND WHO'S ABOUT TO MARRY YOUR FIANCÉE AND SIT ON YOUR THRONE.
IT MUST HAVE OCCURRED TO YOU, BROTHER. IT MUST BE WHAT SENT YOU HERE--
WHOEVER CONTROLS THE PRINCESS CONTROLS THE FUTURE OF ATLANTIS.
AHH!

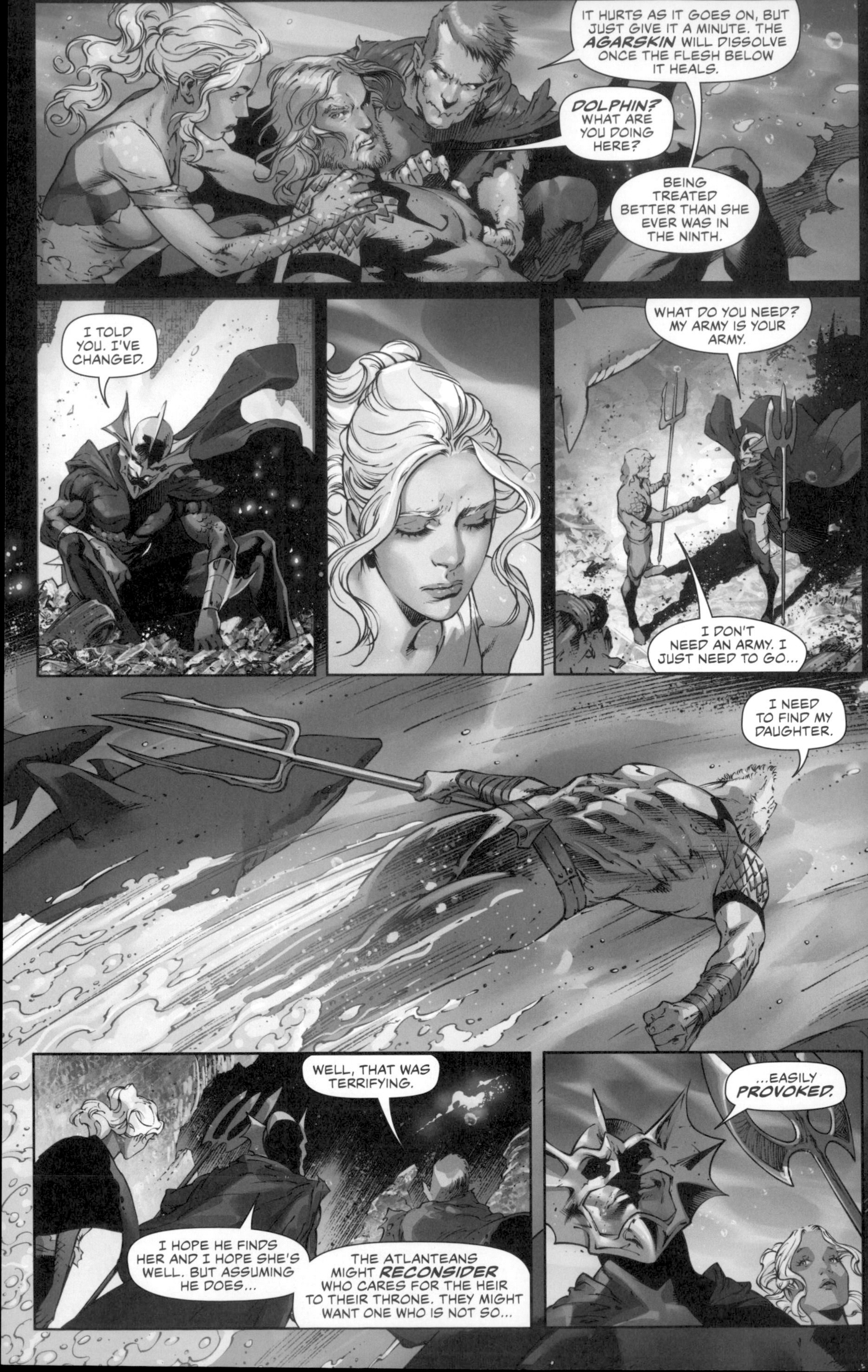

IT HURTS AS IT GOES ON, BUT JUST GIVE IT A MINUTE. THE **AGARSKIN** WILL DISSOLVE ONCE THE FLESH BELOW IT HEALS.
DOLPHIN? WHAT ARE YOU DOING HERE?
BEING TREATED BETTER THAN SHE EVER WAS IN THE NINTH.
I TOLD YOU. I'VE CHANGED.
WHAT DO YOU NEED? MY ARMY IS YOUR ARMY.
I DON'T NEED AN ARMY. I JUST NEED TO GO...
I NEED TO FIND MY DAUGHTER.
WELL, THAT WAS TERRIFYING.
I HOPE HE FINDS HER AND I HOPE SHE'S WELL. BUT ASSUMING HE DOES...
THE ATLANTEANS MIGHT **RECONSIDER** WHO CARES FOR THE HEIR TO THEIR THRONE. THEY MIGHT WANT ONE WHO IS NOT SO...
...EASILY **PROVOKED.**

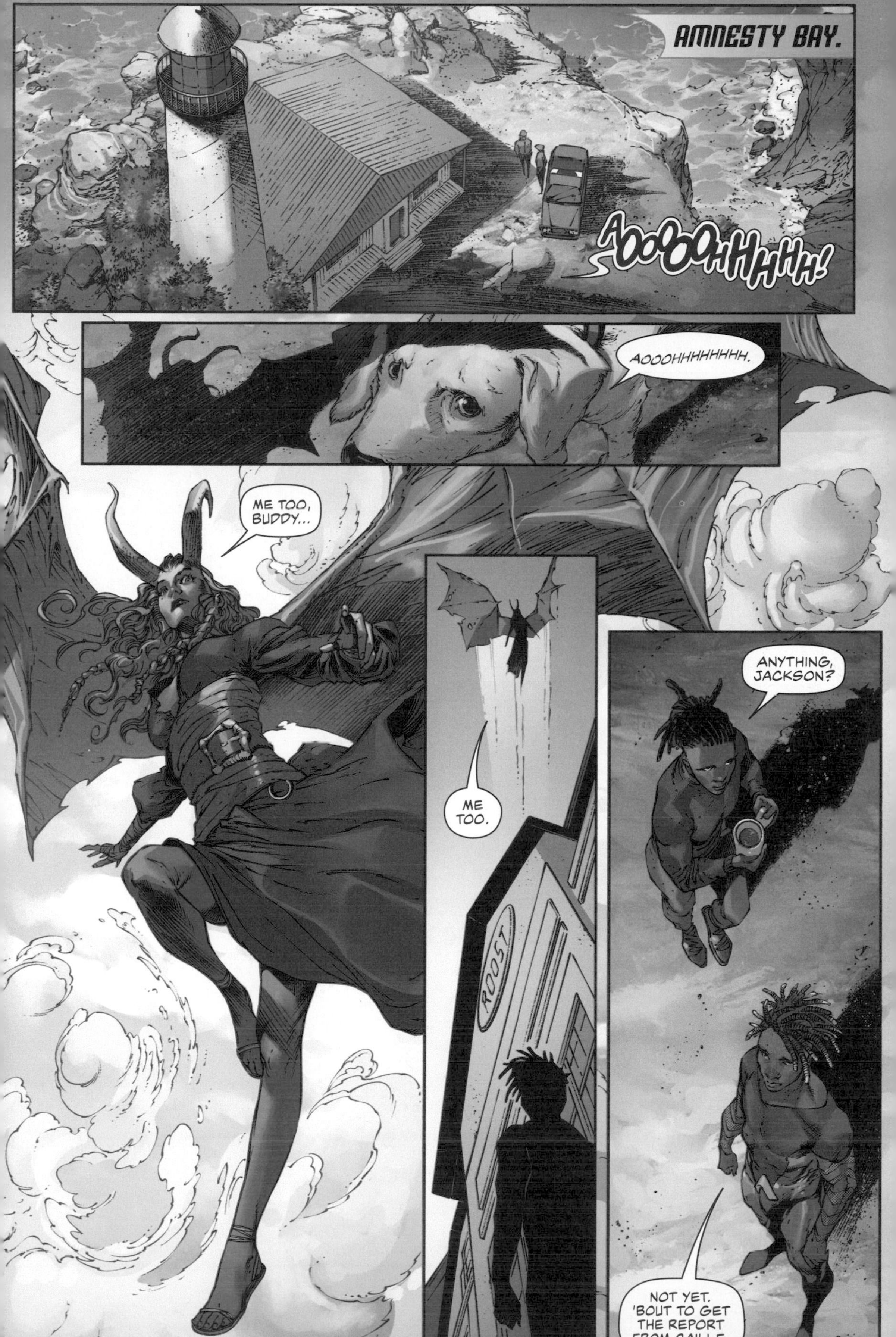
AMNESTY BAY.
AOOOOOHHHHH!
AOOOHHHHHHH.
ME TOO, BUDDY...
ME TOO.
ROOST
ANYTHING, JACKSON?
NOT YET. 'BOUT TO GET THE REPORT FROM CAILLE.

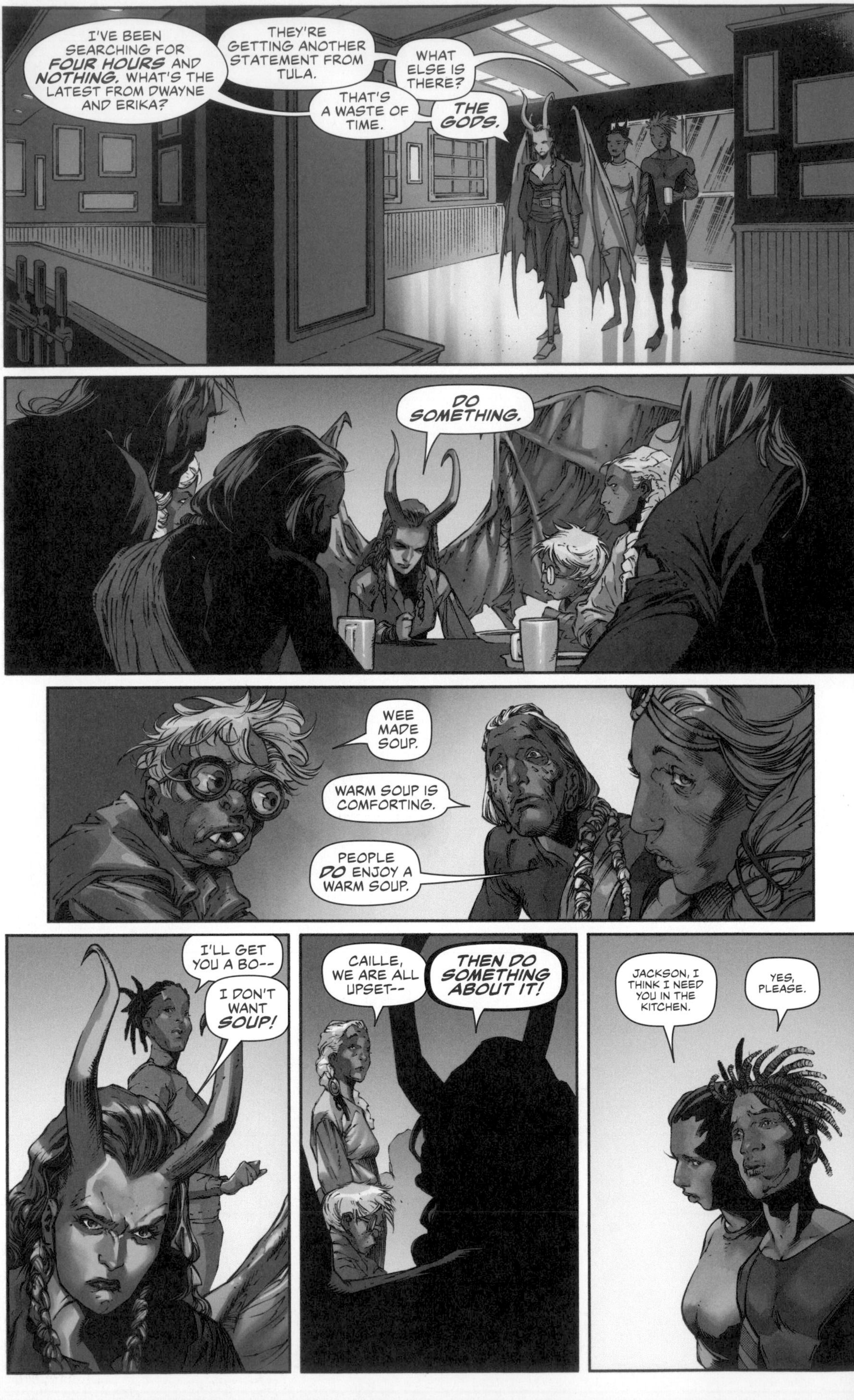

I'VE BEEN SEARCHING FOR FOUR HOURS AND NOTHING. WHAT'S THE LATEST FROM DWAYNE AND ERIKA?
THEY'RE GETTING ANOTHER STATEMENT FROM TULA.
THAT'S A WASTE OF TIME.
WHAT ELSE IS THERE?
THE GODS.
DO SOMETHING.
WEE MADE SOUP.
WARM SOUP IS COMFORTING.
PEOPLE DO ENJOY A WARM SOUP.
I'LL GET YOU A BO--
I DON'T WANT SOUP!
CAILLE, WE ARE ALL UPSET--
THEN DO SOMETHING ABOUT IT!
JACKSON, I THINK I NEED YOU IN THE KITCHEN.
YES, PLEASE.

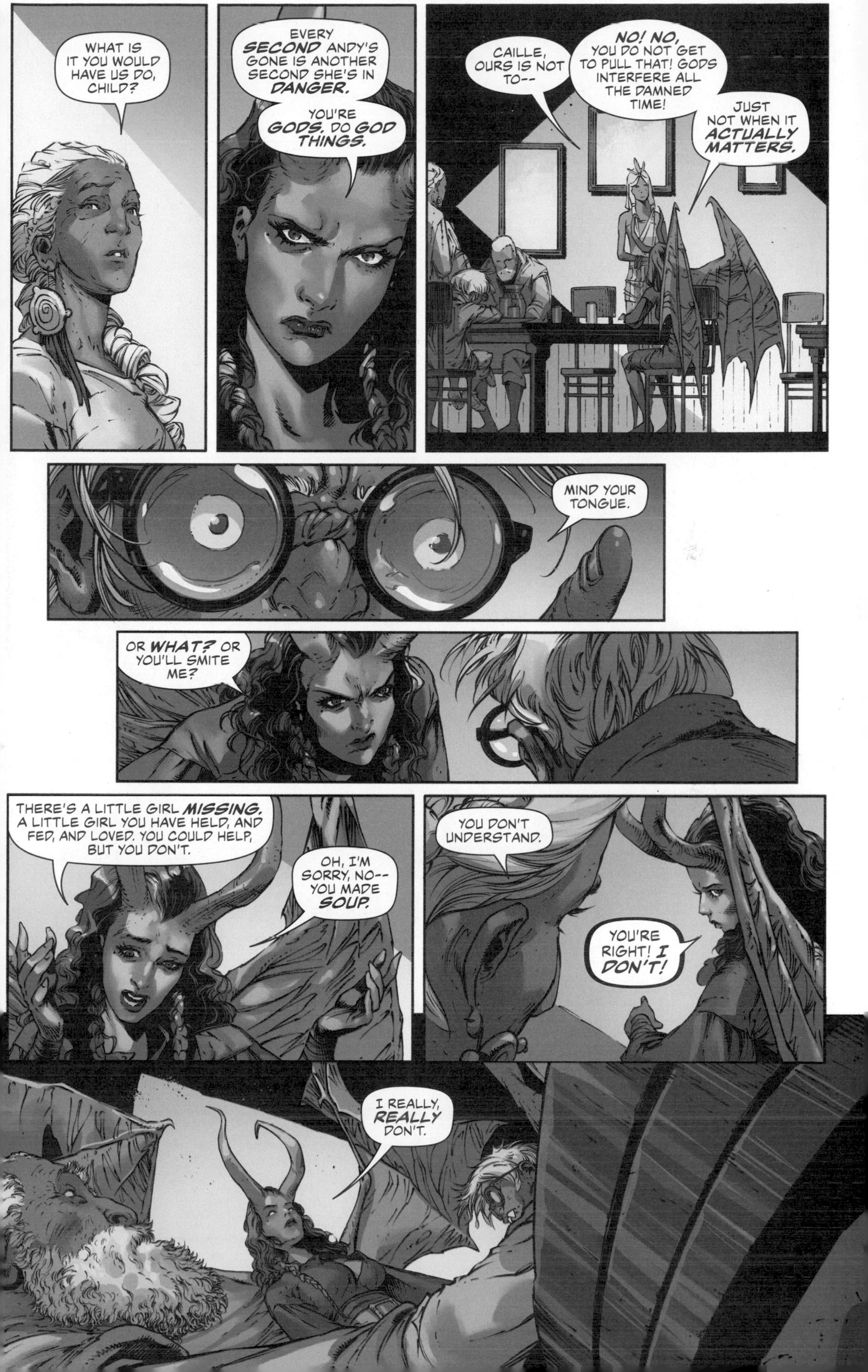
WHAT IS IT YOU WOULD HAVE US DO, CHILD?
EVERY SECOND ANDY'S GONE IS ANOTHER SECOND SHE'S IN DANGER.
YOU'RE GODS. DO GOD THINGS.
CAILLE, OURS IS NOT TO--
NO! NO, YOU DO NOT GET TO PULL THAT! GODS INTERFERE ALL THE DAMNED TIME!
JUST NOT WHEN IT ACTUALLY MATTERS.
MIND YOUR TONGUE.
OR WHAT? OR YOU'LL SMITE ME?
THERE'S A LITTLE GIRL MISSING. A LITTLE GIRL YOU HAVE HELD, AND FED, AND LOVED. YOU COULD HELP, BUT YOU DON'T.
OH, I'M SORRY, NO-- YOU MADE SOUP.
YOU DON'T UNDERSTAND.
YOU'RE RIGHT! I DON'T!
I REALLY, REALLY DON'T.

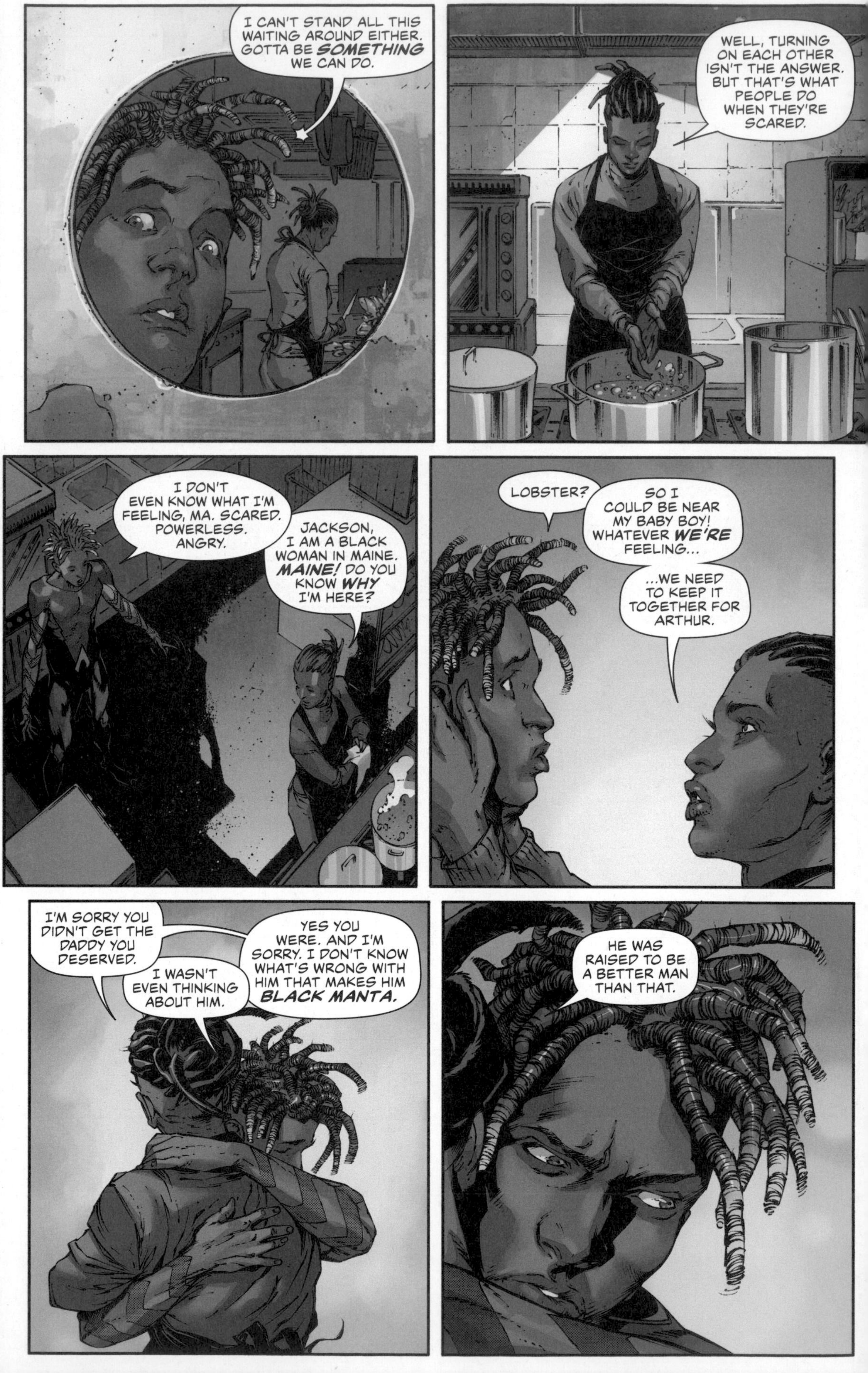
I CAN'T STAND ALL THIS WAITING AROUND EITHER. GOTTA BE SOMETHING WE CAN DO.
WELL, TURNING ON EACH OTHER ISN'T THE ANSWER. BUT THAT'S WHAT PEOPLE DO WHEN THEY'RE SCARED.
I DON'T EVEN KNOW WHAT I'M FEELING, MA. SCARED. POWERLESS. ANGRY.
JACKSON, I AM A BLACK WOMAN IN MAINE. MAINE! DO YOU KNOW WHY I'M HERE?
LOBSTER?
SO I COULD BE NEAR MY BABY BOY! WHATEVER WE'RE FEELING...
...WE NEED TO KEEP IT TOGETHER FOR ARTHUR.
I'M SORRY YOU DIDN'T GET THE DADDY YOU DESERVED.
I WASN'T EVEN THINKING ABOUT HIM.
YES YOU WERE. AND I'M SORRY. I DON'T KNOW WHAT'S WRONG WITH HIM THAT MAKES HIM BLACK MANTA.
HE WAS RAISED TO BE A BETTER MAN THAN THAT.

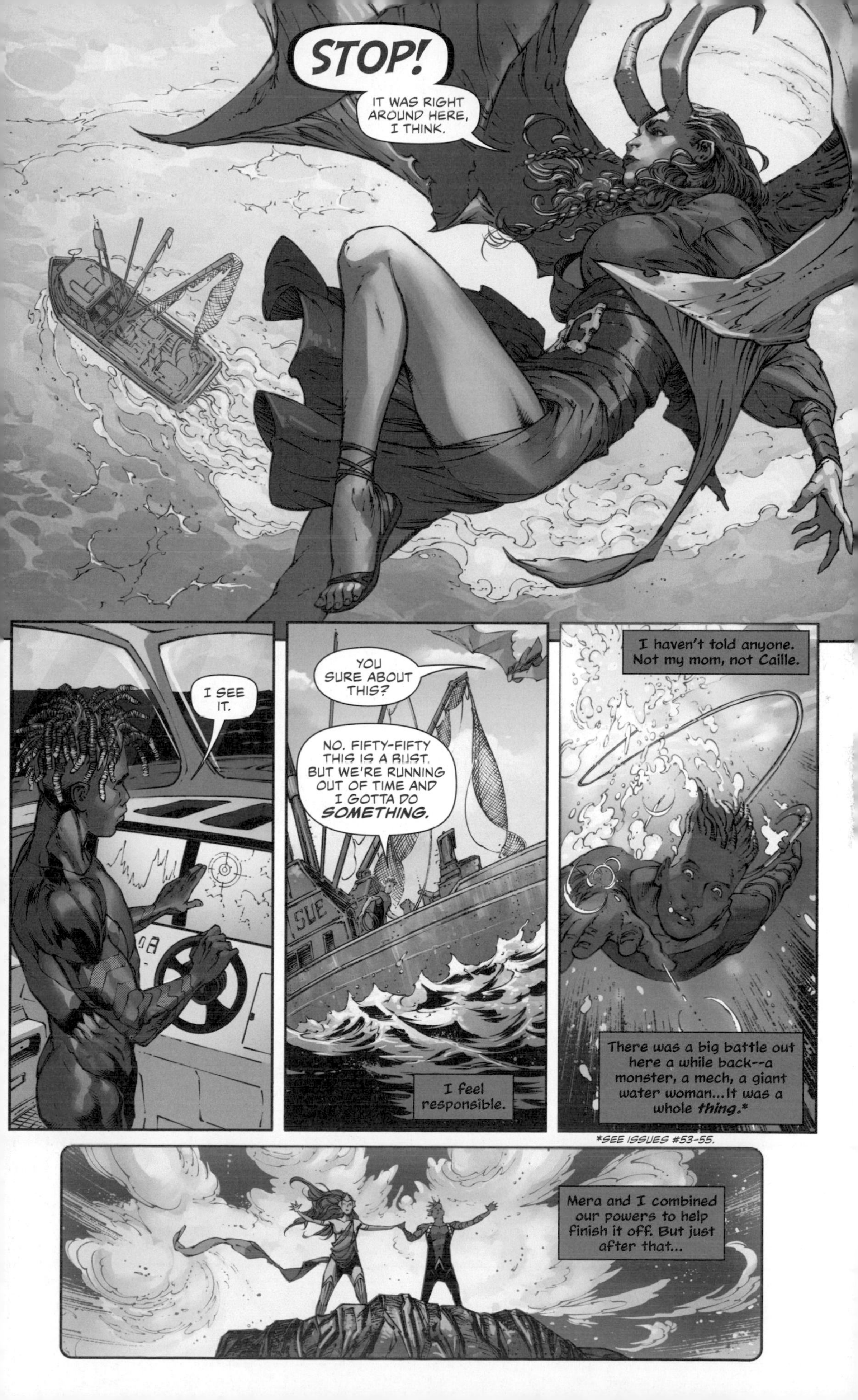
STOP!
IT WAS RIGHT AROUND HERE, I THINK.
I SEE IT.
YOU SURE ABOUT THIS?
NO. FIFTY-FIFTY THIS IS A BUST. BUT WE'RE RUNNING OUT OF TIME AND I GOTTA DO *SOMETHING.*
I feel responsible.
I haven't told anyone. Not my mom, not Caille.
There was a big battle out here a while back--a monster, a mech, a giant water woman...It was a whole ***thing.****
**SEE ISSUES #53-55.*
Mera and I combined our powers to help finish it off. But just after that...

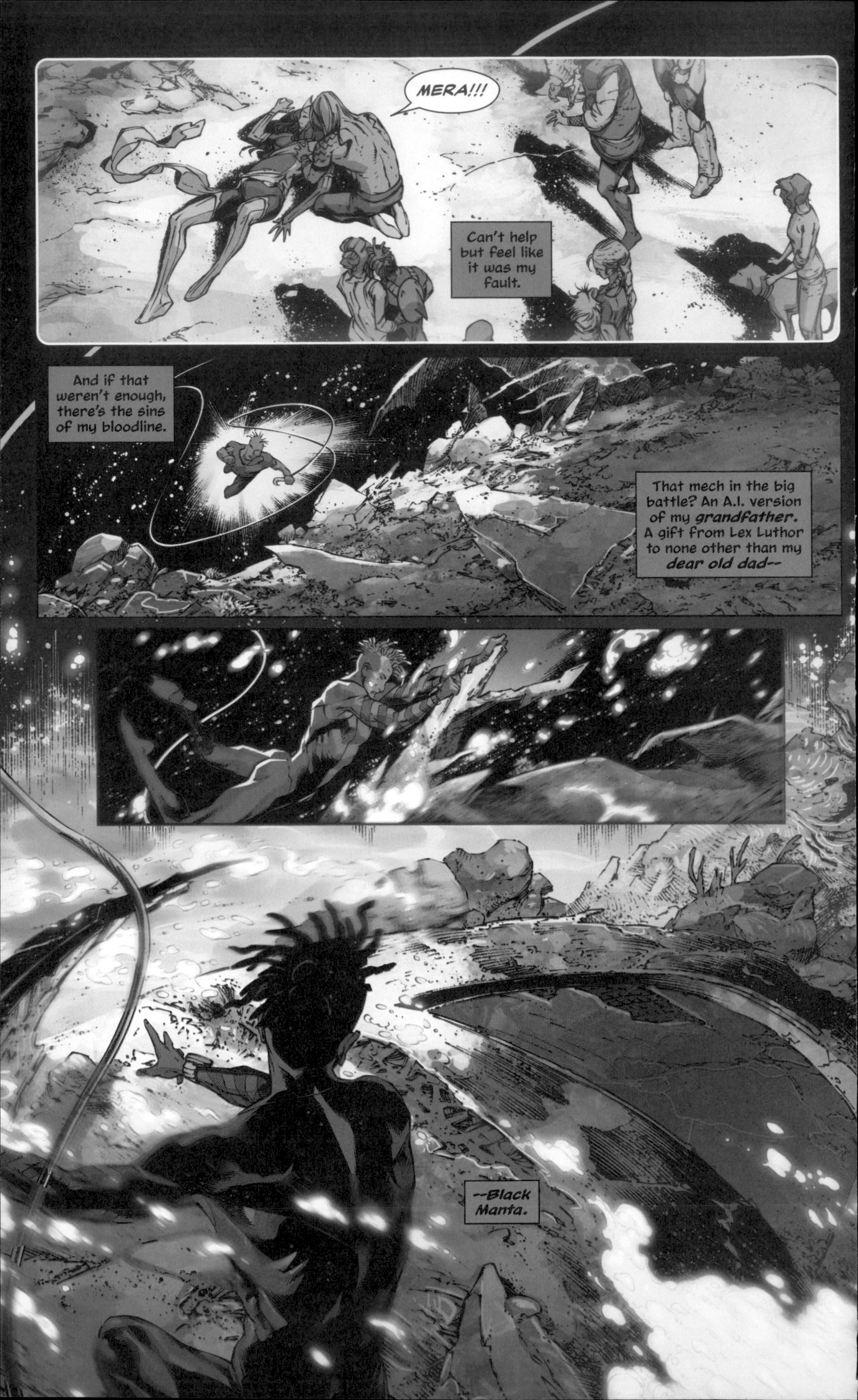
MERA!!!
Can't help but feel like it was my fault.
And if that weren't enough, there's the sins of my bloodline.
That mech in the big battle? An A.I. version of my *grandfather*. A gift from Lex Luthor to none other than my *dear old dad--*
--*Black Manta.*

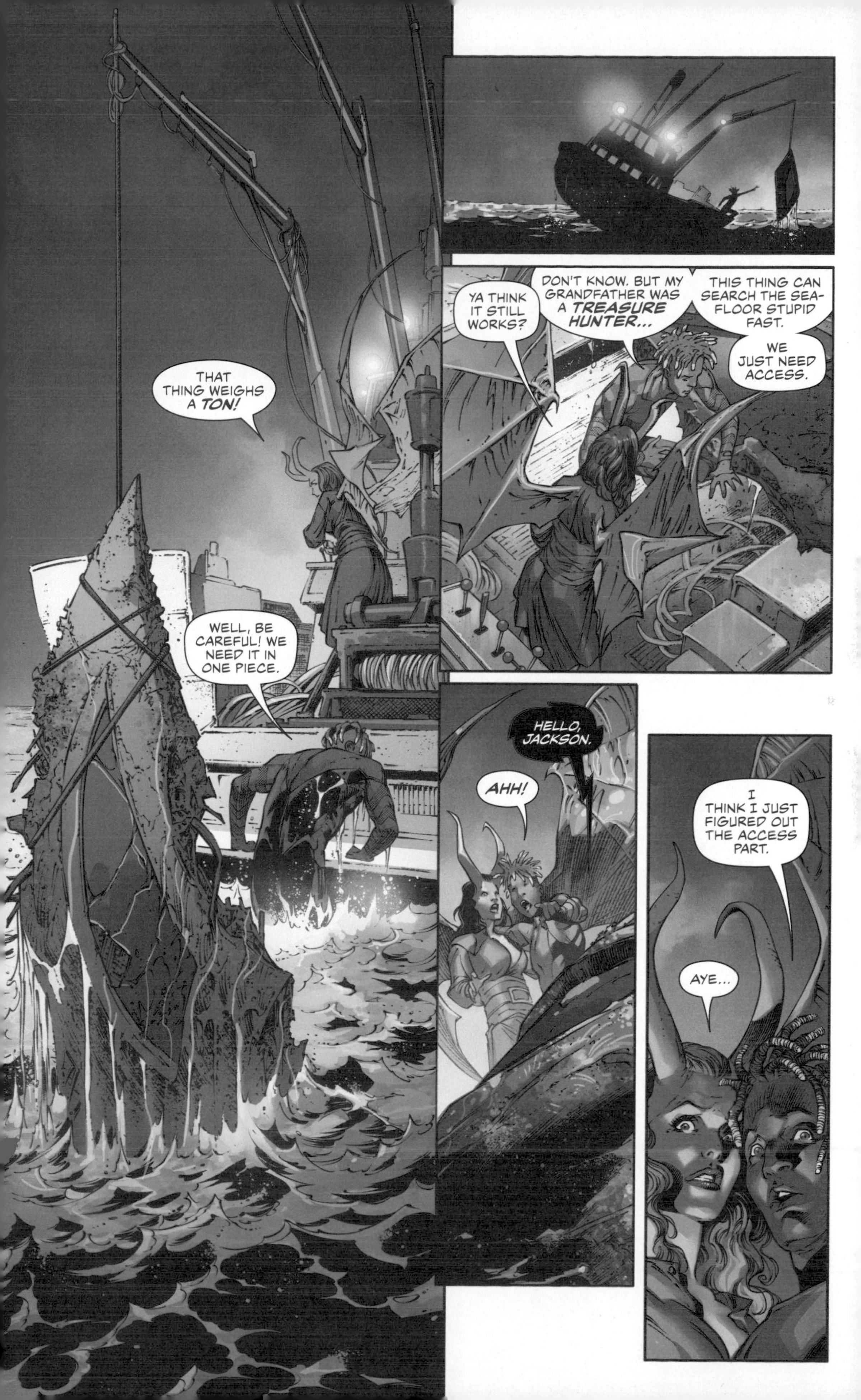
THAT THING WEIGHS A *TON!*
WELL, BE CAREFUL! WE NEED IT IN ONE PIECE.
YA THINK IT STILL WORKS?
DON'T KNOW. BUT MY GRANDFATHER WAS A *TREASURE HUNTER...*
THIS THING CAN SEARCH THE SEA-FLOOR STUPID FAST.
WE JUST NEED ACCESS.
HELLO, JACKSON.
AHH!
I THINK I JUST FIGURED OUT THE ACCESS PART.
AYE...

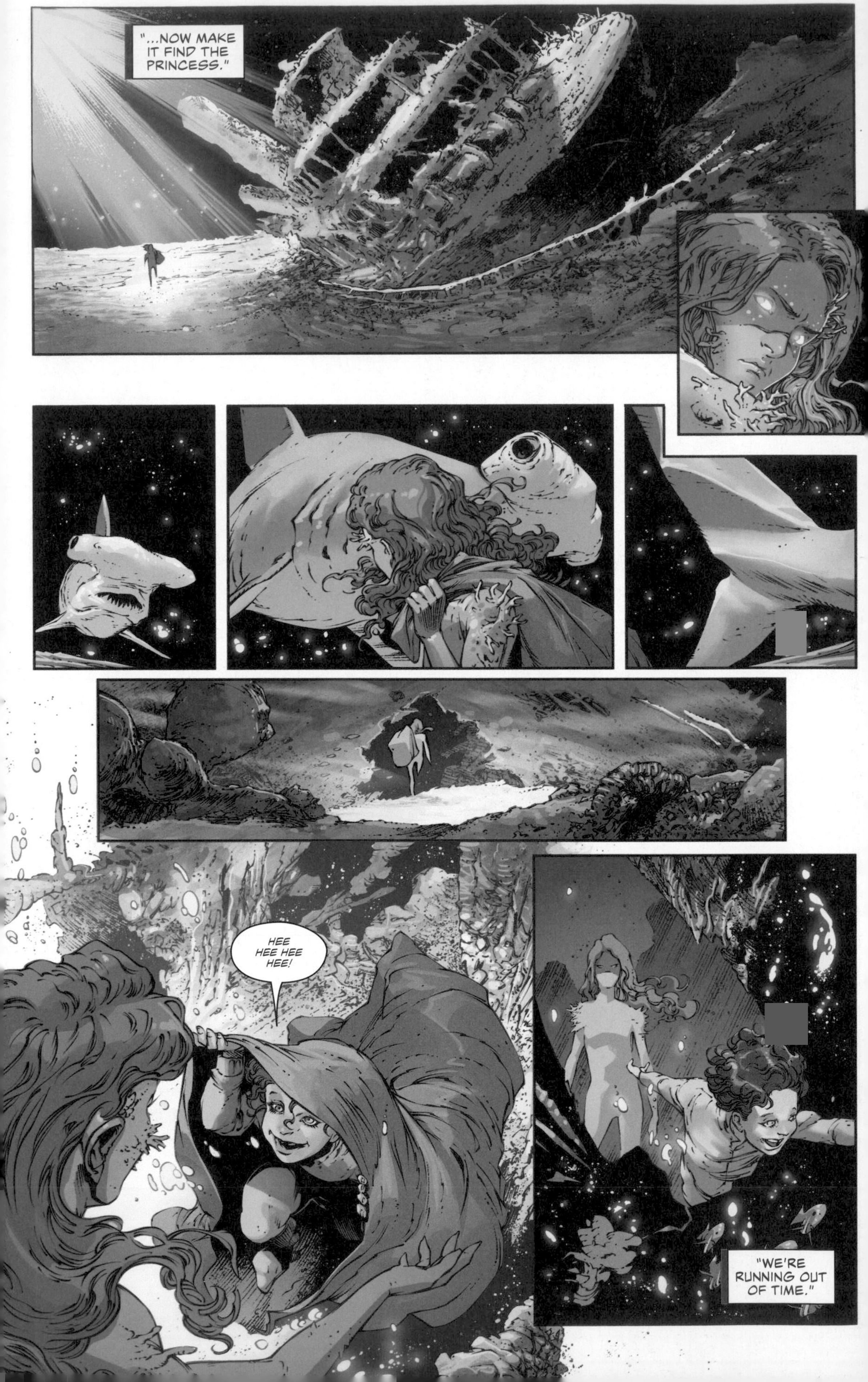
"...NOW MAKE IT FIND THE PRINCESS."
HEE HEE HEE HEE!
"WE'RE RUNNING OUT OF TIME."

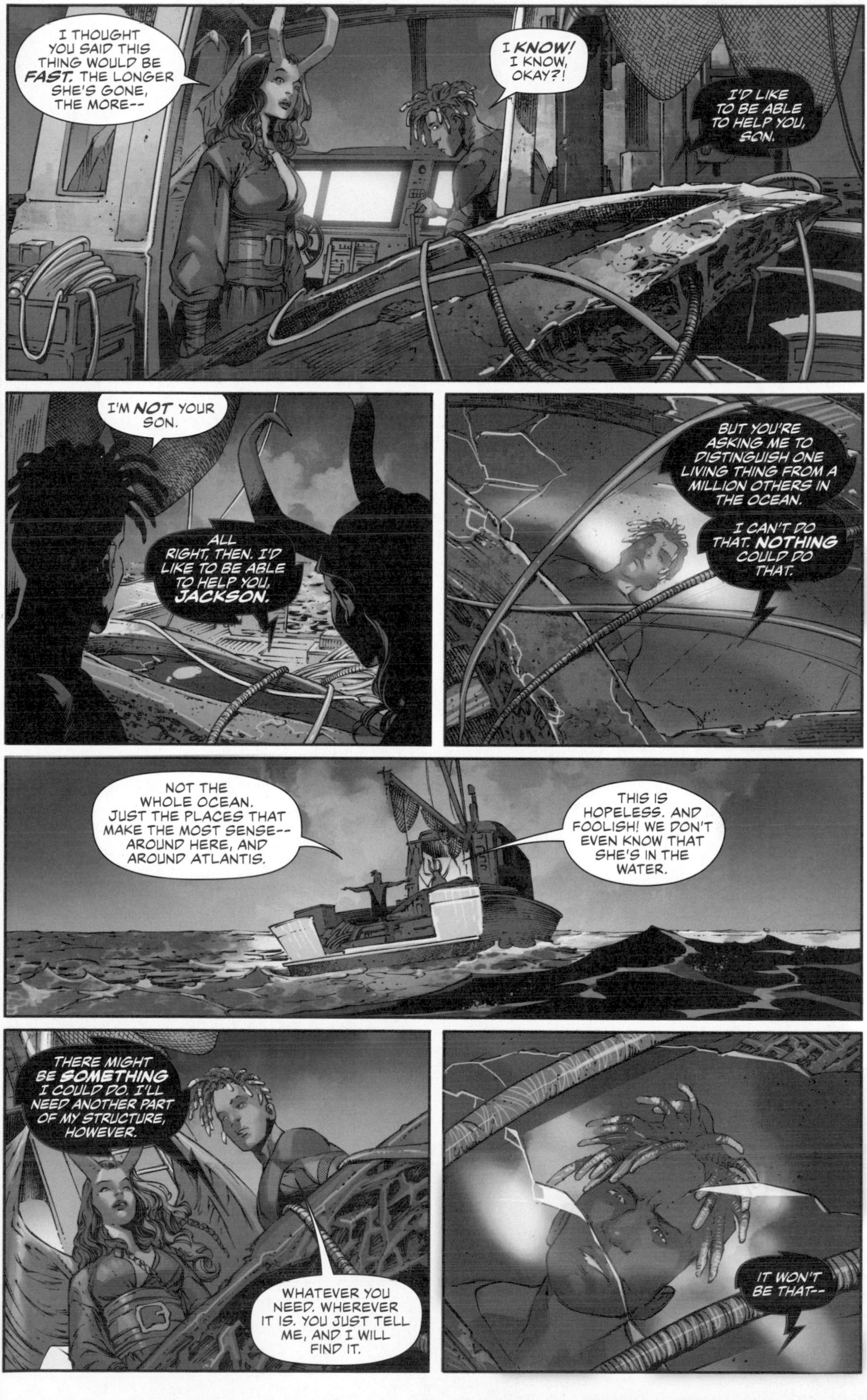

I THOUGHT YOU SAID THIS THING WOULD BE **FAST.** THE LONGER SHE'S GONE, THE MORE--
I **KNOW!** I KNOW, OKAY?!
I'D LIKE TO BE ABLE TO HELP YOU, SON.
I'M **NOT** YOUR SON.
ALL RIGHT, THEN. I'D LIKE TO BE ABLE TO HELP YOU, **JACKSON.**
BUT YOU'RE ASKING ME TO DISTINGUISH ONE LIVING THING FROM A MILLION OTHERS IN THE OCEAN.
I CAN'T DO THAT. **NOTHING** COULD DO THAT.
NOT THE WHOLE OCEAN. JUST THE PLACES THAT MAKE THE MOST SENSE-- AROUND HERE, AND AROUND ATLANTIS.
THIS IS HOPELESS. AND FOOLISH! WE DON'T EVEN KNOW THAT SHE'S IN THE WATER.
THERE MIGHT BE **SOMETHING** I COULD DO. I'LL NEED ANOTHER PART OF MY STRUCTURE, HOWEVER.
WHATEVER YOU NEED. WHEREVER IT IS. YOU JUST TELL ME, AND I WILL FIND IT.
IT WON'T BE THAT--

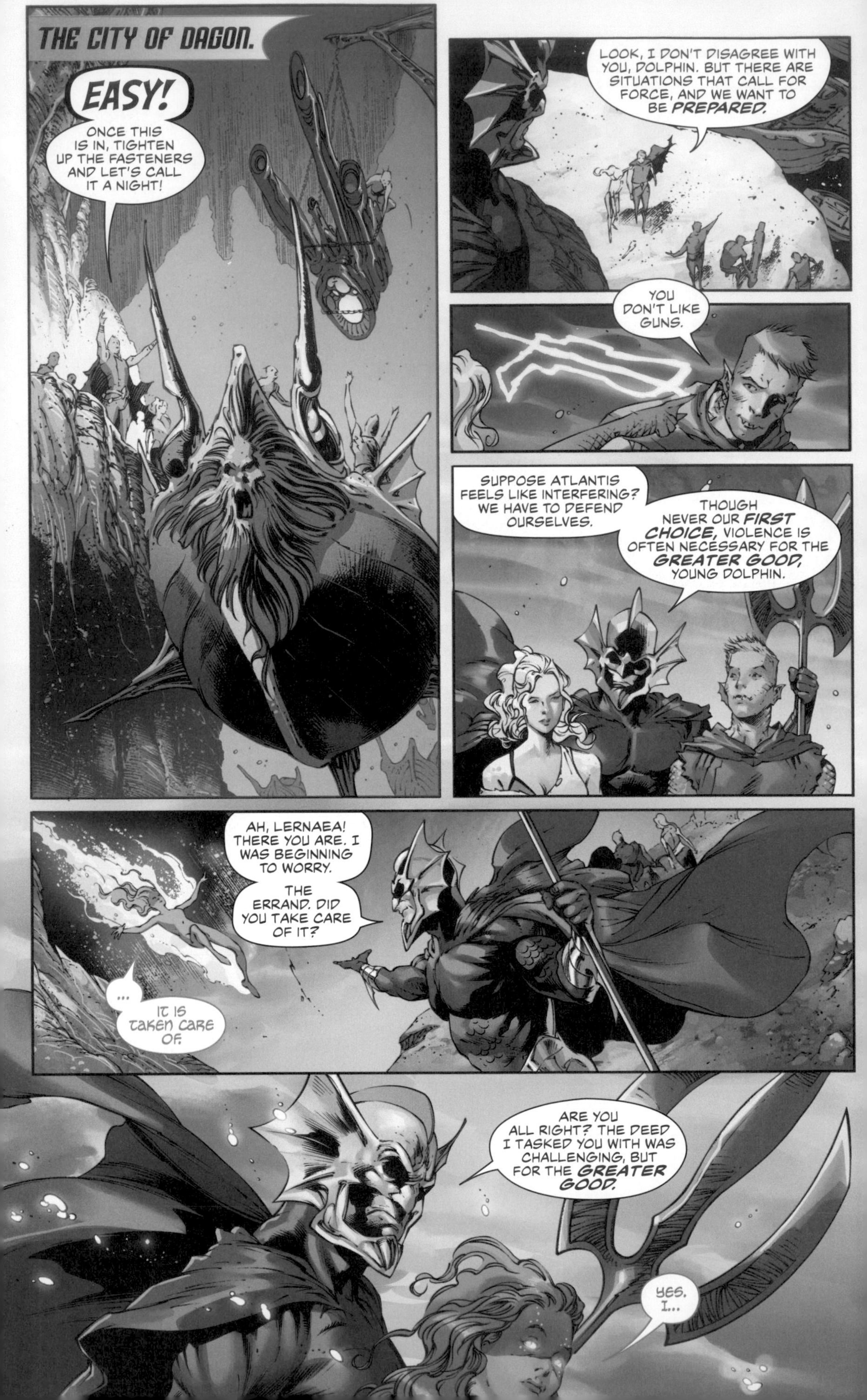
THE CITY OF DAGON.
EASY!
ONCE THIS IS IN, TIGHTEN UP THE FASTENERS AND LET'S CALL IT A NIGHT!
LOOK, I DON'T DISAGREE WITH YOU, DOLPHIN. BUT THERE ARE SITUATIONS THAT CALL FOR FORCE, AND WE WANT TO BE PREPARED.
YOU DON'T LIKE GUNS.
SUPPOSE ATLANTIS FEELS LIKE INTERFERING? WE HAVE TO DEFEND OURSELVES.
THOUGH NEVER OUR FIRST CHOICE, VIOLENCE IS OFTEN NECESSARY FOR THE GREATER GOOD, YOUNG DOLPHIN.
AH, LERNAEA! THERE YOU ARE. I WAS BEGINNING TO WORRY.
THE ERRAND. DID YOU TAKE CARE OF IT?
...
IT IS TAKEN CARE OF.
ARE YOU ALL RIGHT? THE DEED I TASKED YOU WITH WAS CHALLENGING, BUT FOR THE GREATER GOOD.
YES. I...

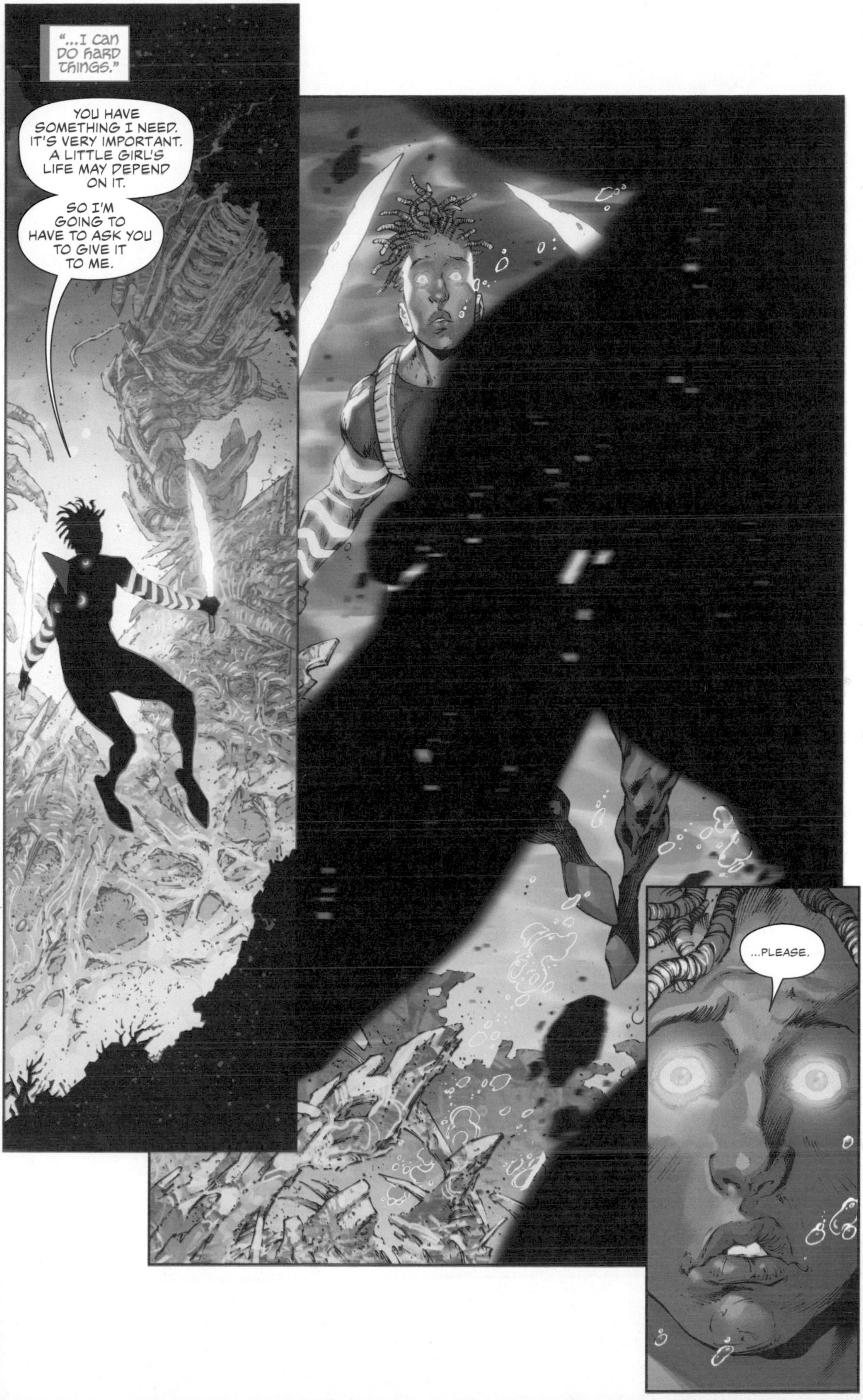
"...I can do hard things."
YOU HAVE SOMETHING I NEED. IT'S VERY IMPORTANT. A LITTLE GIRL'S LIFE MAY DEPEND ON IT.
SO I'M GOING TO HAVE TO ASK YOU TO GIVE IT TO ME.
...PLEASE.

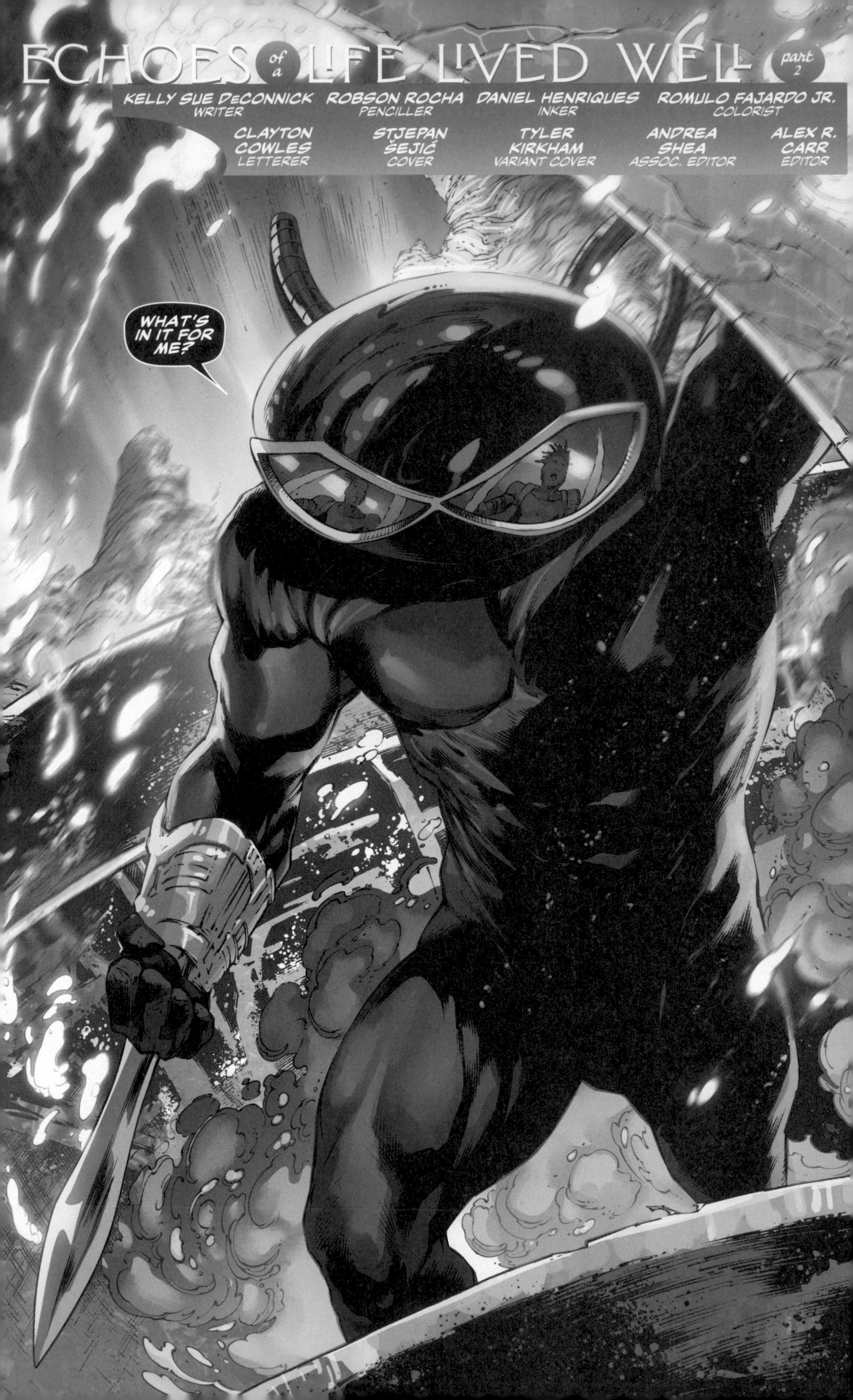
ECHOES of a LIFE LIVED WELL part 2
KELLY SUE DECONNICK WRITER
ROBSON ROCHA PENCILLER
DANIEL HENRIQUES INKER
ROMULO FAJARDO JR. COLORIST
CLAYTON COWLES LETTERER
STJEPAN ŠEJIĆ COVER
TYLER KIRKHAM VARIANT COVER
ANDREA SHEA ASSOC. EDITOR
ALEX R. CARR EDITOR
WHAT'S IN IT FOR ME?

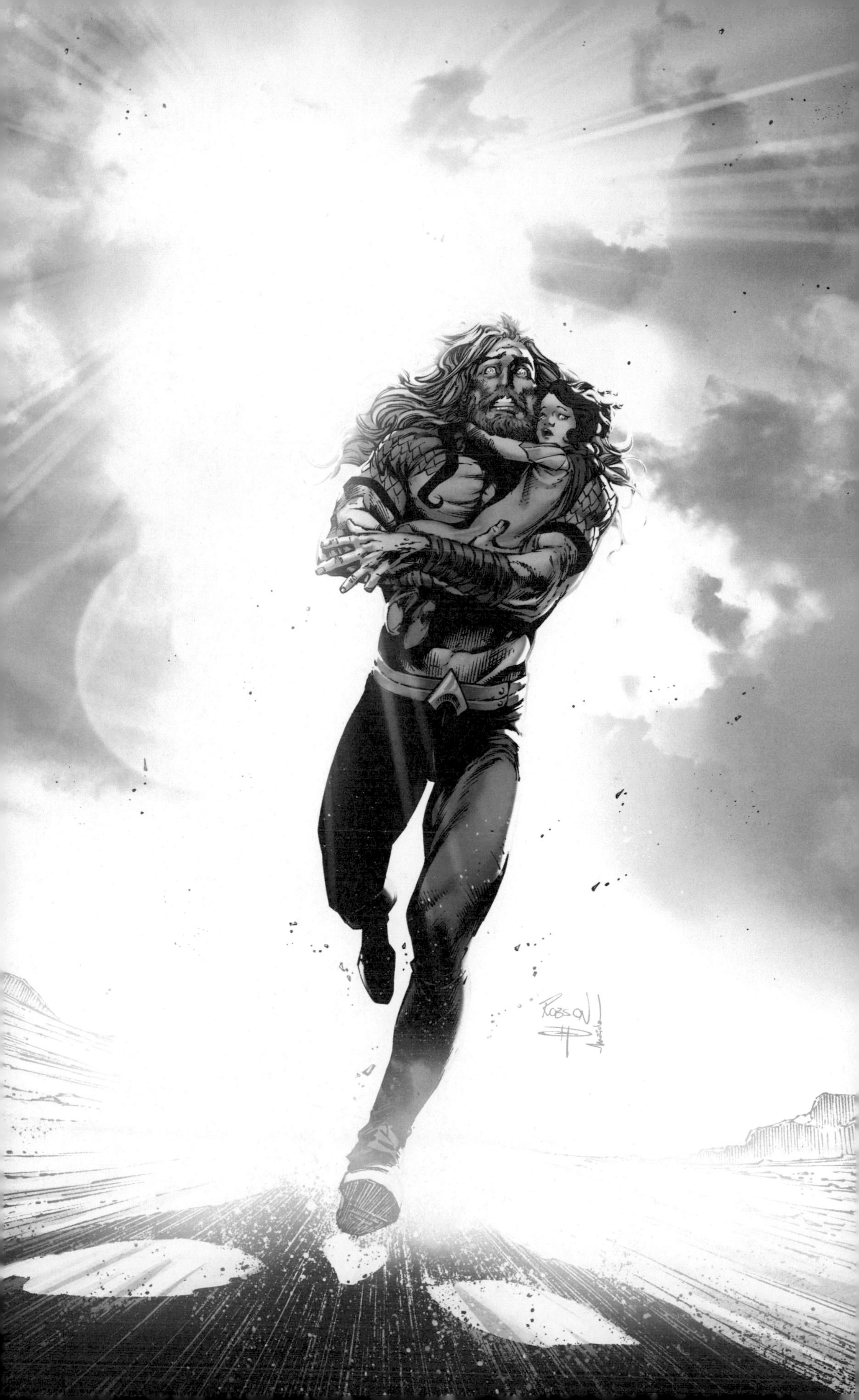

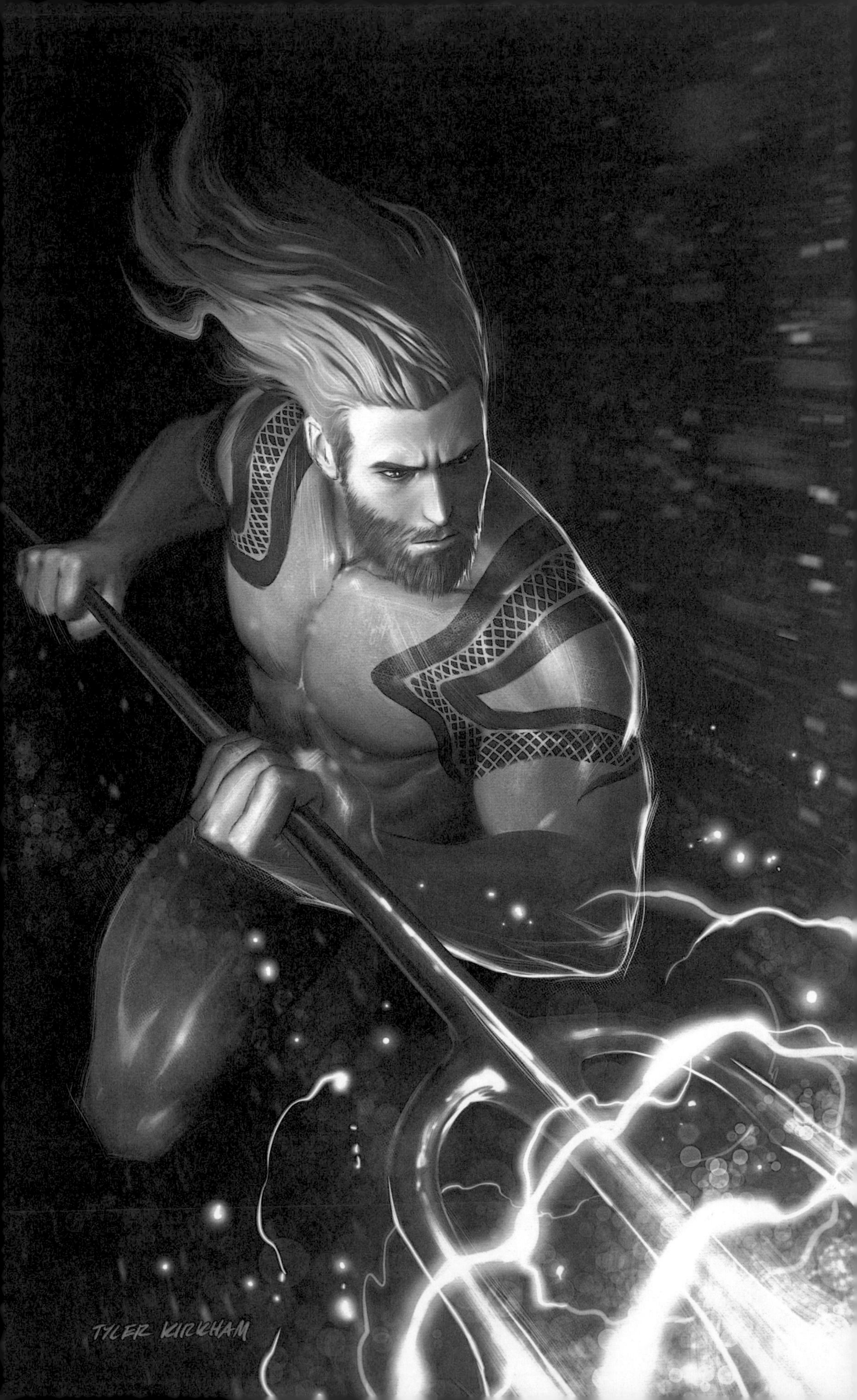
TYLER KIRKHAM

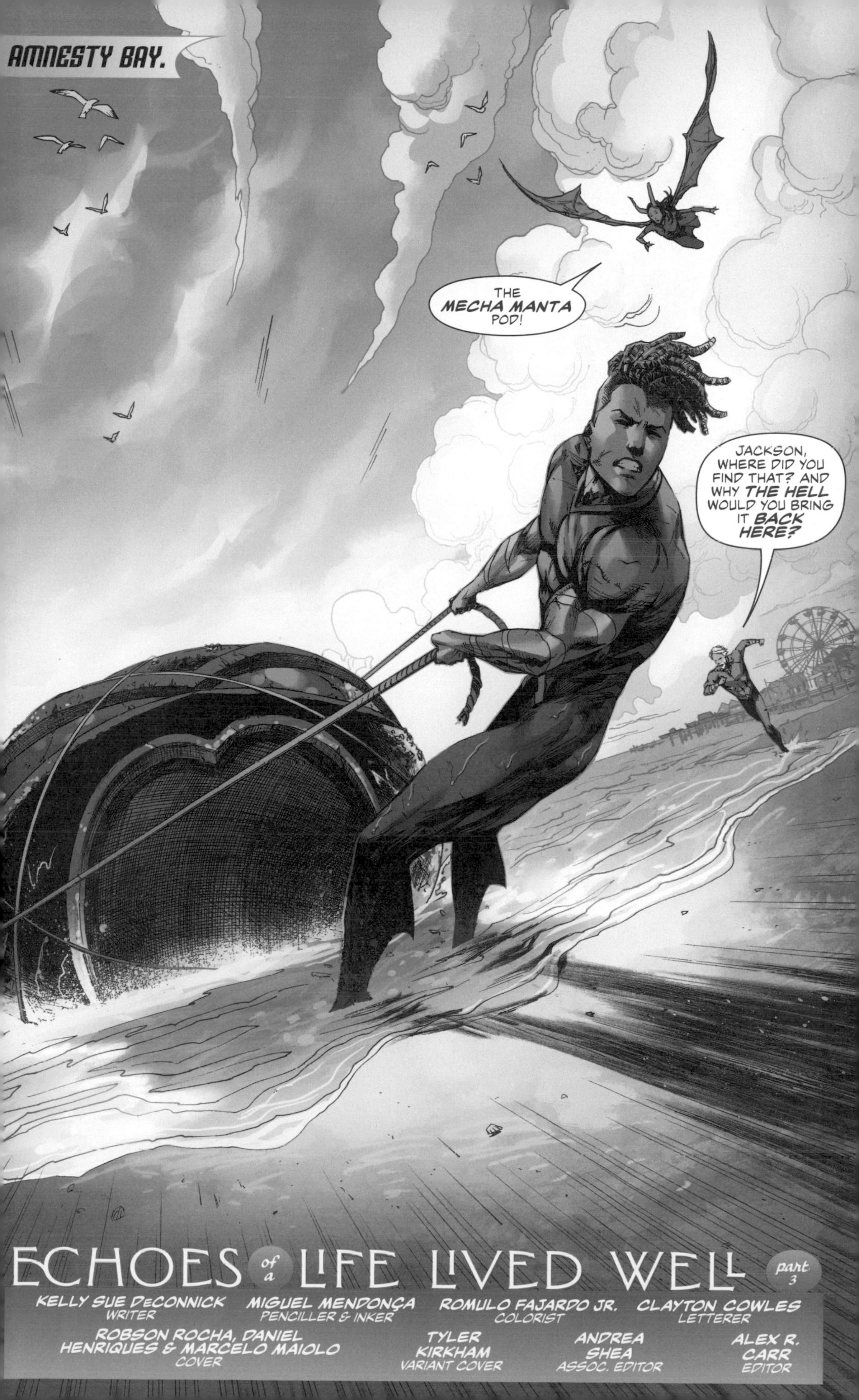
AMNESTY BAY.
THE MECHA MANTA POD!
JACKSON, WHERE DID YOU FIND THAT? AND WHY THE HELL WOULD YOU BRING IT BACK HERE?
ECHOES of a LIFE LIVED WELL part 3
KELLY SUE DeCONNICK WRITER
MIGUEL MENDONÇA PENCILLER & INKER
ROMULO FAJARDO JR. COLORIST
CLAYTON COWLES LETTERER
ROBSON ROCHA, DANIEL HENRIQUES & MARCELO MAIOLO COVER
TYLER KIRKHAM VARIANT COVER
ANDREA SHEA ASSOC. EDITOR
ALEX R. CARR EDITOR

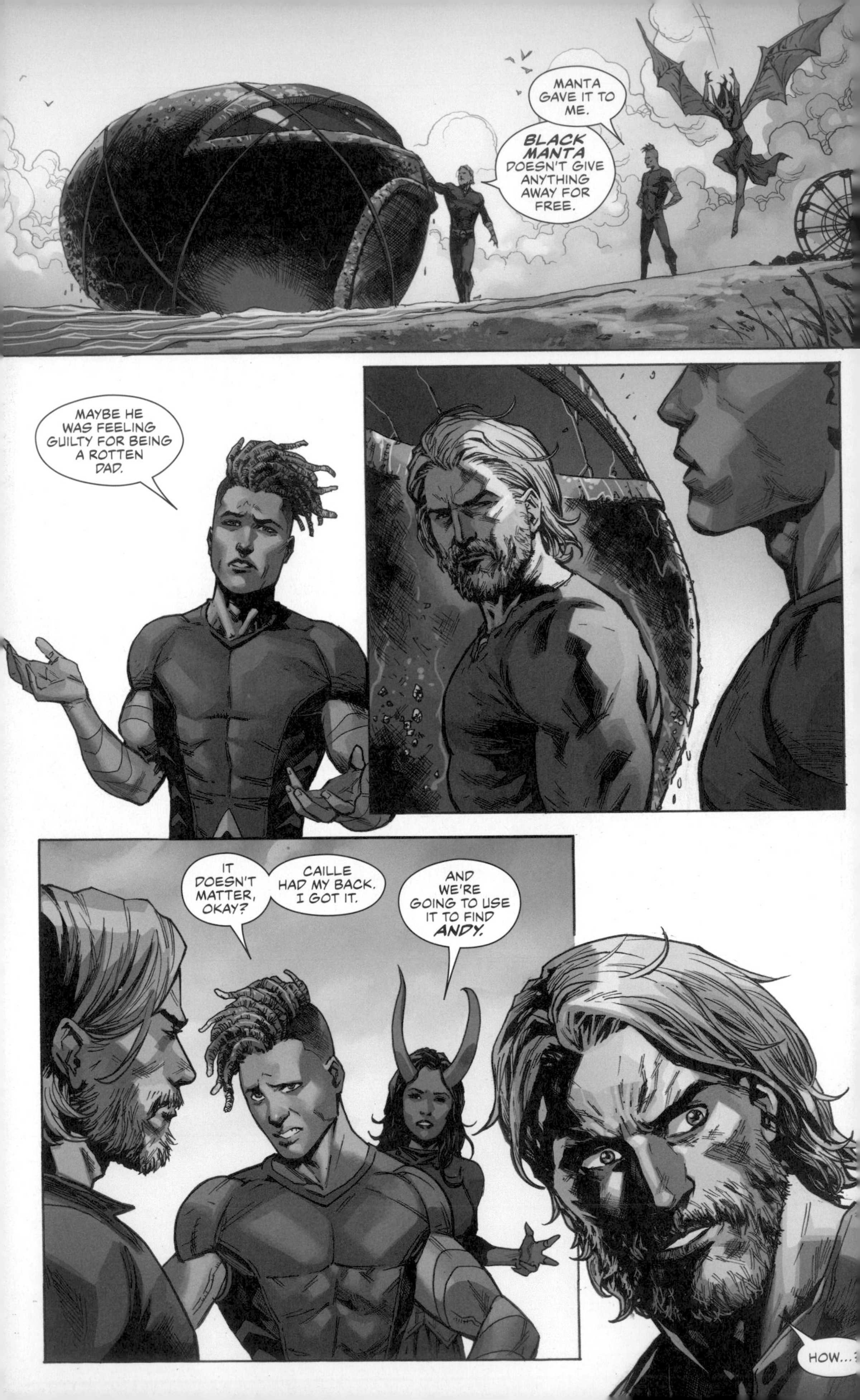
MANTA GAVE IT TO ME.
BLACK MANTA DOESN'T GIVE ANYTHING AWAY FOR FREE.
MAYBE HE WAS FEELING GUILTY FOR BEING A ROTTEN DAD.
IT DOESN'T MATTER, OKAY?
CAILLE HAD MY BACK. I GOT IT.
AND WE'RE GOING TO USE IT TO FIND ANDY.
HOW...?

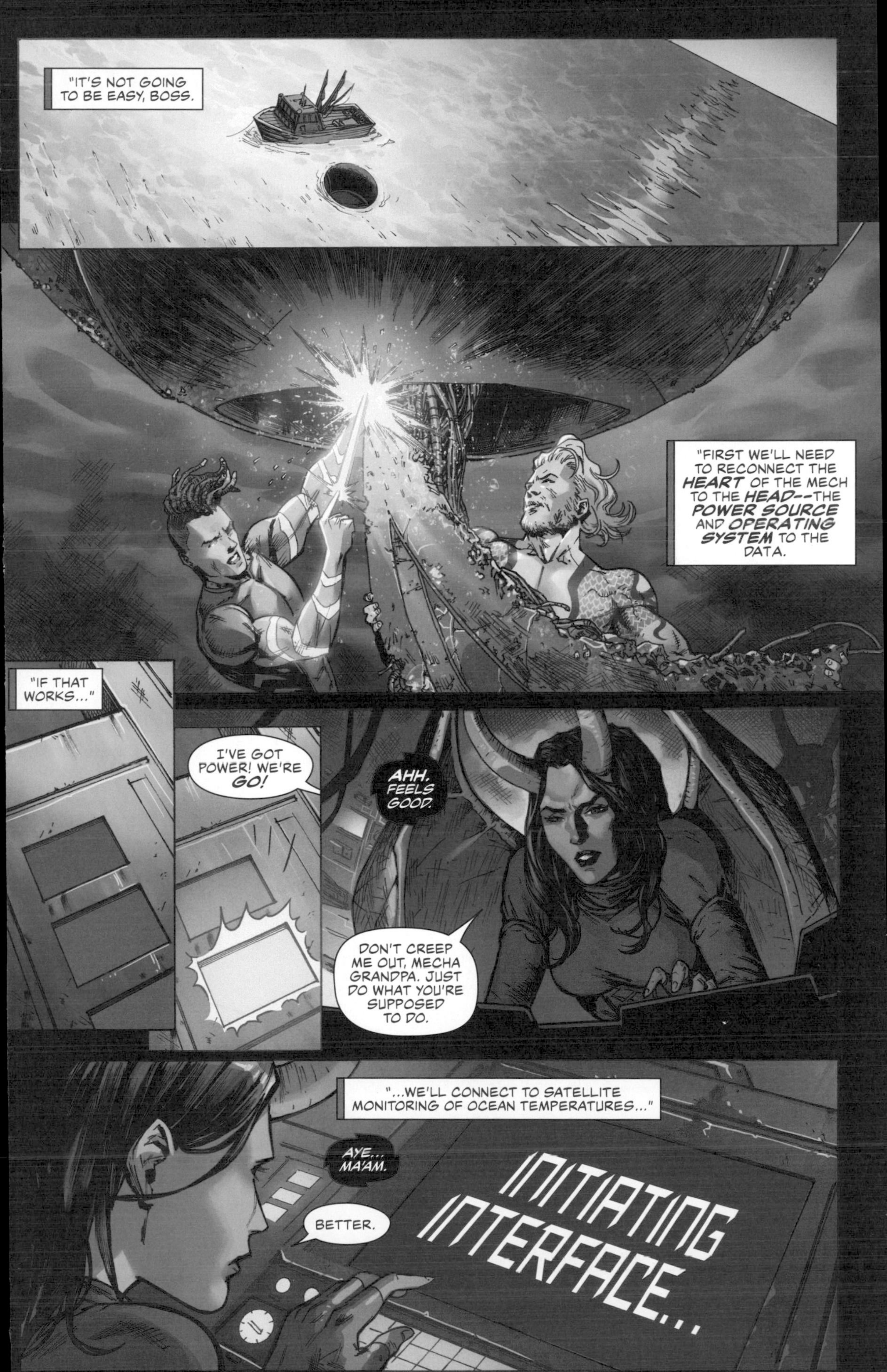
"IT'S NOT GOING TO BE EASY, BOSS.
"FIRST WE'LL NEED TO RECONNECT THE HEART OF THE MECH TO THE HEAD--THE POWER SOURCE AND OPERATING SYSTEM TO THE DATA.
"IF THAT WORKS..."
I'VE GOT POWER! WE'RE GO!
AHH. FEELS GOOD.
DON'T CREEP ME OUT, MECHA GRANDPA. JUST DO WHAT YOU'RE SUPPOSED TO DO.
"...WE'LL CONNECT TO SATELLITE MONITORING OF OCEAN TEMPERATURES..."
AYE... MA'AM.
BETTER.
INITIATING INTERFACE...

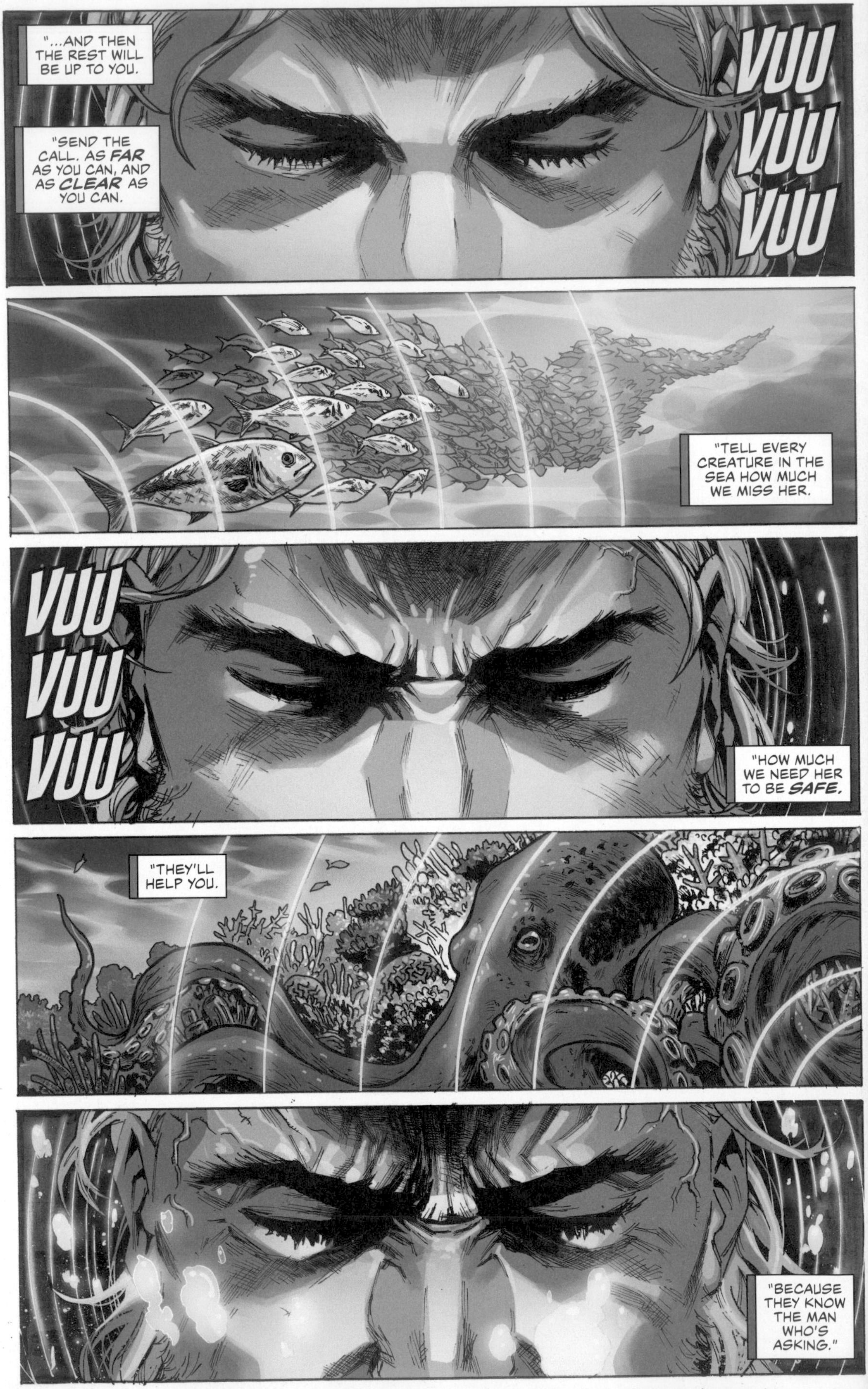
"...AND THEN THE REST WILL BE UP TO YOU.
"SEND THE CALL. AS FAR AS YOU CAN, AND AS CLEAR AS YOU CAN.
VUU VUU VUU
"TELL EVERY CREATURE IN THE SEA HOW MUCH WE MISS HER.
VUU VUU VUU
"HOW MUCH WE NEED HER TO BE SAFE.
"THEY'LL HELP YOU.
"BECAUSE THEY KNOW THE MAN WHO'S ASKING."

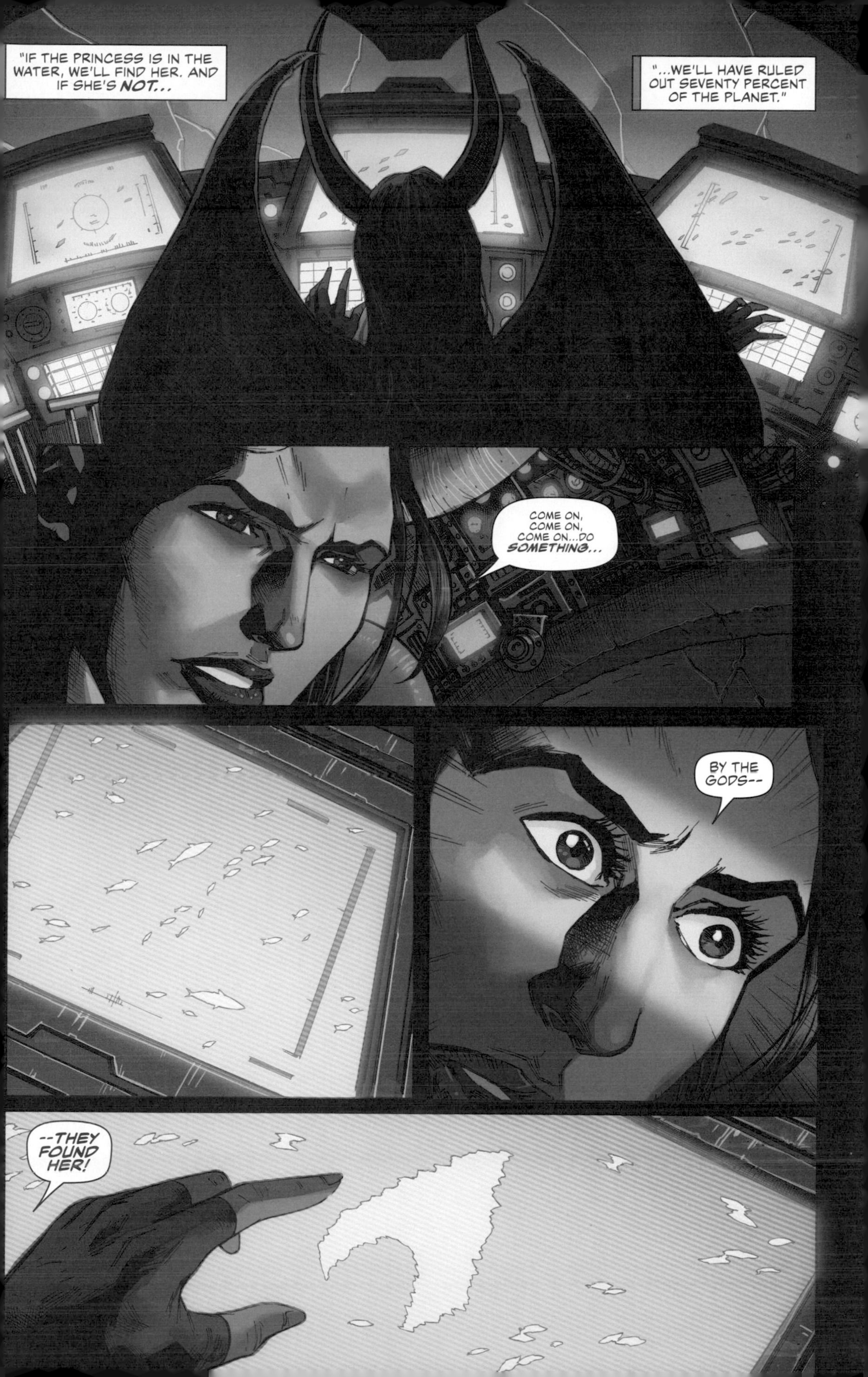
"IF THE PRINCESS IS IN THE WATER, WE'LL FIND HER. AND IF SHE'S NOT...
"...WE'LL HAVE RULED OUT SEVENTY PERCENT OF THE PLANET."
COME ON, COME ON, COME ON...DO SOMETHING...
BY THE GODS--
--THEY FOUND HER!

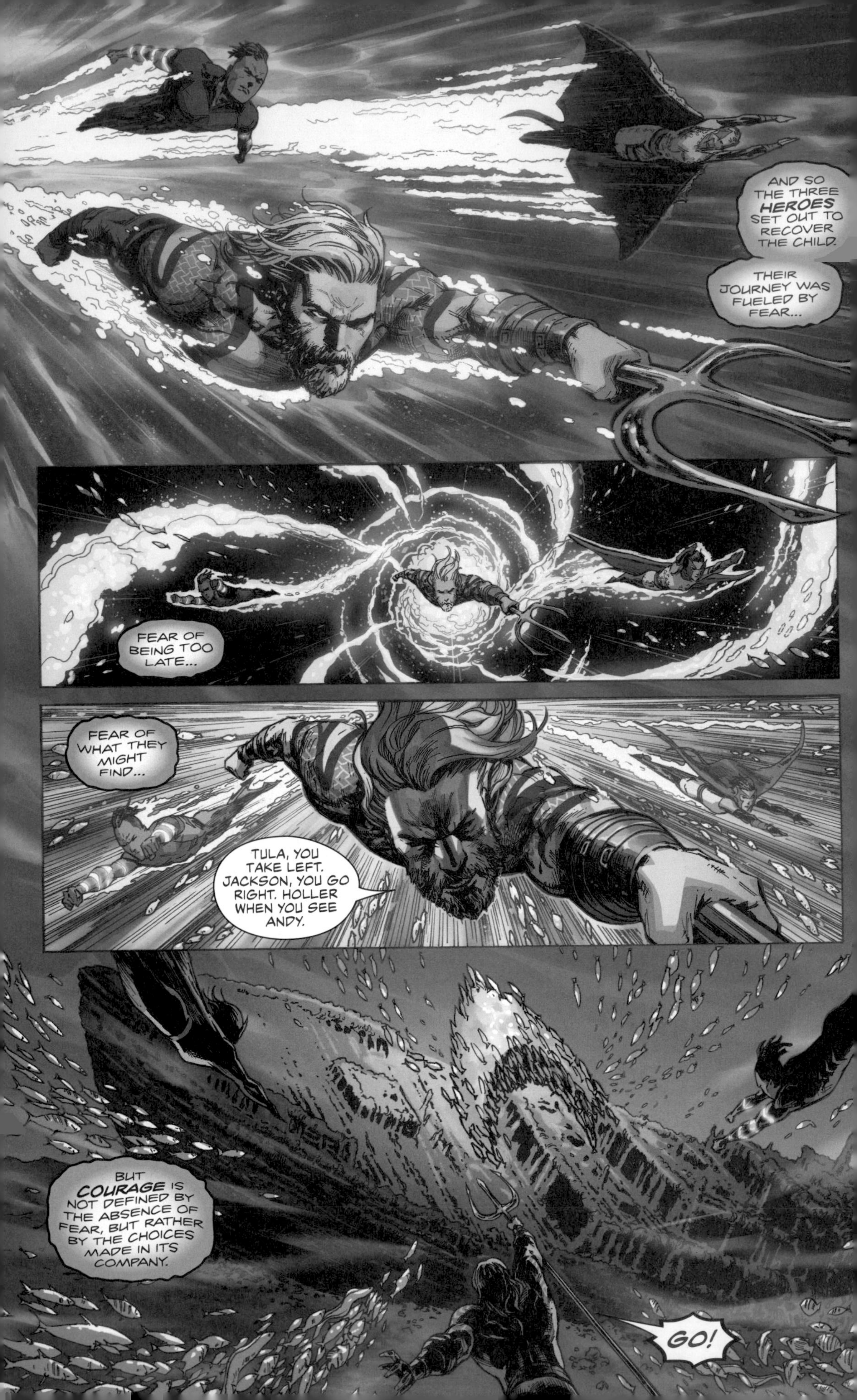
AND SO THE THREE **HEROES** SET OUT TO RECOVER THE CHILD.
THEIR JOURNEY WAS FUELED BY FEAR...
FEAR OF BEING TOO LATE...
FEAR OF WHAT THEY MIGHT FIND...
TULA, YOU TAKE LEFT. JACKSON, YOU GO RIGHT. HOLLER WHEN YOU SEE ANDY.
BUT **COURAGE** IS NOT DEFINED BY THE ABSENCE OF FEAR, BUT RATHER BY THE CHOICES MADE IN ITS COMPANY.
GO!

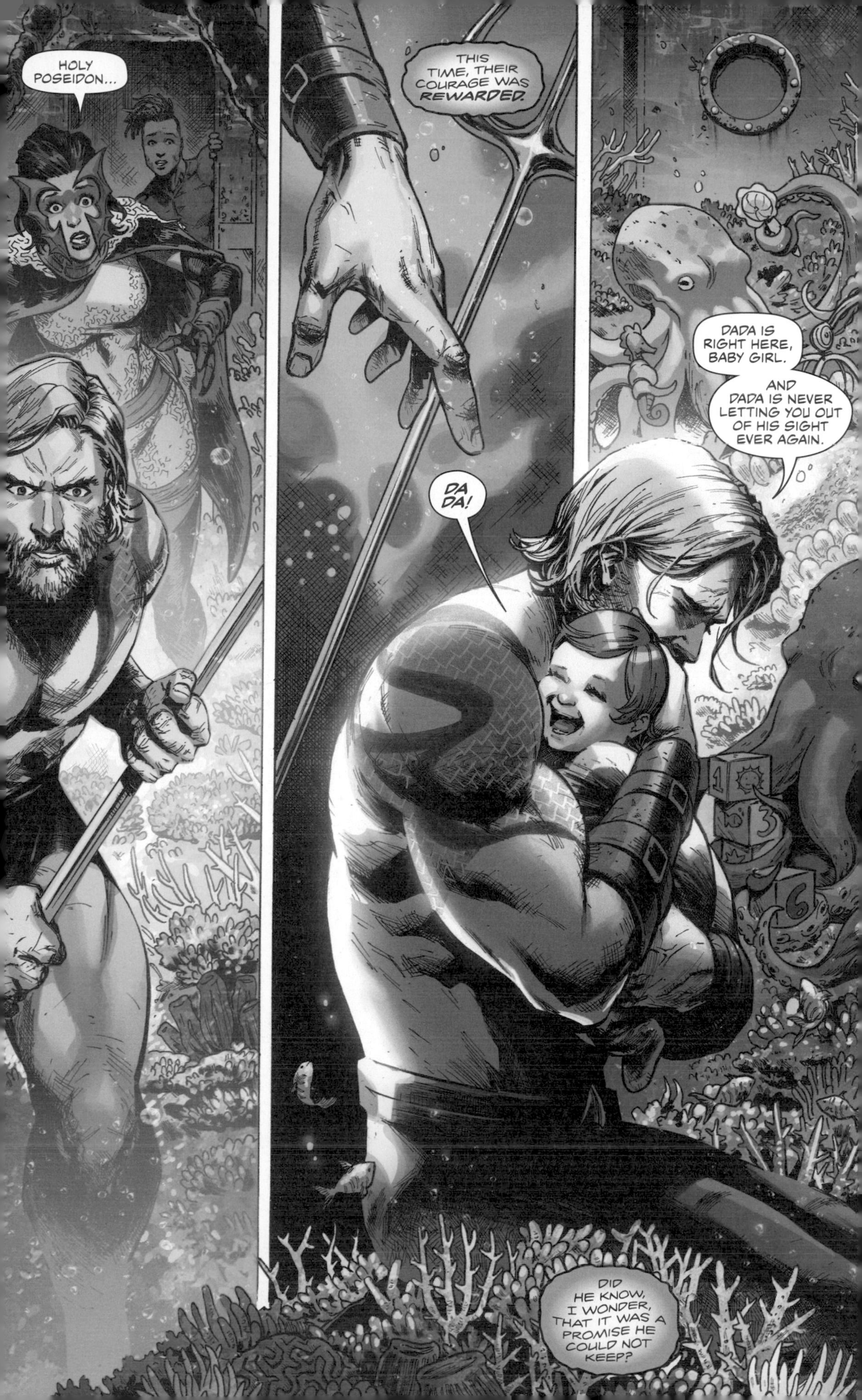
HOLY POSEIDON...
THIS TIME, THEIR COURAGE WAS REWARDED.
DA DA!
DADA IS RIGHT HERE, BABY GIRL.
AND DADA IS NEVER LETTING YOU OUT OF HIS SIGHT EVER AGAIN.
DID HE KNOW, I WONDER, THAT IT WAS A PROMISE HE COULD NOT KEEP?

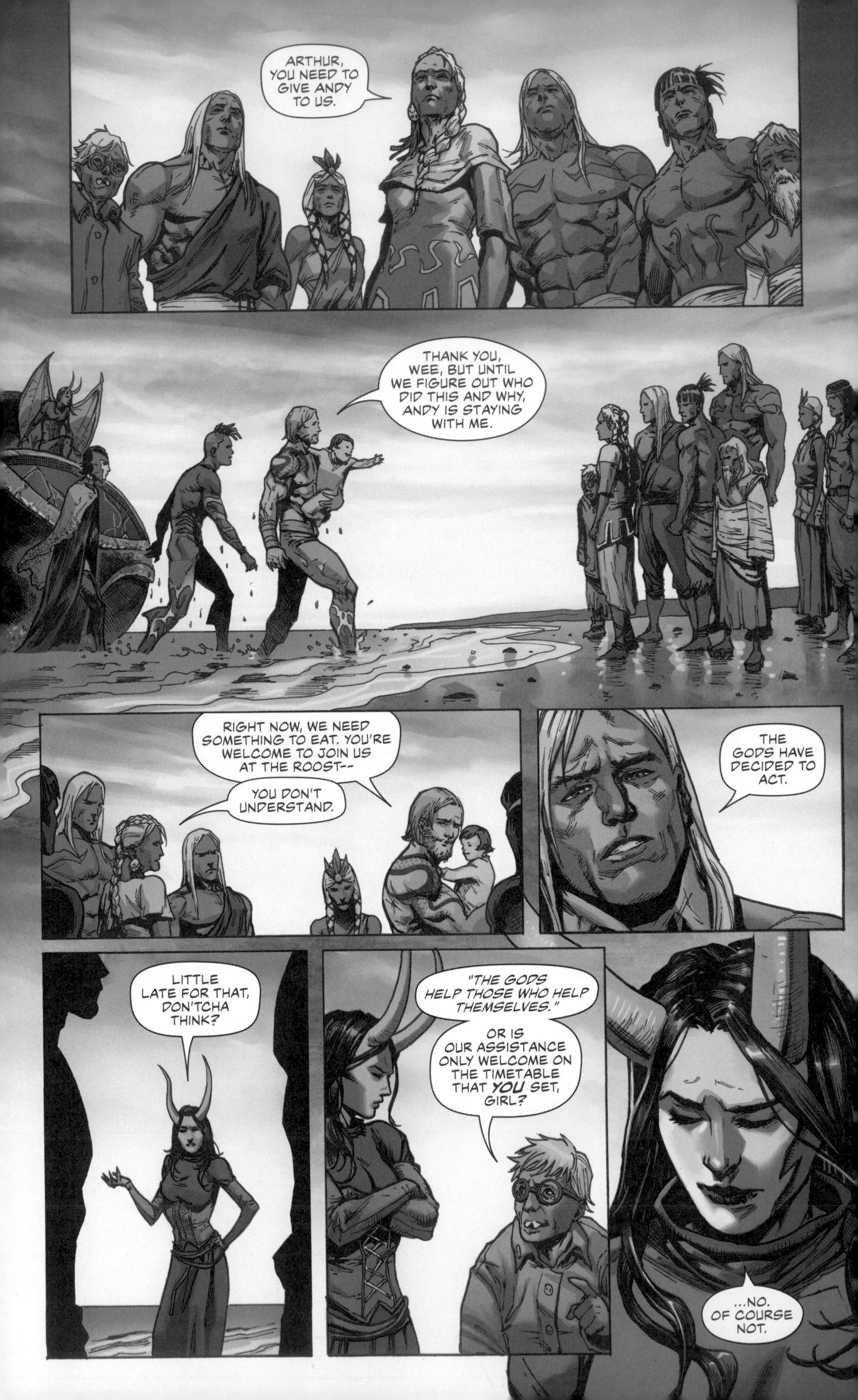
ARTHUR, YOU NEED TO GIVE ANDY TO US.
THANK YOU, WEE, BUT UNTIL WE FIGURE OUT WHO DID THIS AND WHY, ANDY IS STAYING WITH ME.
RIGHT NOW, WE NEED SOMETHING TO EAT. YOU'RE WELCOME TO JOIN US AT THE ROOST--
YOU DON'T UNDERSTAND.
THE GODS HAVE DECIDED TO ACT.
LITTLE LATE FOR THAT, DON'TCHA THINK?
"THE GODS HELP THOSE WHO HELP THEMSELVES."
OR IS OUR ASSISTANCE ONLY WELCOME ON THE TIMETABLE THAT YOU SET, GIRL?
...NO. OF COURSE NOT.

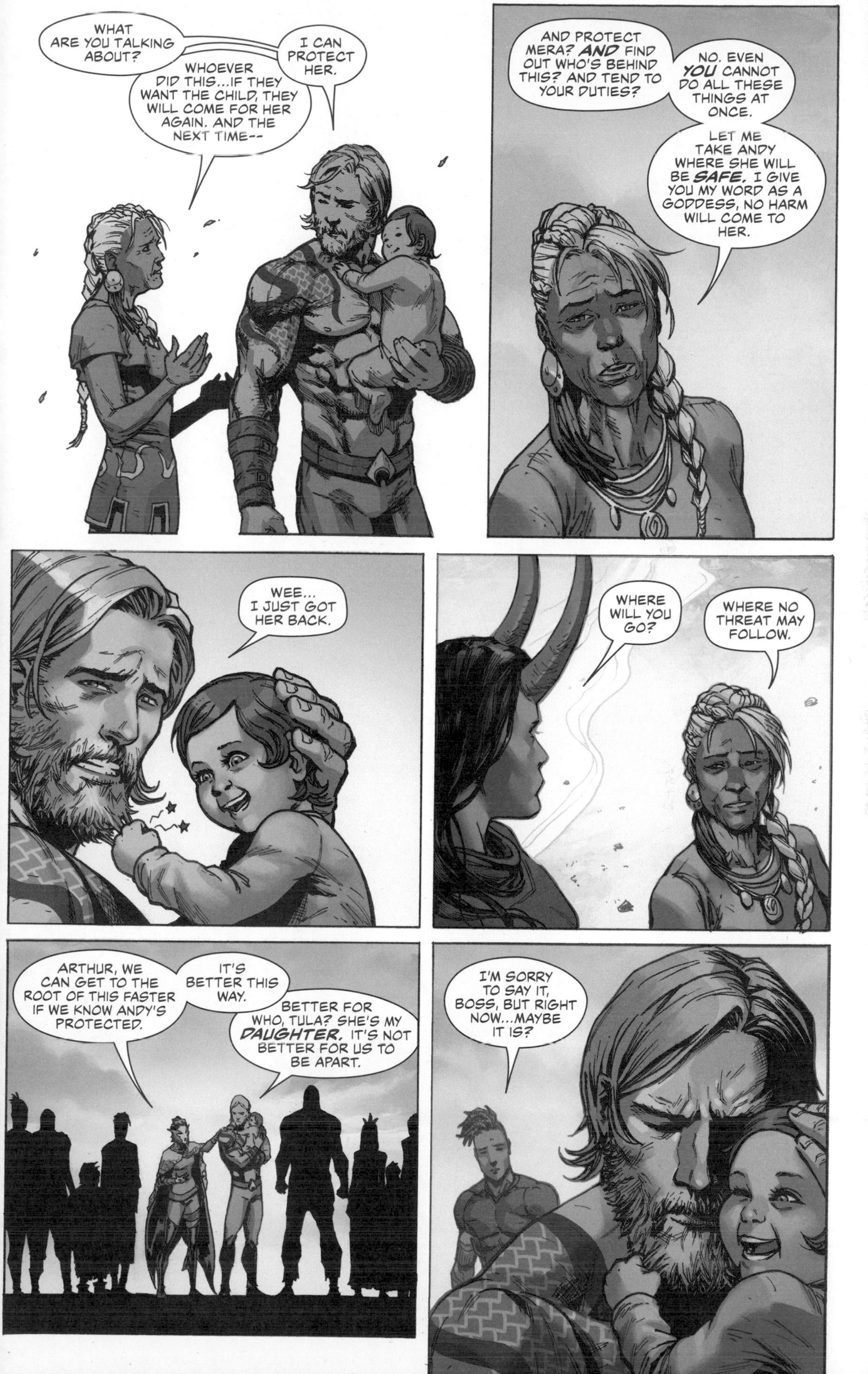
WHAT ARE YOU TALKING ABOUT?
I CAN PROTECT HER.
WHOEVER DID THIS...IF THEY WANT THE CHILD, THEY WILL COME FOR HER AGAIN. AND THE NEXT TIME--
AND PROTECT MERA? AND FIND OUT WHO'S BEHIND THIS? AND TEND TO YOUR DUTIES?
NO. EVEN YOU CANNOT DO ALL THESE THINGS AT ONCE.
LET ME TAKE ANDY WHERE SHE WILL BE SAFE. I GIVE YOU MY WORD AS A GODDESS, NO HARM WILL COME TO HER.
WEE... I JUST GOT HER BACK.
WHERE WILL YOU GO?
WHERE NO THREAT MAY FOLLOW.
ARTHUR, WE CAN GET TO THE ROOT OF THIS FASTER IF WE KNOW ANDY'S PROTECTED.
IT'S BETTER THIS WAY.
BETTER FOR WHO, TULA? SHE'S MY DAUGHTER. IT'S NOT BETTER FOR US TO BE APART.
I'M SORRY TO SAY IT, BOSS, BUT RIGHT NOW...MAYBE IT IS?

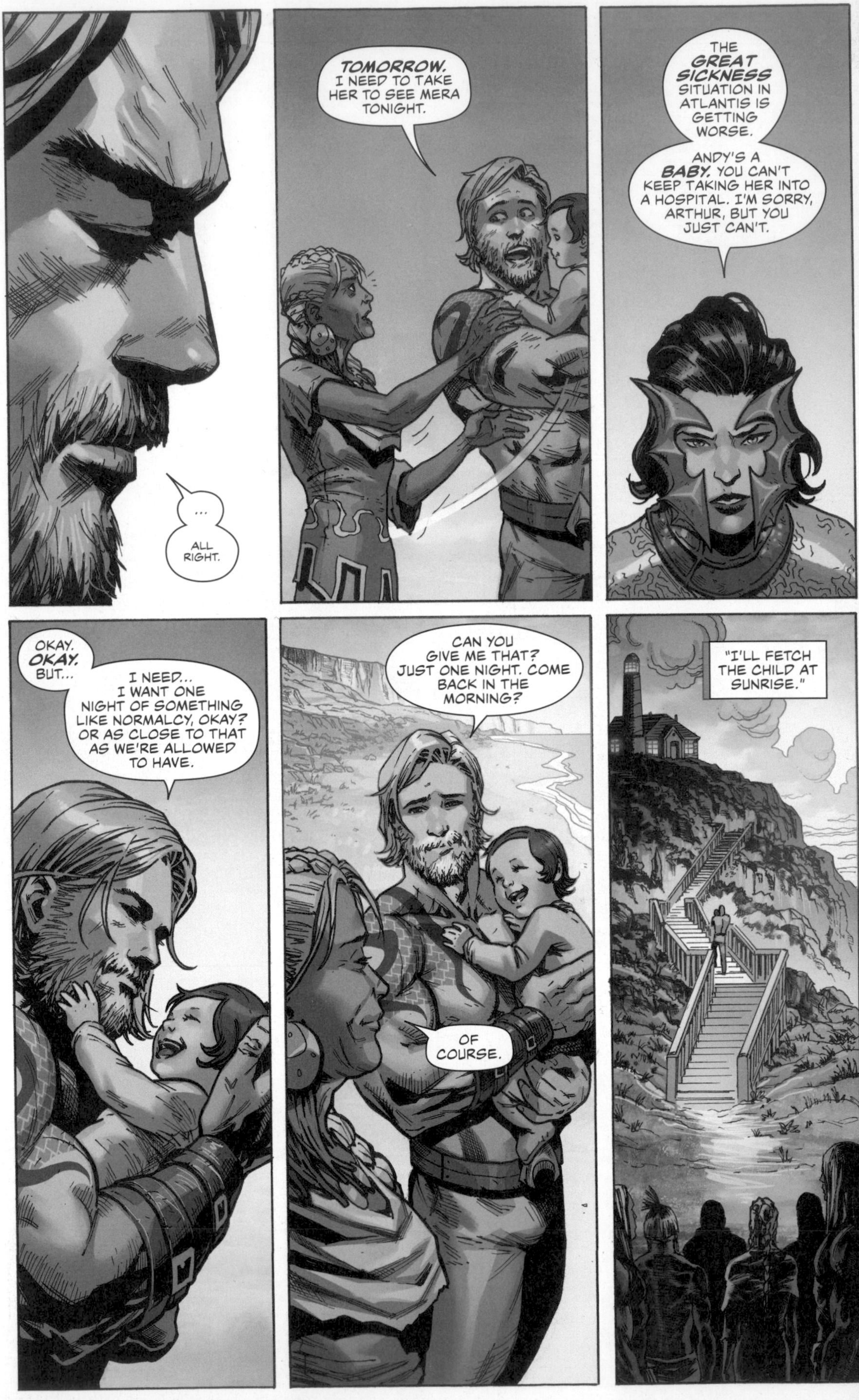

...
ALL RIGHT.
TOMORROW. I NEED TO TAKE HER TO SEE MERA TONIGHT.
THE GREAT SICKNESS SITUATION IN ATLANTIS IS GETTING WORSE.
ANDY'S A BABY. YOU CAN'T KEEP TAKING HER INTO A HOSPITAL. I'M SORRY, ARTHUR, BUT YOU JUST CAN'T.
OKAY. OKAY. BUT...
I NEED... I WANT ONE NIGHT OF SOMETHING LIKE NORMALCY, OKAY? OR AS CLOSE TO THAT AS WE'RE ALLOWED TO HAVE.
CAN YOU GIVE ME THAT? JUST ONE NIGHT. COME BACK IN THE MORNING?
OF COURSE.
"I'LL FETCH THE CHILD AT SUNRISE."

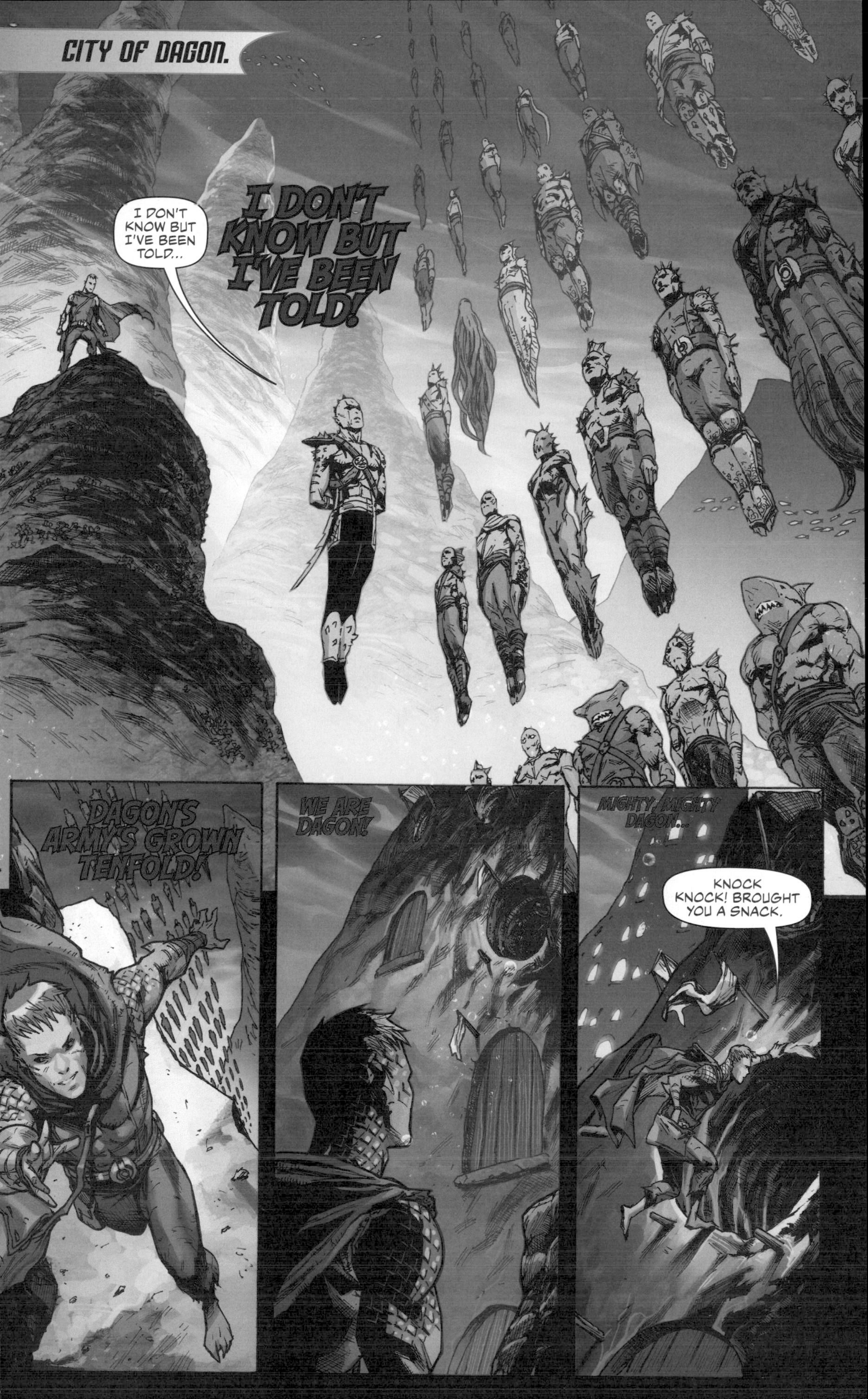
CITY OF DAGON.
I DON'T KNOW BUT I'VE BEEN TOLD...
I DON'T KNOW BUT I'VE BEEN TOLD!
DAGON'S ARMY'S GROWN TENFOLD!
WE ARE DAGON!
MIGHTY, MIGHTY DAGON...
KNOCK KNOCK! BROUGHT YOU A SNACK.

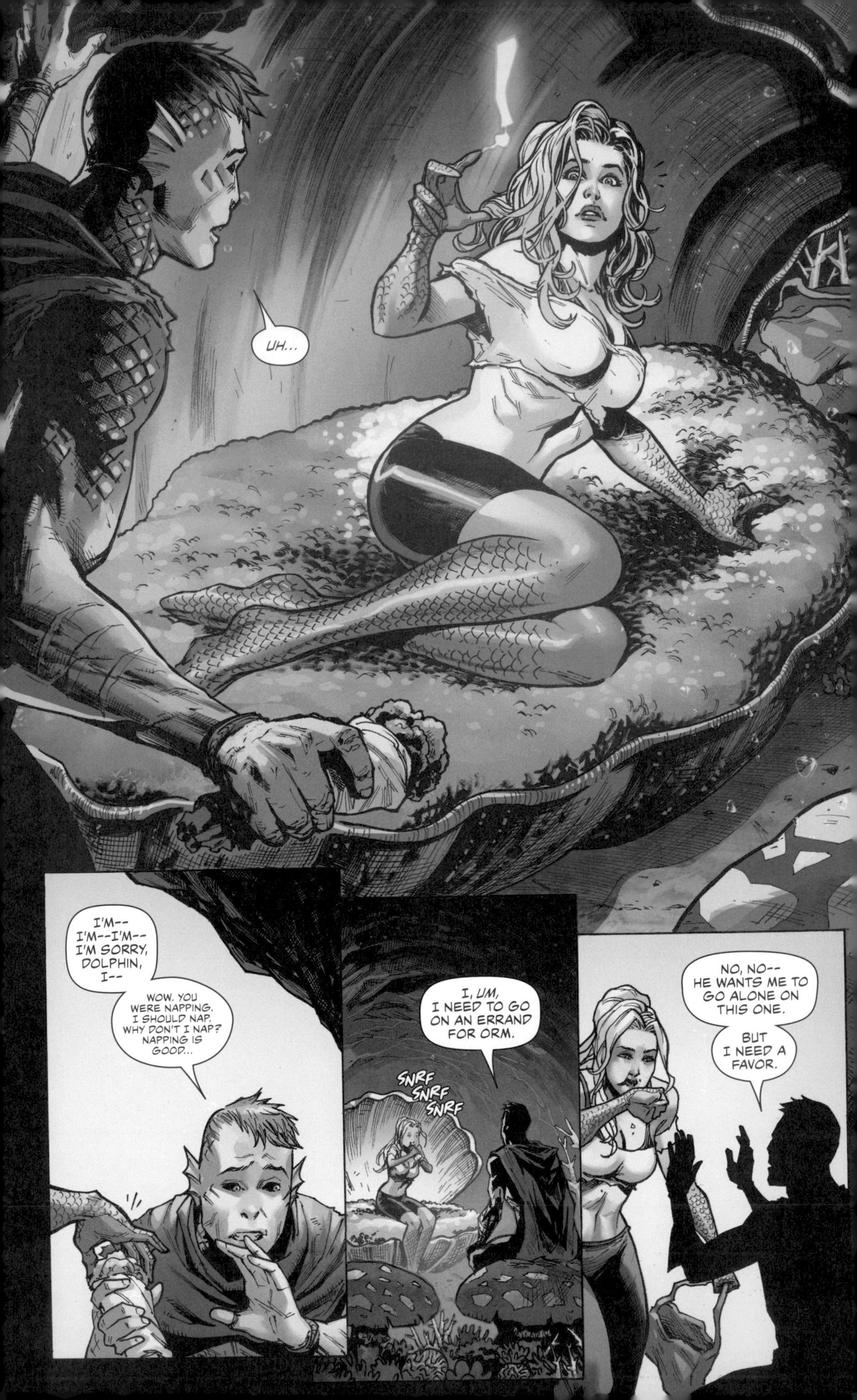
!
UH...
I'M--
I'M--I'M--
I'M SORRY,
DOLPHIN,
I--
WOW. YOU
WERE NAPPING.
I SHOULD NAP.
WHY DON'T I NAP?
NAPPING IS
GOOD...
I, UM,
I NEED TO GO
ON AN ERRAND
FOR ORM.
SNRF
SNRF
SNRF
NO, NO--
HE WANTS ME TO
GO ALONE ON
THIS ONE.
BUT
I NEED A
FAVOR.

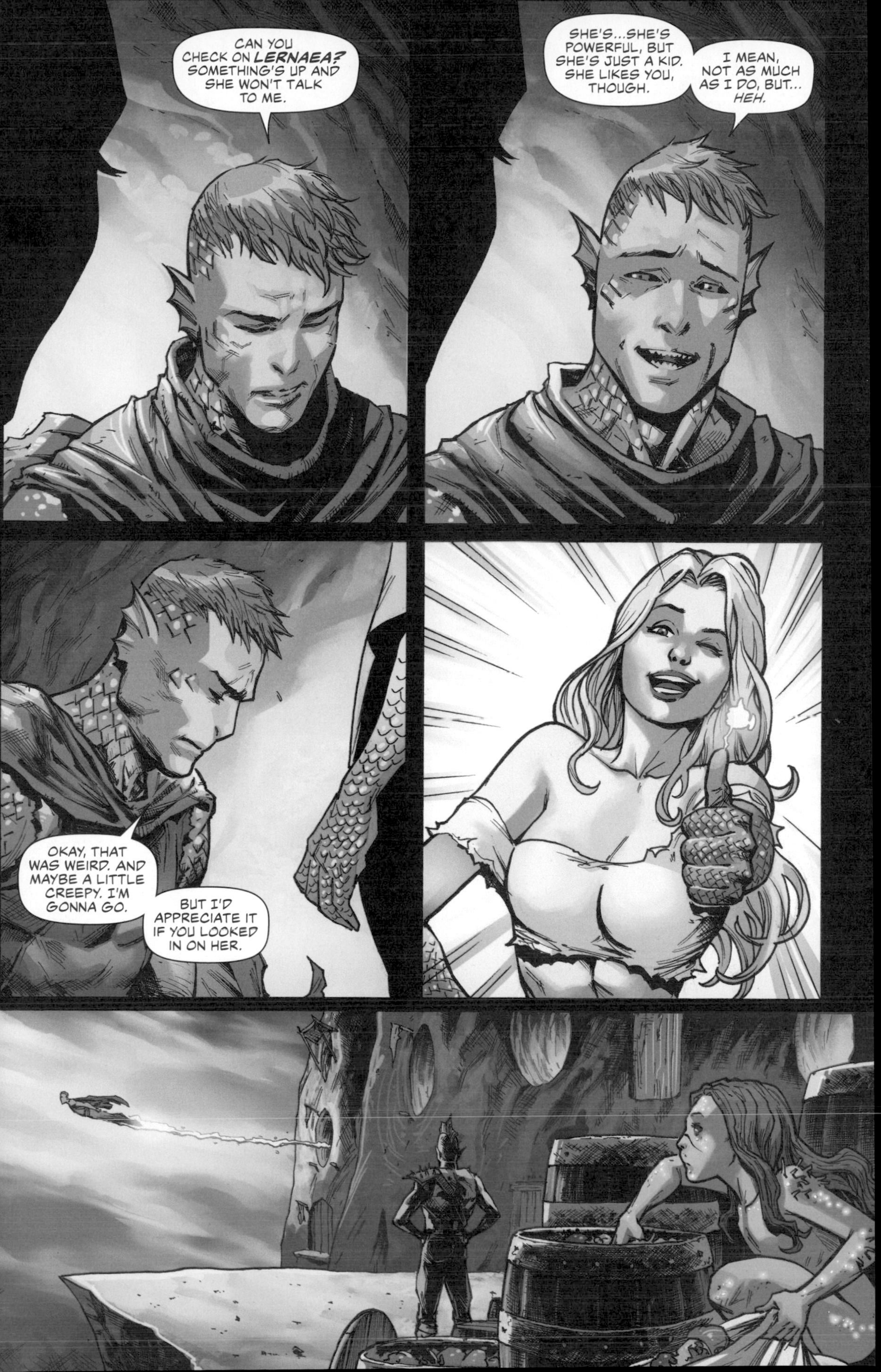
CAN YOU CHECK ON LERNAEA? SOMETHING'S UP AND SHE WON'T TALK TO ME.
SHE'S...SHE'S POWERFUL, BUT SHE'S JUST A KID. SHE LIKES YOU, THOUGH.
I MEAN, NOT AS MUCH AS I DO, BUT... HEH.
OKAY, THAT WAS WEIRD. AND MAYBE A LITTLE CREEPY. I'M GONNA GO.
BUT I'D APPRECIATE IT IF YOU LOOKED IN ON HER.

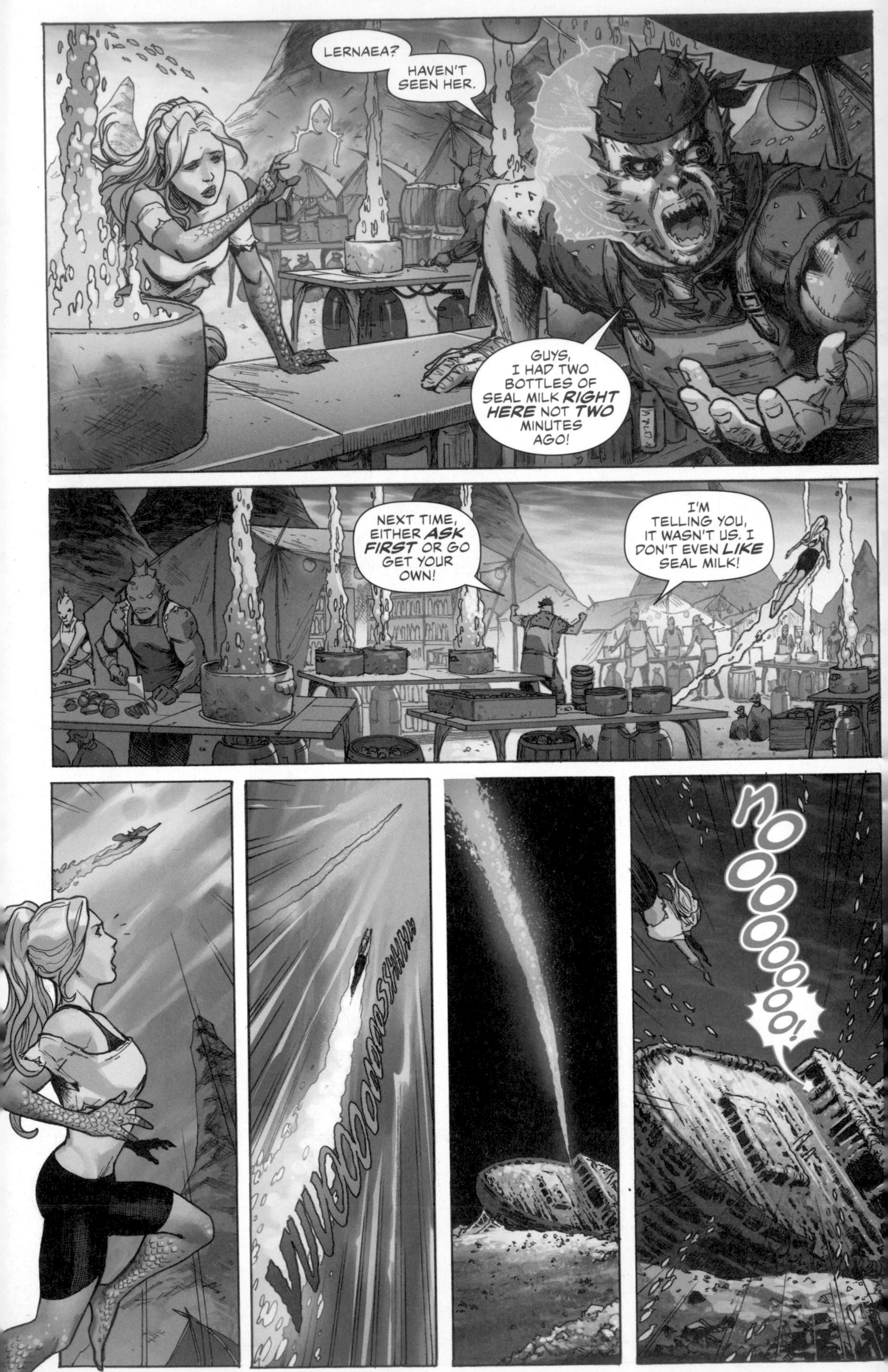
LERNAEA?
HAVEN'T SEEN HER.
GUYS, I HAD TWO BOTTLES OF SEAL MILK RIGHT HERE NOT TWO MINUTES AGO!
NEXT TIME, EITHER ASK FIRST OR GO GET YOUR OWN!
I'M TELLING YOU, IT WASN'T US. I DON'T EVEN LIKE SEAL MILK!
nOOOOOOOO!

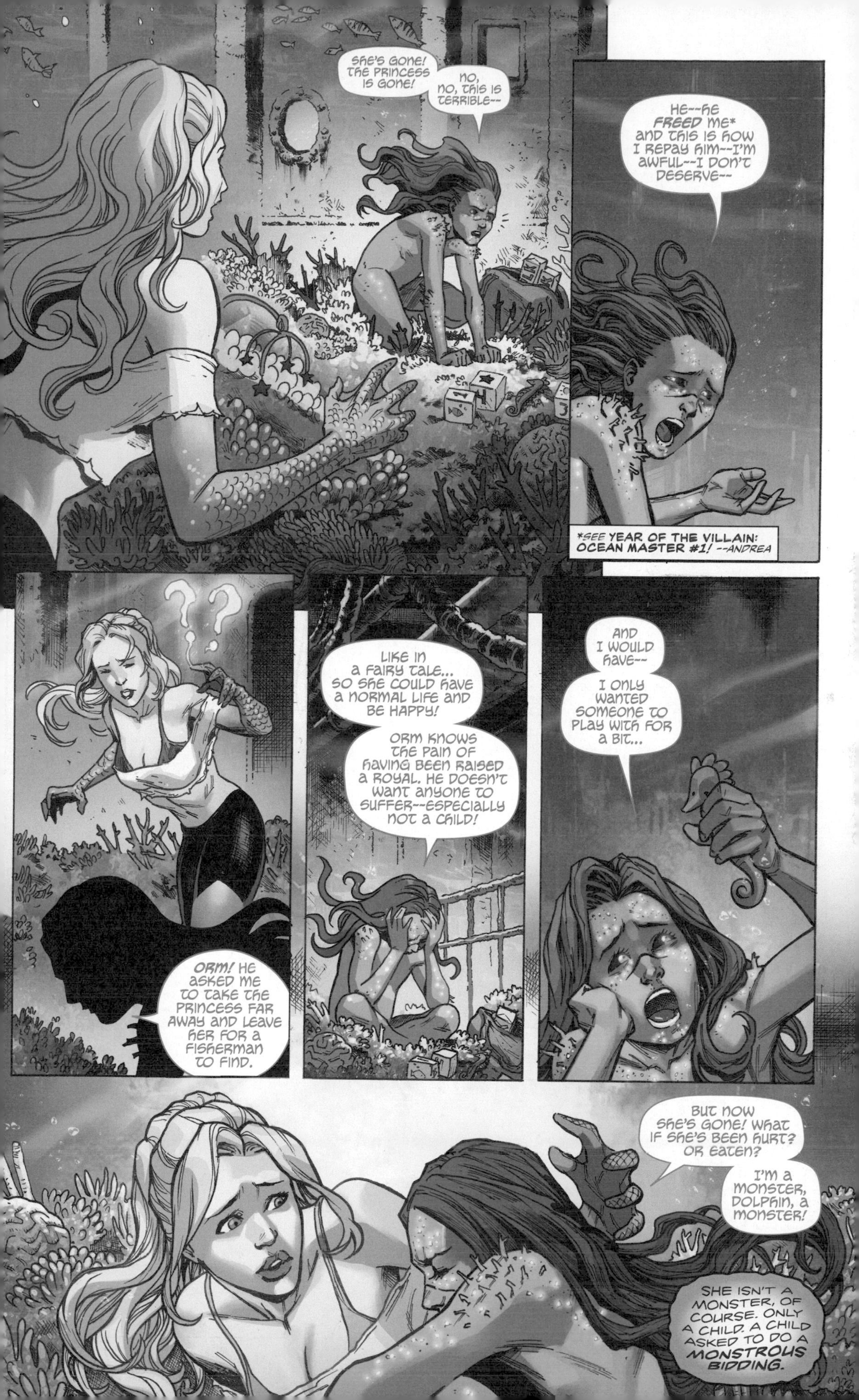
SHE'S GONE! THE PRINCESS IS GONE!
NO, NO, THIS IS TERRIBLE--
HE--HE FREED ME* AND THIS IS HOW I REPAY HIM--I'M AWFUL--I DON'T DESERVE--
*SEE YEAR OF THE VILLAIN: OCEAN MASTER #1! --ANDREA
ORM! HE ASKED ME TO TAKE THE PRINCESS FAR AWAY AND LEAVE HER FOR A FISHERMAN TO FIND.
LIKE IN A FAIRY TALE... SO SHE COULD HAVE A NORMAL LIFE AND BE HAPPY!
ORM KNOWS THE PAIN OF HAVING BEEN RAISED A ROYAL. HE DOESN'T WANT ANYONE TO SUFFER--ESPECIALLY NOT A CHILD!
AND I WOULD HAVE--
I ONLY WANTED SOMEONE TO PLAY WITH FOR A BIT...
BUT NOW SHE'S GONE! WHAT IF SHE'S BEEN HURT? OR EATEN?
I'M A MONSTER, DOLPHIN, A MONSTER!
SHE ISN'T A MONSTER, OF COURSE. ONLY A CHILD. A CHILD ASKED TO DO A MONSTROUS BIDDING.

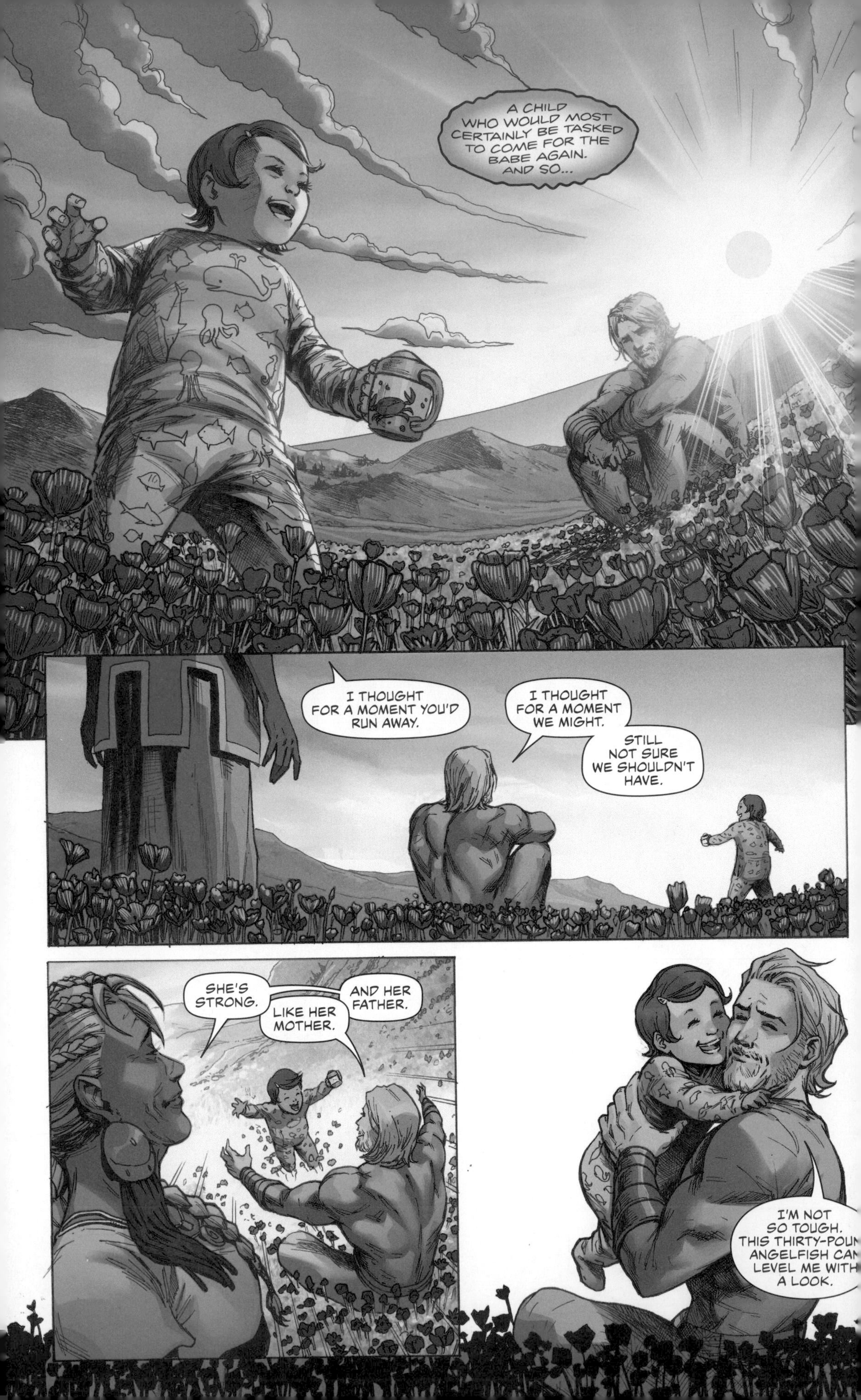
A CHILD WHO WOULD MOST CERTAINLY BE TASKED TO COME FOR THE BABE AGAIN. AND SO...
I THOUGHT FOR A MOMENT YOU'D RUN AWAY.
I THOUGHT FOR A MOMENT WE MIGHT.
STILL NOT SURE WE SHOULDN'T HAVE.
SHE'S STRONG.
LIKE HER MOTHER.
AND HER FATHER.
I'M NOT SO TOUGH. THIS THIRTY-POUN ANGELFISH CAN LEVEL ME WITH A LOOK.

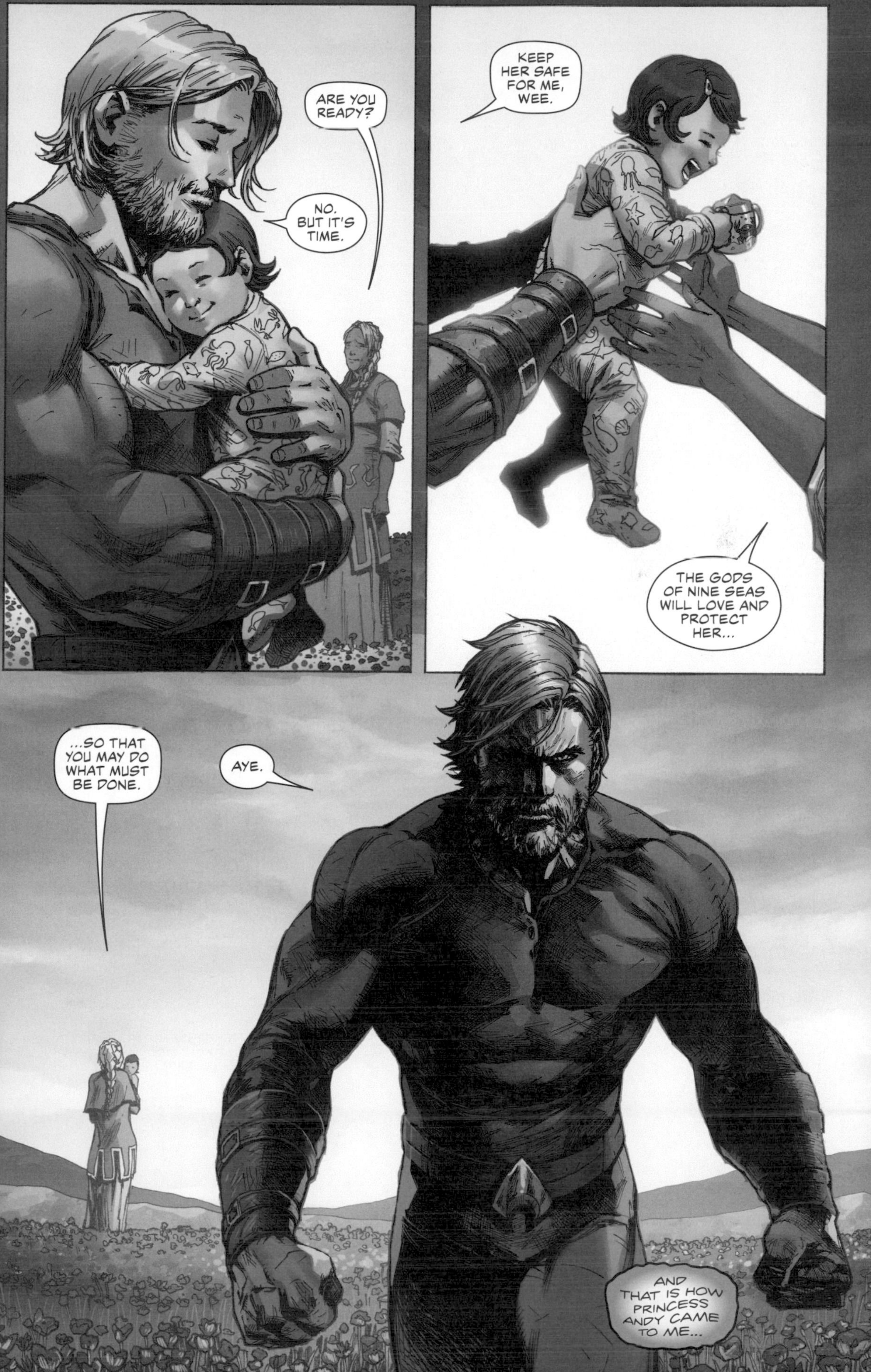
ARE YOU READY?
NO. BUT IT'S TIME.
KEEP HER SAFE FOR ME, WEE.
THE GODS OF NINE SEAS WILL LOVE AND PROTECT HER...
...SO THAT YOU MAY DO WHAT MUST BE DONE.
AYE.
AND THAT IS HOW PRINCESS ANDY CAME TO ME...

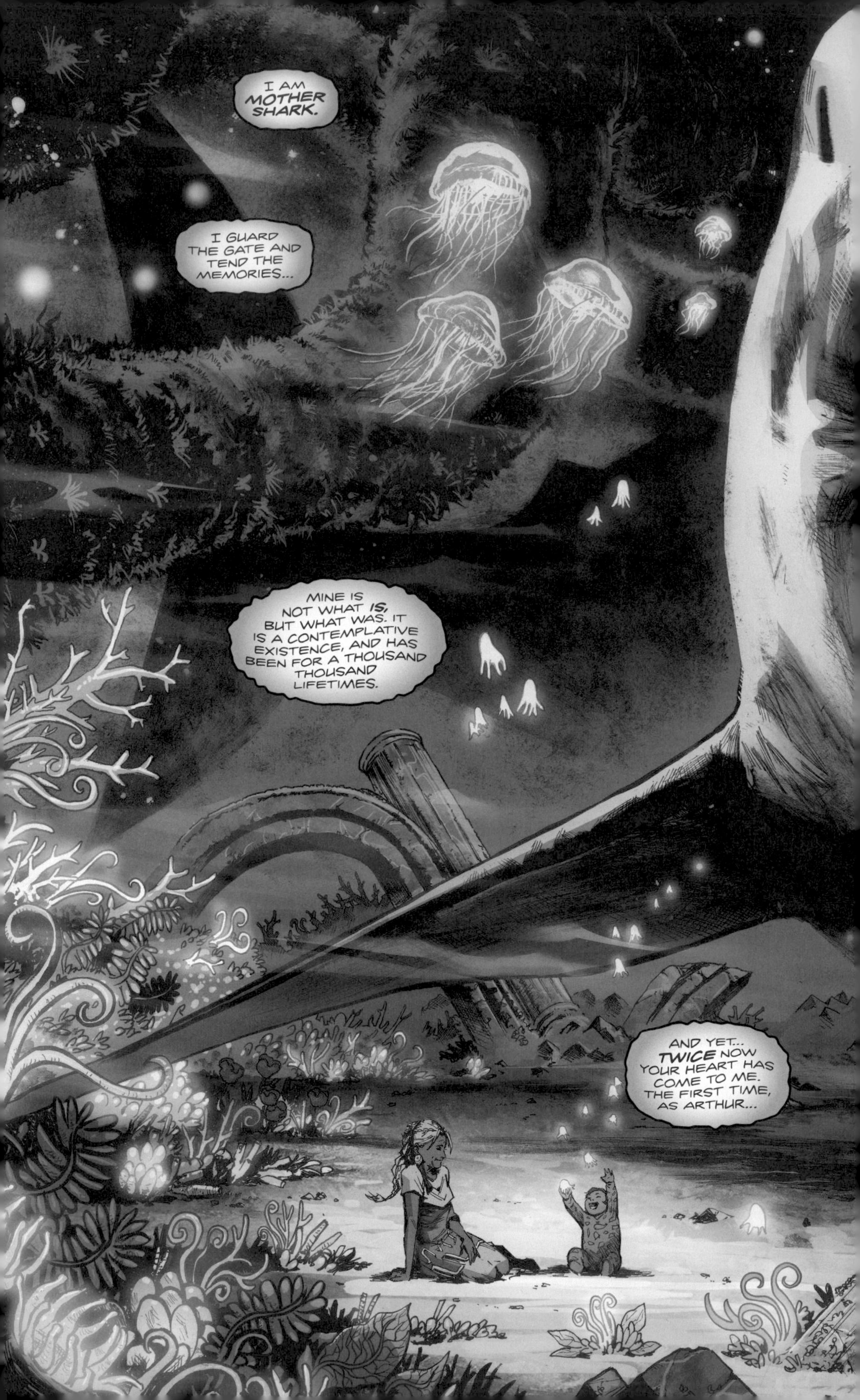
I AM MOTHER SHARK.
I GUARD THE GATE AND TEND THE MEMORIES...
MINE IS NOT WHAT IS, BUT WHAT WAS. IT IS A CONTEMPLATIVE EXISTENCE, AND HAS BEEN FOR A THOUSAND THOUSAND LIFETIMES.
AND YET... TWICE NOW YOUR HEART HAS COME TO ME. THE FIRST TIME, AS ARTHUR...

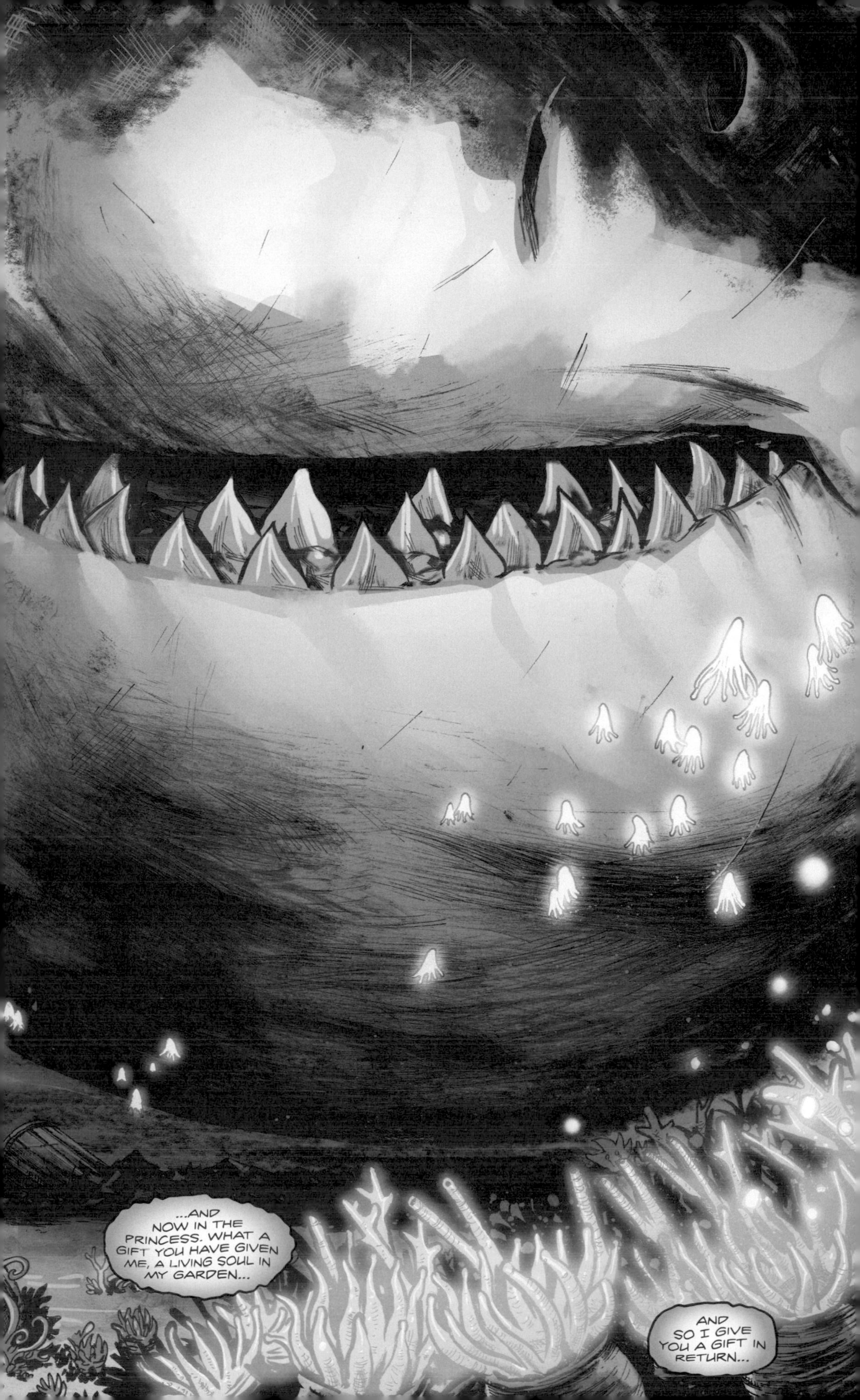
...AND NOW IN THE PRINCESS. WHAT A GIFT YOU HAVE GIVEN ME, A LIVING SOUL IN MY GARDEN...
AND SO I GIVE YOU A GIFT IN RETURN...

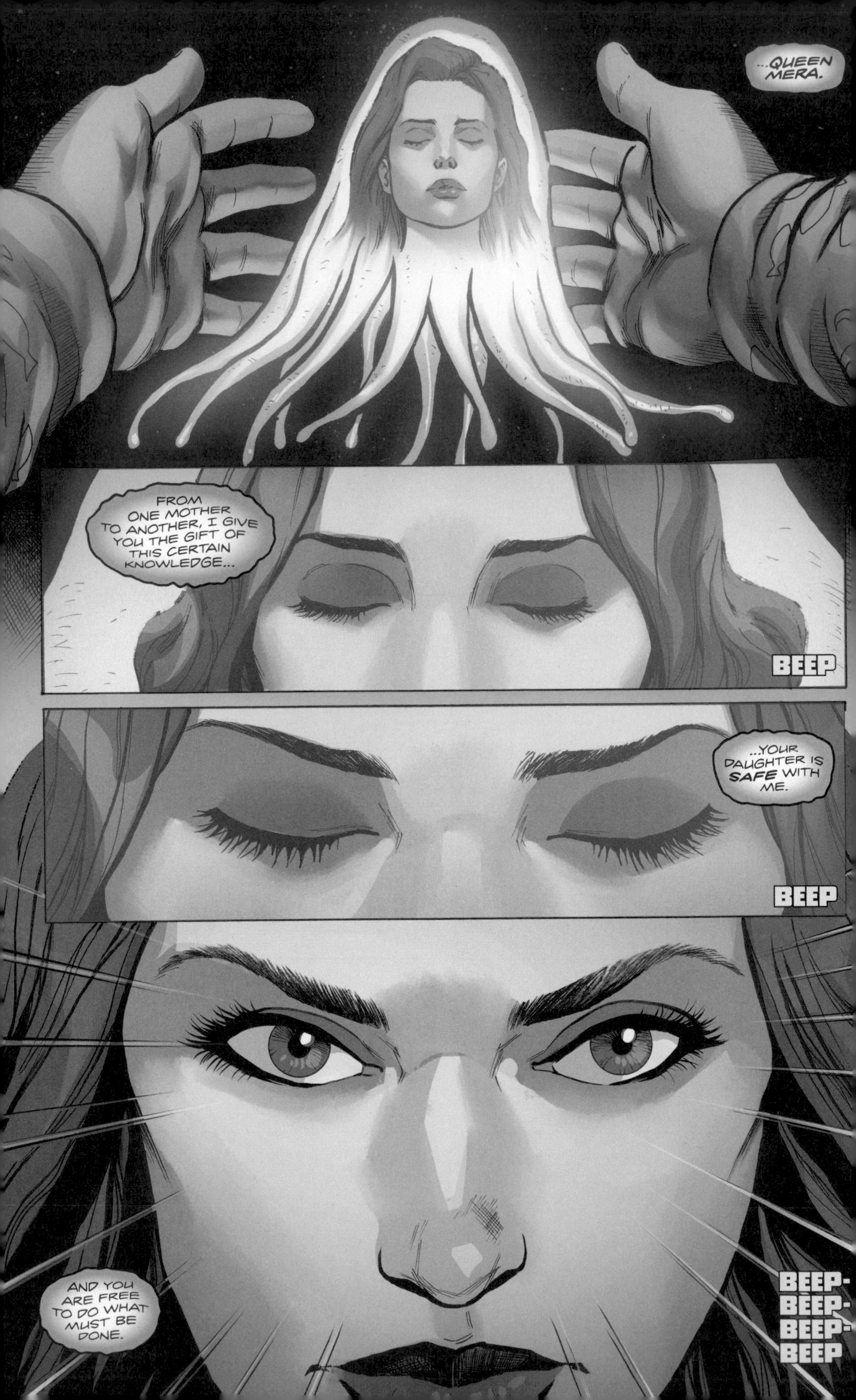
...QUEEN MERA.
FROM ONE MOTHER TO ANOTHER, I GIVE YOU THE GIFT OF THIS CERTAIN KNOWLEDGE...
BEEP
...YOUR DAUGHTER IS SAFE WITH ME.
BEEP
AND YOU ARE FREE TO DO WHAT MUST BE DONE.
BEEP-BEEP-BEEP-BEEP

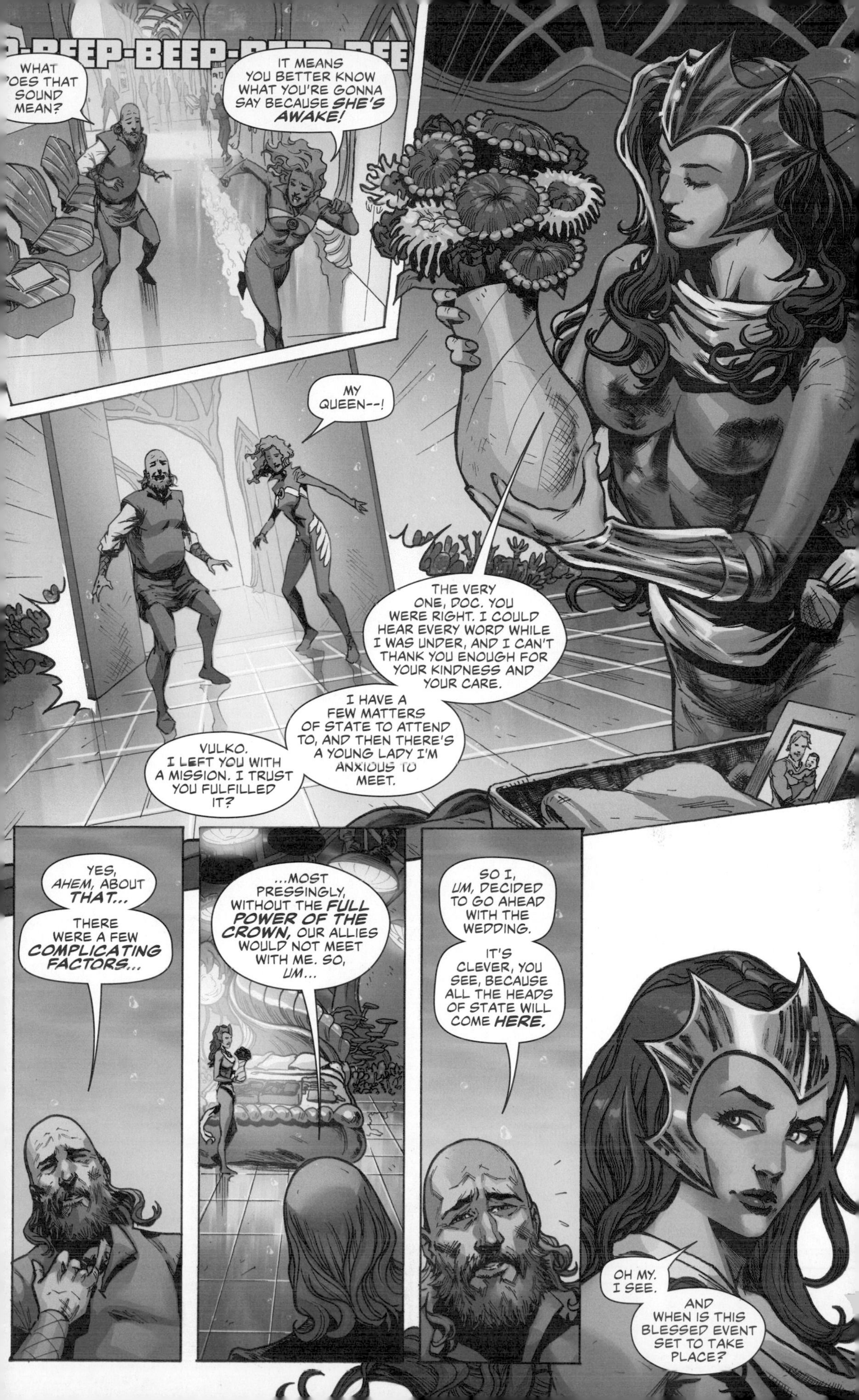

-BEEP-BEEP-
WHAT DOES THAT SOUND MEAN?
IT MEANS YOU BETTER KNOW WHAT YOU'RE GONNA SAY BECAUSE SHE'S AWAKE!
MY QUEEN--!
THE VERY ONE, DOC. YOU WERE RIGHT. I COULD HEAR EVERY WORD WHILE I WAS UNDER, AND I CAN'T THANK YOU ENOUGH FOR YOUR KINDNESS AND YOUR CARE.
I HAVE A FEW MATTERS OF STATE TO ATTEND TO, AND THEN THERE'S A YOUNG LADY I'M ANXIOUS TO MEET.
VULKO. I LEFT YOU WITH A MISSION. I TRUST YOU FULFILLED IT?
YES, AHEM, ABOUT THAT...
THERE WERE A FEW COMPLICATING FACTORS...
...MOST PRESSINGLY, WITHOUT THE FULL POWER OF THE CROWN, OUR ALLIES WOULD NOT MEET WITH ME. SO, UM...
SO I, UM, DECIDED TO GO AHEAD WITH THE WEDDING.
IT'S CLEVER, YOU SEE, BECAUSE ALL THE HEADS OF STATE WILL COME HERE.
OH MY. I SEE.
AND WHEN IS THIS BLESSED EVENT SET TO TAKE PLACE?

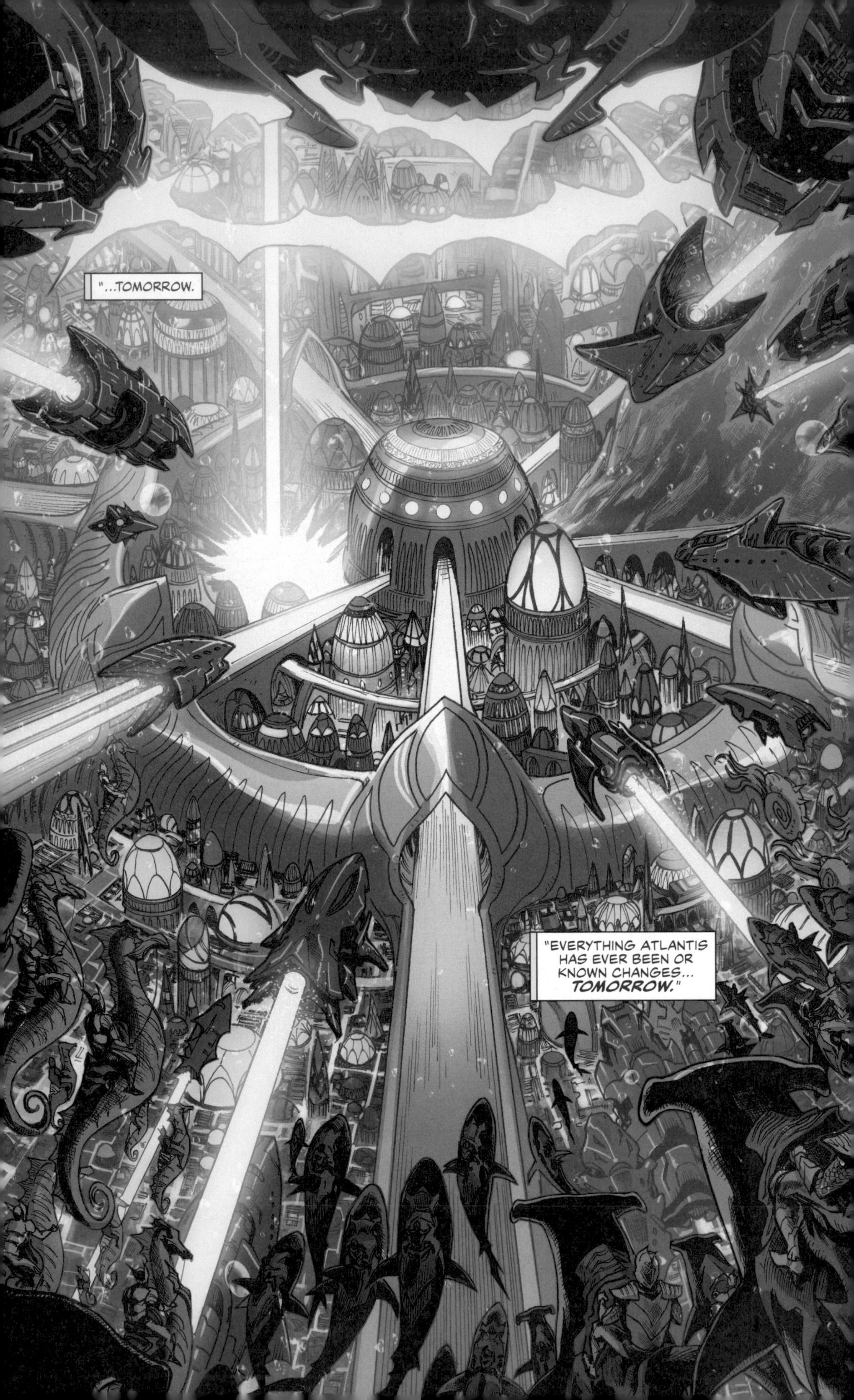
"...TOMORROW.
"EVERYTHING ATLANTIS HAS EVER BEEN OR KNOWN CHANGES... ***TOMORROW.***"

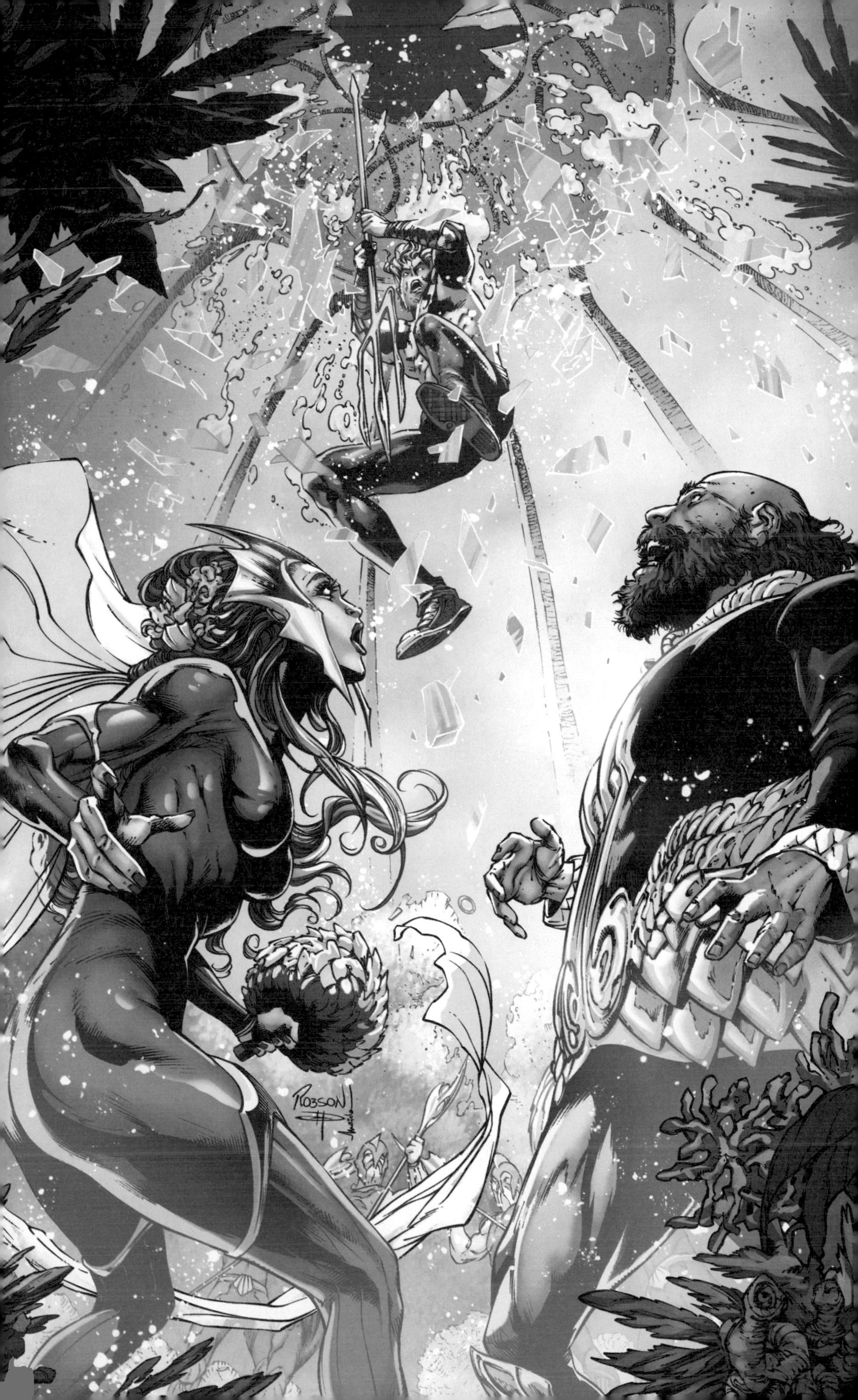
ROBSON

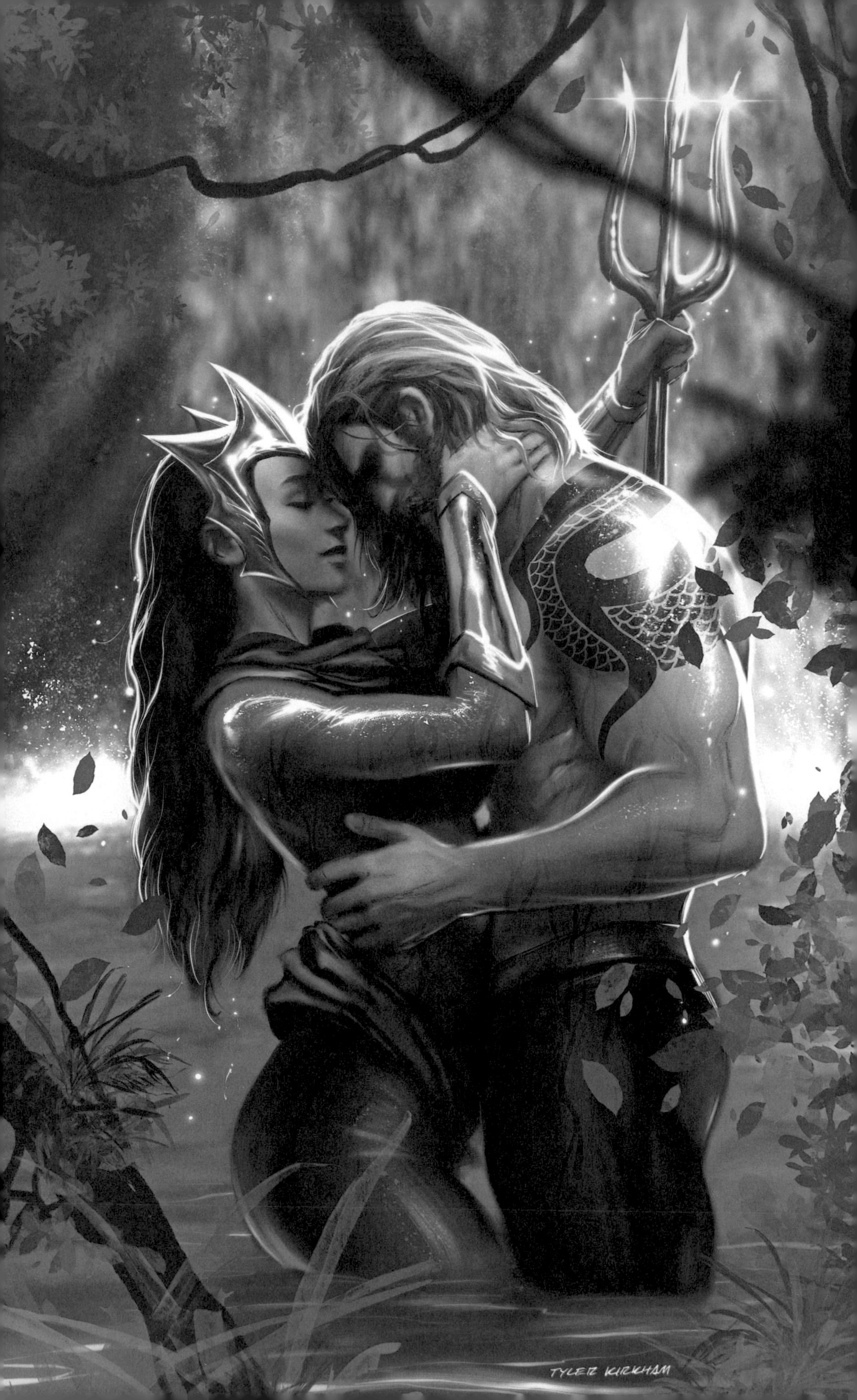
TYLER KIRKHAM

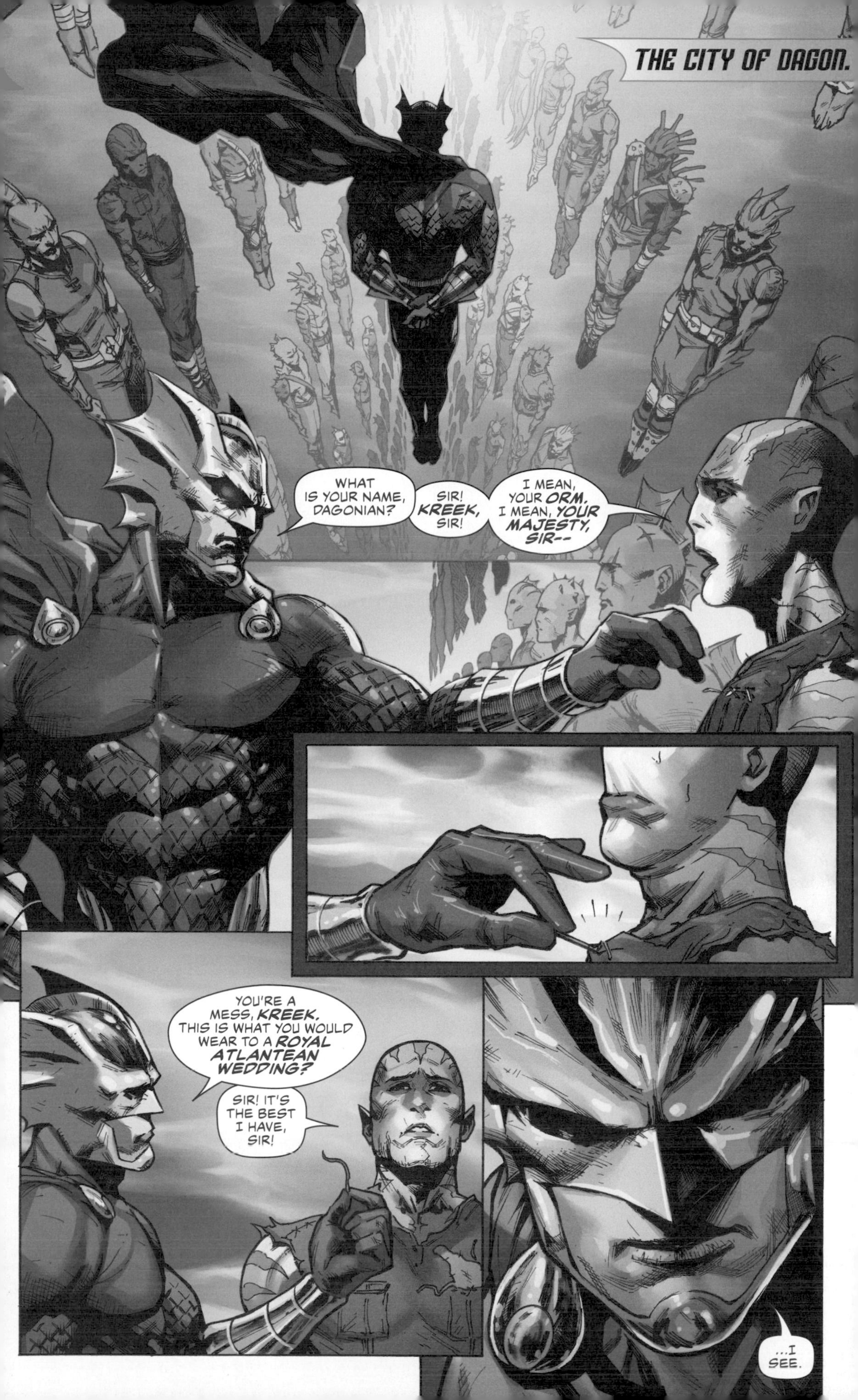
THE CITY OF DAGON.
WHAT IS YOUR NAME, DAGONIAN?
SIR! KREEK, SIR!
I MEAN, YOUR ORM. I MEAN, YOUR MAJESTY, SIR--
YOU'RE A MESS, KREEK. THIS IS WHAT YOU WOULD WEAR TO A ROYAL ATLANTEAN WEDDING?
SIR! IT'S THE BEST I HAVE, SIR!
...I SEE.

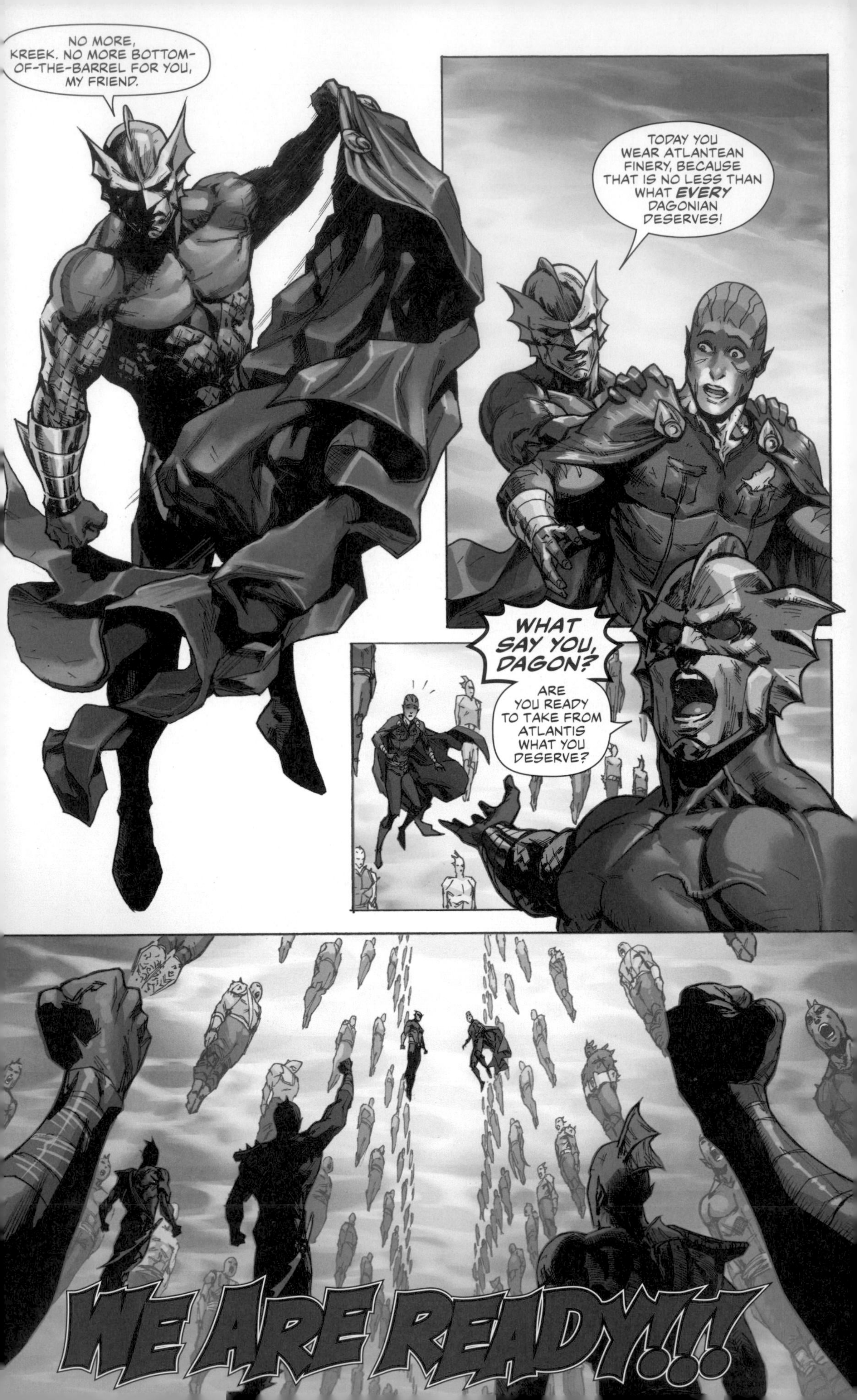
NO MORE, KREEK. NO MORE BOTTOM-OF-THE-BARREL FOR YOU, MY FRIEND.
TODAY YOU WEAR ATLANTEAN FINERY, BECAUSE THAT IS NO LESS THAN WHAT EVERY DAGONIAN DESERVES!
WHAT SAY YOU, DAGON?
ARE YOU READY TO TAKE FROM ATLANTIS WHAT YOU DESERVE?
WE ARE READY!!!

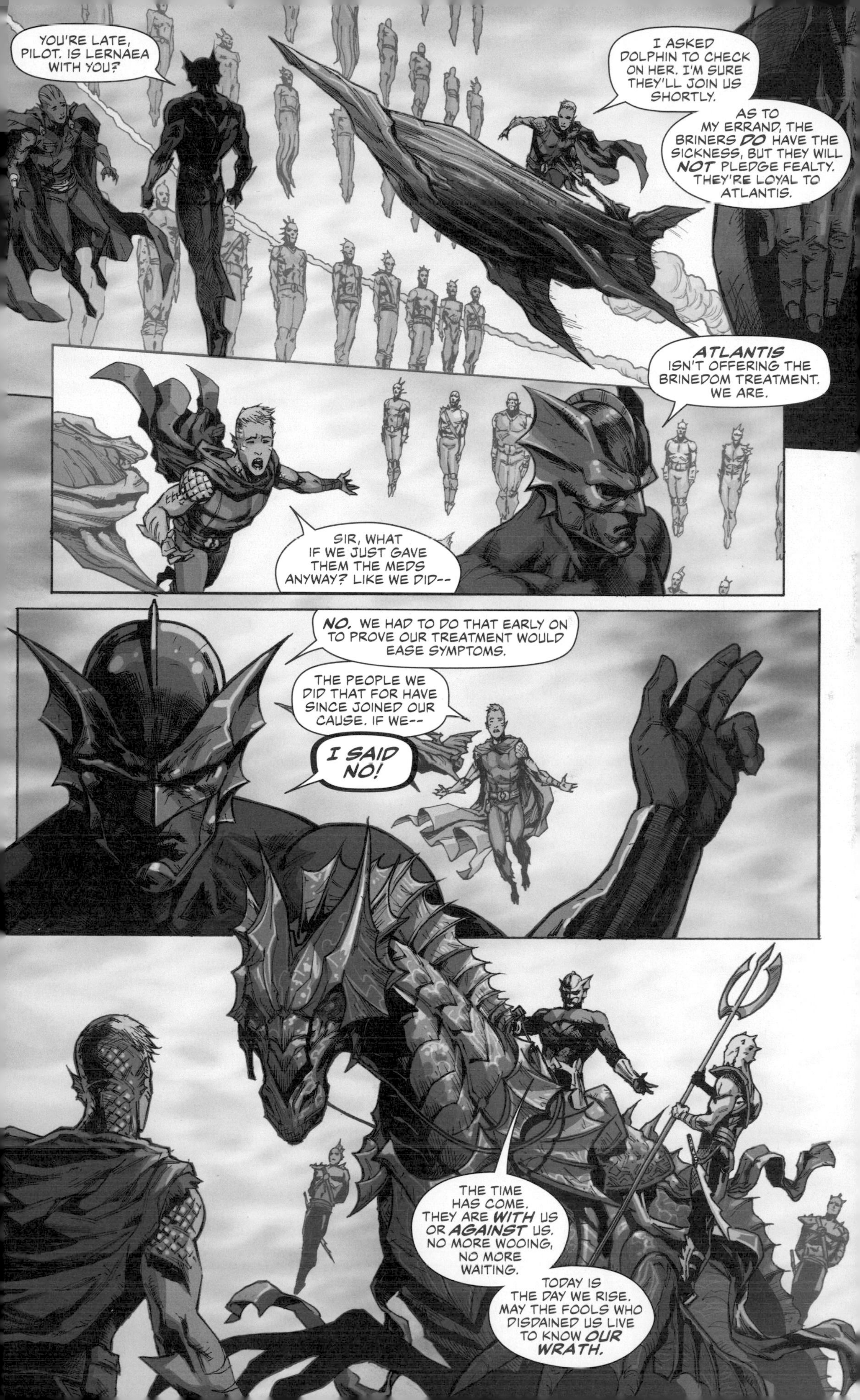
YOU'RE LATE, PILOT. IS LERNAEA WITH YOU?
I ASKED DOLPHIN TO CHECK ON HER. I'M SURE THEY'LL JOIN US SHORTLY.
AS TO MY ERRAND, THE BRINERS DO HAVE THE SICKNESS, BUT THEY WILL NOT PLEDGE FEALTY. THEY'RE LOYAL TO ATLANTIS.
ATLANTIS ISN'T OFFERING THE BRINEDOM TREATMENT. WE ARE.
SIR, WHAT IF WE JUST GAVE THEM THE MEDS ANYWAY? LIKE WE DID--
NO. WE HAD TO DO THAT EARLY ON TO PROVE OUR TREATMENT WOULD EASE SYMPTOMS.
THE PEOPLE WE DID THAT FOR HAVE SINCE JOINED OUR CAUSE. IF WE--
I SAID NO!
THE TIME HAS COME. THEY ARE WITH US OR AGAINST US. NO MORE WOOING, NO MORE WAITING.
TODAY IS THE DAY WE RISE. MAY THE FOOLS WHO DISDAINED US LIVE TO KNOW OUR WRATH.

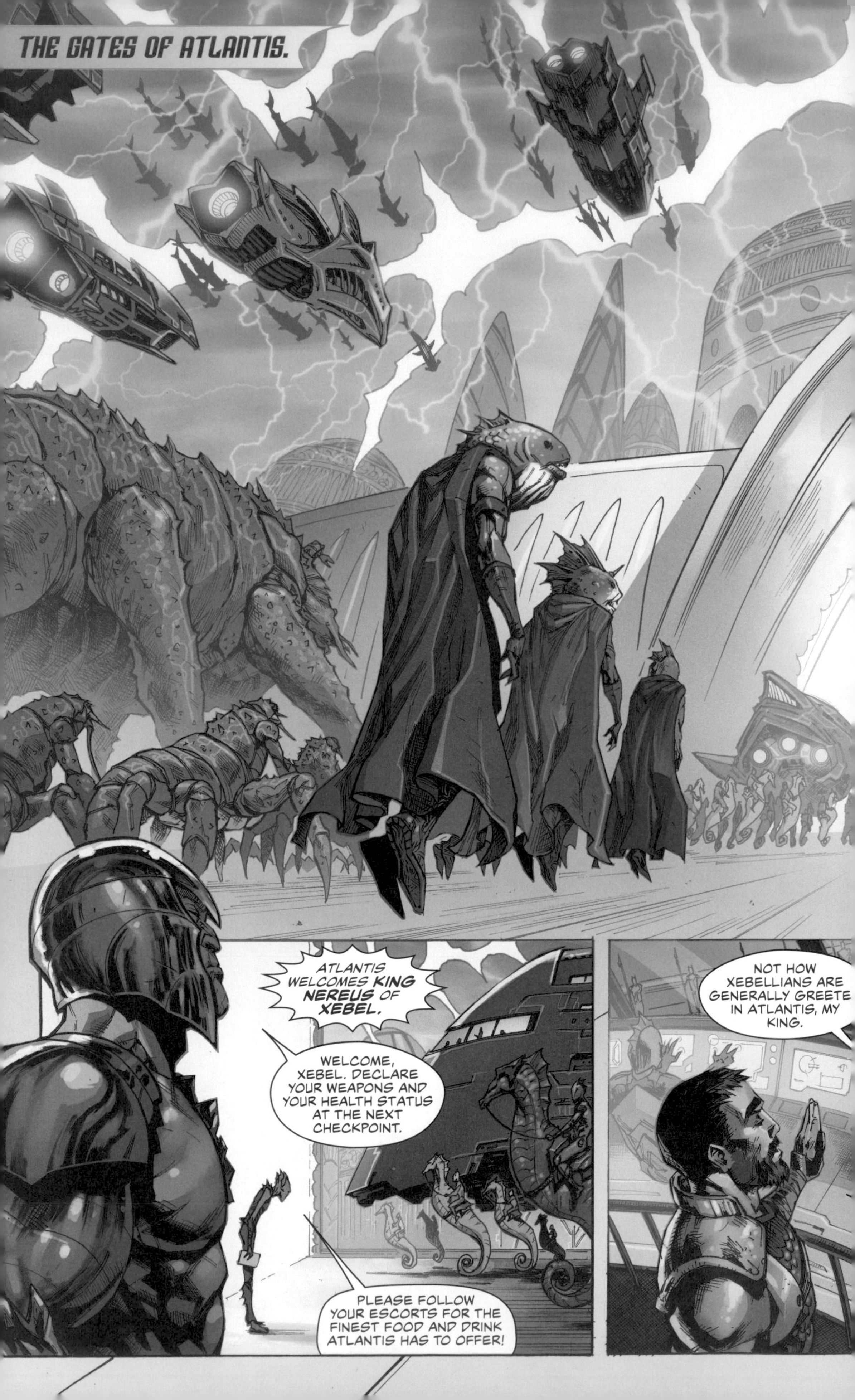
THE GATES OF ATLANTIS.
ATLANTIS WELCOMES KING NEREUS OF XEBEL.
WELCOME, XEBEL. DECLARE YOUR WEAPONS AND YOUR HEALTH STATUS AT THE NEXT CHECKPOINT.
PLEASE FOLLOW YOUR ESCORTS FOR THE FINEST FOOD AND DRINK ATLANTIS HAS TO OFFER!
NOT HOW XEBELLIANS ARE GENERALLY GREETE IN ATLANTIS, MY KING.

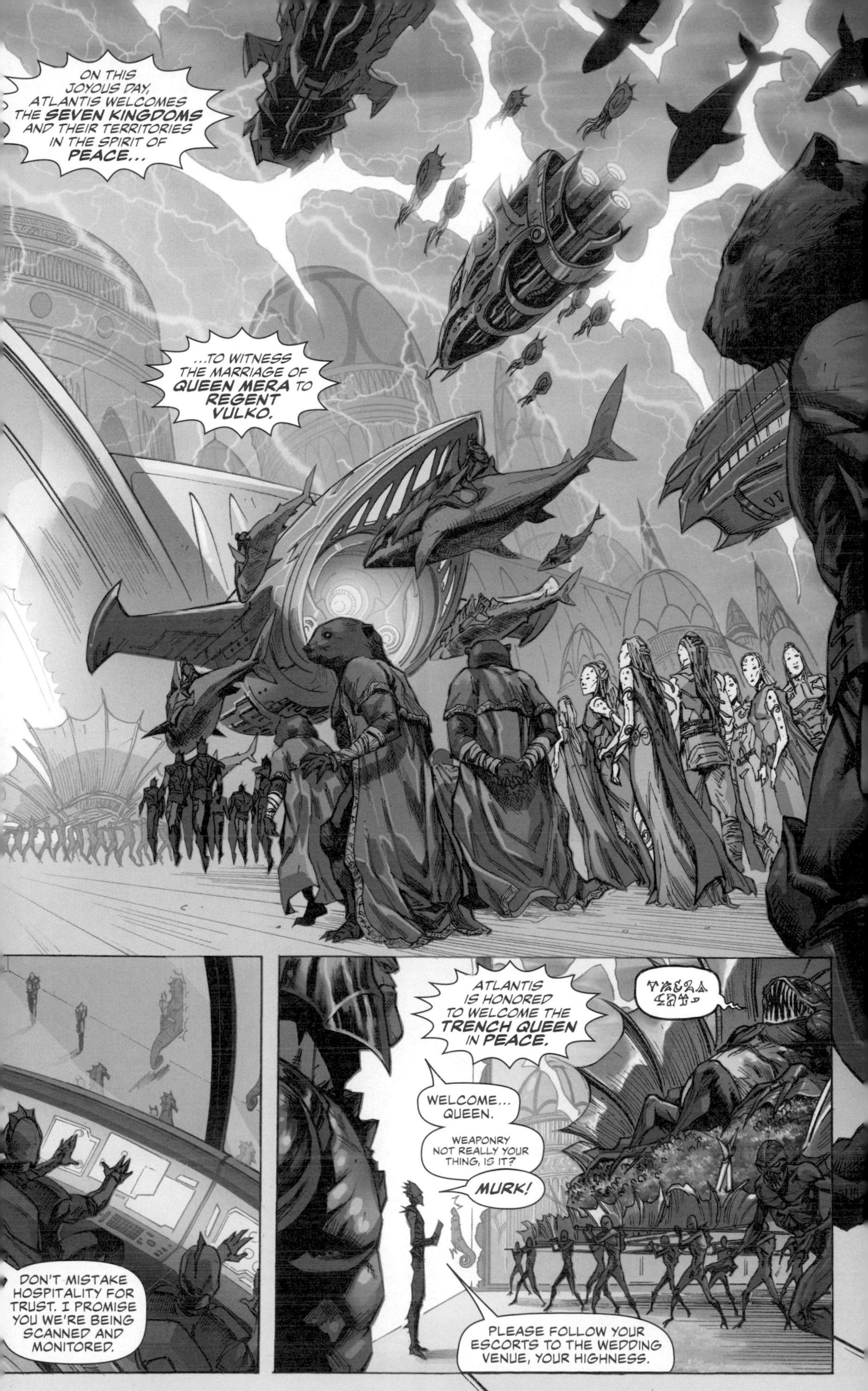
ON THIS JOYOUS DAY, ATLANTIS WELCOMES THE SEVEN KINGDOMS AND THEIR TERRITORIES IN THE SPIRIT OF PEACE...
...TO WITNESS THE MARRIAGE OF QUEEN MERA TO REGENT VULKO.
DON'T MISTAKE HOSPITALITY FOR TRUST. I PROMISE YOU WE'RE BEING SCANNED AND MONITORED.
ATLANTIS IS HONORED TO WELCOME THE TRENCH QUEEN IN PEACE.
WELCOME... QUEEN.
WEAPONRY NOT REALLY YOUR THING, IS IT?
MURK!
PLEASE FOLLOW YOUR ESCORTS TO THE WEDDING VENUE, YOUR HIGHNESS.

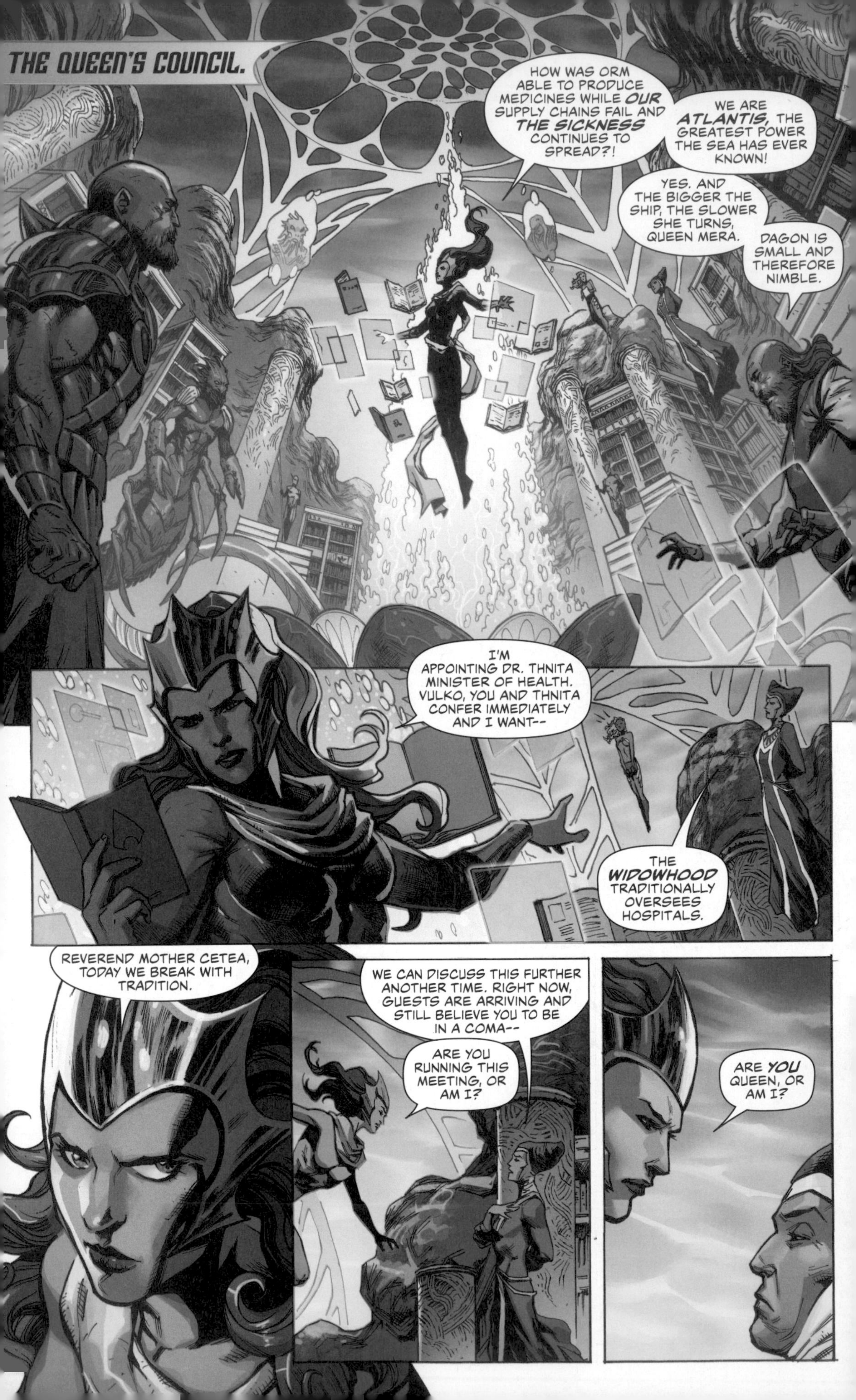
THE QUEEN'S COUNCIL.
HOW WAS ORM ABLE TO PRODUCE MEDICINES WHILE OUR SUPPLY CHAINS FAIL AND THE SICKNESS CONTINUES TO SPREAD?!
WE ARE ATLANTIS, THE GREATEST POWER THE SEA HAS EVER KNOWN!
YES. AND THE BIGGER THE SHIP, THE SLOWER SHE TURNS, QUEEN MERA.
DAGON IS SMALL AND THEREFORE NIMBLE.
I'M APPOINTING DR. THNITA MINISTER OF HEALTH. VULKO, YOU AND THNITA CONFER IMMEDIATELY AND I WANT--
THE WIDOWHOOD TRADITIONALLY OVERSEES HOSPITALS.
REVEREND MOTHER CETEA, TODAY WE BREAK WITH TRADITION.
WE CAN DISCUSS THIS FURTHER ANOTHER TIME. RIGHT NOW, GUESTS ARE ARRIVING AND STILL BELIEVE YOU TO BE IN A COMA--
ARE YOU RUNNING THIS MEETING, OR AM I?
ARE YOU QUEEN, OR AM I?

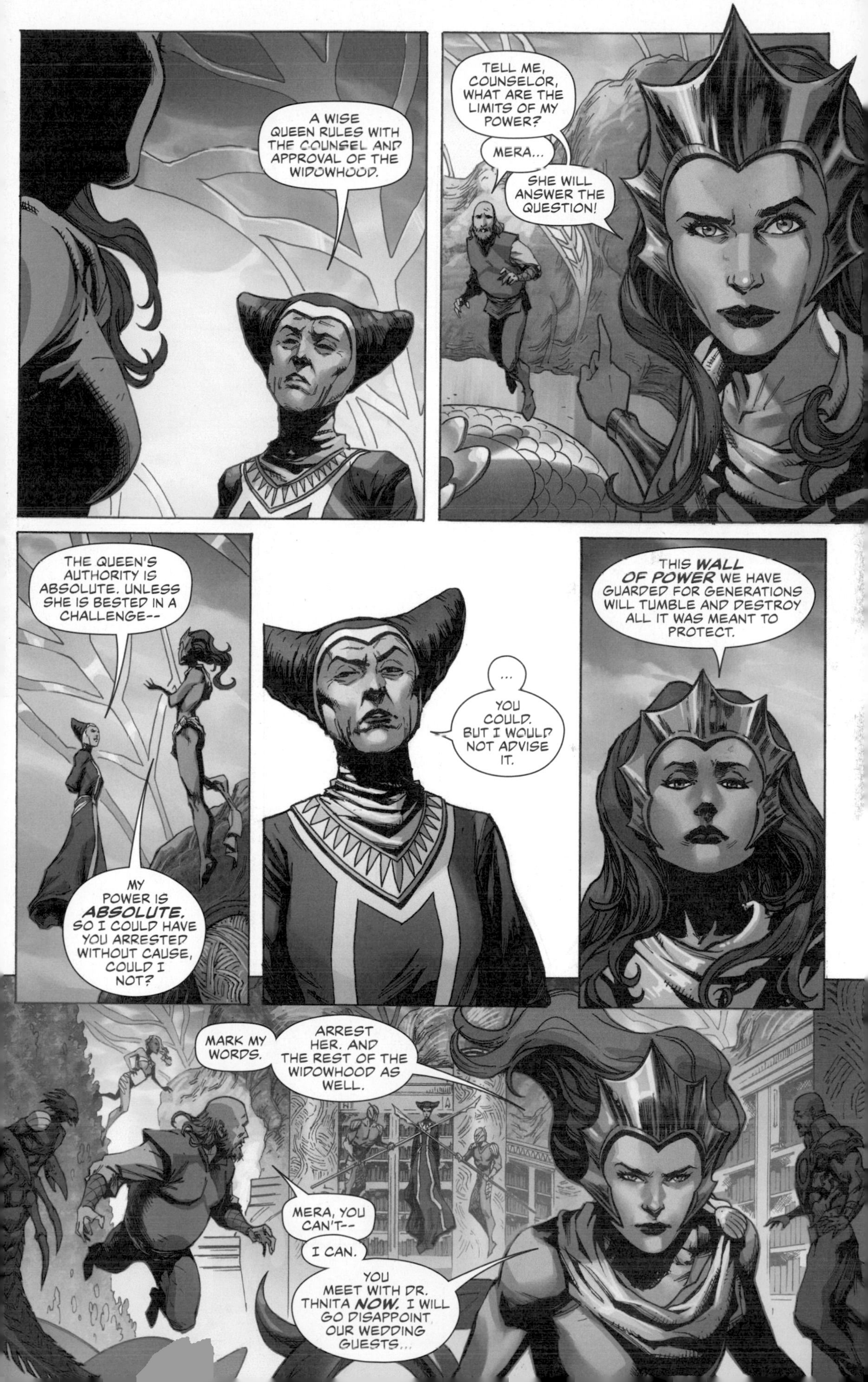
A WISE QUEEN RULES WITH THE COUNSEL AND APPROVAL OF THE WIDOWHOOD.
TELL ME, COUNSELOR, WHAT ARE THE LIMITS OF MY POWER?
MERA...
SHE WILL ANSWER THE QUESTION!
THE QUEEN'S AUTHORITY IS ABSOLUTE. UNLESS SHE IS BESTED IN A CHALLENGE--
MY POWER IS ABSOLUTE. SO I COULD HAVE YOU ARRESTED WITHOUT CAUSE, COULD I NOT?
...
YOU COULD. BUT I WOULD NOT ADVISE IT.
THIS WALL OF POWER WE HAVE GUARDED FOR GENERATIONS WILL TUMBLE AND DESTROY ALL IT WAS MEANT TO PROTECT.
MARK MY WORDS.
ARREST HER. AND THE REST OF THE WIDOWHOOD AS WELL.
MERA, YOU CAN'T--
I CAN.
YOU MEET WITH DR. THNITA NOW. I WILL GO DISAPPOINT OUR WEDDING GUESTS...

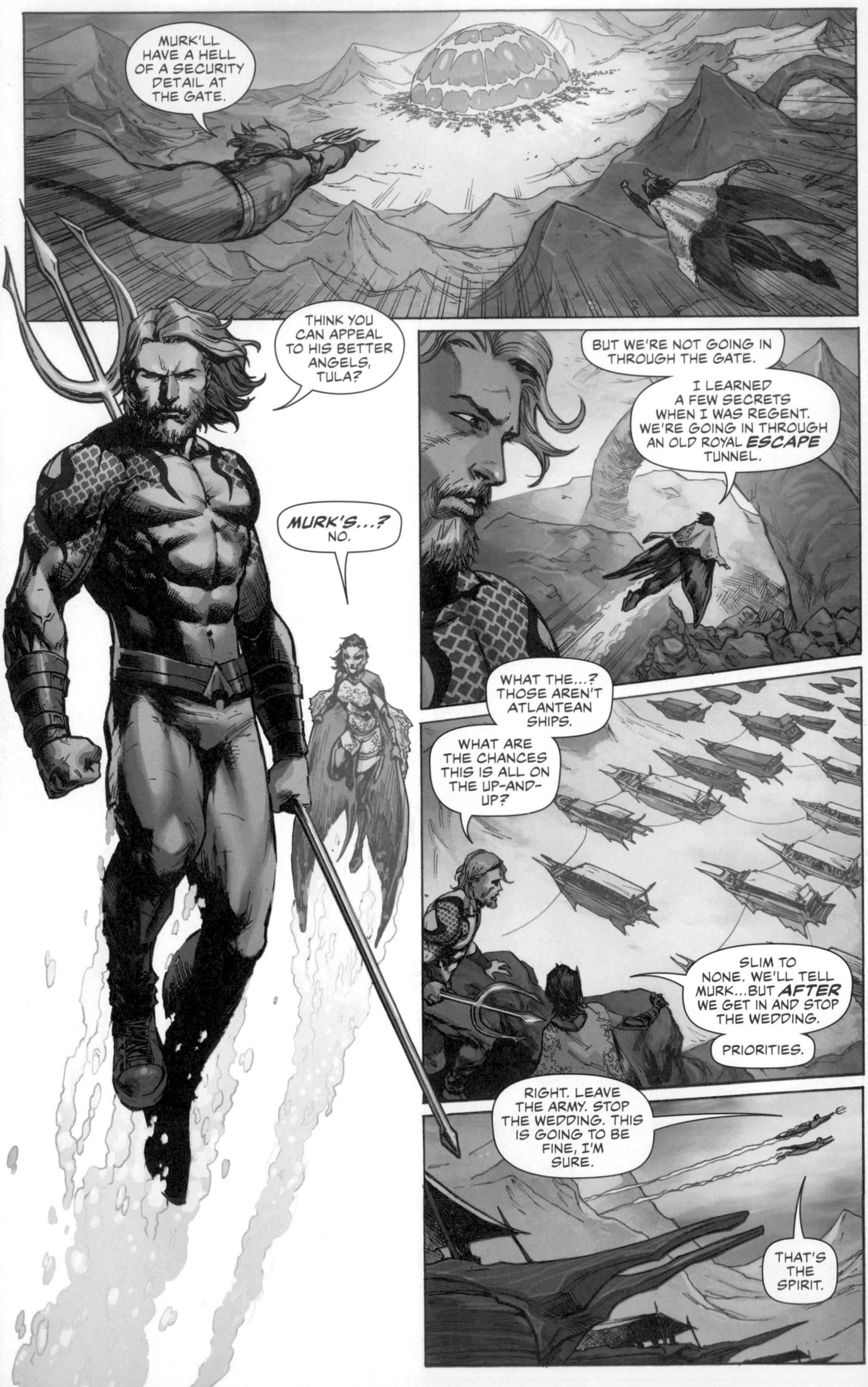
MURK'LL HAVE A HELL OF A SECURITY DETAIL AT THE GATE.
THINK YOU CAN APPEAL TO HIS BETTER ANGELS, TULA?
MURK'S...? NO.
BUT WE'RE NOT GOING IN THROUGH THE GATE.
I LEARNED A FEW SECRETS WHEN I WAS REGENT. WE'RE GOING IN THROUGH AN OLD ROYAL ESCAPE TUNNEL.
WHAT THE...? THOSE AREN'T ATLANTEAN SHIPS.
WHAT ARE THE CHANCES THIS IS ALL ON THE UP-AND-UP?
SLIM TO NONE. WE'LL TELL MURK...BUT AFTER WE GET IN AND STOP THE WEDDING.
PRIORITIES.
RIGHT. LEAVE THE ARMY. STOP THE WEDDING. THIS IS GOING TO BE FINE, I'M SURE.
THAT'S THE SPIRIT.

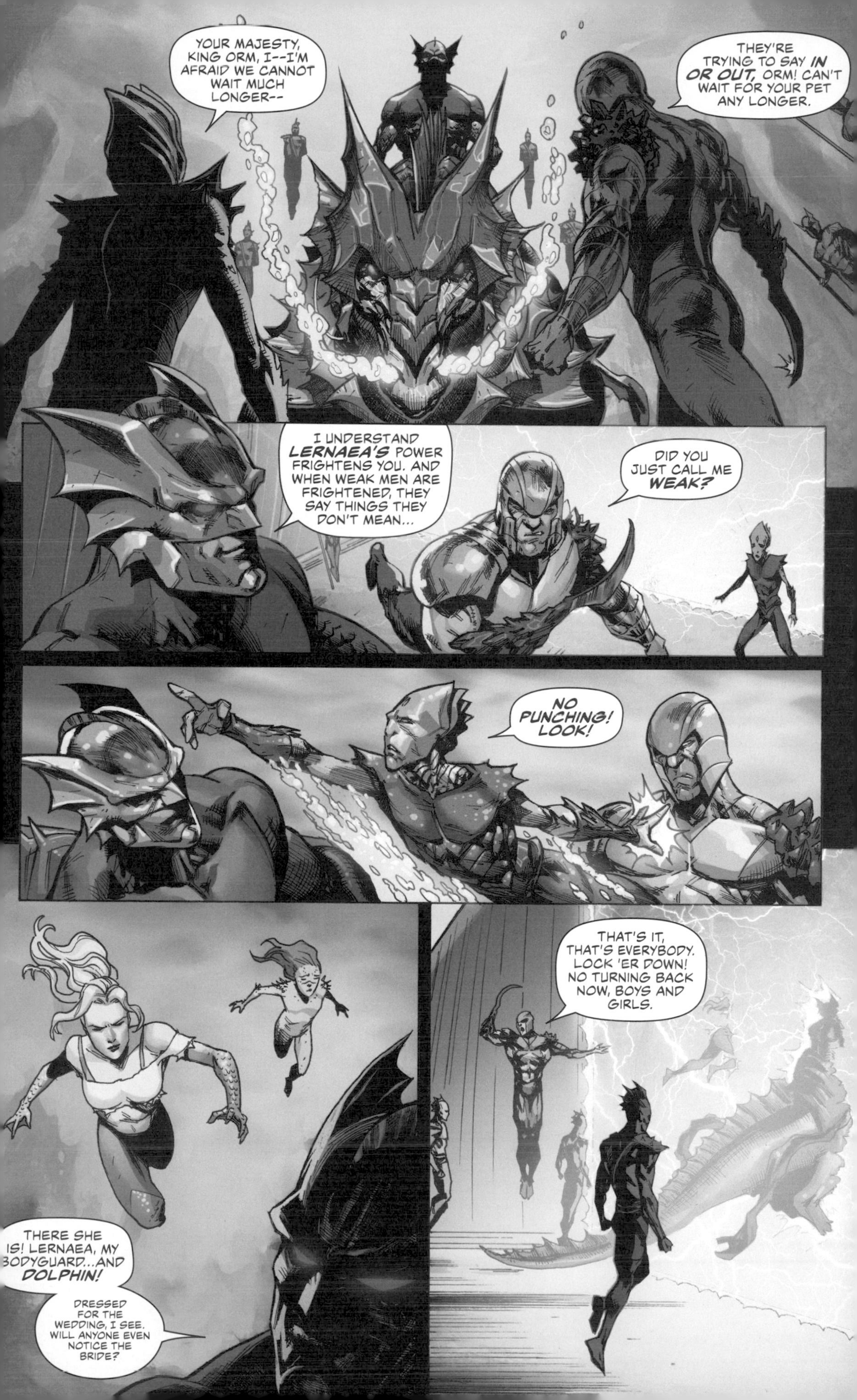
YOUR MAJESTY, KING ORM, I--I'M AFRAID WE CANNOT WAIT MUCH LONGER--
THEY'RE TRYING TO SAY IN OR OUT, ORM! CAN'T WAIT FOR YOUR PET ANY LONGER.
I UNDERSTAND LERNAEA'S POWER FRIGHTENS YOU. AND WHEN WEAK MEN ARE FRIGHTENED, THEY SAY THINGS THEY DON'T MEAN...
DID YOU JUST CALL ME WEAK?
NO PUNCHING! LOOK!
THERE SHE IS! LERNAEA, MY BODYGUARD...AND DOLPHIN!
DRESSED FOR THE WEDDING, I SEE. WILL ANYONE EVEN NOTICE THE BRIDE?
THAT'S IT, THAT'S EVERYBODY. LOCK 'ER DOWN! NO TURNING BACK NOW, BOYS AND GIRLS.

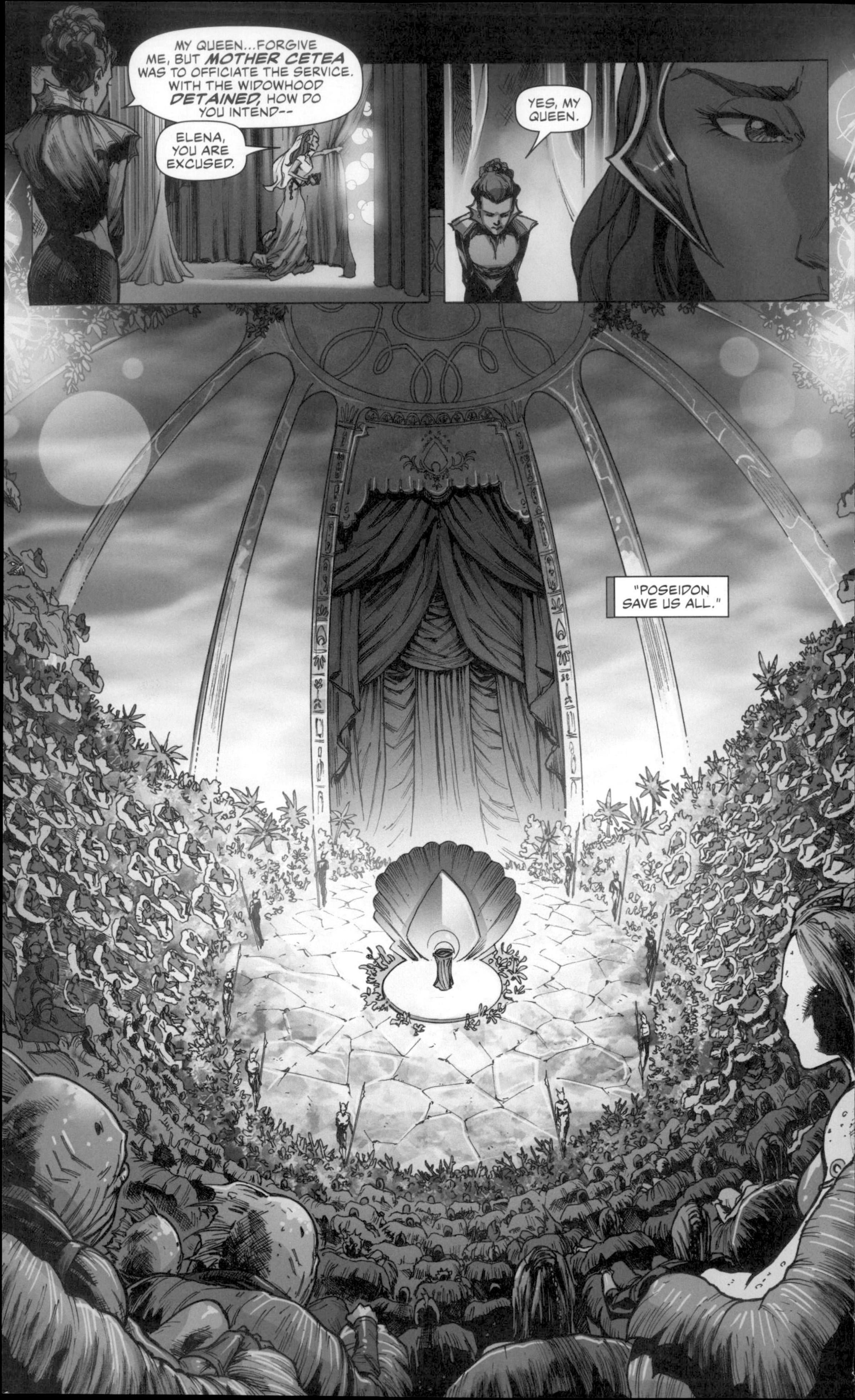
MY QUEEN...FORGIVE ME, BUT MOTHER CETEA WAS TO OFFICIATE THE SERVICE. WITH THE WIDOWHOOD DETAINED, HOW DO YOU INTEND--
ELENA, YOU ARE EXCUSED.
YES, MY QUEEN.
"POSEIDON SAVE US ALL."

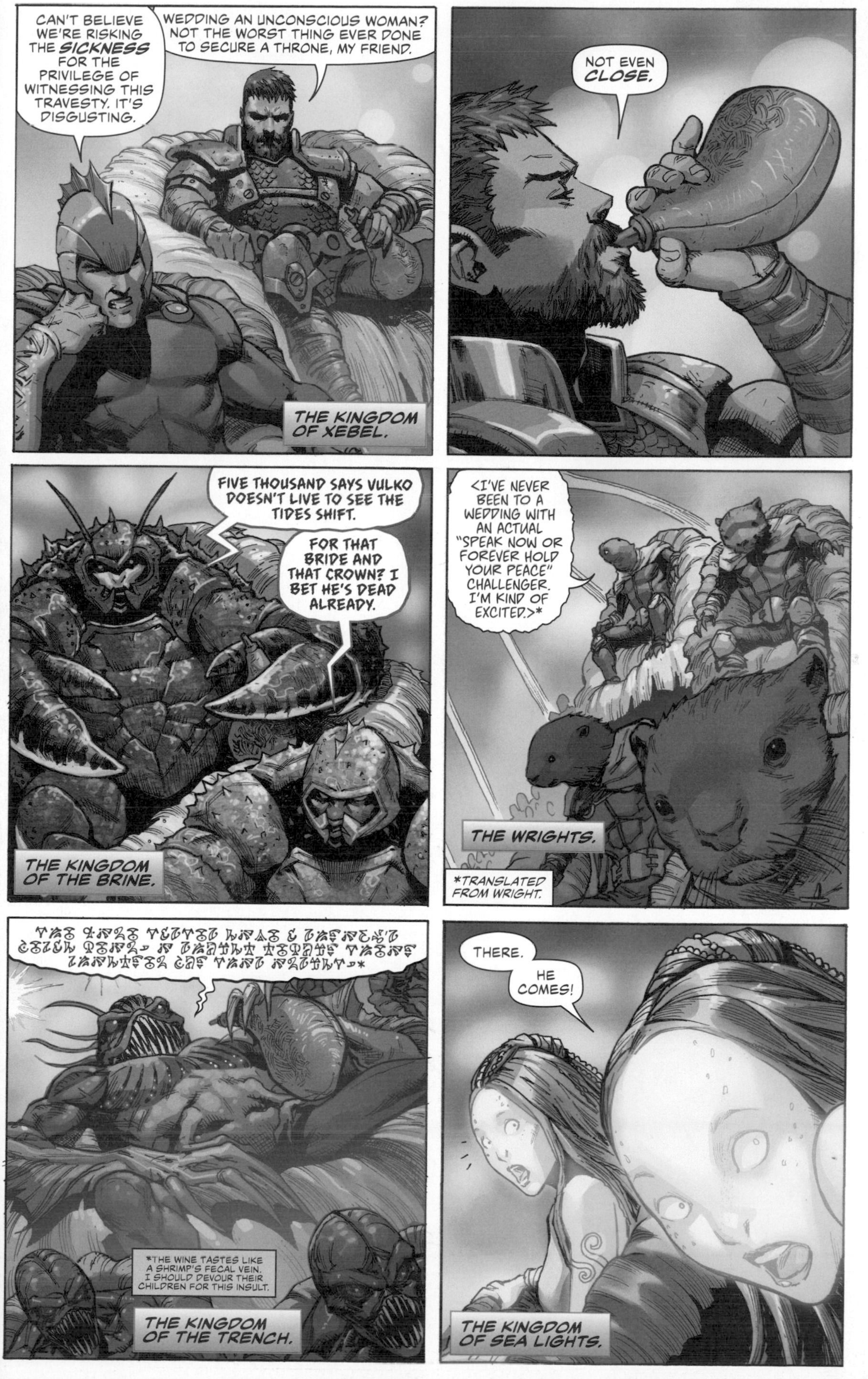
CAN'T BELIEVE WE'RE RISKING THE SICKNESS FOR THE PRIVILEGE OF WITNESSING THIS TRAVESTY. IT'S DISGUSTING.
WEDDING AN UNCONSCIOUS WOMAN? NOT THE WORST THING EVER DONE TO SECURE A THRONE, MY FRIEND.
THE KINGDOM OF XEBEL.
NOT EVEN CLOSE.
FIVE THOUSAND SAYS VULKO DOESN'T LIVE TO SEE THE TIDES SHIFT.
FOR THAT BRIDE AND THAT CROWN? I BET HE'S DEAD ALREADY.
THE KINGDOM OF THE BRINE.
<I'VE NEVER BEEN TO A WEDDING WITH AN ACTUAL "SPEAK NOW OR FOREVER HOLD YOUR PEACE" CHALLENGER. I'M KIND OF EXCITED.>*
THE WRIGHTS.
*TRANSLATED FROM WRIGHT.
*THE WINE TASTES LIKE A SHRIMP'S FECAL VEIN. I SHOULD DEVOUR THEIR CHILDREN FOR THIS INSULT.
THE KINGDOM OF THE TRENCH.
THERE.
HE COMES!
THE KINGDOM OF SEA LIGHTS.

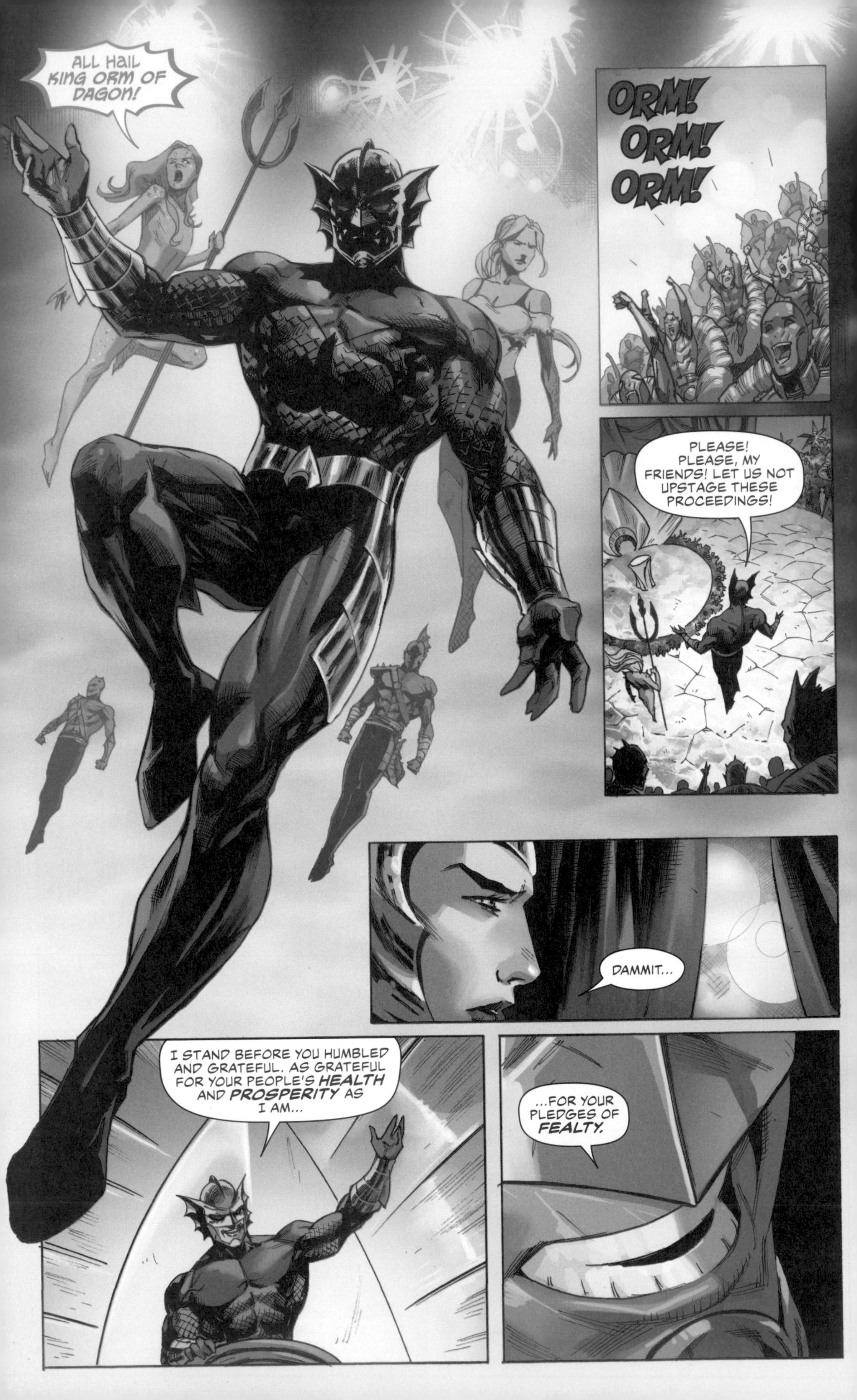
ALL HAIL KING ORM OF DAGON!
ORM! ORM! ORM!
PLEASE! PLEASE, MY FRIENDS! LET US NOT UPSTAGE THESE PROCEEDINGS!
DAMMIT...
I STAND BEFORE YOU HUMBLED AND GRATEFUL. AS GRATEFUL FOR YOUR PEOPLE'S HEALTH AND PROSPERITY AS I AM...
...FOR YOUR PLEDGES OF FEALTY.

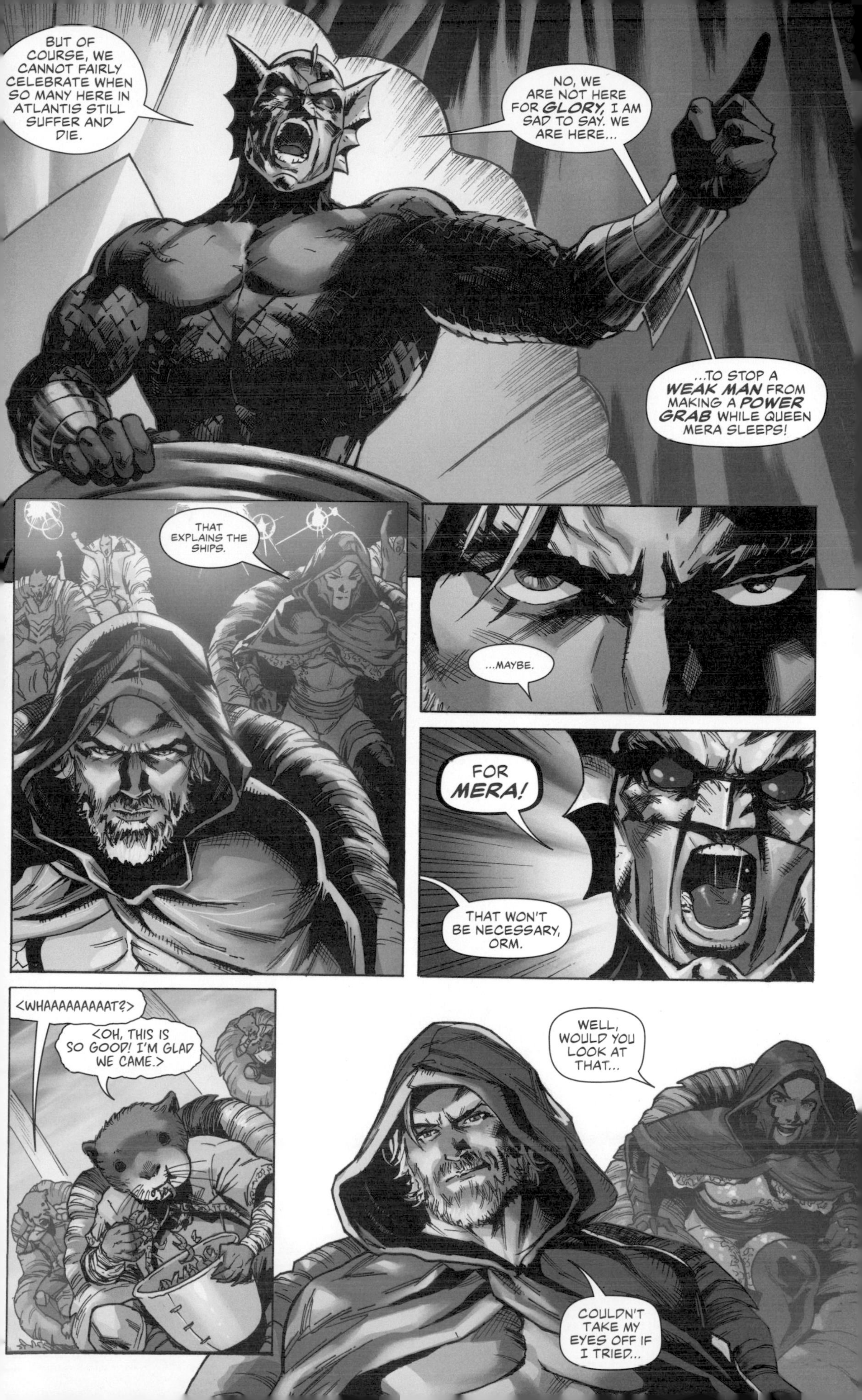
BUT OF COURSE, WE CANNOT FAIRLY CELEBRATE WHEN SO MANY HERE IN ATLANTIS STILL SUFFER AND DIE.
NO, WE ARE NOT HERE FOR GLORY, I AM SAD TO SAY. WE ARE HERE...
...TO STOP A WEAK MAN FROM MAKING A POWER GRAB WHILE QUEEN MERA SLEEPS!
THAT EXPLAINS THE SHIPS.
...MAYBE.
FOR MERA!
THAT WON'T BE NECESSARY, ORM.
<WHAAAAAAAAAT?>
<OH, THIS IS SO GOOD! I'M GLAD WE CAME.>
WELL, WOULD YOU LOOK AT THAT...
COULDN'T TAKE MY EYES OFF IF I TRIED...

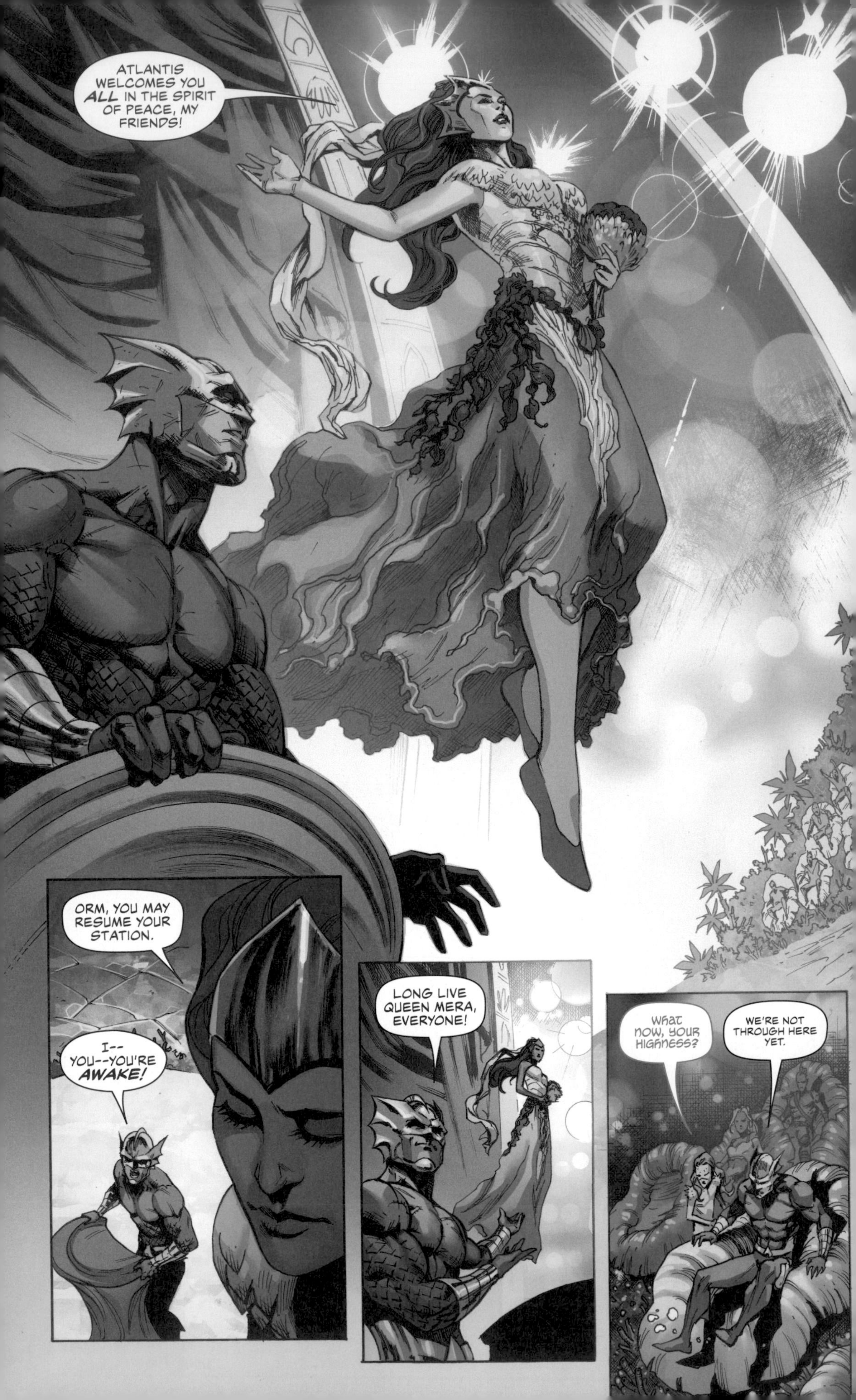
ATLANTIS WELCOMES YOU ALL IN THE SPIRIT OF PEACE, MY FRIENDS!
ORM, YOU MAY RESUME YOUR STATION.
I-- YOU--YOU'RE AWAKE!
LONG LIVE QUEEN MERA, EVERYONE!
WHAT NOW, YOUR HIGHNESS?
WE'RE NOT THROUGH HERE YET.

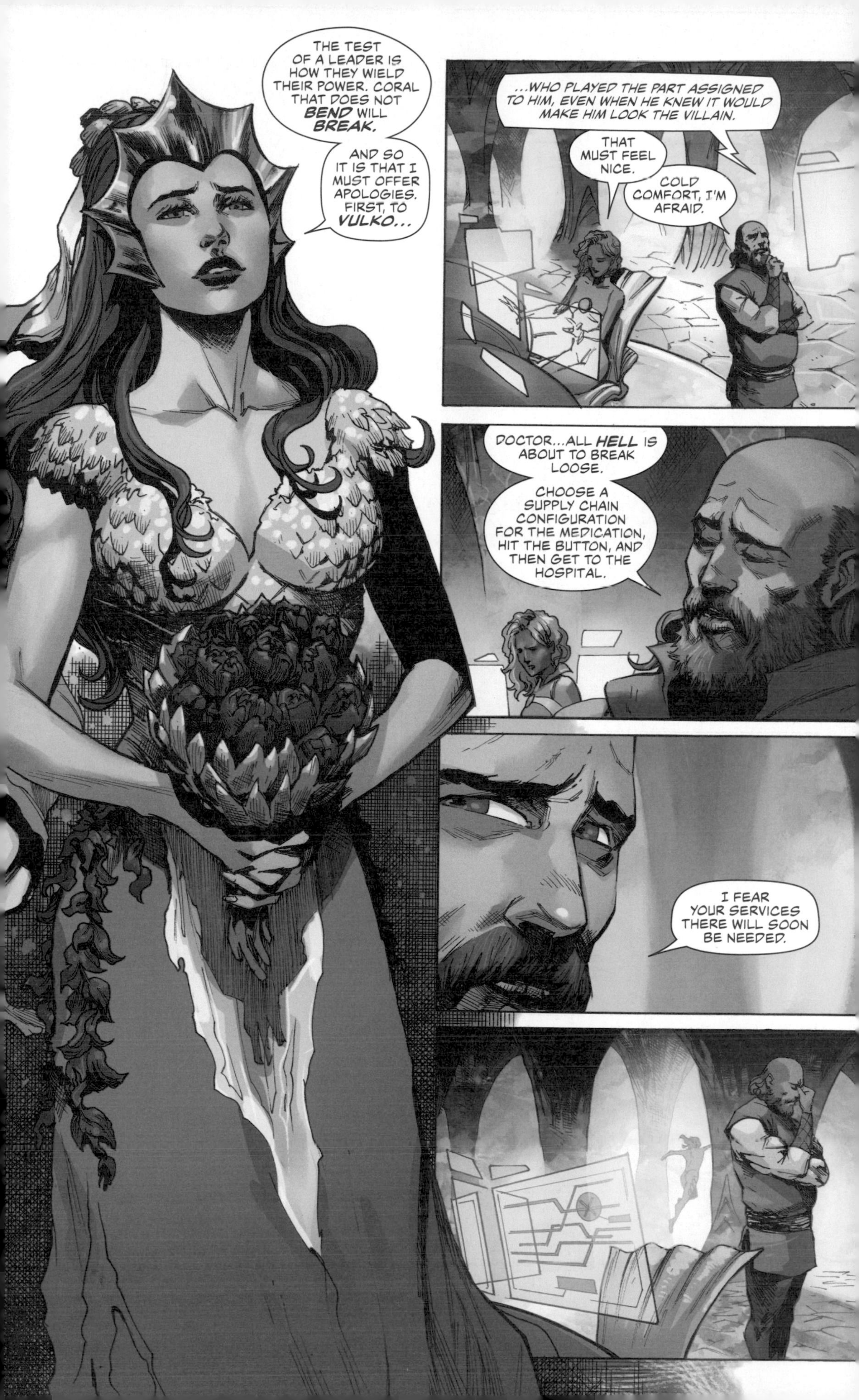
THE TEST OF A LEADER IS HOW THEY WIELD THEIR POWER. CORAL THAT DOES NOT BEND WILL BREAK.
AND SO IT IS THAT I MUST OFFER APOLOGIES. FIRST, TO VULKO...
...WHO PLAYED THE PART ASSIGNED TO HIM, EVEN WHEN HE KNEW IT WOULD MAKE HIM LOOK THE VILLAIN.
THAT MUST FEEL NICE.
COLD COMFORT, I'M AFRAID.
DOCTOR...ALL HELL IS ABOUT TO BREAK LOOSE.
CHOOSE A SUPPLY CHAIN CONFIGURATION FOR THE MEDICATION, HIT THE BUTTON, AND THEN GET TO THE HOSPITAL.
I FEAR YOUR SERVICES THERE WILL SOON BE NEEDED.

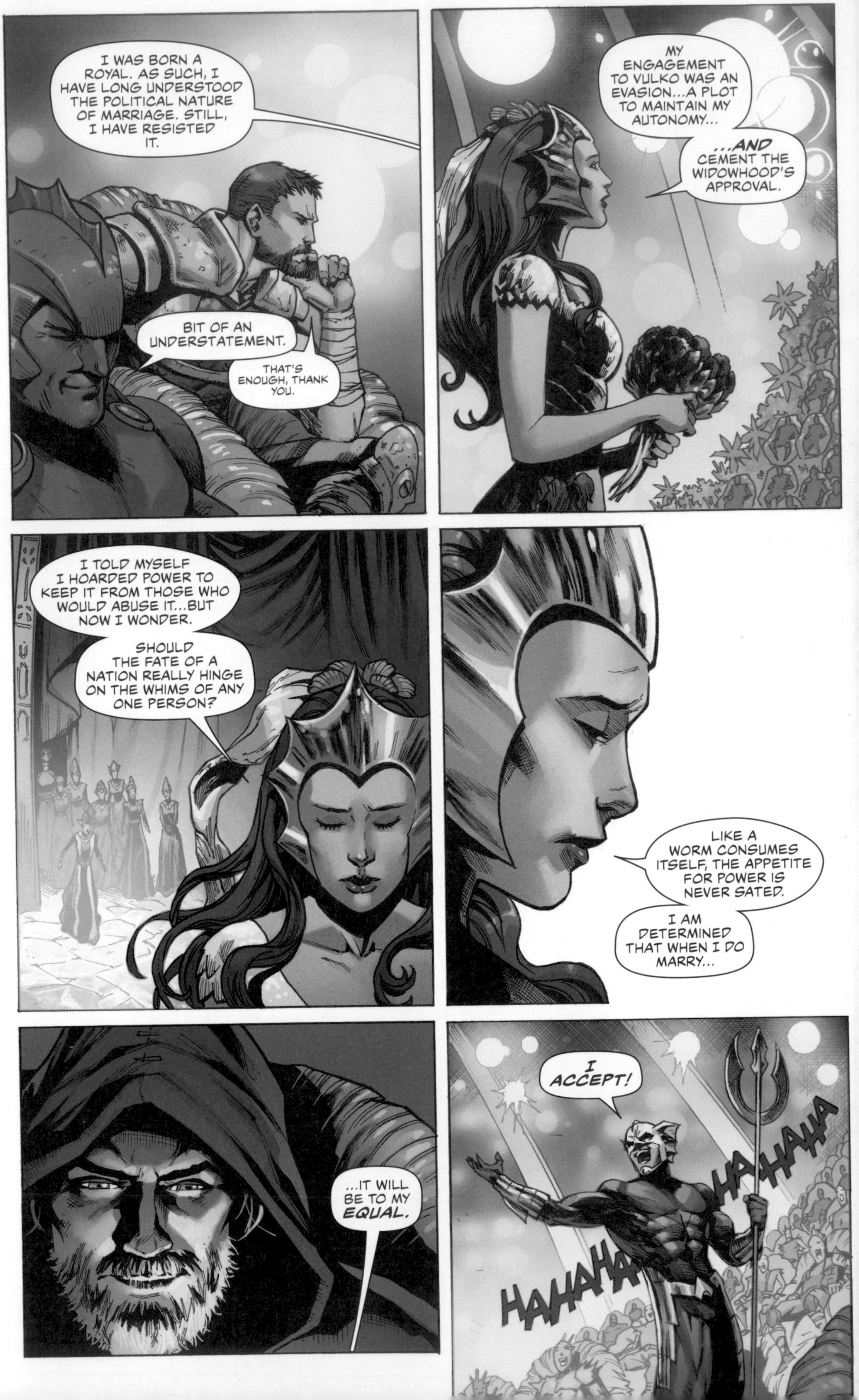
I WAS BORN A ROYAL. AS SUCH, I HAVE LONG UNDERSTOOD THE POLITICAL NATURE OF MARRIAGE. STILL, I HAVE RESISTED IT.
BIT OF AN UNDERSTATEMENT.
THAT'S ENOUGH, THANK YOU.
MY ENGAGEMENT TO VULKO WAS AN EVASION...A PLOT TO MAINTAIN MY AUTONOMY...
...AND CEMENT THE WIDOWHOOD'S APPROVAL.
I TOLD MYSELF I HOARDED POWER TO KEEP IT FROM THOSE WHO WOULD ABUSE IT...BUT NOW I WONDER.
SHOULD THE FATE OF A NATION REALLY HINGE ON THE WHIMS OF ANY ONE PERSON?
LIKE A WORM CONSUMES ITSELF, THE APPETITE FOR POWER IS NEVER SATED.
I AM DETERMINED THAT WHEN I DO MARRY...
...IT WILL BE TO MY EQUAL.
I ACCEPT!
HAHAHAHA
HAHAHAHA

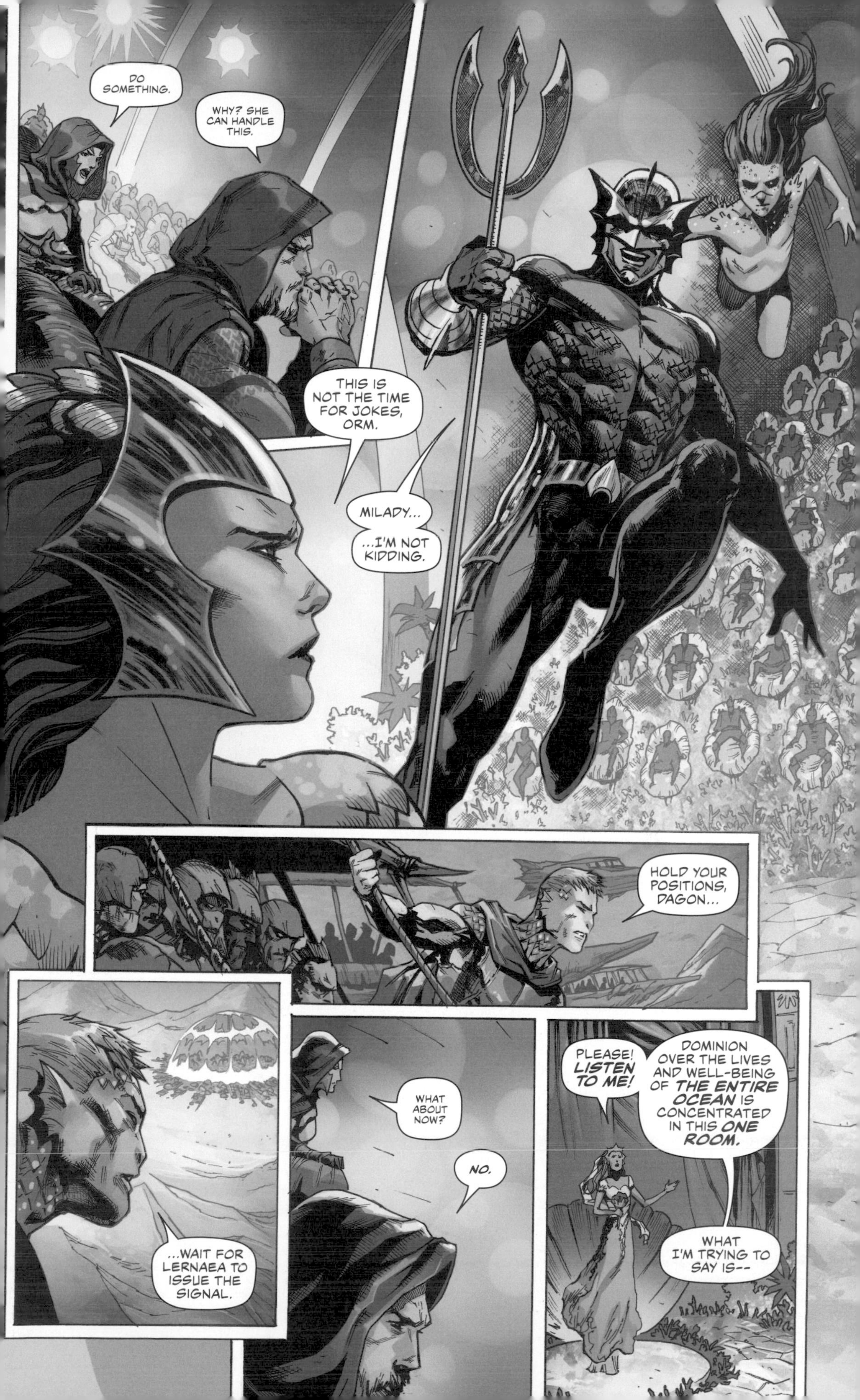
DO SOMETHING.
WHY? SHE CAN HANDLE THIS.
THIS IS NOT THE TIME FOR JOKES, ORM.
MILADY...
...I'M NOT KIDDING.
HOLD YOUR POSITIONS, DAGON...
...WAIT FOR LERNAEA TO ISSUE THE SIGNAL.
WHAT ABOUT NOW?
NO.
PLEASE! LISTEN TO ME!
DOMINION OVER THE LIVES AND WELL-BEING OF THE ENTIRE OCEAN IS CONCENTRATED IN THIS ONE ROOM.
WHAT I'M TRYING TO SAY IS--

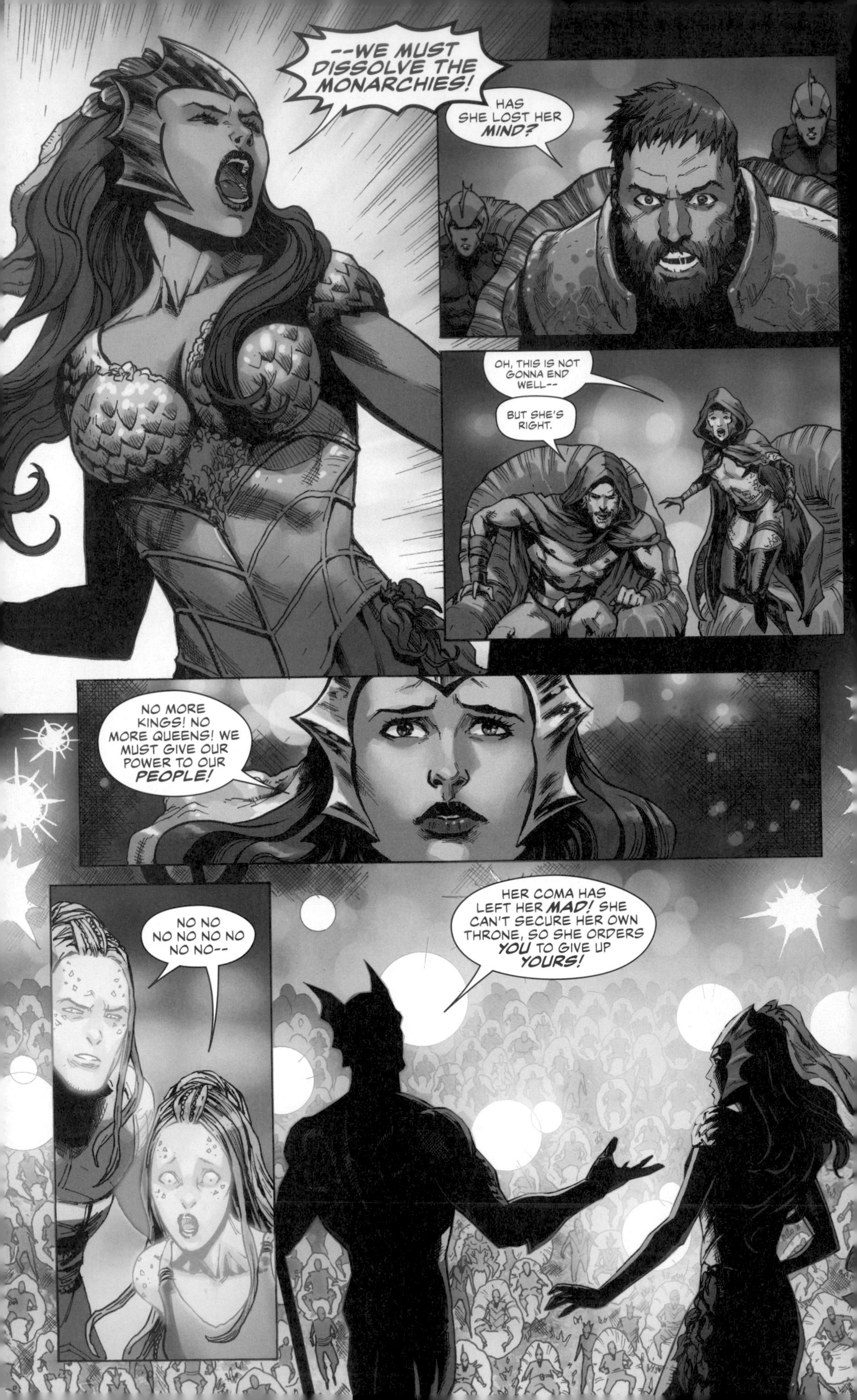
--WE MUST DISSOLVE THE MONARCHIES!
HAS SHE LOST HER MIND?
OH, THIS IS NOT GONNA END WELL--
BUT SHE'S RIGHT.
NO MORE KINGS! NO MORE QUEENS! WE MUST GIVE OUR POWER TO OUR PEOPLE!
NO NO NO NO NO NO NO NO--
HER COMA HAS LEFT HER MAD! SHE CAN'T SECURE HER OWN THRONE, SO SHE ORDERS YOU TO GIVE UP YOURS!

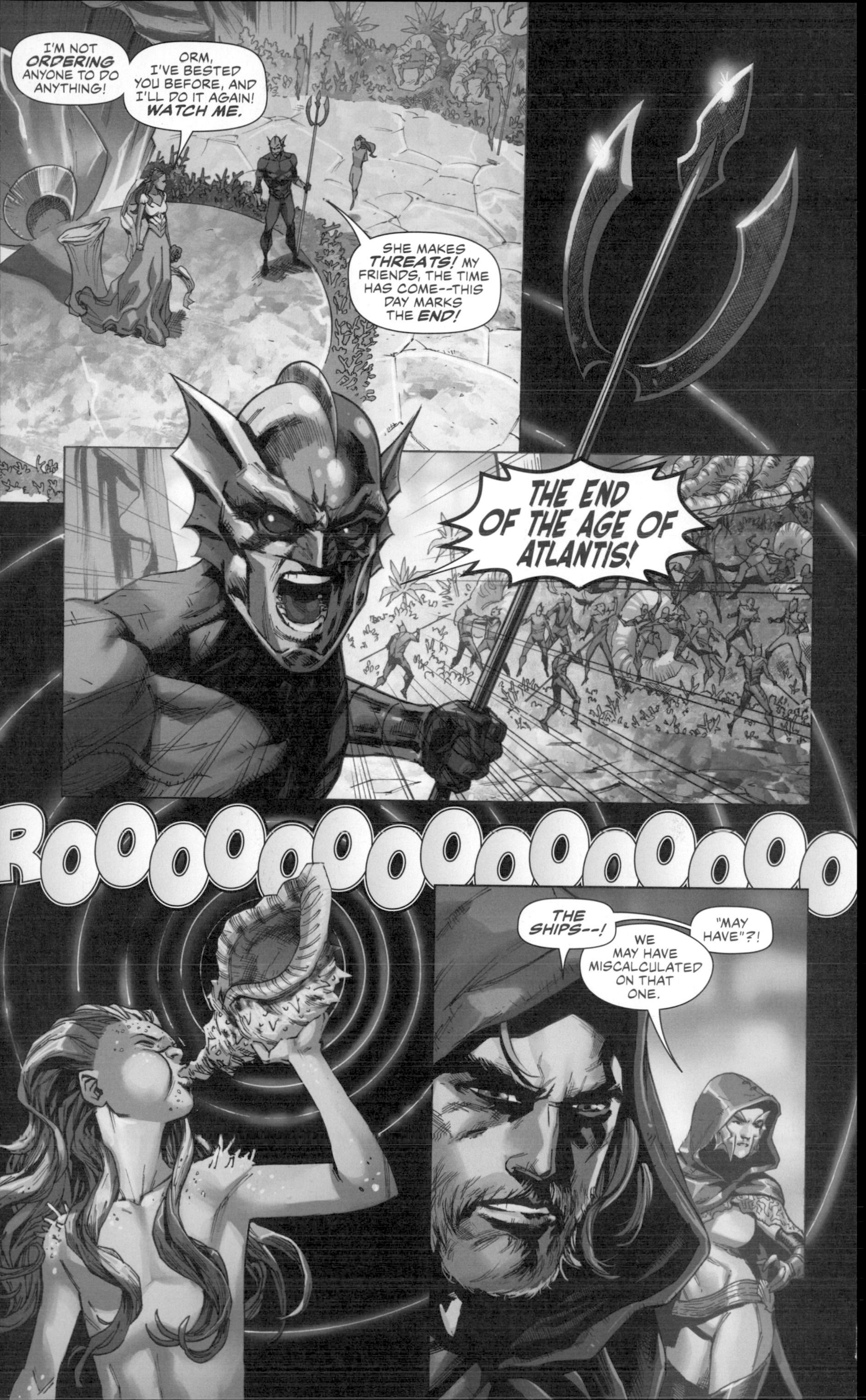
I'M NOT ORDERING ANYONE TO DO ANYTHING!
ORM, I'VE BESTED YOU BEFORE, AND I'LL DO IT AGAIN! WATCH ME.
SHE MAKES THREATS! MY FRIENDS, THE TIME HAS COME--THIS DAY MARKS THE END!
THE END OF THE AGE OF ATLANTIS!
ROOOOOOOOOOOOOOOO
THE SHIPS--!
"MAY HAVE"?!
WE MAY HAVE MISCALCULATED ON THAT ONE.

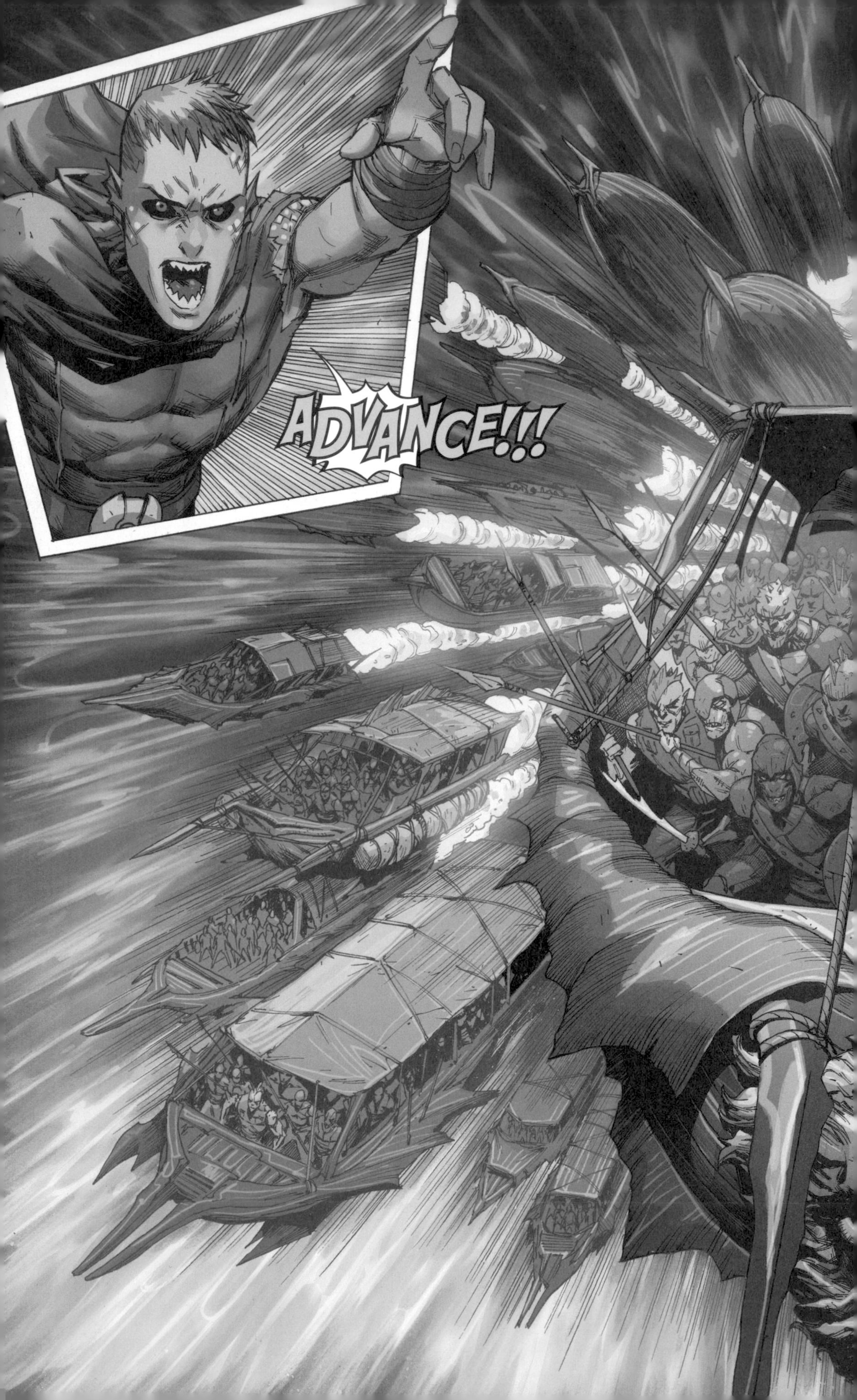
ADVANCE!!!

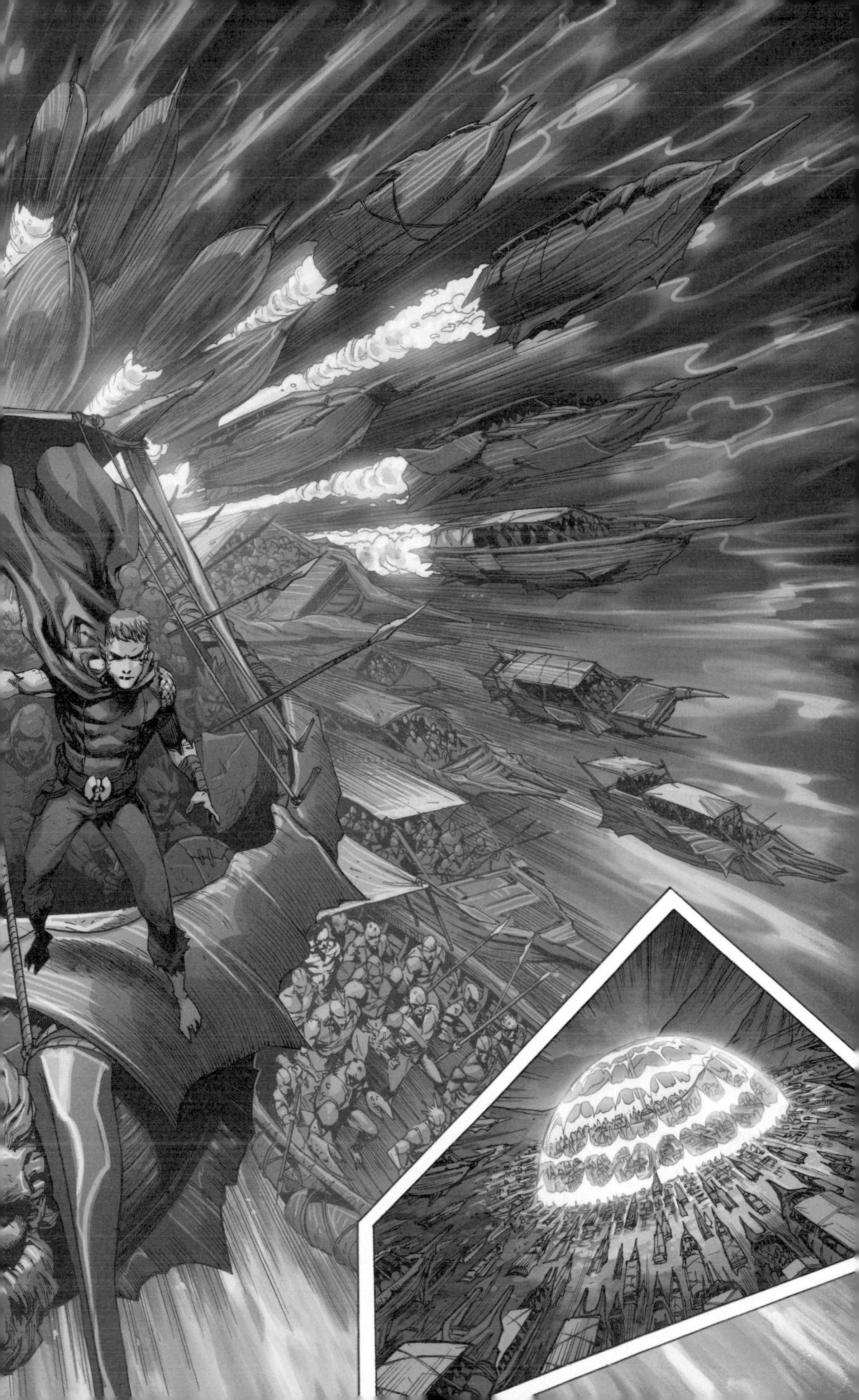

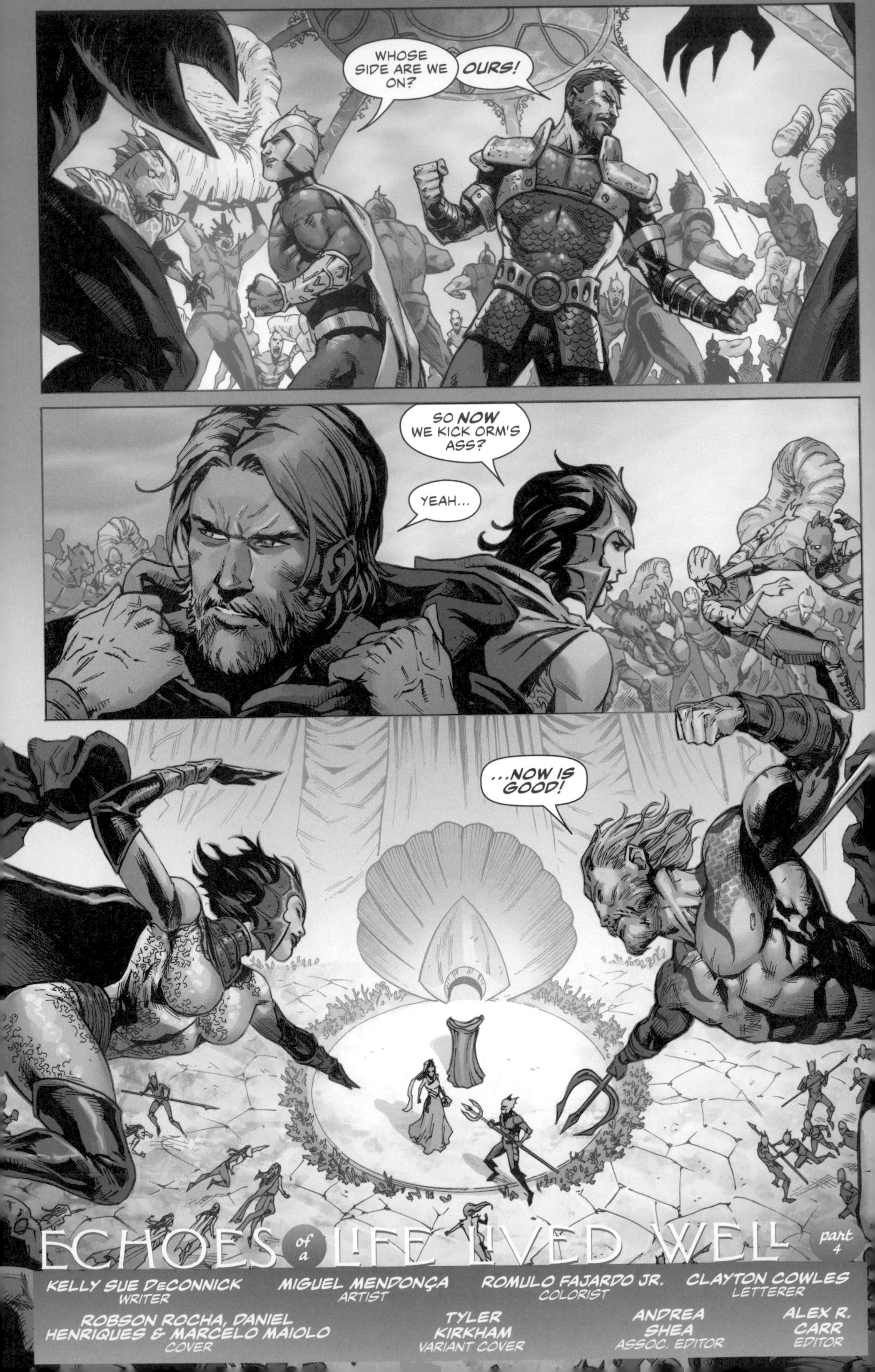
WHOSE SIDE ARE WE ON?
OURS!
SO NOW WE KICK ORM'S ASS?
YEAH...
...NOW IS GOOD!
ECHOES of a LIFE LIVED WELL part 4
KELLY SUE DeCONNICK WRITER
MIGUEL MENDONÇA ARTIST
ROMULO FAJARDO JR. COLORIST
CLAYTON COWLES LETTERER
ROBSON ROCHA, DANIEL HENRIQUES & MARCELO MAIOLO COVER
TYLER KIRKHAM VARIANT COVER
ANDREA SHEA ASSOC. EDITOR
ALEX R. CARR EDITOR

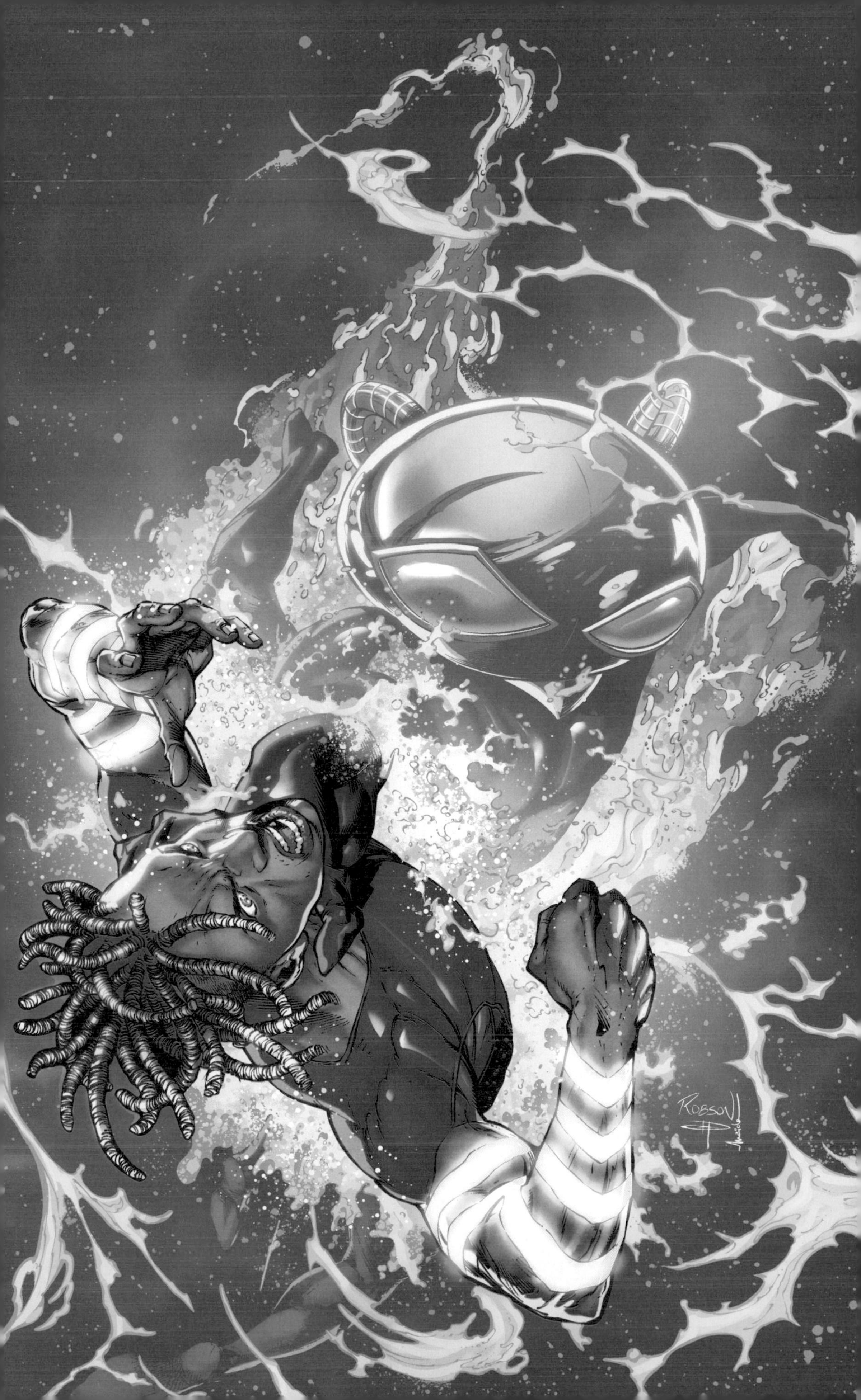

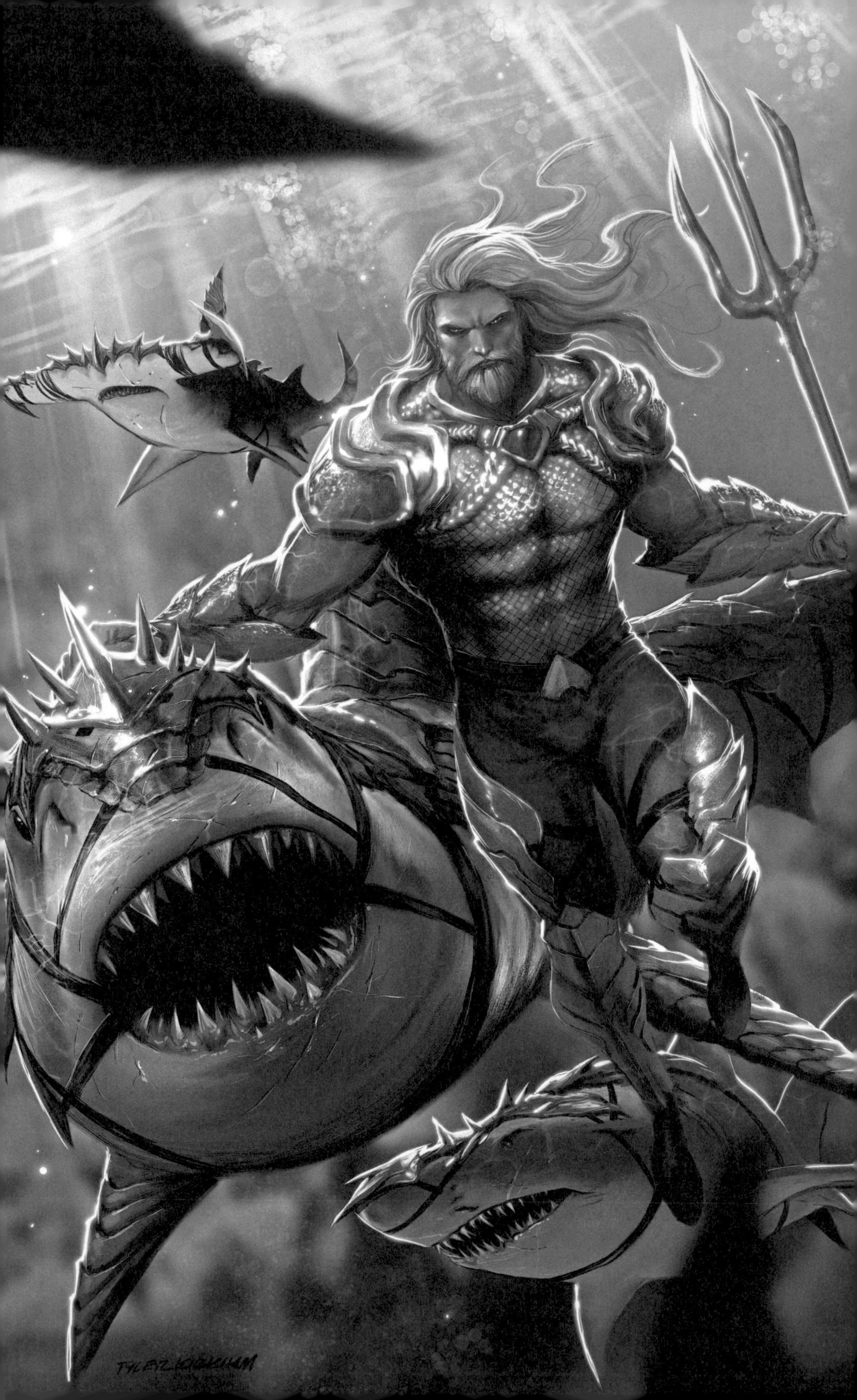
TYLER KIRKHAM

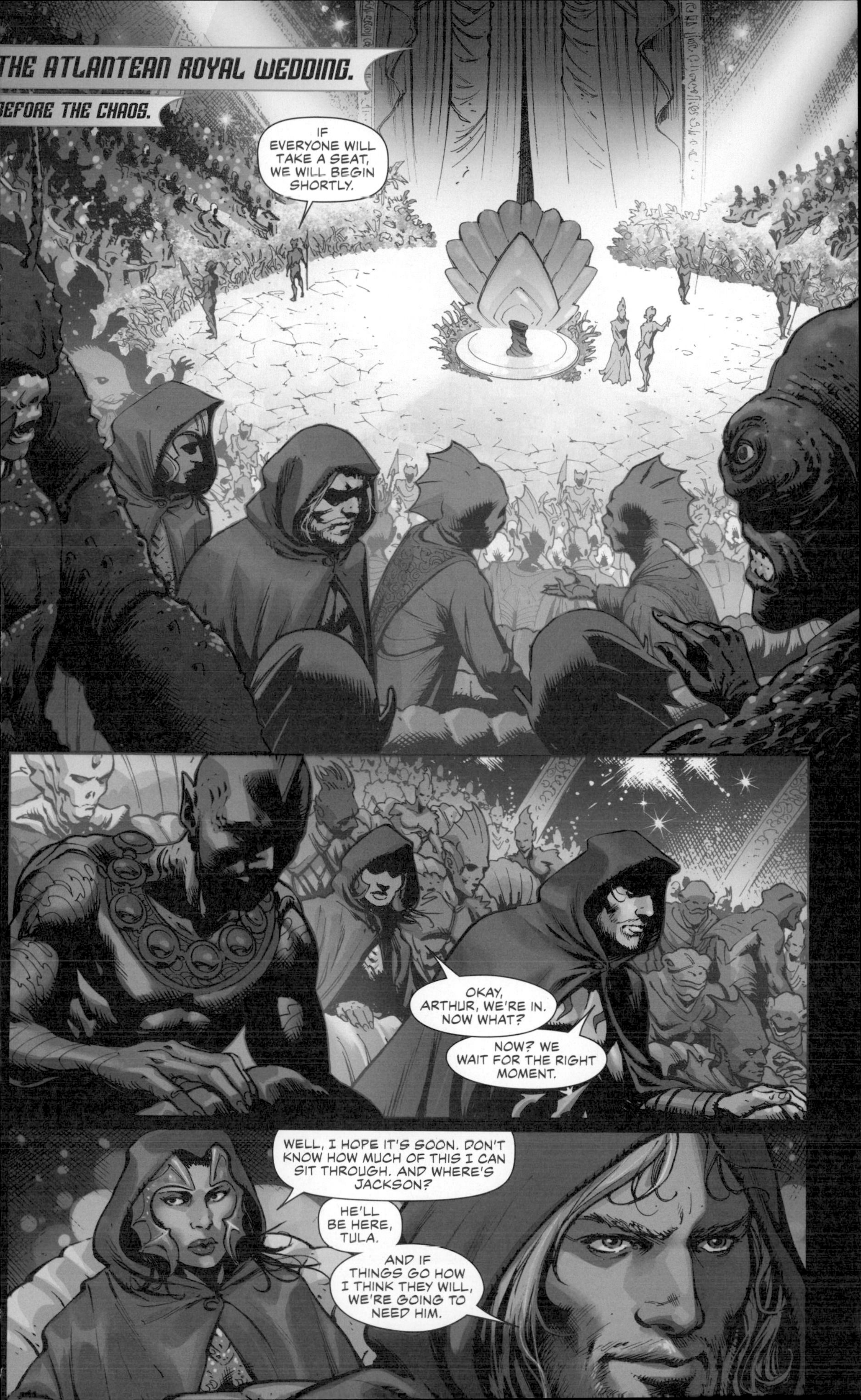
THE ATLANTEAN ROYAL WEDDING.
BEFORE THE CHAOS.
IF EVERYONE WILL TAKE A SEAT, WE WILL BEGIN SHORTLY.
OKAY, ARTHUR, WE'RE IN. NOW WHAT?
NOW? WE WAIT FOR THE RIGHT MOMENT.
WELL, I HOPE IT'S SOON. DON'T KNOW HOW MUCH OF THIS I CAN SIT THROUGH. AND WHERE'S JACKSON?
HE'LL BE HERE, TULA.
AND IF THINGS GO HOW I THINK THEY WILL, WE'RE GOING TO NEED HIM.

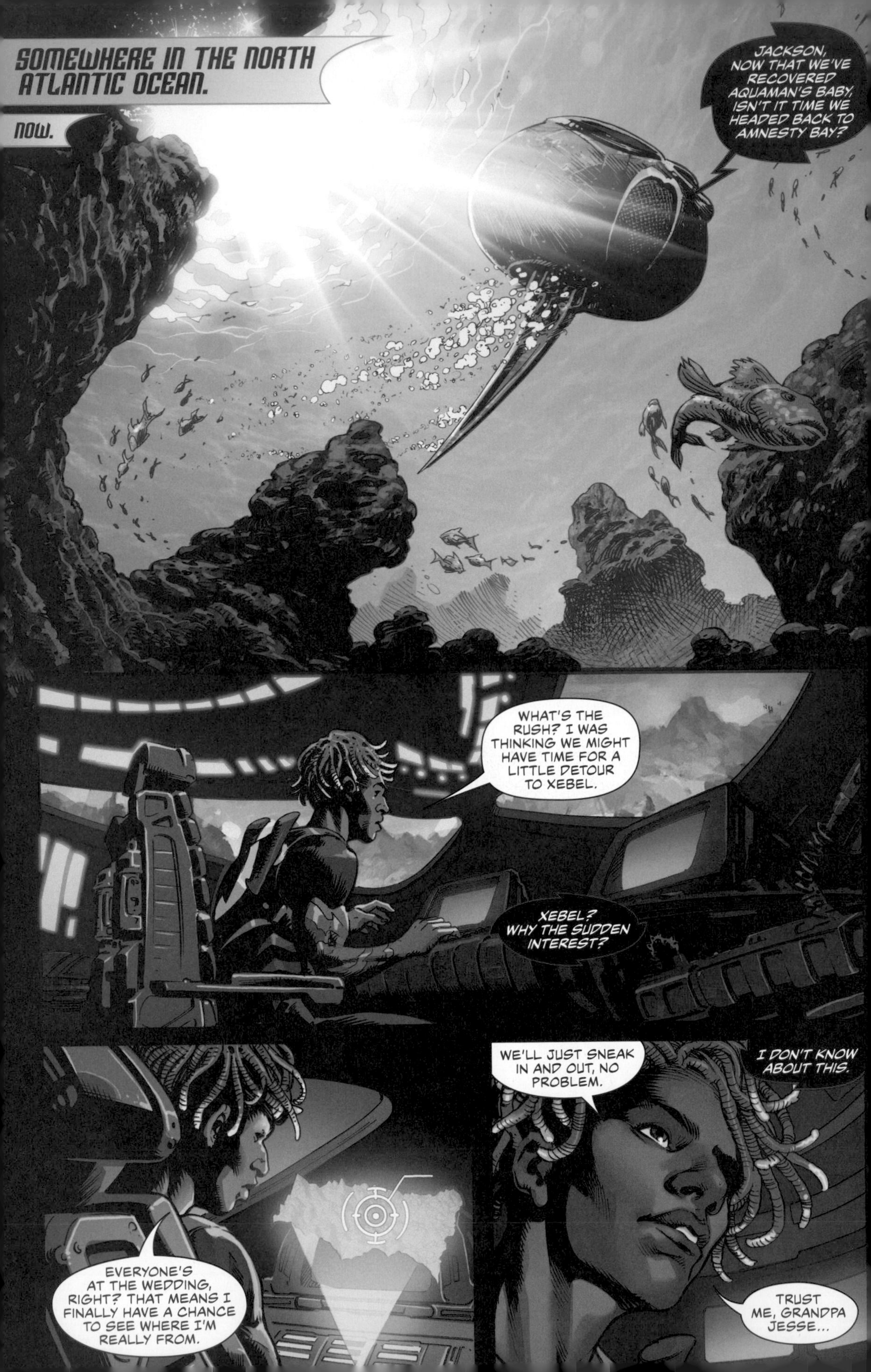
SOMEWHERE IN THE NORTH ATLANTIC OCEAN.
NOW.
JACKSON, NOW THAT WE'VE RECOVERED AQUAMAN'S BABY, ISN'T IT TIME WE HEADED BACK TO AMNESTY BAY?
WHAT'S THE RUSH? I WAS THINKING WE MIGHT HAVE TIME FOR A LITTLE DETOUR TO XEBEL.
XEBEL? WHY THE SUDDEN INTEREST?
EVERYONE'S AT THE WEDDING, RIGHT? THAT MEANS I FINALLY HAVE A CHANCE TO SEE WHERE I'M REALLY FROM.
WE'LL JUST SNEAK IN AND OUT, NO PROBLEM.
I DON'T KNOW ABOUT THIS.
TRUST ME, GRANDPA JESSE...

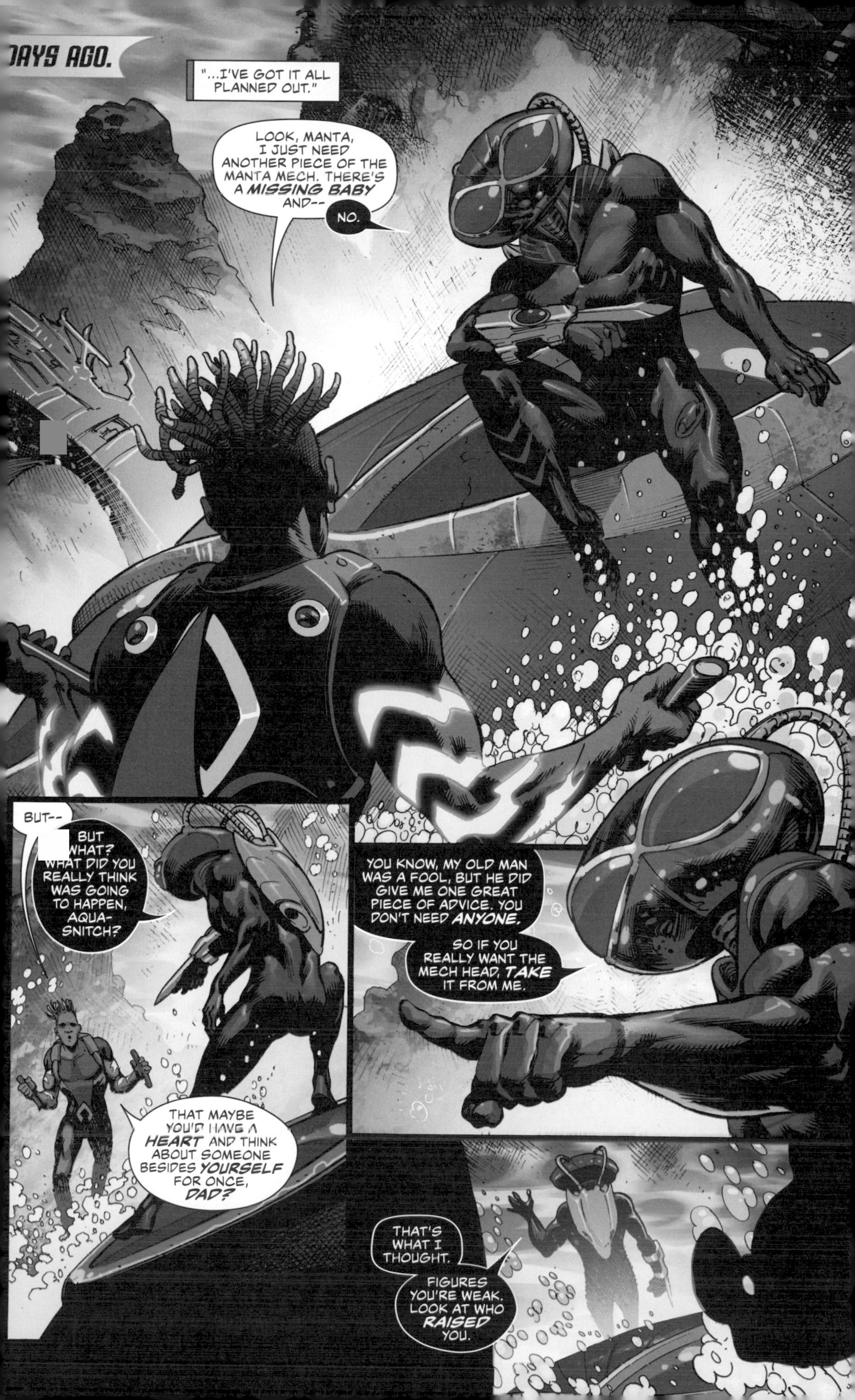
DAYS AGO.
"...I'VE GOT IT ALL PLANNED OUT."
LOOK, MANTA, I JUST NEED ANOTHER PIECE OF THE MANTA MECH. THERE'S A MISSING BABY AND--
NO.
BUT--
BUT WHAT? WHAT DID YOU REALLY THINK WAS GOING TO HAPPEN, AQUA-SNITCH?
THAT MAYBE YOU'D HAVE A HEART AND THINK ABOUT SOMEONE BESIDES YOURSELF FOR ONCE, DAD?
YOU KNOW, MY OLD MAN WAS A FOOL, BUT HE DID GIVE ME ONE GREAT PIECE OF ADVICE. YOU DON'T NEED ANYONE.
SO IF YOU REALLY WANT THE MECH HEAD, TAKE IT FROM ME.
THAT'S WHAT I THOUGHT.
FIGURES YOU'RE WEAK. LOOK AT WHO RAISED YOU.

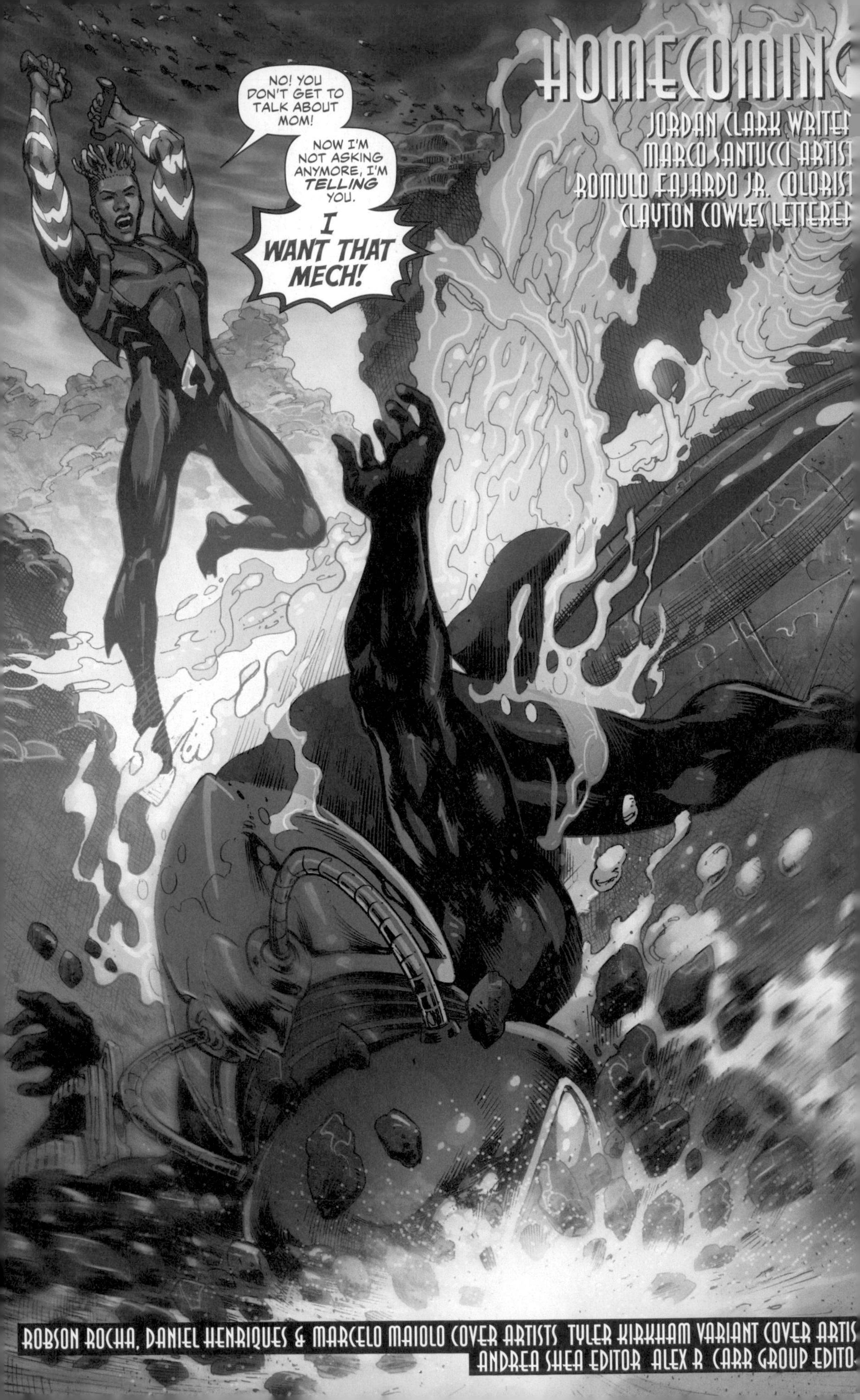
HOMECOMING
JORDAN CLARK WRITER
MARCO SANTUCCI ARTIST
ROMULO FAJARDO JR. COLORIST
CLAYTON COWLES LETTERER
NO! YOU DON'T GET TO TALK ABOUT MOM!
NOW I'M NOT ASKING ANYMORE, I'M *TELLING* YOU.
I WANT THAT MECH!
ROBSON ROCHA, DANIEL HENRIQUES & MARCELO MAIOLO COVER ARTISTS TYLER KIRKHAM VARIANT COVER ARTIS
ANDREA SHEA EDITOR ALEX R CARR GROUP EDITO

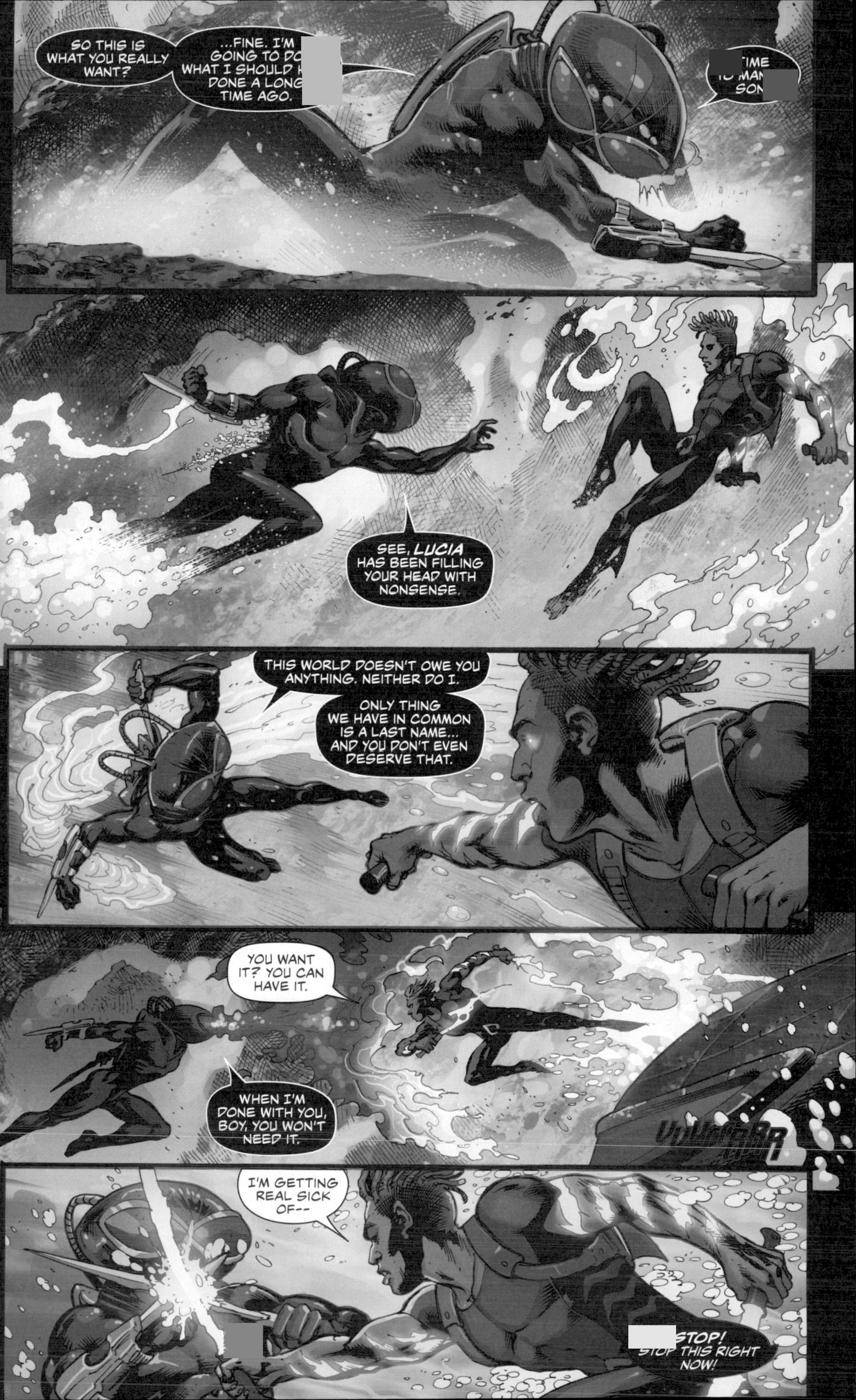
SO THIS IS WHAT YOU REALLY WANT?
...FINE. I'M GOING TO DO[redacted] WHAT I SHOULD H[redacted] DONE A LONG[redacted] TIME AGO.
[redacted]TIME [redacted]MAN[redacted] SON[redacted]
SEE, LUCIA HAS BEEN FILLING YOUR HEAD WITH NONSENSE.
THIS WORLD DOESN'T OWE YOU ANYTHING. NEITHER DO I.
ONLY THING WE HAVE IN COMMON IS A LAST NAME... AND YOU DON'T EVEN DESERVE THAT.
YOU WANT IT? YOU CAN HAVE IT.
WHEN I'M DONE WITH YOU, BOY, YOU WON'T NEED IT.
I'M GETTING REAL SICK OF--
[redacted]STOP! STOP THIS RIGHT NOW!

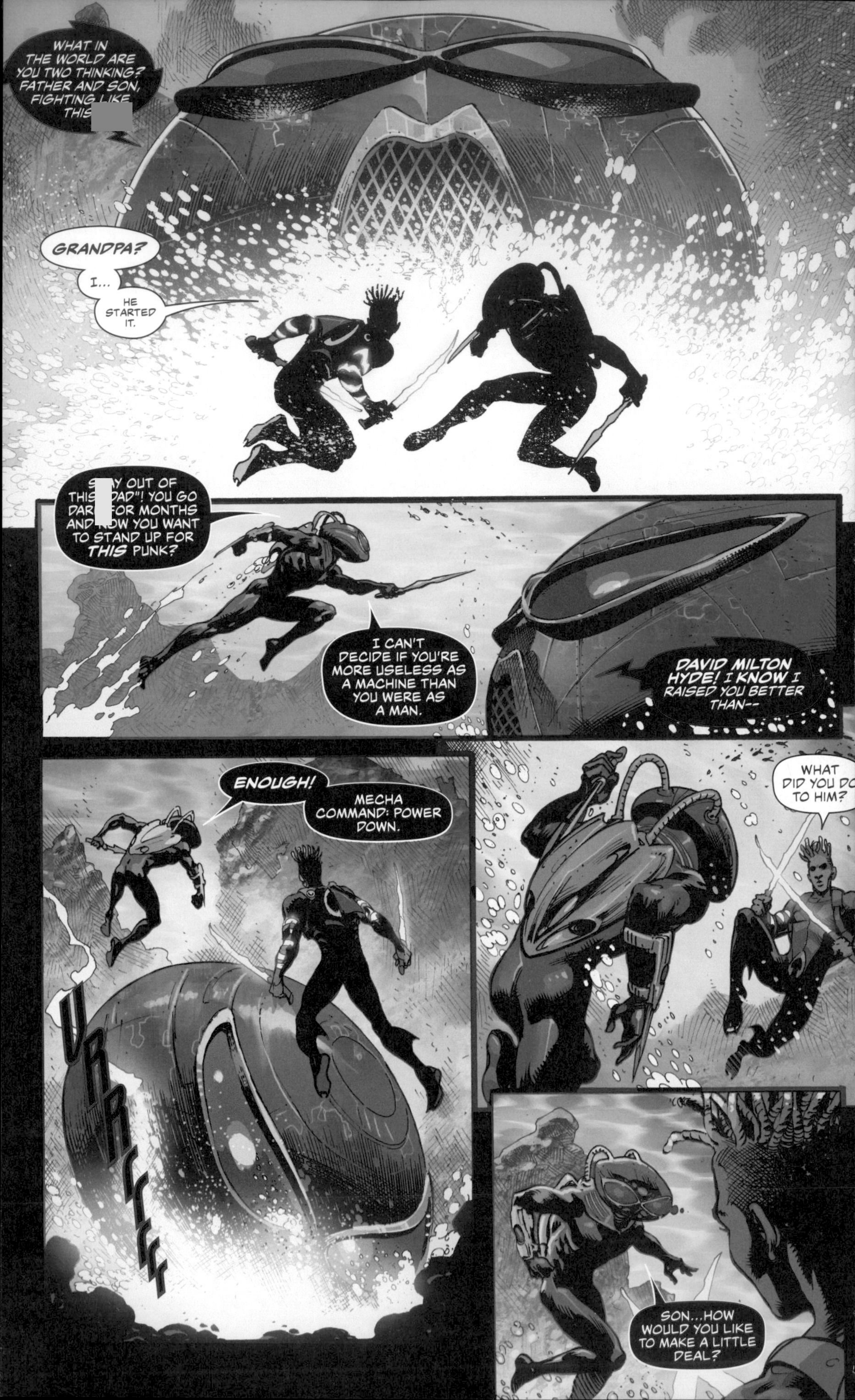
WHAT IN THE WORLD ARE YOU TWO THINKING? FATHER AND SON, FIGHTING LIKE THIS[redacted]
GRANDPA?
I...
HE STARTED IT.
S[redacted]AY OUT OF THIS[redacted]DAD"! YOU GO DAR[redacted]FOR MONTHS AND[redacted]OW YOU WANT TO STAND UP FOR THIS PUNK?
I CAN'T DECIDE IF YOU'RE MORE USELESS AS A MACHINE THAN YOU WERE AS A MAN.
DAVID MILTON HYDE! I KNOW I RAISED YOU BETTER THAN--
ENOUGH!
MECHA COMMAND: POWER DOWN.
URRRCCCCC
WHAT DID YOU DO TO HIM?
SON...HOW WOULD YOU LIKE TO MAKE A LITTLE DEAL?

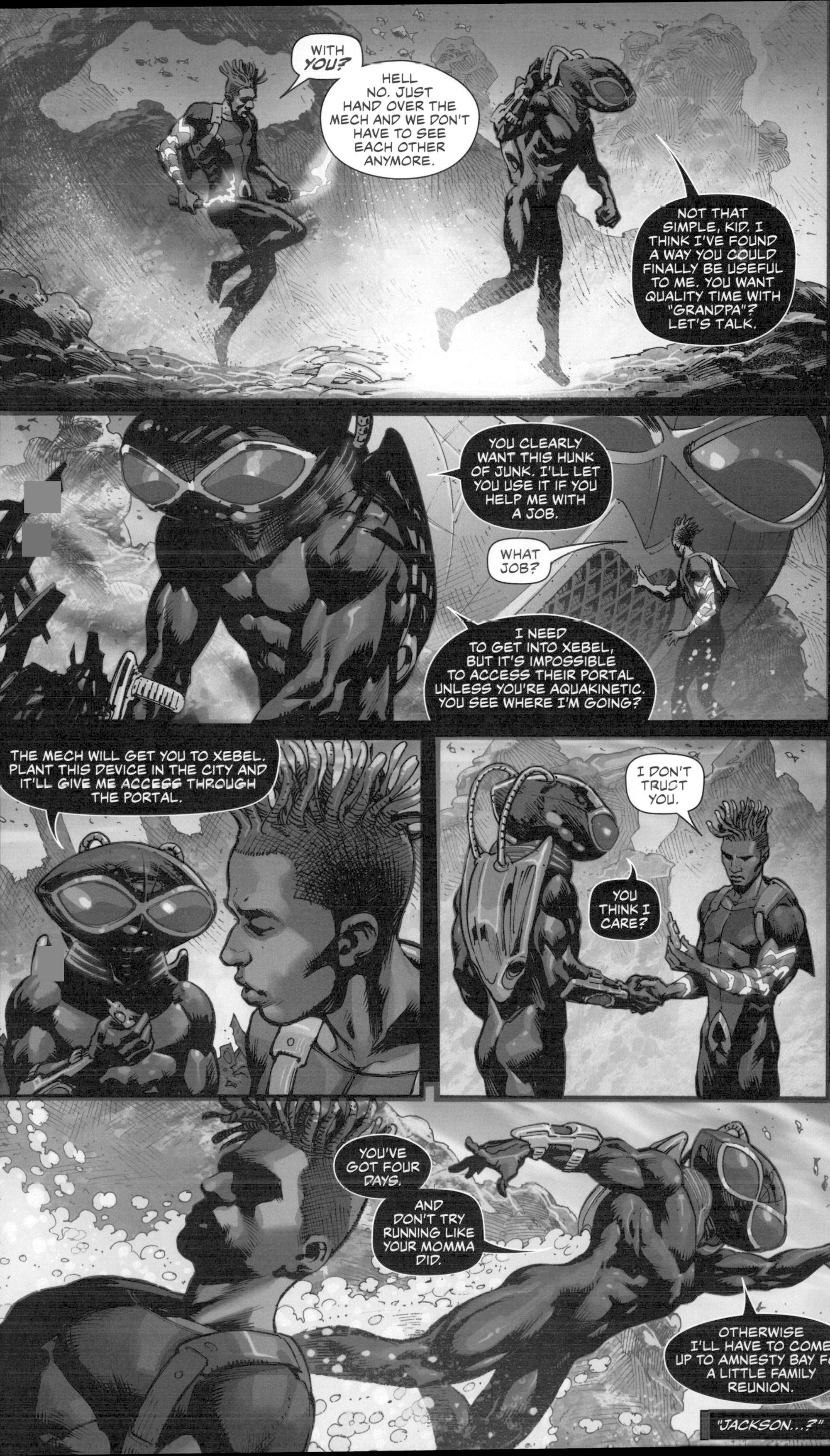
WITH YOU?
HELL NO. JUST HAND OVER THE MECH AND WE DON'T HAVE TO SEE EACH OTHER ANYMORE.
NOT THAT SIMPLE, KID. I THINK I'VE FOUND A WAY YOU COULD FINALLY BE USEFUL TO ME. YOU WANT QUALITY TIME WITH "GRANDPA"? LET'S TALK.
YOU CLEARLY WANT THIS HUNK OF JUNK. I'LL LET YOU USE IT IF YOU HELP ME WITH A JOB.
WHAT JOB?
I NEED TO GET INTO XEBEL, BUT IT'S IMPOSSIBLE TO ACCESS THEIR PORTAL UNLESS YOU'RE AQUAKINETIC. YOU SEE WHERE I'M GOING?
THE MECH WILL GET YOU TO XEBEL. PLANT THIS DEVICE IN THE CITY AND IT'LL GIVE ME ACCESS THROUGH THE PORTAL.
I DON'T TRUST YOU.
YOU THINK I CARE?
YOU'VE GOT FOUR DAYS.
AND DON'T TRY RUNNING LIKE YOUR MOMMA DID.
OTHERWISE I'LL HAVE TO COME UP TO AMNESTY BAY FOR A LITTLE FAMILY REUNION.
"JACKSON...?"

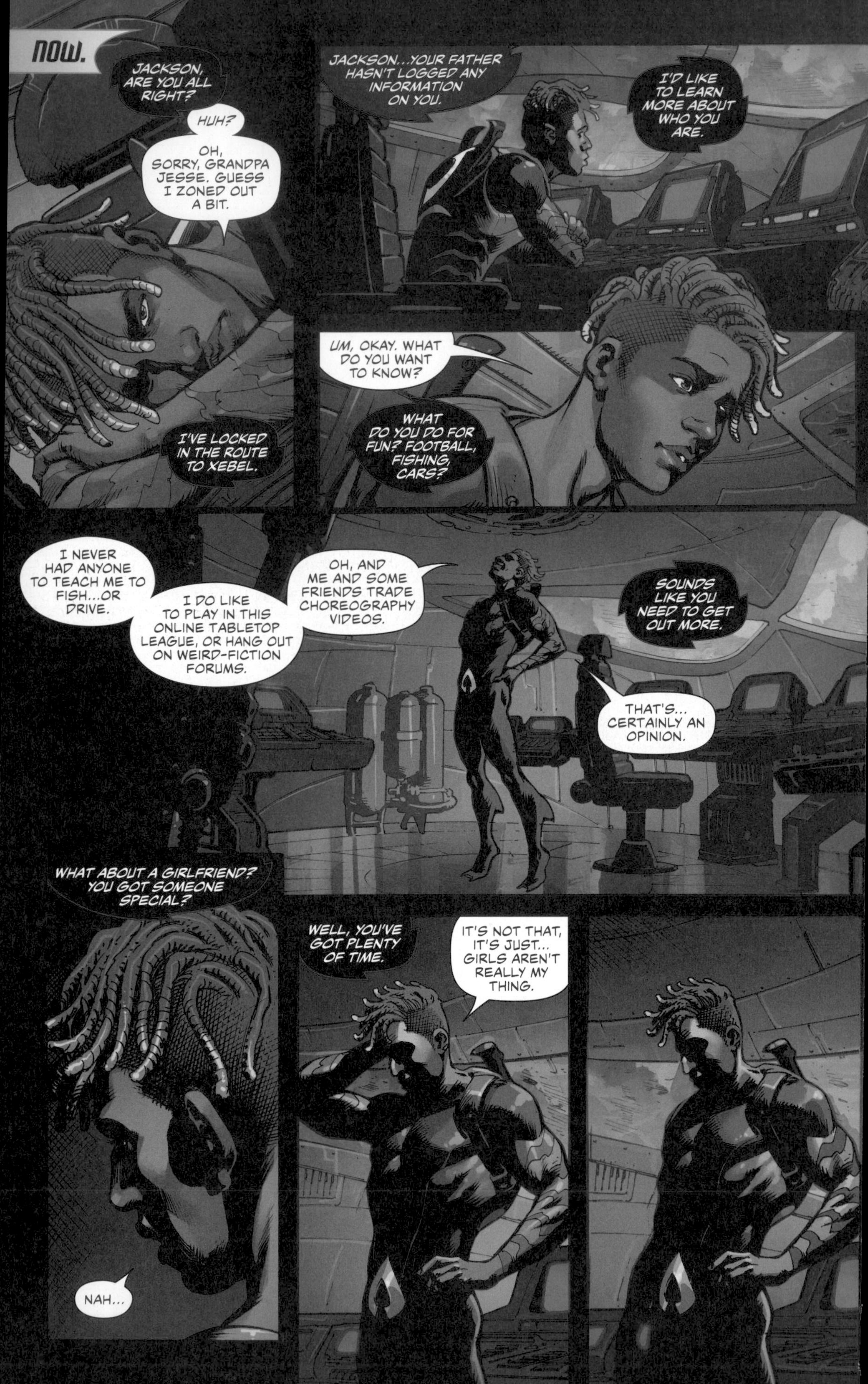
NOW.
JACKSON, ARE YOU ALL RIGHT?
HUH?
OH, SORRY, GRANDPA JESSE. GUESS I ZONED OUT A BIT.
JACKSON...YOUR FATHER HASN'T LOGGED ANY INFORMATION ON YOU.
I'D LIKE TO LEARN MORE ABOUT WHO YOU ARE.
I'VE LOCKED IN THE ROUTE TO XEBEL.
UM, OKAY. WHAT DO YOU WANT TO KNOW?
WHAT DO YOU DO FOR FUN? FOOTBALL, FISHING, CARS?
I NEVER HAD ANYONE TO TEACH ME TO FISH...OR DRIVE.
I DO LIKE TO PLAY IN THIS ONLINE TABLETOP LEAGUE, OR HANG OUT ON WEIRD-FICTION FORUMS.
OH, AND ME AND SOME FRIENDS TRADE CHOREOGRAPHY VIDEOS.
SOUNDS LIKE YOU NEED TO GET OUT MORE.
THAT'S... CERTAINLY AN OPINION.
WHAT ABOUT A GIRLFRIEND? YOU GOT SOMEONE SPECIAL?
NAH...
WELL, YOU'VE GOT PLENTY OF TIME.
IT'S NOT THAT, IT'S JUST... GIRLS AREN'T REALLY MY THING.

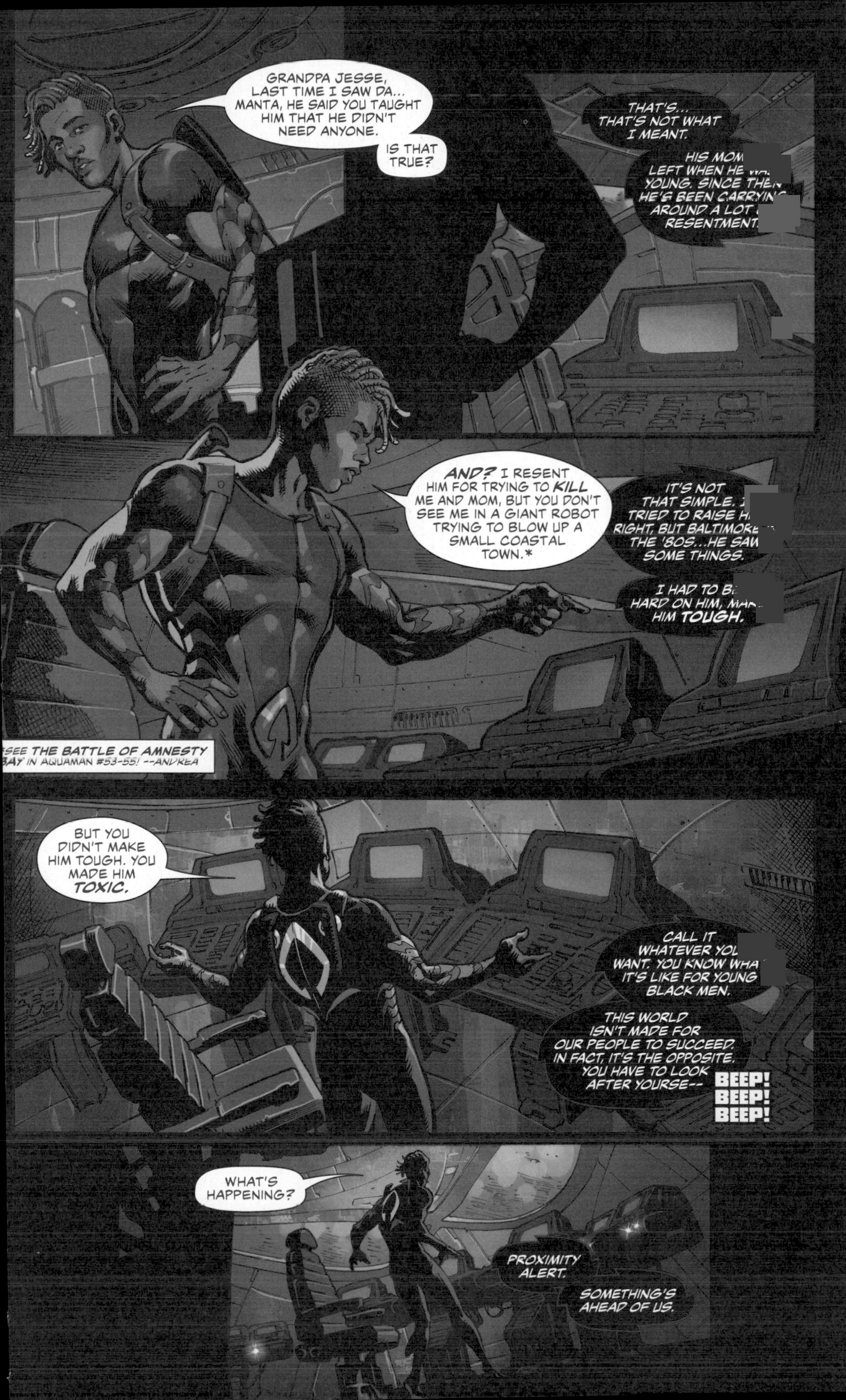
GRANDPA JESSE, LAST TIME I SAW DA... MANTA, HE SAID YOU TAUGHT HIM THAT HE DIDN'T NEED ANYONE.
IS THAT TRUE?
THAT'S... THAT'S NOT WHAT I MEANT.
HIS MOM [redacted] LEFT WHEN HE WA [redacted] YOUNG. SINCE THEN HE'S BEEN CARRYIN [redacted] AROUND A LOT [redacted] RESENTMENT [redacted]
AND? I RESENT HIM FOR TRYING TO KILL ME AND MOM, BUT YOU DON'T SEE ME IN A GIANT ROBOT TRYING TO BLOW UP A SMALL COASTAL TOWN.*
IT'S NOT THAT SIMPLE. I [redacted] TRIED TO RAISE H [redacted] RIGHT, BUT BALTIMORE [redacted] THE '80S...HE SAW [redacted] SOME THINGS.
I HAD TO BE [redacted] HARD ON HIM, MAK [redacted] HIM TOUGH.
*SEE THE BATTLE OF AMNESTY BAY IN AQUAMAN #53-55! --ANDREA
BUT YOU DIDN'T MAKE HIM TOUGH. YOU MADE HIM TOXIC.
CALL IT WHATEVER YOU [redacted] WANT. YOU KNOW WHAT [redacted] IT'S LIKE FOR YOUNG [redacted] BLACK MEN.
THIS WORLD ISN'T MADE FOR OUR PEOPLE TO SUCCEED. IN FACT, IT'S THE OPPOSITE. YOU HAVE TO LOOK AFTER YOURSE--
BEEP! BEEP! BEEP!
WHAT'S HAPPENING?
PROXIMITY ALERT.
SOMETHING'S AHEAD OF US.

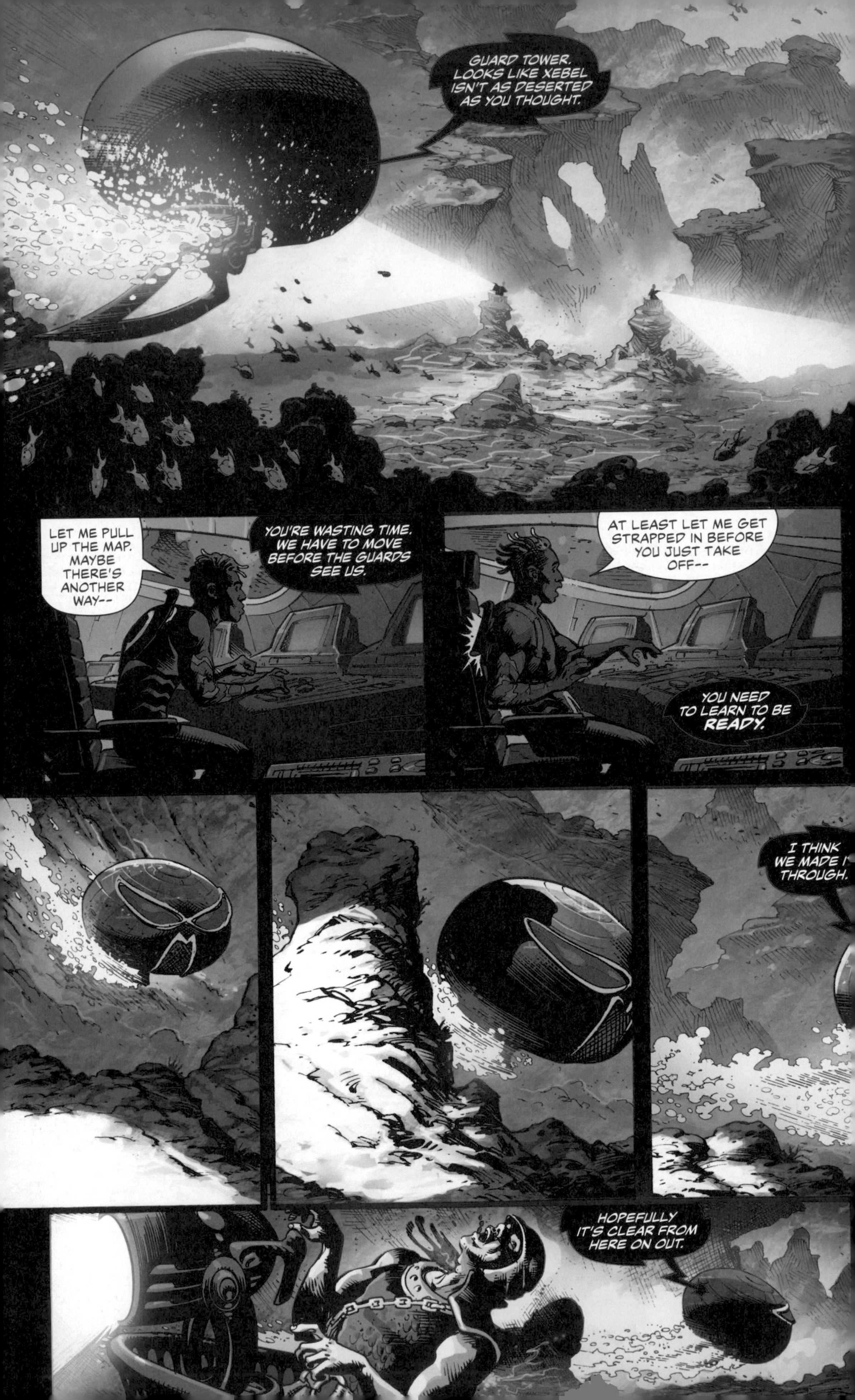
GUARD TOWER. LOOKS LIKE XEBEL ISN'T AS DESERTED AS YOU THOUGHT.
LET ME PULL UP THE MAP. MAYBE THERE'S ANOTHER WAY--
YOU'RE WASTING TIME. WE HAVE TO MOVE BEFORE THE GUARDS SEE US.
AT LEAST LET ME GET STRAPPED IN BEFORE YOU JUST TAKE OFF--
YOU NEED TO LEARN TO BE **READY.**
I THINK WE MADE I THROUGH.
HOPEFULLY IT'S CLEAR FROM HERE ON OUT.

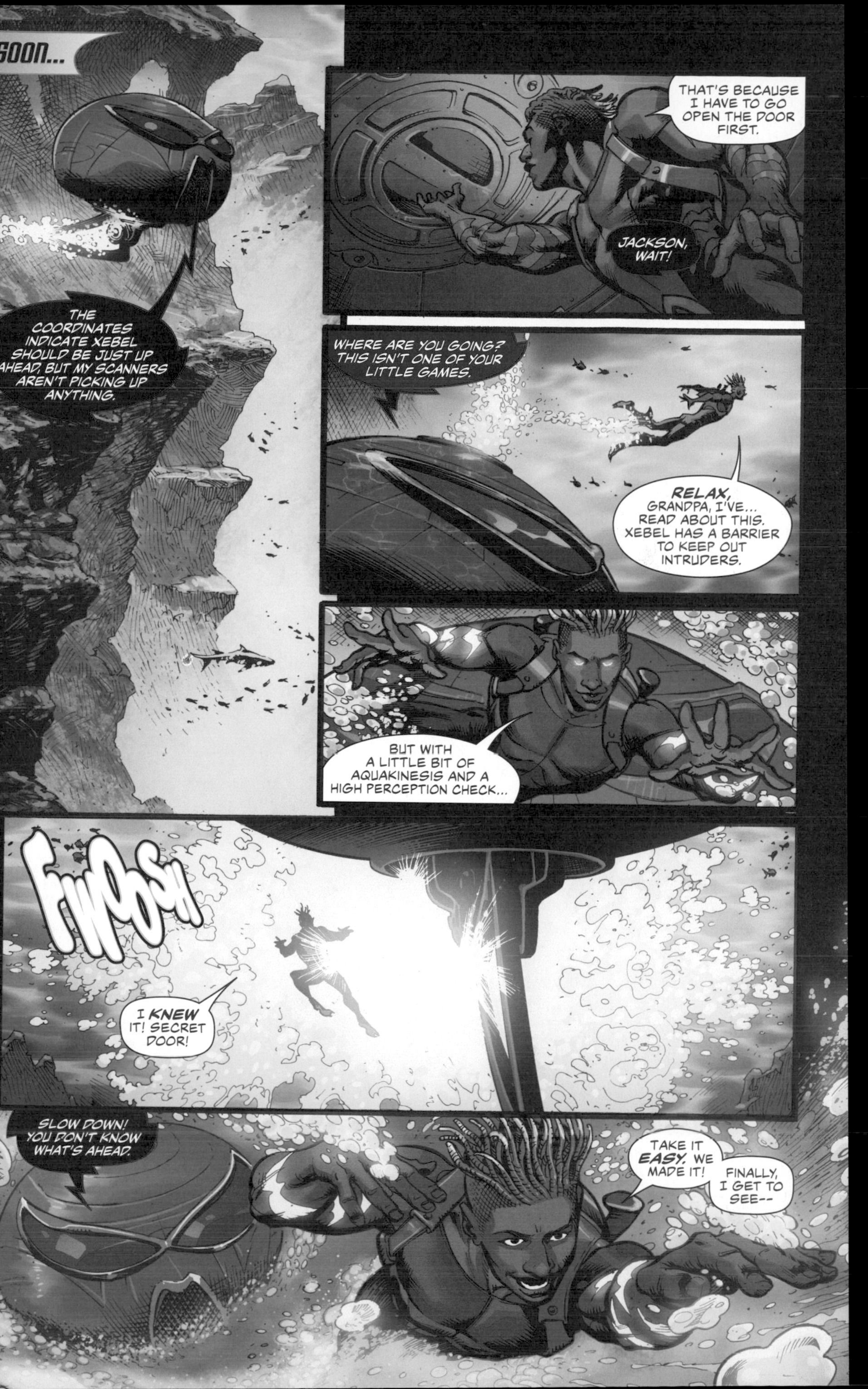
SOON...
THE COORDINATES INDICATE XEBEL SHOULD BE JUST UP AHEAD, BUT MY SCANNERS AREN'T PICKING UP ANYTHING.
THAT'S BECAUSE I HAVE TO GO OPEN THE DOOR FIRST.
JACKSON, WAIT!
WHERE ARE YOU GOING? THIS ISN'T ONE OF YOUR LITTLE GAMES.
RELAX, GRANDPA, I'VE... READ ABOUT THIS. XEBEL HAS A BARRIER TO KEEP OUT INTRUDERS.
BUT WITH A LITTLE BIT OF AQUAKINESIS AND A HIGH PERCEPTION CHECK...
FWOOSH
I KNEW IT! SECRET DOOR!
SLOW DOWN! YOU DON'T KNOW WHAT'S AHEAD.
TAKE IT EASY. WE MADE IT!
FINALLY, I GET TO SEE--

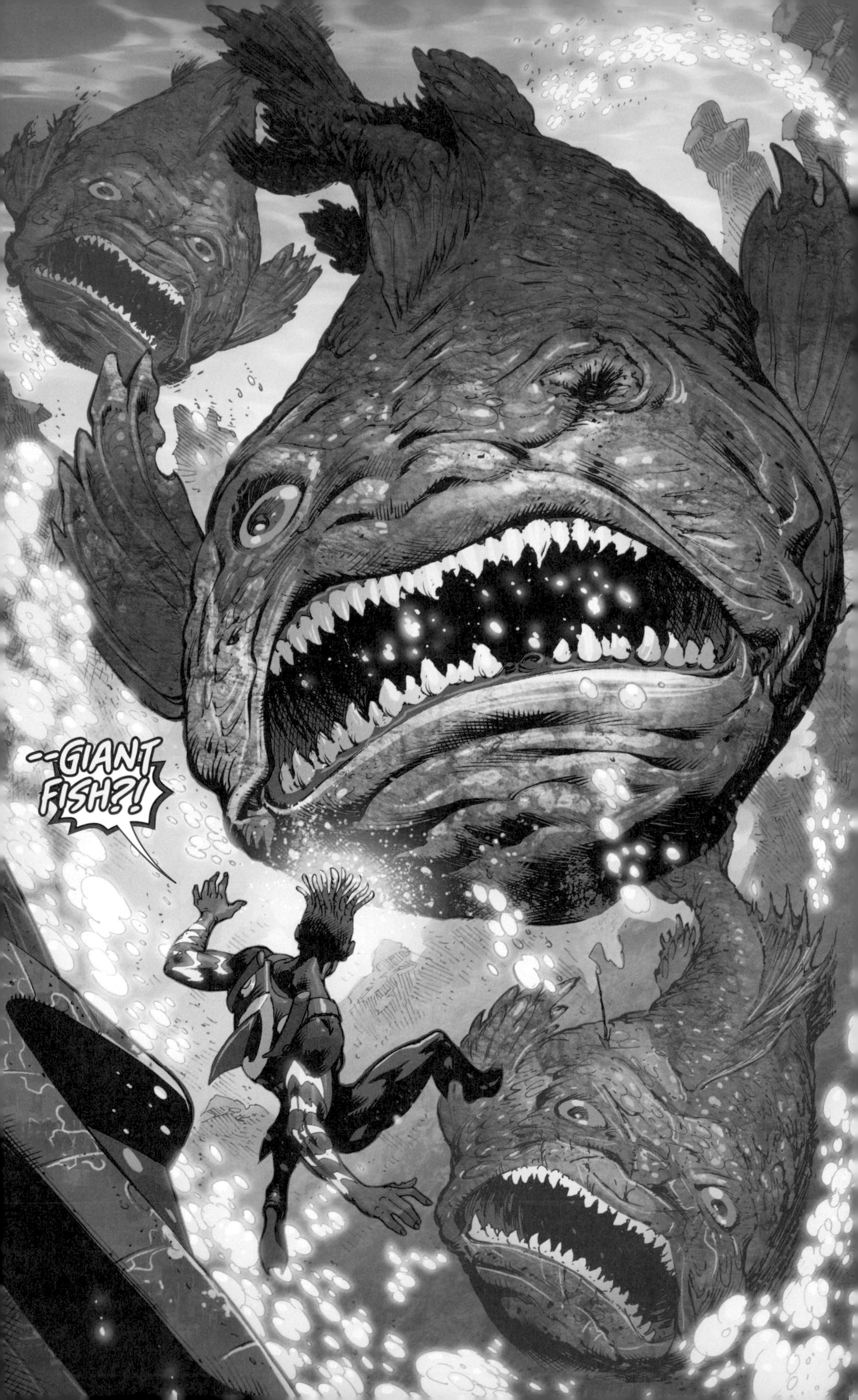
--GIANT FISH?!

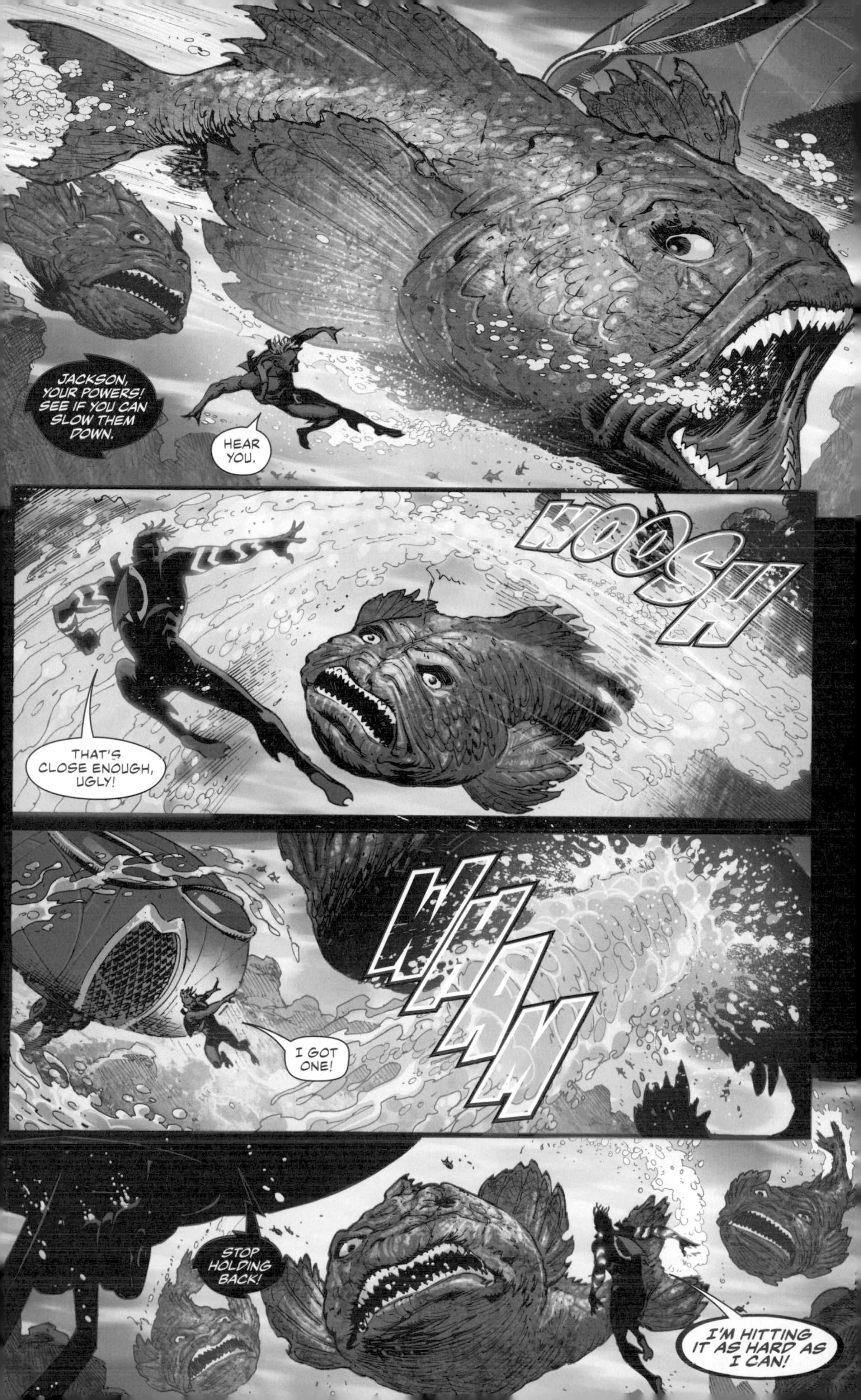
JACKSON, YOUR POWERS! SEE IF YOU CAN SLOW THEM DOWN.
HEAR YOU.
WOOSH
THAT'S CLOSE ENOUGH, UGLY!
I GOT ONE!
STOP HOLDING BACK!
I'M HITTING IT AS HARD AS I CAN!

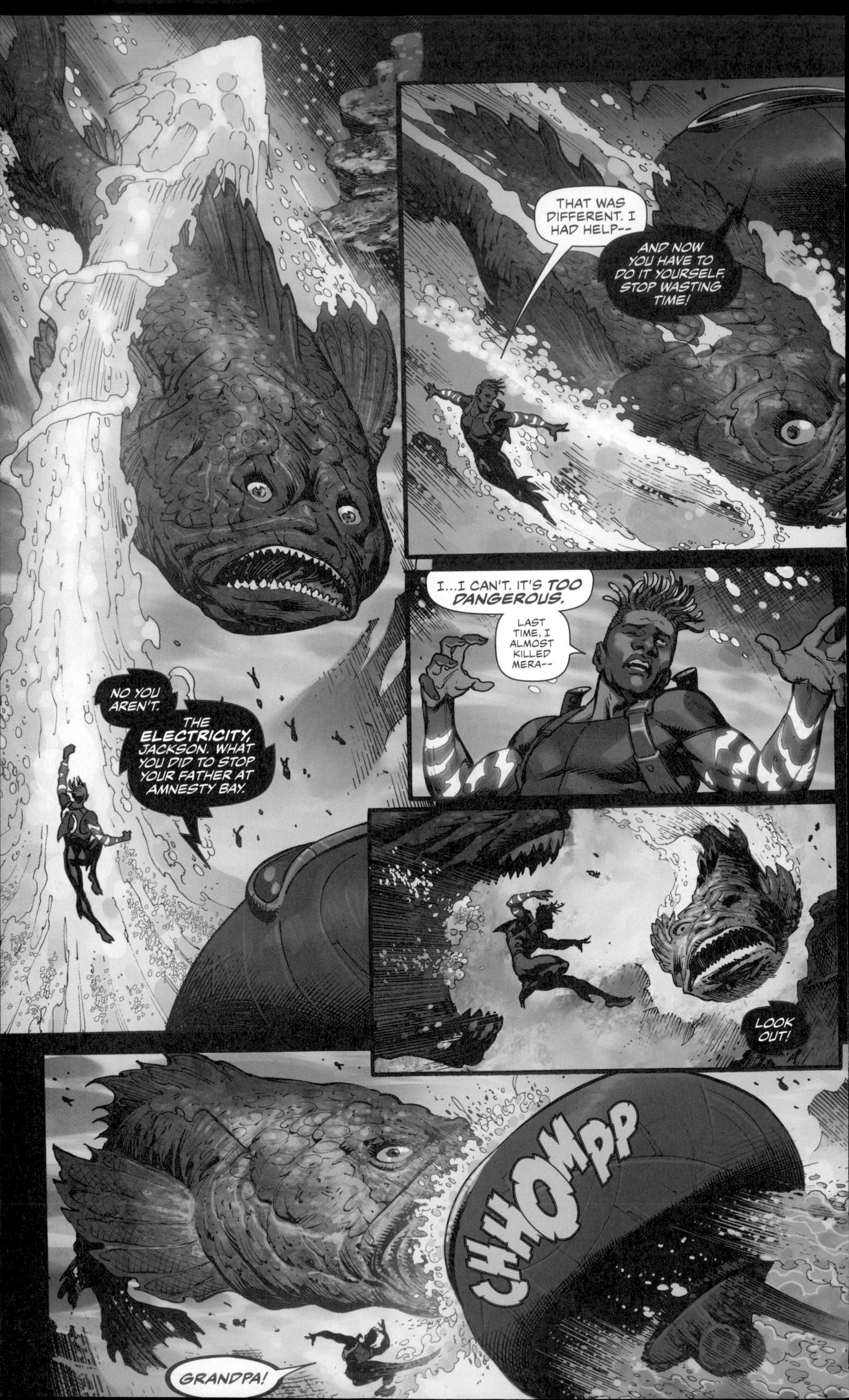
THAT WAS DIFFERENT. I HAD HELP--
AND NOW YOU HAVE TO DO IT YOURSELF. STOP WASTING TIME!
I...I CAN'T. IT'S TOO DANGEROUS.
LAST TIME, I ALMOST KILLED MERA--
NO YOU AREN'T.
THE ELECTRICITY, JACKSON. WHAT YOU DID TO STOP YOUR FATHER AT AMNESTY BAY.
LOOK OUT!
CHHOMPP
GRANDPA!

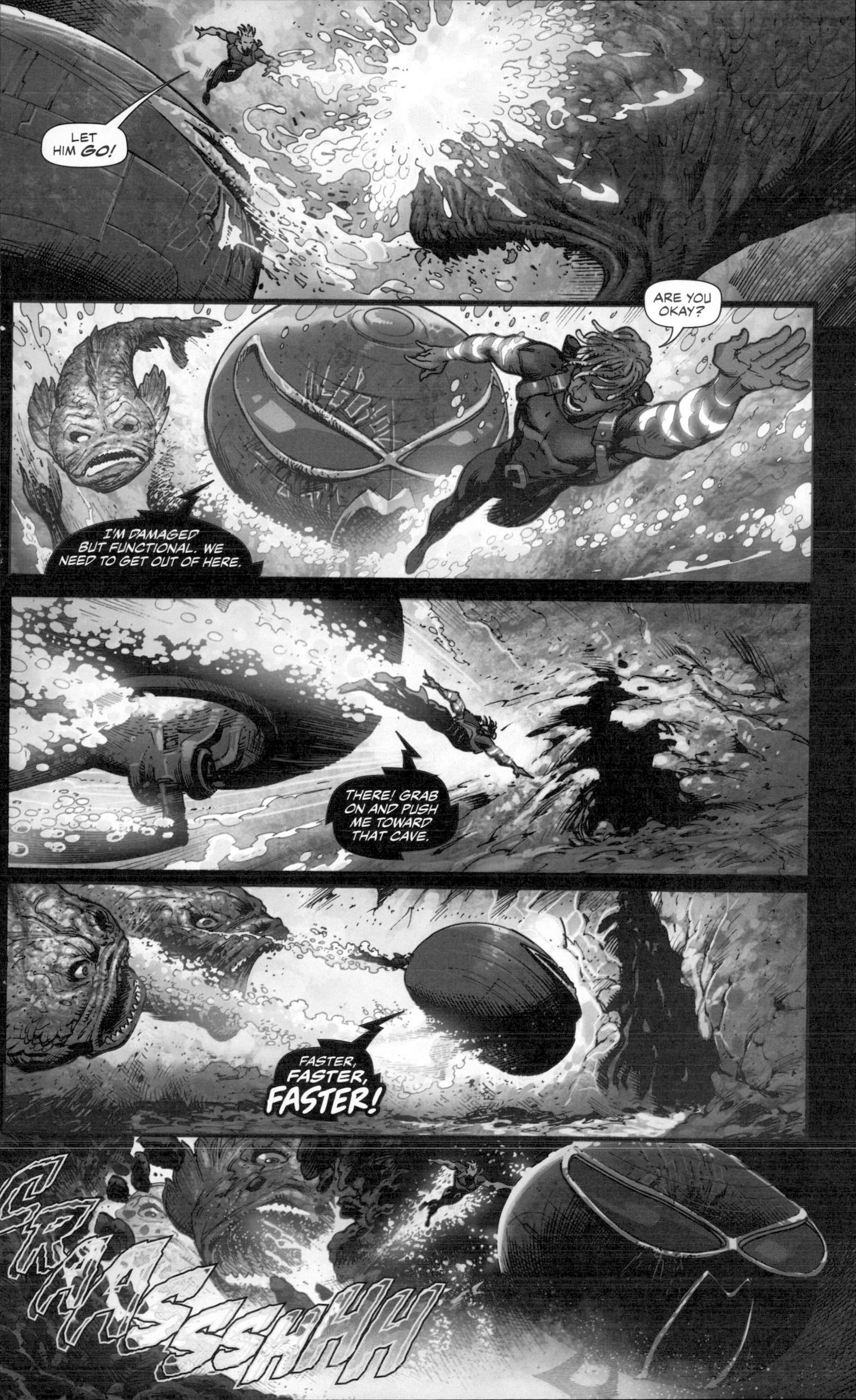
LET HIM GO!
ARE YOU OKAY?
I'M DAMAGED BUT FUNCTIONAL. WE NEED TO GET OUT OF HERE.
THERE! GRAB ON AND PUSH ME TOWARD THAT CAVE.
FASTER, FASTER, FASTER!
SKRAASSHHH

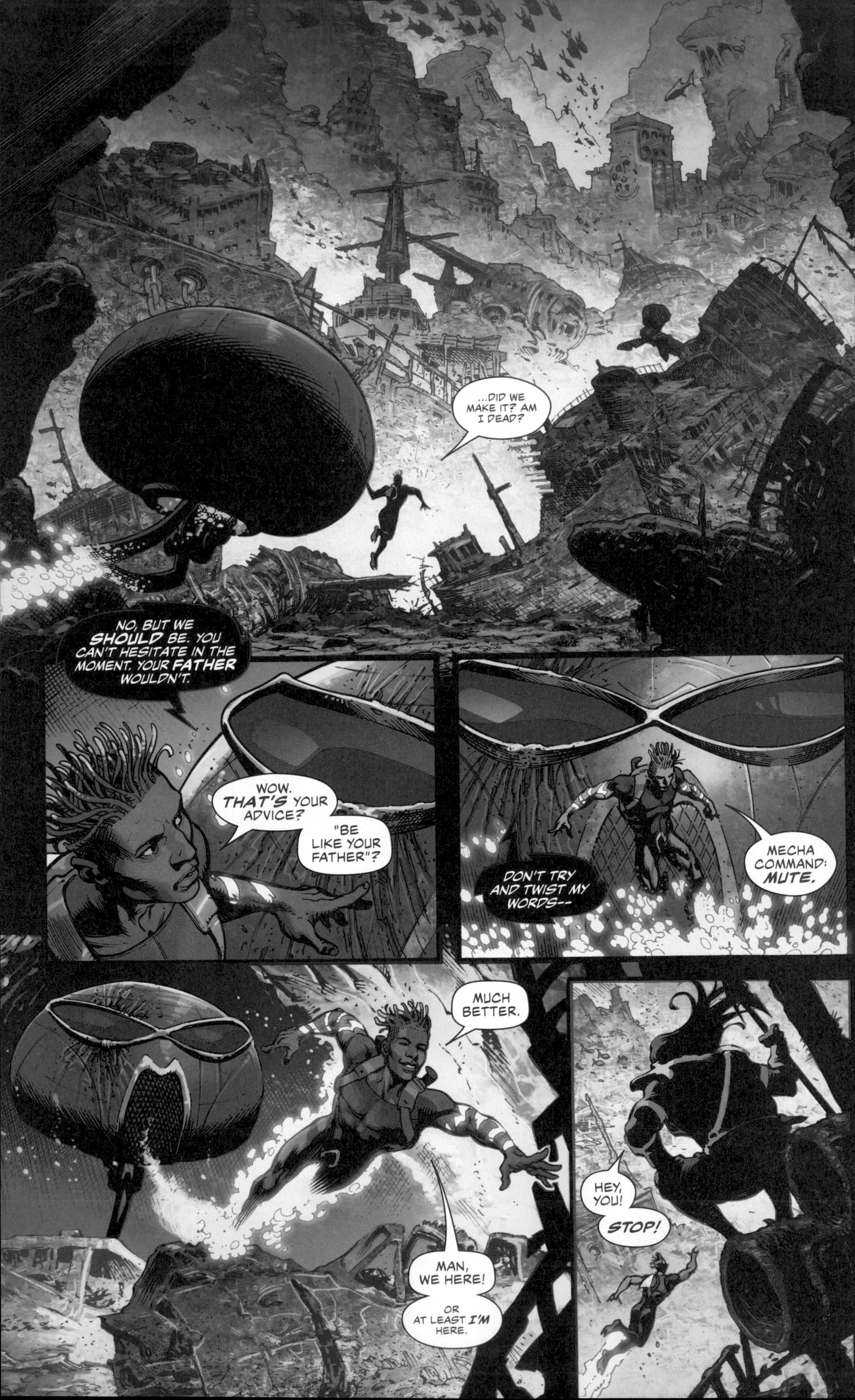
...DID WE MAKE IT? AM I DEAD?
NO, BUT WE SHOULD BE. YOU CAN'T HESITATE IN THE MOMENT. YOUR FATHER WOULDN'T.
WOW. THAT'S YOUR ADVICE?
"BE LIKE YOUR FATHER"?
DON'T TRY AND TWIST MY WORDS--
MECHA COMMAND: MUTE.
MUCH BETTER.
MAN, WE HERE!
OR AT LEAST I'M HERE.
HEY, YOU!
STOP!

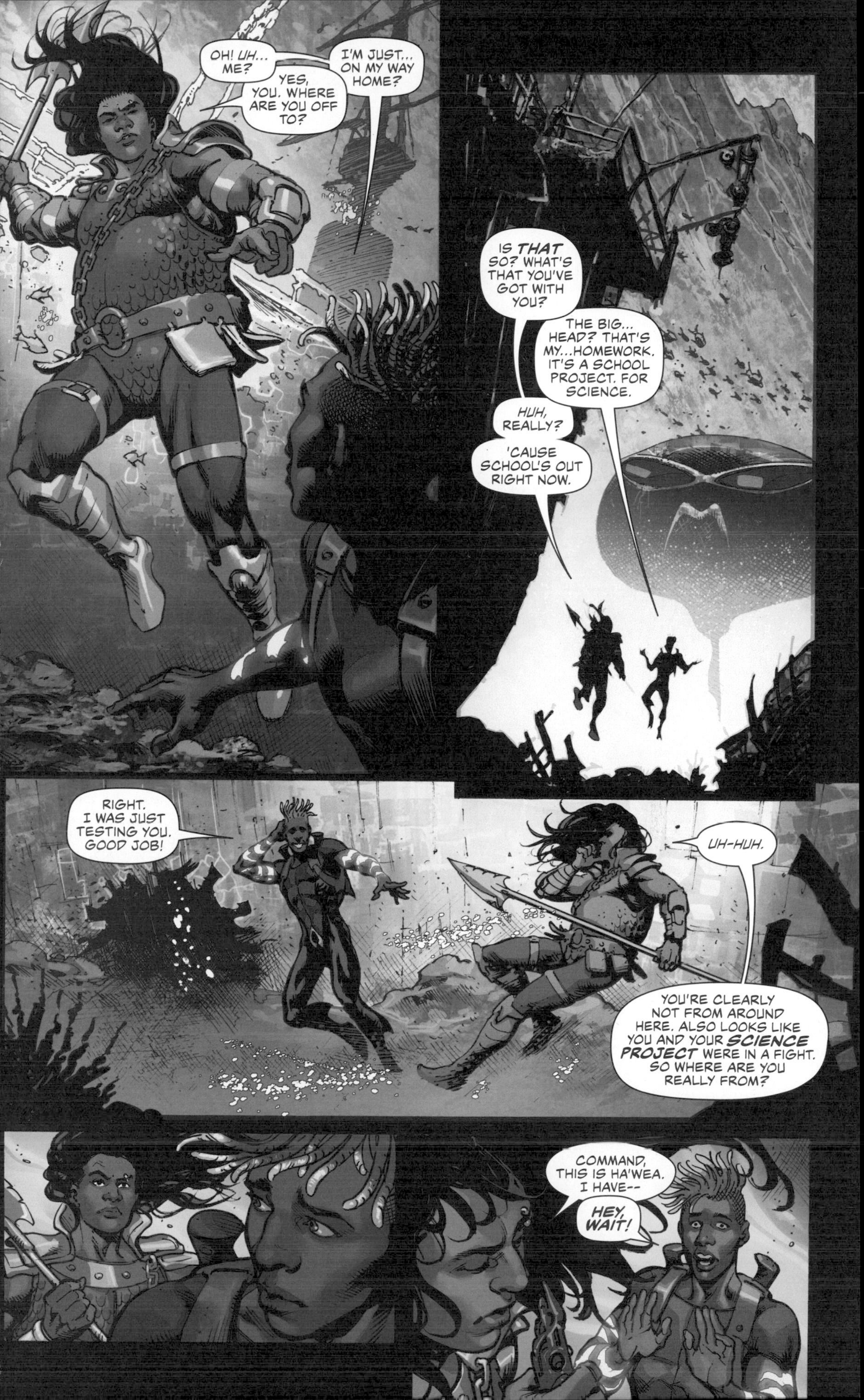
OH! UH... ME?
YES, YOU. WHERE ARE YOU OFF TO?
I'M JUST... ON MY WAY HOME?
IS THAT SO? WHAT'S THAT YOU'VE GOT WITH YOU?
THE BIG... HEAD? THAT'S MY...HOMEWORK. IT'S A SCHOOL PROJECT. FOR SCIENCE.
HUH, REALLY?
'CAUSE SCHOOL'S OUT RIGHT NOW.
RIGHT. I WAS JUST TESTING YOU. GOOD JOB!
UH-HUH.
YOU'RE CLEARLY NOT FROM AROUND HERE. ALSO LOOKS LIKE YOU AND YOUR SCIENCE PROJECT WERE IN A FIGHT. SO WHERE ARE YOU REALLY FROM?
COMMAND, THIS IS HA'WEA. I HAVE--
HEY, WAIT!

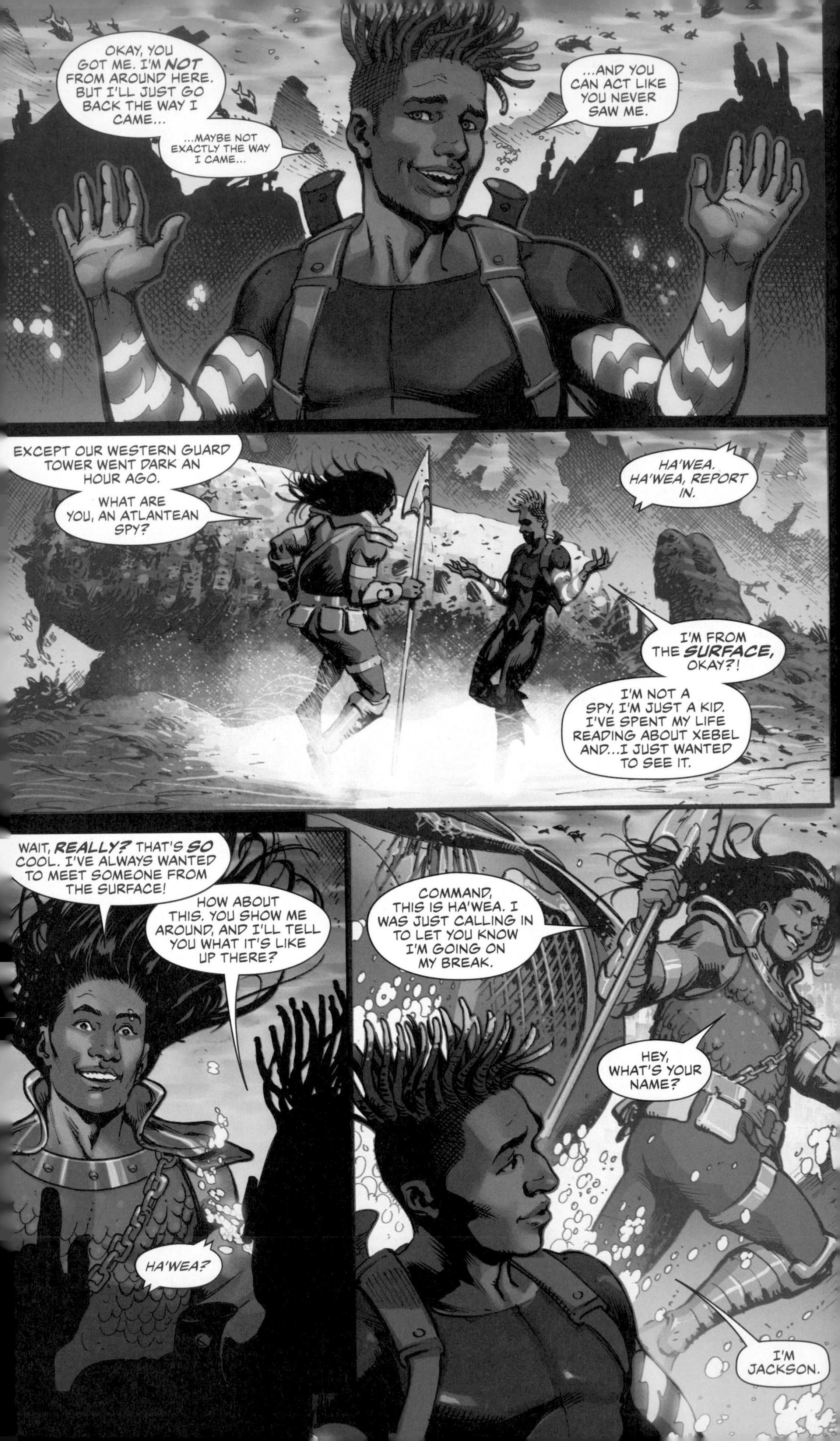
OKAY, YOU GOT ME. I'M ***NOT*** FROM AROUND HERE. BUT I'LL JUST GO BACK THE WAY I CAME...
...MAYBE NOT EXACTLY THE WAY I CAME...
...AND YOU CAN ACT LIKE YOU NEVER SAW ME.
EXCEPT OUR WESTERN GUARD TOWER WENT DARK AN HOUR AGO.
WHAT ARE YOU, AN ATLANTEAN SPY?
HA'WEA. HA'WEA, REPORT IN.
I'M FROM THE ***SURFACE,*** OKAY?!
I'M NOT A SPY, I'M JUST A KID. I'VE SPENT MY LIFE READING ABOUT XEBEL AND...I JUST WANTED TO SEE IT.
WAIT, ***REALLY?*** THAT'S ***SO*** COOL. I'VE ALWAYS WANTED TO MEET SOMEONE FROM THE SURFACE!
HOW ABOUT THIS. YOU SHOW ME AROUND, AND I'LL TELL YOU WHAT IT'S LIKE UP THERE?
HA'WEA?
COMMAND, THIS IS HA'WEA. I WAS JUST CALLING IN TO LET YOU KNOW I'M GOING ON MY BREAK.
HEY, WHAT'S YOUR NAME?
I'M JACKSON.

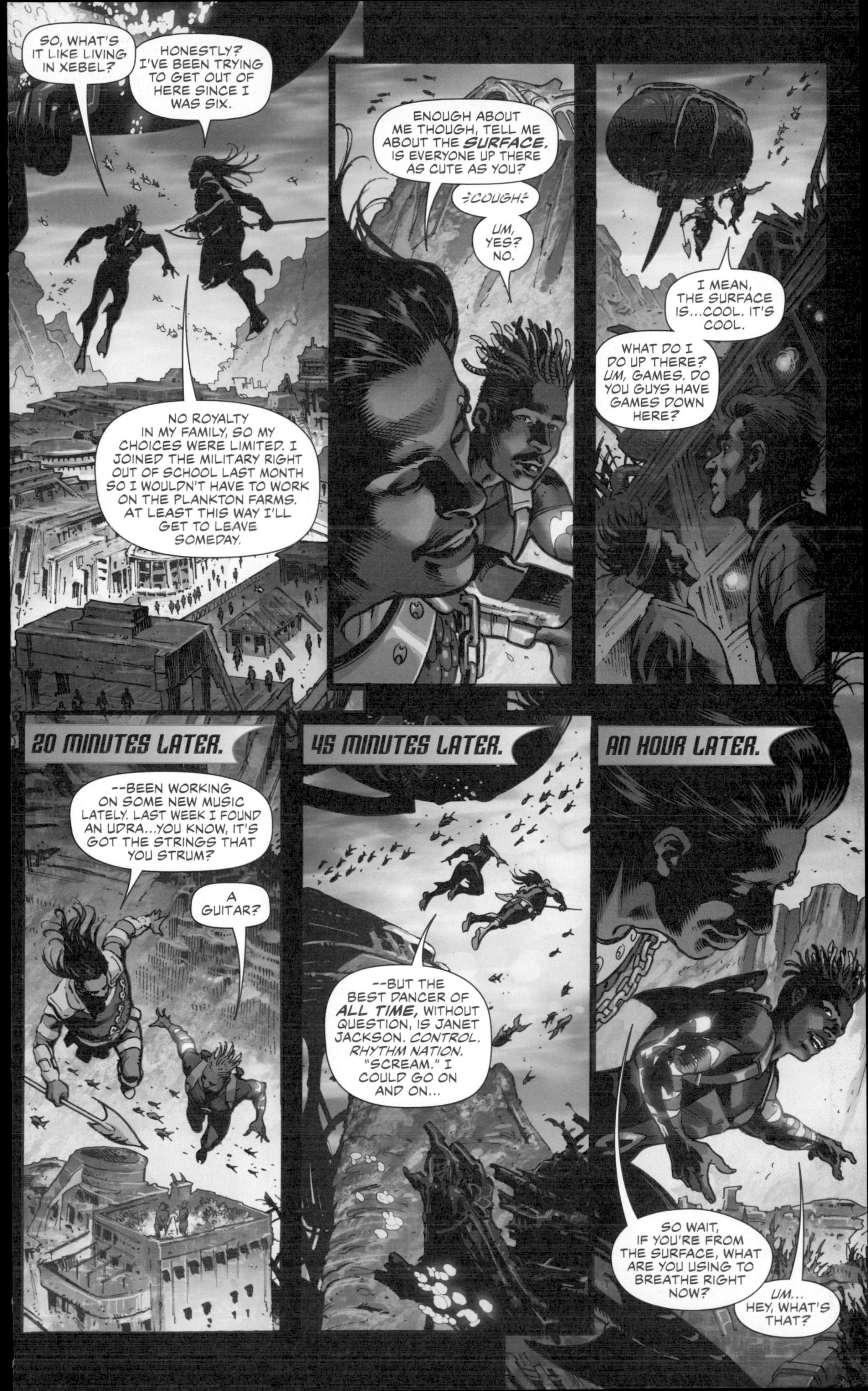
SO, WHAT'S IT LIKE LIVING IN XEBEL?
HONESTLY? I'VE BEEN TRYING TO GET OUT OF HERE SINCE I WAS SIX.
NO ROYALTY IN MY FAMILY, SO MY CHOICES WERE LIMITED. I JOINED THE MILITARY RIGHT OUT OF SCHOOL LAST MONTH SO I WOULDN'T HAVE TO WORK ON THE PLANKTON FARMS. AT LEAST THIS WAY I'LL GET TO LEAVE SOMEDAY.
ENOUGH ABOUT ME THOUGH, TELL ME ABOUT THE SURFACE. IS EVERYONE UP THERE AS CUTE AS YOU?
COUGH
UM, YES? NO.
I MEAN, THE SURFACE IS...COOL. IT'S COOL.
WHAT DO I DO UP THERE? UM, GAMES. DO YOU GUYS HAVE GAMES DOWN HERE?
20 MINUTES LATER.
--BEEN WORKING ON SOME NEW MUSIC LATELY. LAST WEEK I FOUND AN UDRA...YOU KNOW, IT'S GOT THE STRINGS THAT YOU STRUM?
A GUITAR?
45 MINUTES LATER.
--BUT THE BEST DANCER OF ALL TIME, WITHOUT QUESTION, IS JANET JACKSON. CONTROL. RHYTHM NATION. "SCREAM." I COULD GO ON AND ON...
AN HOUR LATER.
SO WAIT, IF YOU'RE FROM THE SURFACE, WHAT ARE YOU USING TO BREATHE RIGHT NOW?
UM... HEY, WHAT'S THAT?

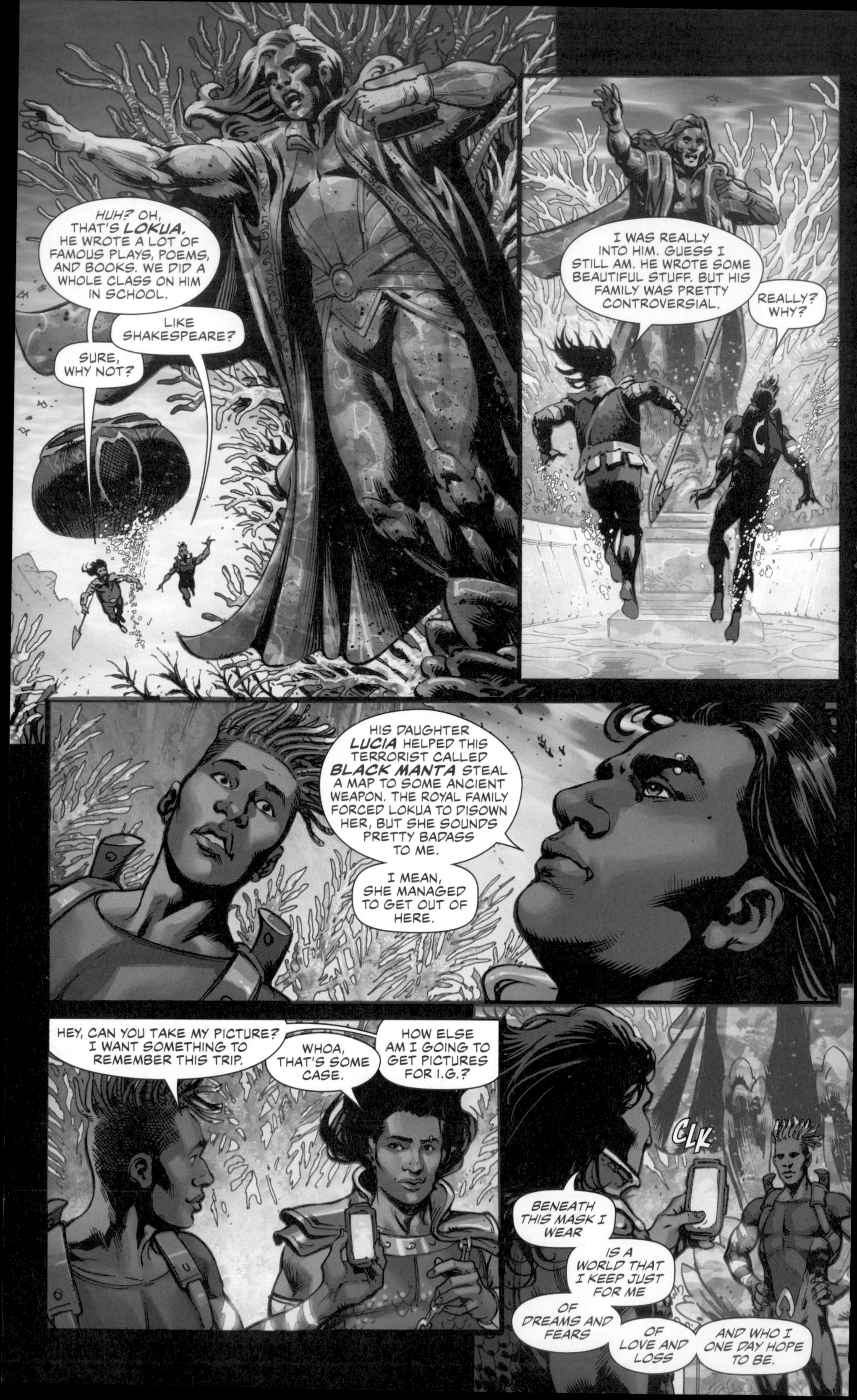
HUH? OH, THAT'S LOKUA. HE WROTE A LOT OF FAMOUS PLAYS, POEMS, AND BOOKS. WE DID A WHOLE CLASS ON HIM IN SCHOOL.
LIKE SHAKESPEARE?
SURE, WHY NOT?
I WAS REALLY INTO HIM. GUESS I STILL AM. HE WROTE SOME BEAUTIFUL STUFF. BUT HIS FAMILY WAS PRETTY CONTROVERSIAL.
REALLY? WHY?
HIS DAUGHTER LUCIA HELPED THIS TERRORIST CALLED BLACK MANTA STEAL A MAP TO SOME ANCIENT WEAPON. THE ROYAL FAMILY FORCED LOKUA TO DISOWN HER, BUT SHE SOUNDS PRETTY BADASS TO ME.
I MEAN, SHE MANAGED TO GET OUT OF HERE.
HEY, CAN YOU TAKE MY PICTURE? I WANT SOMETHING TO REMEMBER THIS TRIP.
WHOA, THAT'S SOME CASE.
HOW ELSE AM I GOING TO GET PICTURES FOR I.G.?
CLK
BENEATH THIS MASK I WEAR
IS A WORLD THAT I KEEP JUST FOR ME
OF DREAMS AND FEARS
OF LOVE AND LOSS
AND WHO I ONE DAY HOPE TO BE.

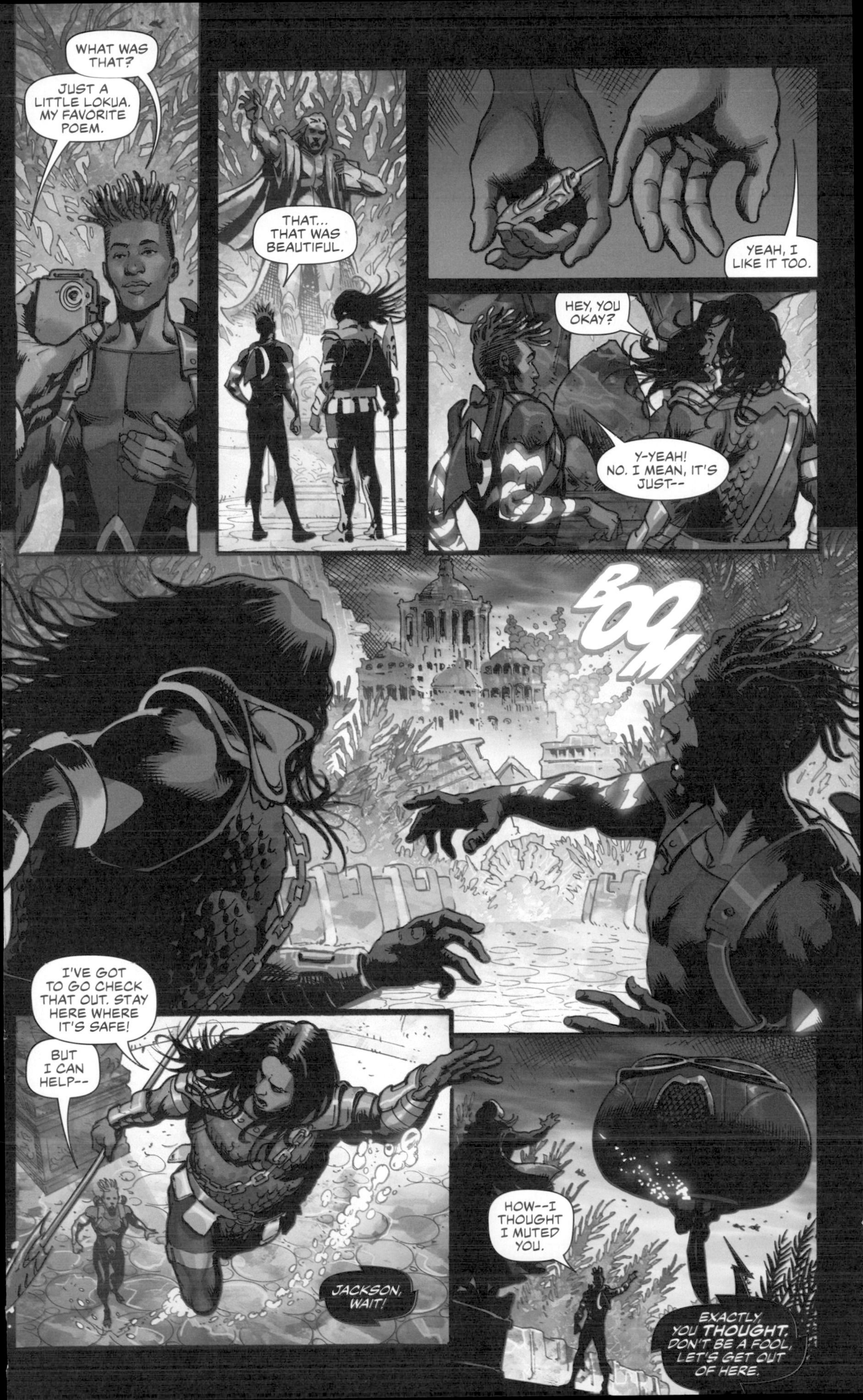
WHAT WAS THAT?
JUST A LITTLE LOKUA. MY FAVORITE POEM.
THAT... THAT WAS BEAUTIFUL.
YEAH, I LIKE IT TOO.
HEY, YOU OKAY?
Y-YEAH! NO. I MEAN, IT'S JUST--
BOOM
I'VE GOT TO GO CHECK THAT OUT. STAY HERE WHERE IT'S SAFE!
BUT I CAN HELP--
JACKSON, WAIT!
HOW--I THOUGHT I MUTED YOU.
EXACTLY. YOU THOUGHT. DON'T BE A FOOL. LET'S GET OUT OF HERE.

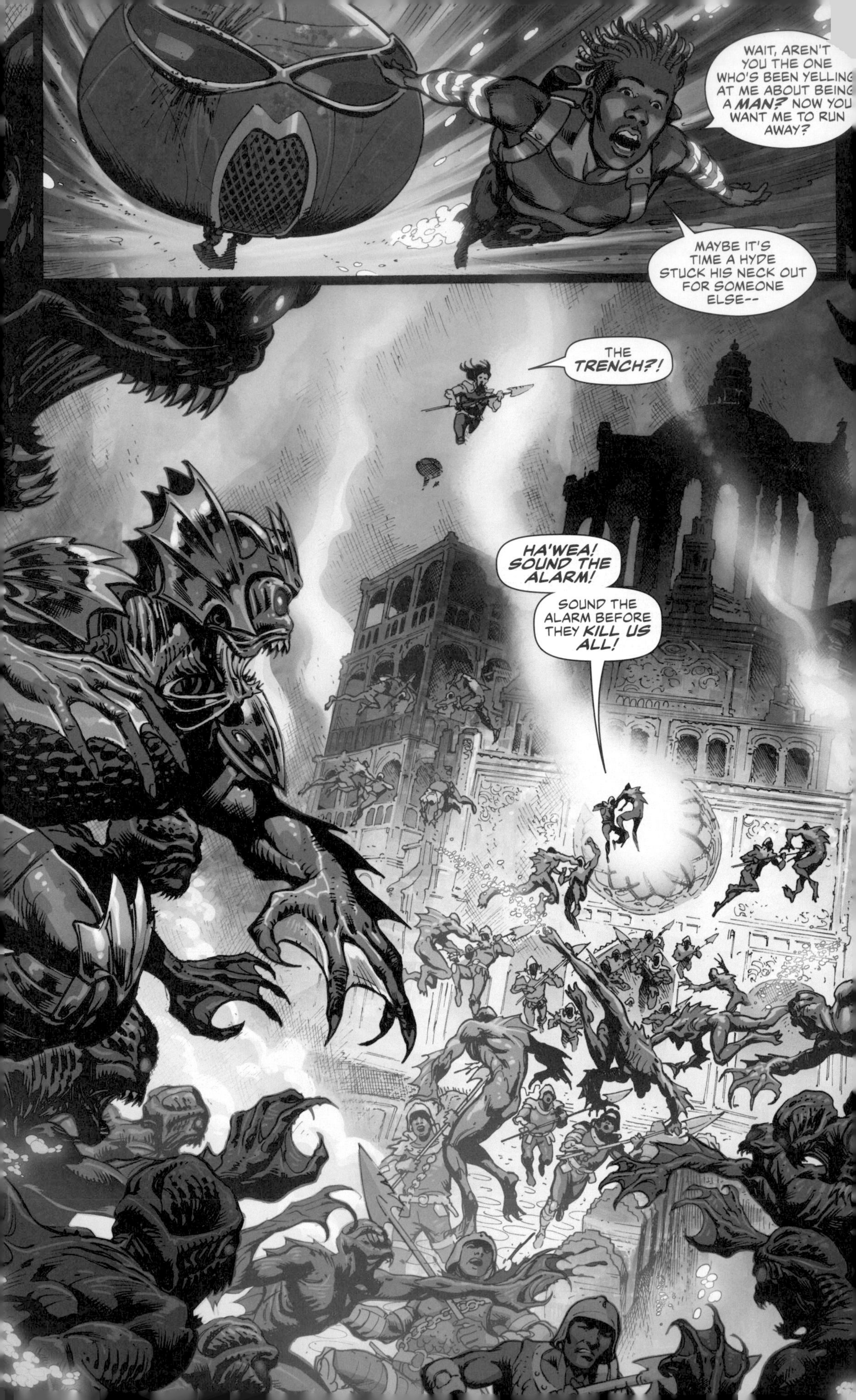
WAIT, AREN'T YOU THE ONE WHO'S BEEN YELLING AT ME ABOUT BEING A MAN? NOW YOU WANT ME TO RUN AWAY?
MAYBE IT'S TIME A HYDE STUCK HIS NECK OUT FOR SOMEONE ELSE--
THE TRENCH?!
HA'WEA! SOUND THE ALARM!
SOUND THE ALARM BEFORE THEY KILL US ALL!

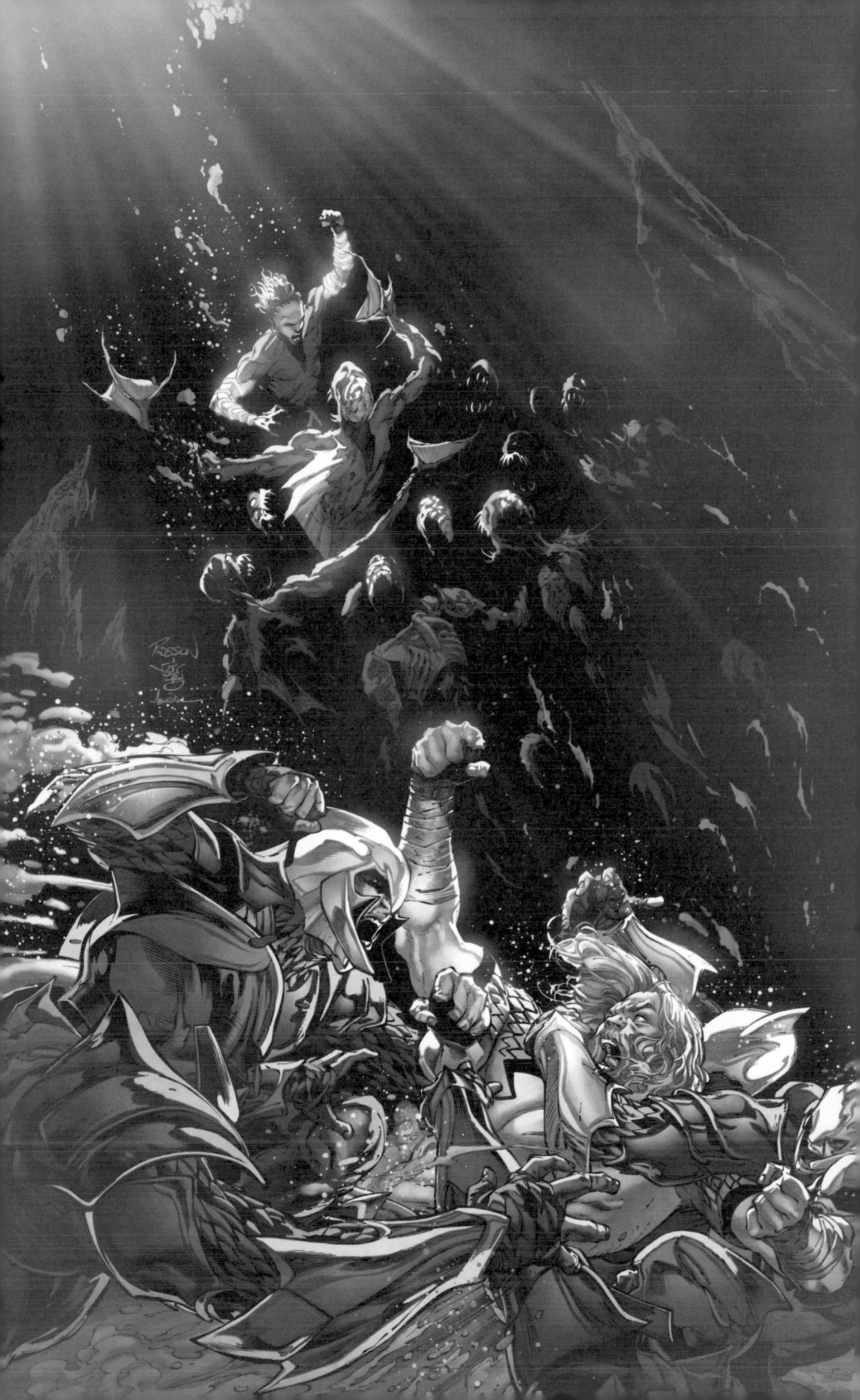

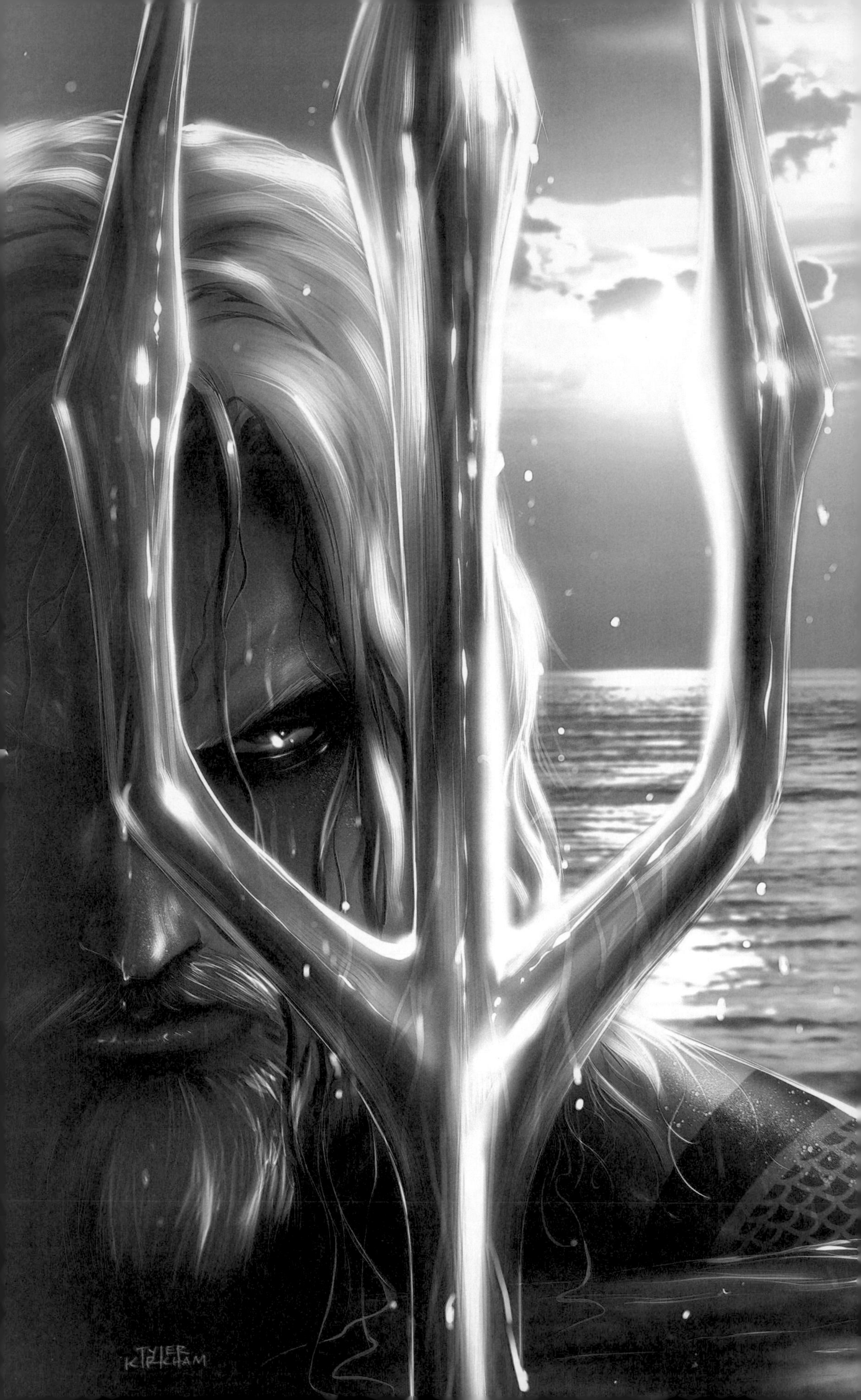
TYLER KIRKHAM

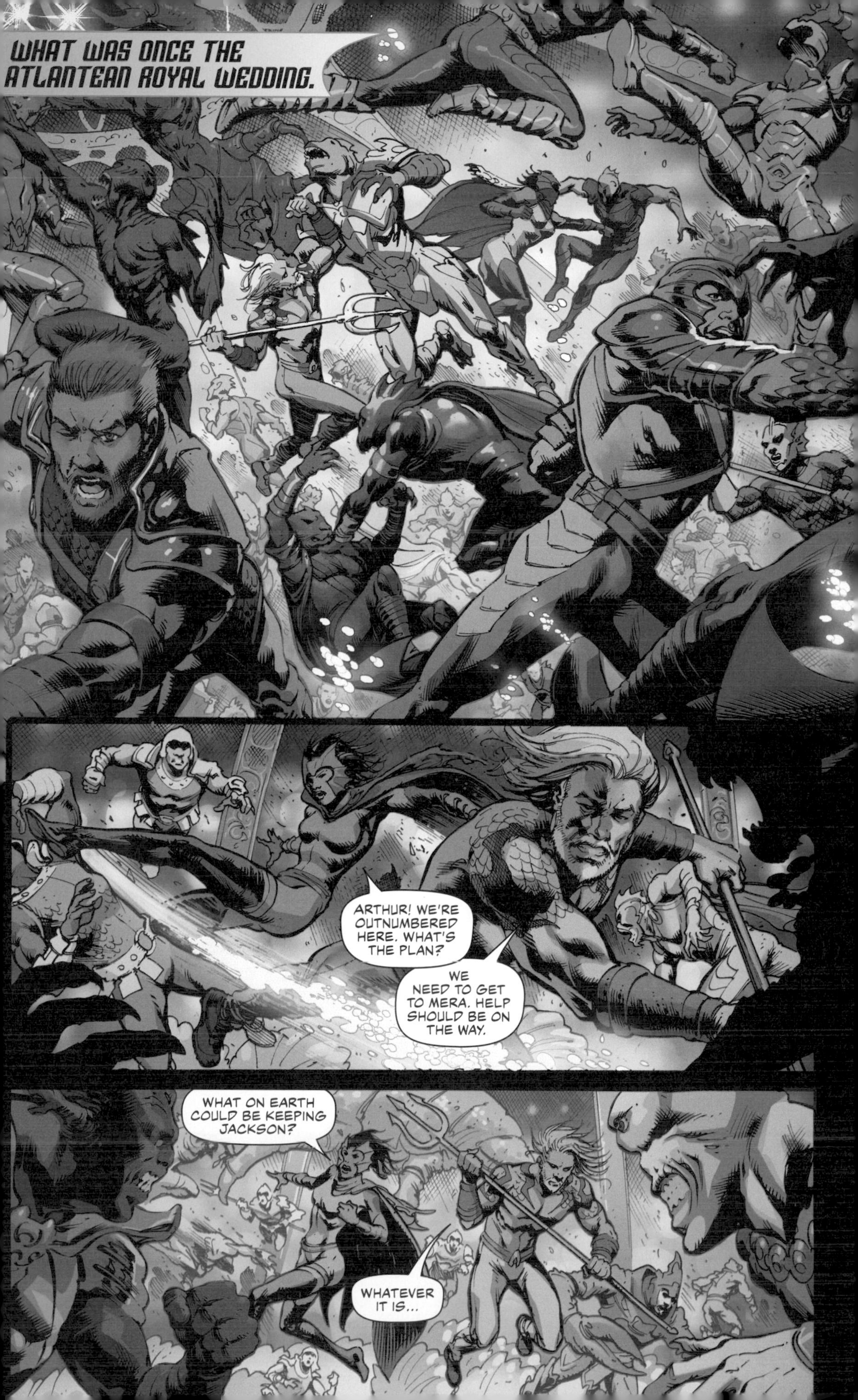
WHAT WAS ONCE THE ATLANTEAN ROYAL WEDDING.
ARTHUR! WE'RE OUTNUMBERED HERE. WHAT'S THE PLAN?
WE NEED TO GET TO MERA. HELP SHOULD BE ON THE WAY.
WHAT ON EARTH COULD BE KEEPING JACKSON?
WHATEVER IT IS...

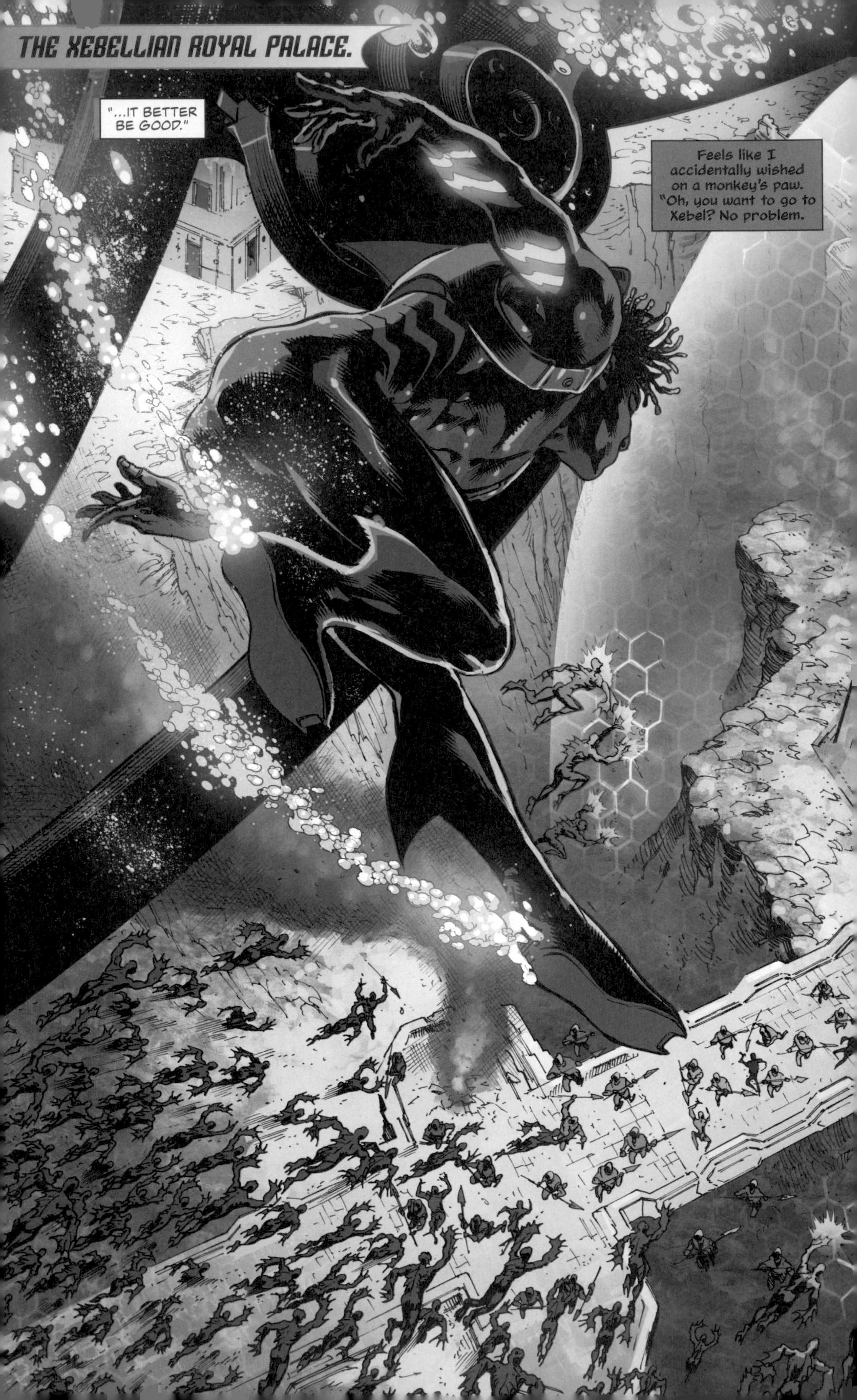
THE XEBELLIAN ROYAL PALACE.
"...IT BETTER BE GOOD."
Feels like I accidentally wished on a monkey's paw. "Oh, you want to go to Xebel? No problem.

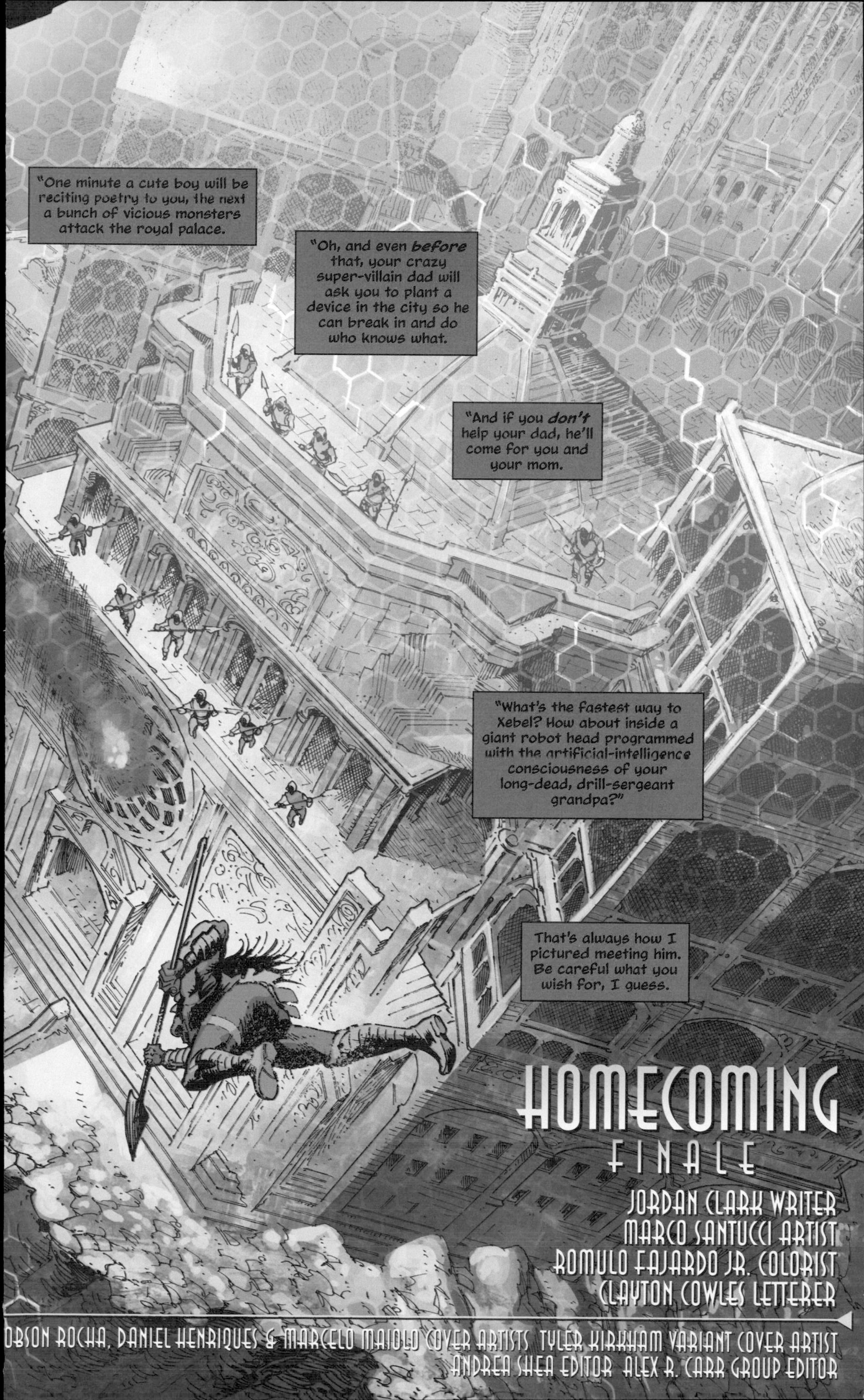
"One minute a cute boy will be reciting poetry to you, the next a bunch of vicious monsters attack the royal palace.
"Oh, and even *before* that, your crazy super-villain dad will ask you to plant a device in the city so he can break in and do who knows what.
"And if you *don't* help your dad, he'll come for you and your mom.
"What's the fastest way to Xebel? How about inside a giant robot head programmed with the artificial-intelligence consciousness of your long-dead, drill-sergeant grandpa?"
That's always how I pictured meeting him. Be careful what you wish for, I guess.
HOMECOMING
FINALE
JORDAN CLARK WRITER
MARCO SANTUCCI ARTIST
ROMULO FAJARDO JR. COLORIST
CLAYTON COWLES LETTERER
OBSON ROCHA, DANIEL HENRIQUES & MARCELO MAIOLO COVER ARTISTS TYLER KIRKHAM VARIANT COVER ARTIST
ANDREA SHEA EDITOR ALEX R. CARR GROUP EDITOR

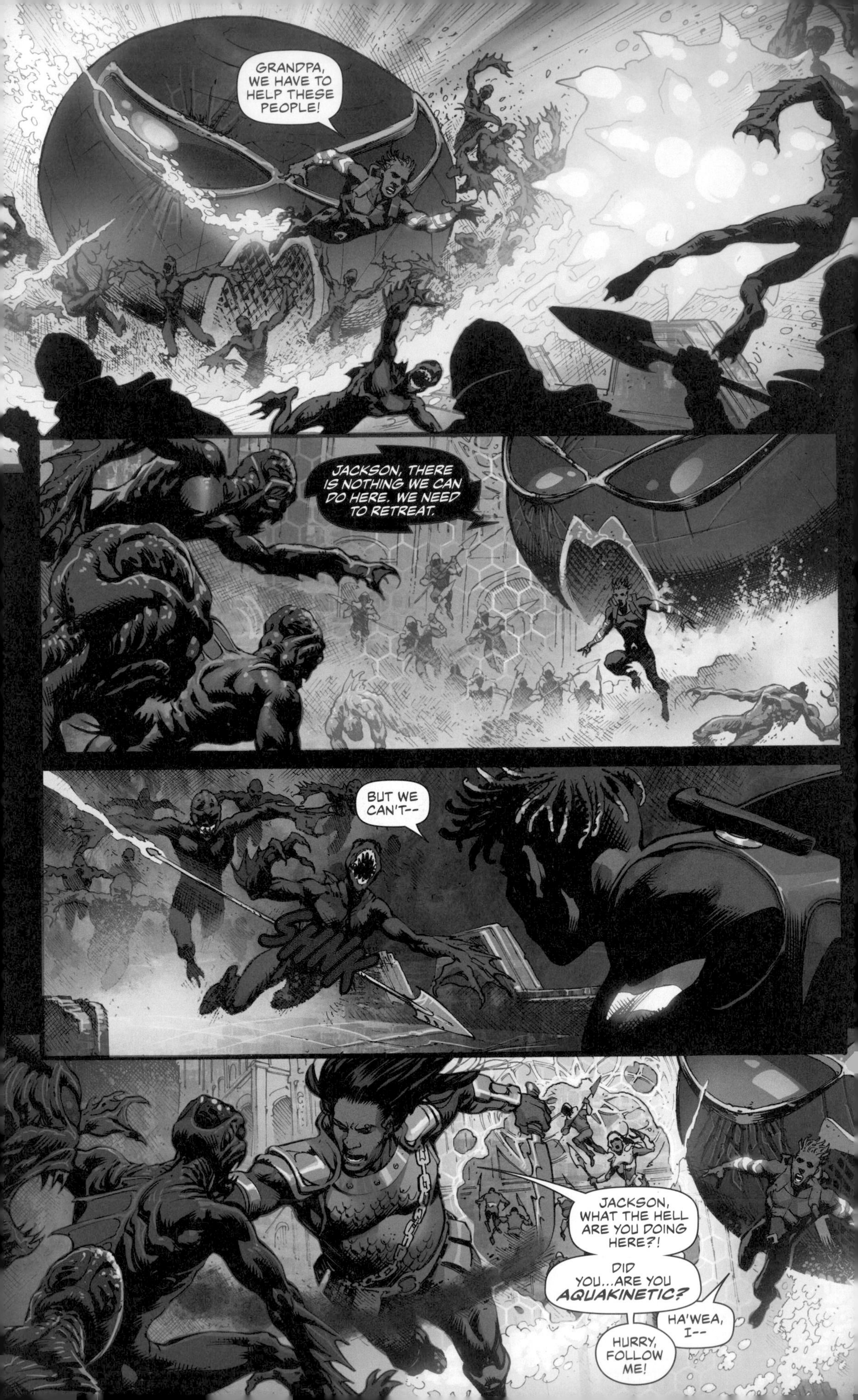
GRANDPA, WE HAVE TO HELP THESE PEOPLE!
JACKSON, THERE IS NOTHING WE CAN DO HERE. WE NEED TO RETREAT.
BUT WE CAN'T--
JACKSON, WHAT THE HELL ARE YOU DOING HERE?!
DID YOU...ARE YOU AQUAKINETIC?
HA'WEA, I--
HURRY, FOLLOW ME!

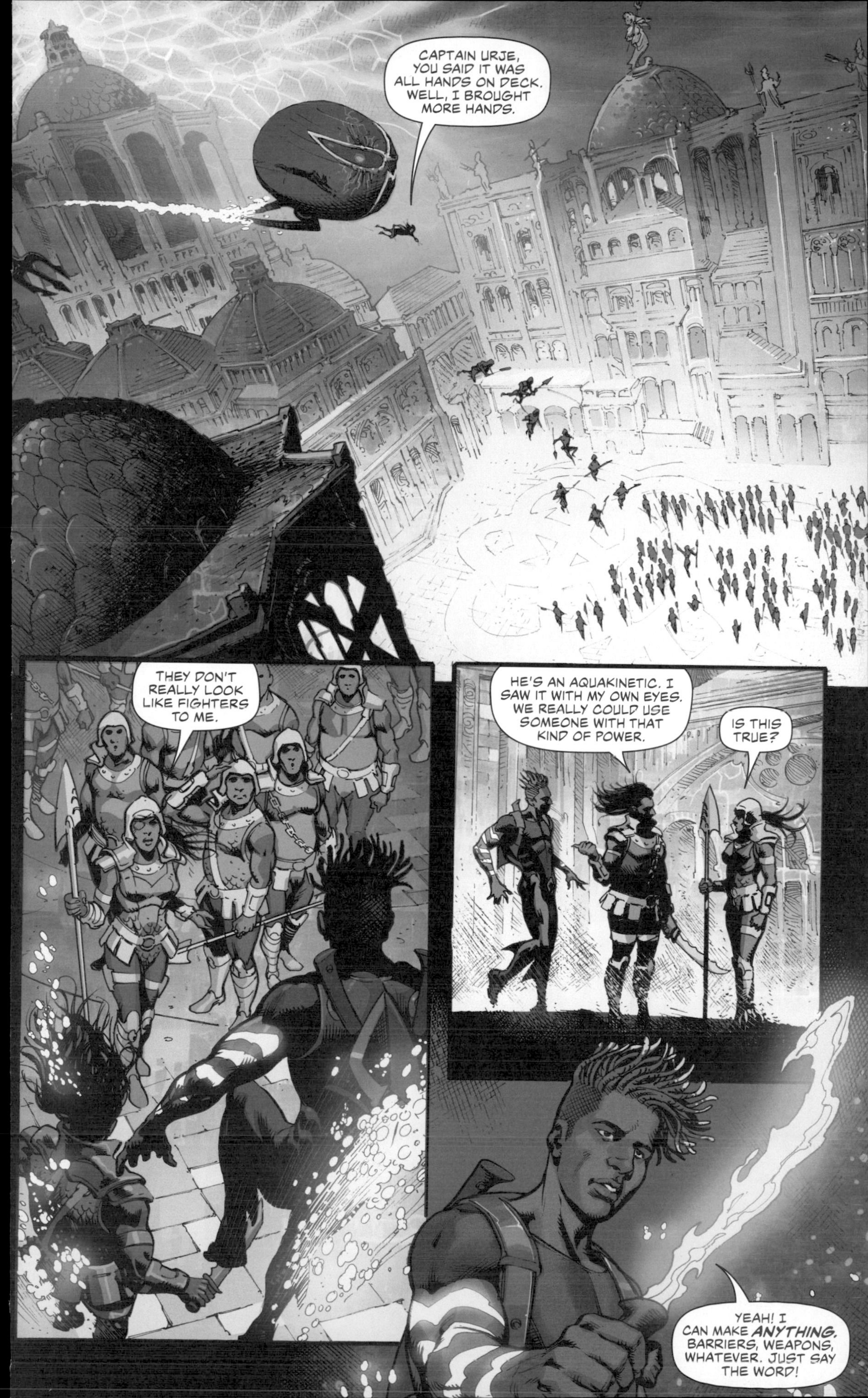
CAPTAIN URJE, YOU SAID IT WAS ALL HANDS ON DECK. WELL, I BROUGHT MORE HANDS.
THEY DON'T REALLY LOOK LIKE FIGHTERS TO ME.
HE'S AN AQUAKINETIC. I SAW IT WITH MY OWN EYES. WE REALLY COULD USE SOMEONE WITH THAT KIND OF POWER.
IS THIS TRUE?
YEAH! I CAN MAKE *ANYTHING.* BARRIERS, WEAPONS, WHATEVER. JUST SAY THE WORD!

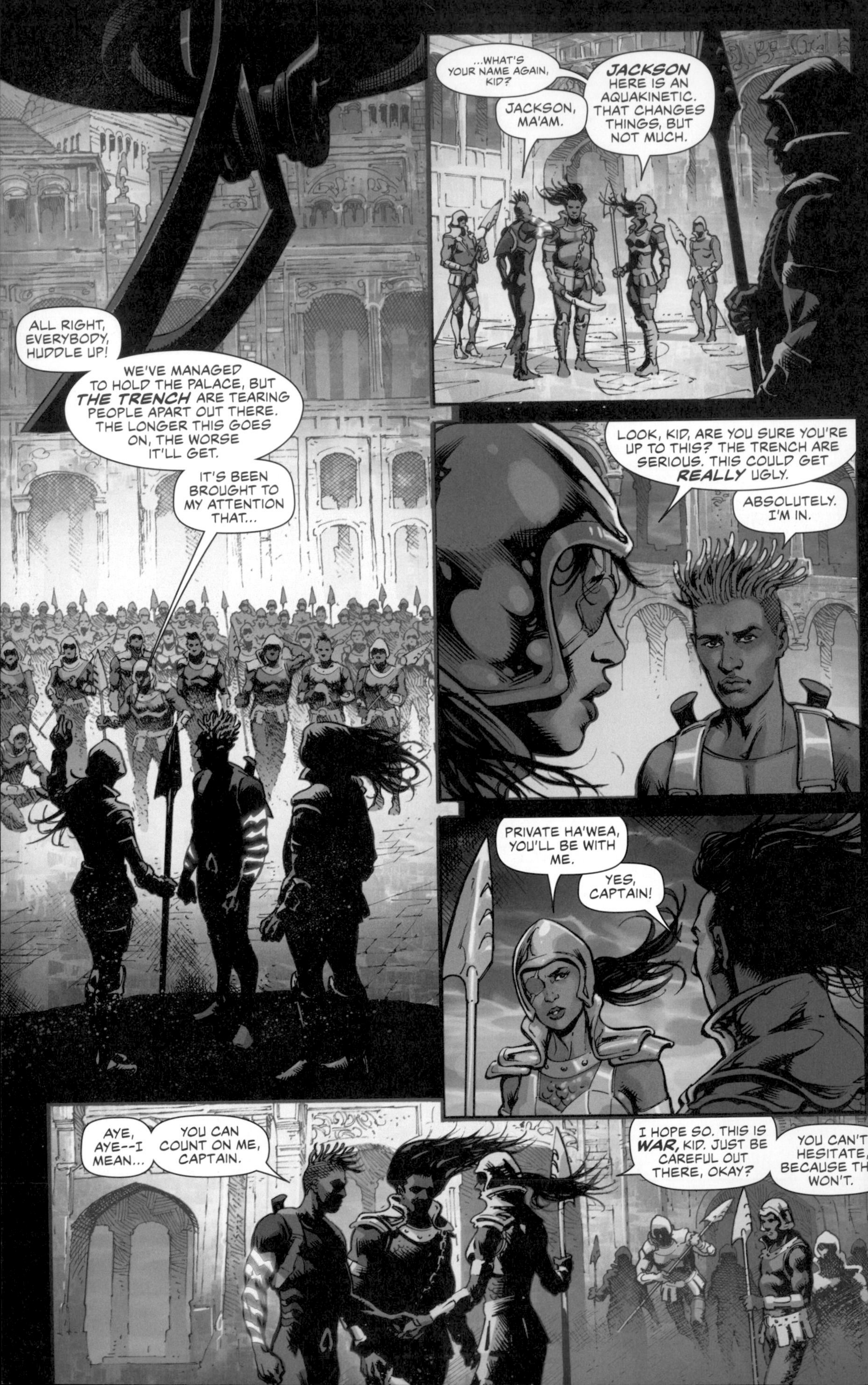

ALL RIGHT, EVERYBODY, HUDDLE UP!
WE'VE MANAGED TO HOLD THE PALACE, BUT THE TRENCH ARE TEARING PEOPLE APART OUT THERE. THE LONGER THIS GOES ON, THE WORSE IT'LL GET.
IT'S BEEN BROUGHT TO MY ATTENTION THAT...
...WHAT'S YOUR NAME AGAIN, KID?
JACKSON, MA'AM.
JACKSON HERE IS AN AQUAKINETIC. THAT CHANGES THINGS, BUT NOT MUCH.
LOOK, KID, ARE YOU SURE YOU'RE UP TO THIS? THE TRENCH ARE SERIOUS. THIS COULD GET REALLY UGLY.
ABSOLUTELY. I'M IN.
PRIVATE HA'WEA, YOU'LL BE WITH ME.
YES, CAPTAIN!
AYE, AYE--I MEAN...
YOU CAN COUNT ON ME, CAPTAIN.
I HOPE SO. THIS IS WAR, KID. JUST BE CAREFUL OUT THERE, OKAY?

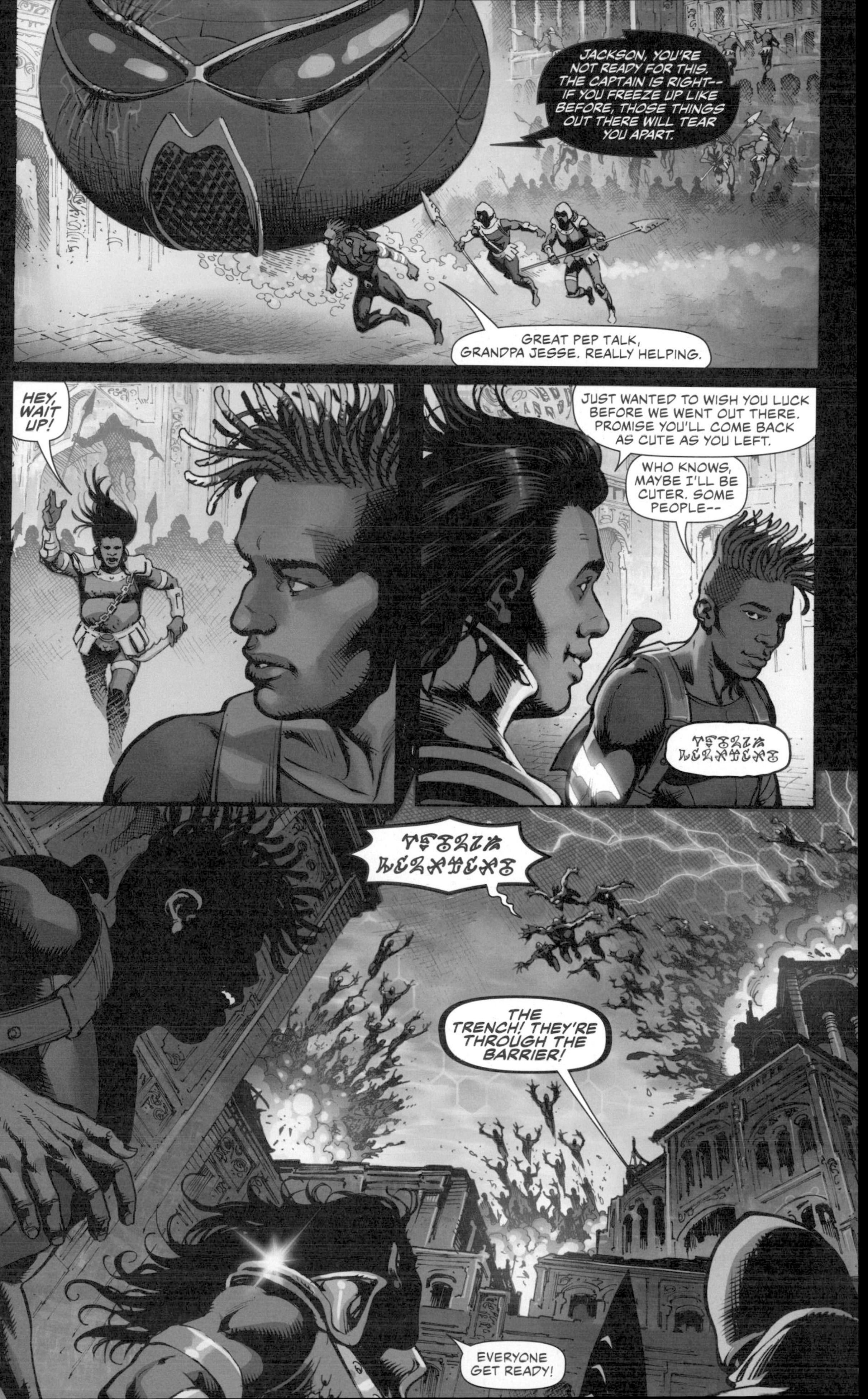
JACKSON, YOU'RE NOT READY FOR THIS. THE CAPTAIN IS RIGHT-- IF YOU FREEZE UP LIKE BEFORE, THOSE THINGS OUT THERE WILL TEAR YOU APART.
GREAT PEP TALK, GRANDPA JESSE. REALLY HELPING.
HEY, WAIT UP!
JUST WANTED TO WISH YOU LUCK BEFORE WE WENT OUT THERE. PROMISE YOU'LL COME BACK AS CUTE AS YOU LEFT.
WHO KNOWS, MAYBE I'LL BE CUTER. SOME PEOPLE--
THE TRENCH! THEY'RE THROUGH THE BARRIER!
EVERYONE GET READY!

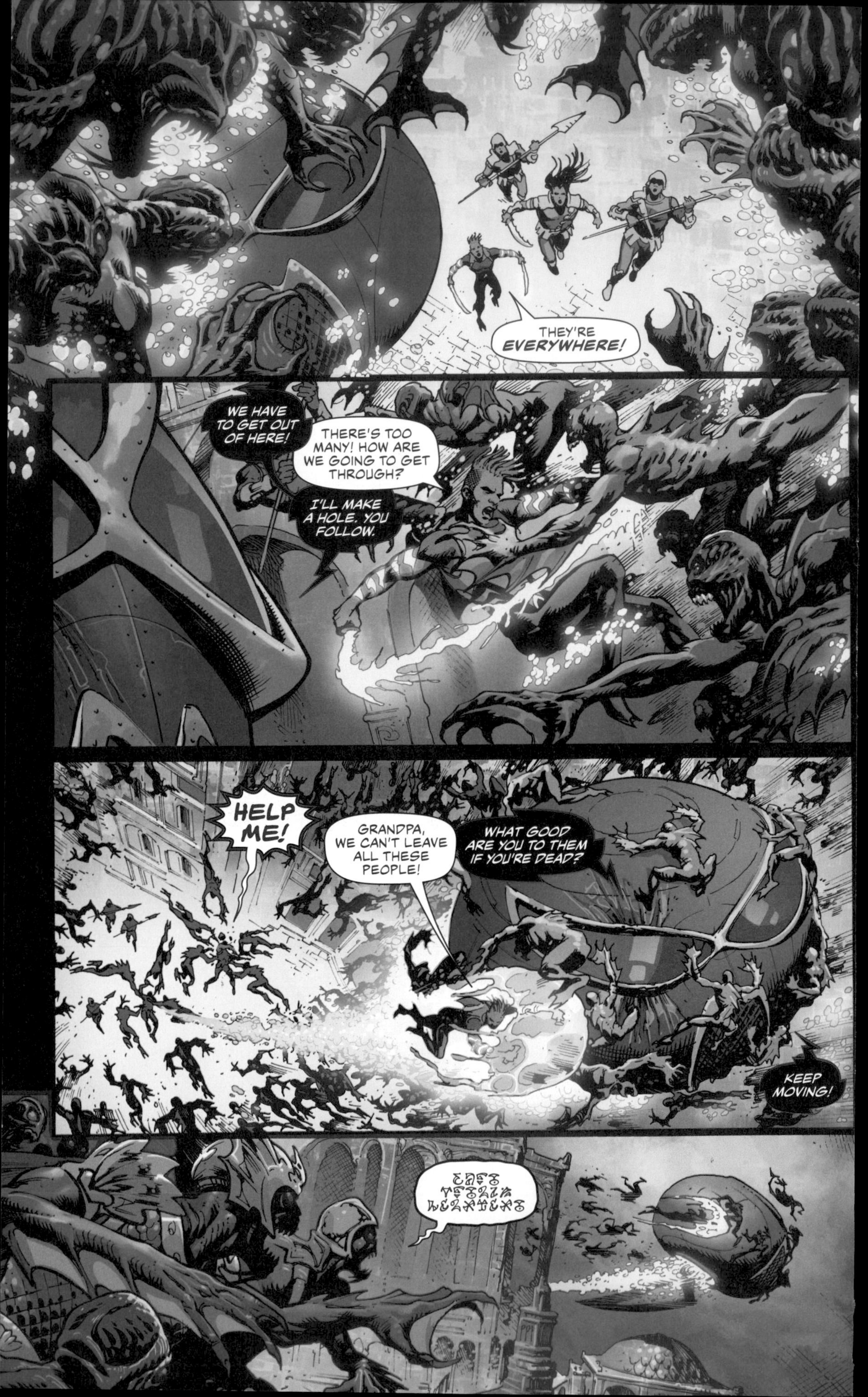
THEY'RE EVERYWHERE!
WE HAVE TO GET OUT OF HERE!
THERE'S TOO MANY! HOW ARE WE GOING TO GET THROUGH?
I'LL MAKE A HOLE. YOU FOLLOW.
HELP ME!
GRANDPA, WE CAN'T LEAVE ALL THESE PEOPLE!
WHAT GOOD ARE YOU TO THEM IF YOU'RE DEAD?
KEEP MOVING!

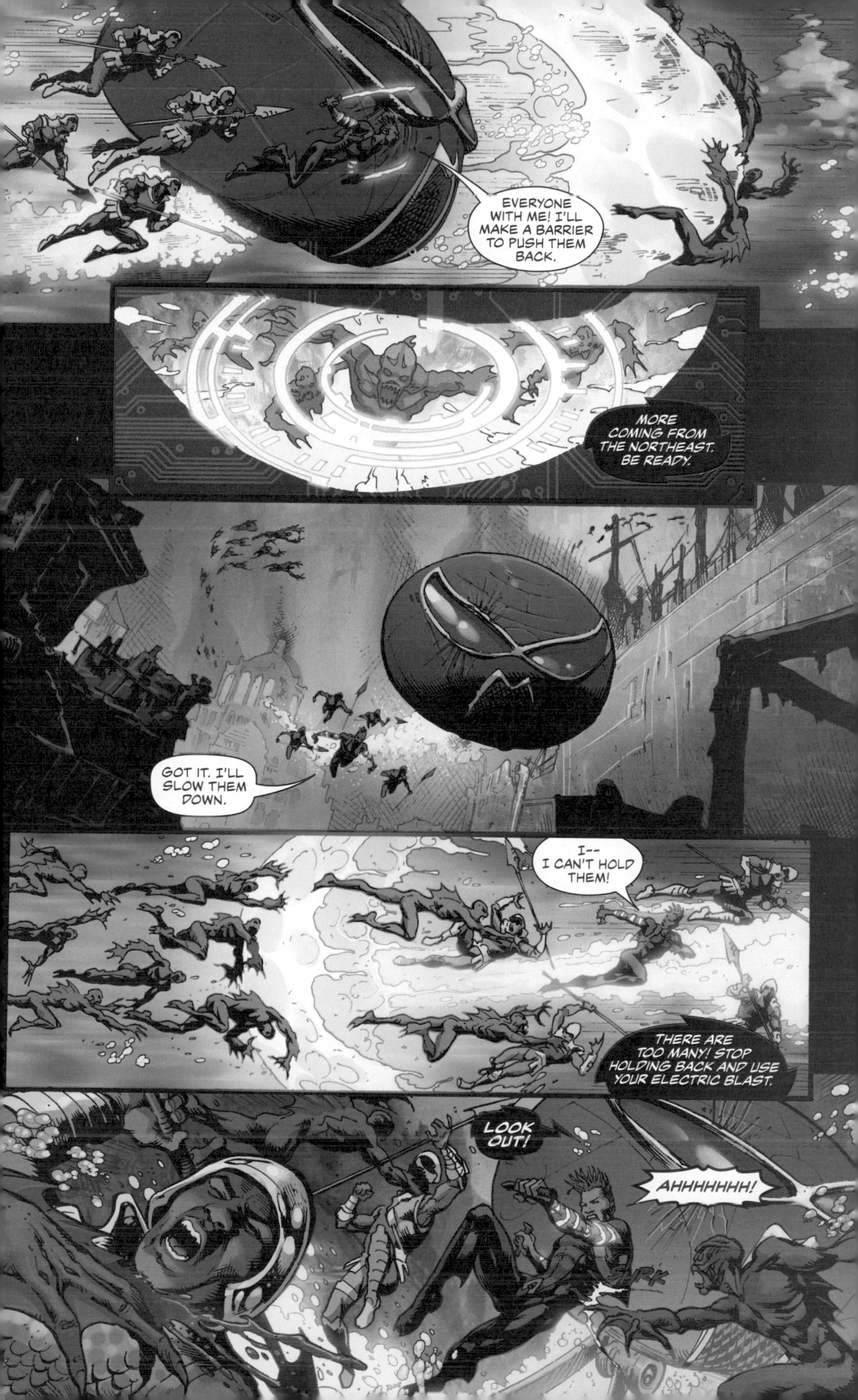
EVERYONE WITH ME! I'LL MAKE A BARRIER TO PUSH THEM BACK.
MORE COMING FROM THE NORTHEAST. BE READY.
GOT IT. I'LL SLOW THEM DOWN.
I-- I CAN'T HOLD THEM!
THERE ARE TOO MANY! STOP HOLDING BACK AND USE YOUR ELECTRIC BLAST.
LOOK OUT!
AHHHHHHH!

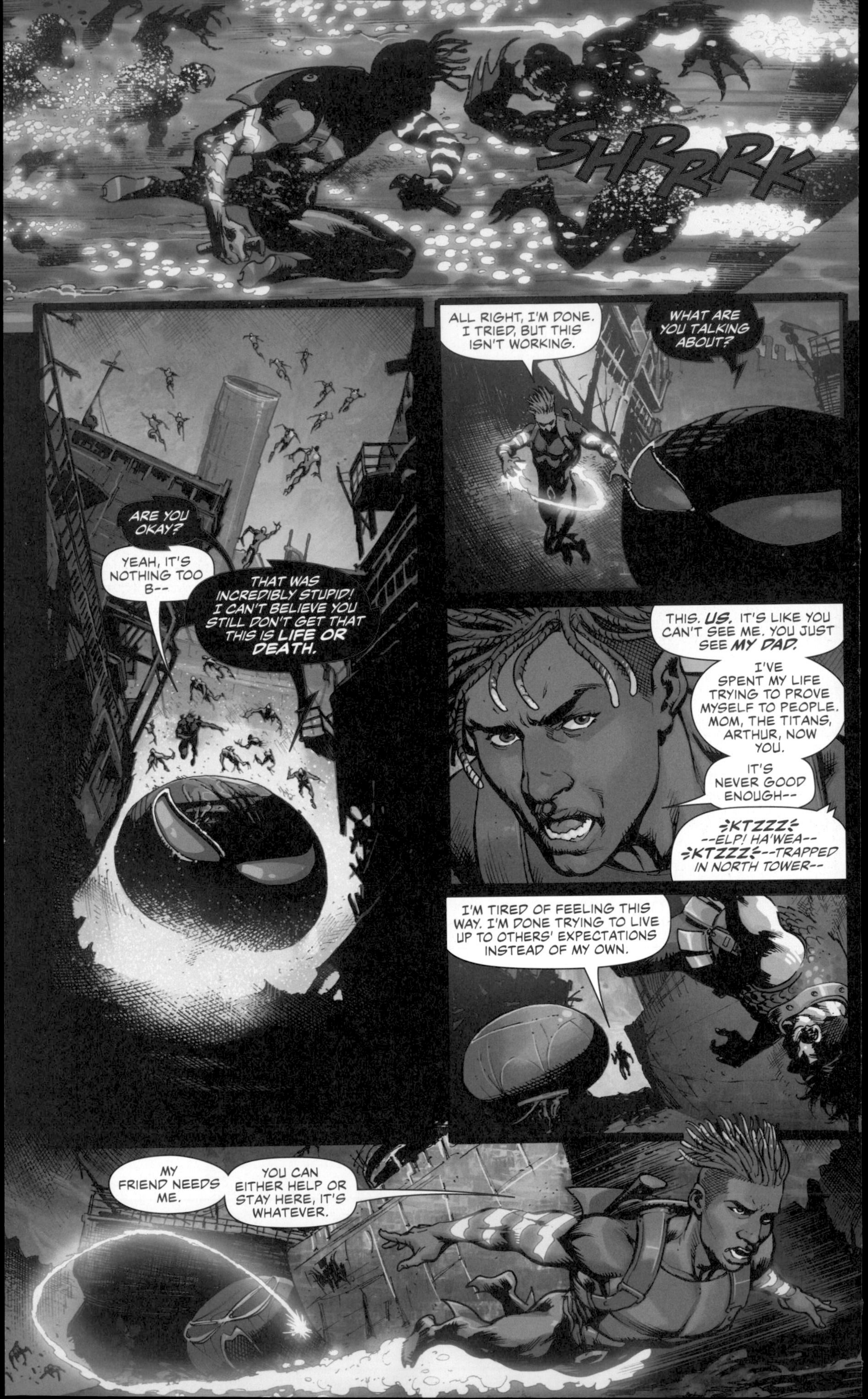
SHRRRK
ARE YOU OKAY?
YEAH, IT'S NOTHING TOO B--
THAT WAS INCREDIBLY STUPID! I CAN'T BELIEVE YOU STILL DON'T GET THAT THIS IS LIFE OR DEATH.
ALL RIGHT, I'M DONE. I TRIED, BUT THIS ISN'T WORKING.
WHAT ARE YOU TALKING ABOUT?
THIS. US. IT'S LIKE YOU CAN'T SEE ME. YOU JUST SEE MY DAD.
I'VE SPENT MY LIFE TRYING TO PROVE MYSELF TO PEOPLE. MOM, THE TITANS, ARTHUR, NOW YOU.
IT'S NEVER GOOD ENOUGH--
KTZZZ --ELP! HA'WEA-- KTZZZ --TRAPPED IN NORTH TOWER--
I'M TIRED OF FEELING THIS WAY. I'M DONE TRYING TO LIVE UP TO OTHERS' EXPECTATIONS INSTEAD OF MY OWN.
MY FRIEND NEEDS ME.
YOU CAN EITHER HELP OR STAY HERE, IT'S WHATEVER.

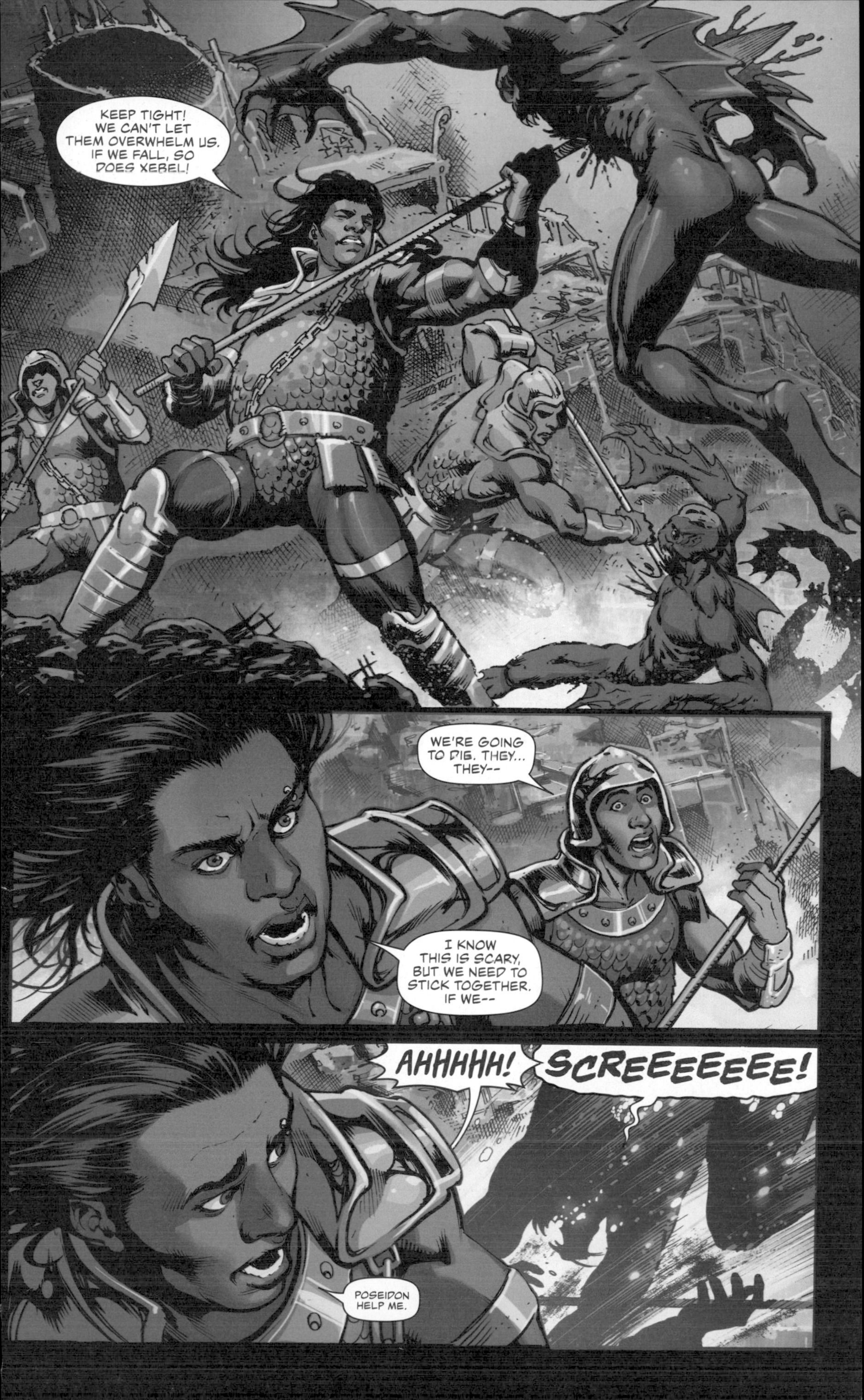
KEEP TIGHT! WE CAN'T LET THEM OVERWHELM US. IF WE FALL, SO DOES XEBEL!
WE'RE GOING TO DIE. THEY... THEY--
I KNOW THIS IS SCARY, BUT WE NEED TO STICK TOGETHER. IF WE--
AHHHHH!
SCREEEEEEEE!
POSEIDON HELP ME.

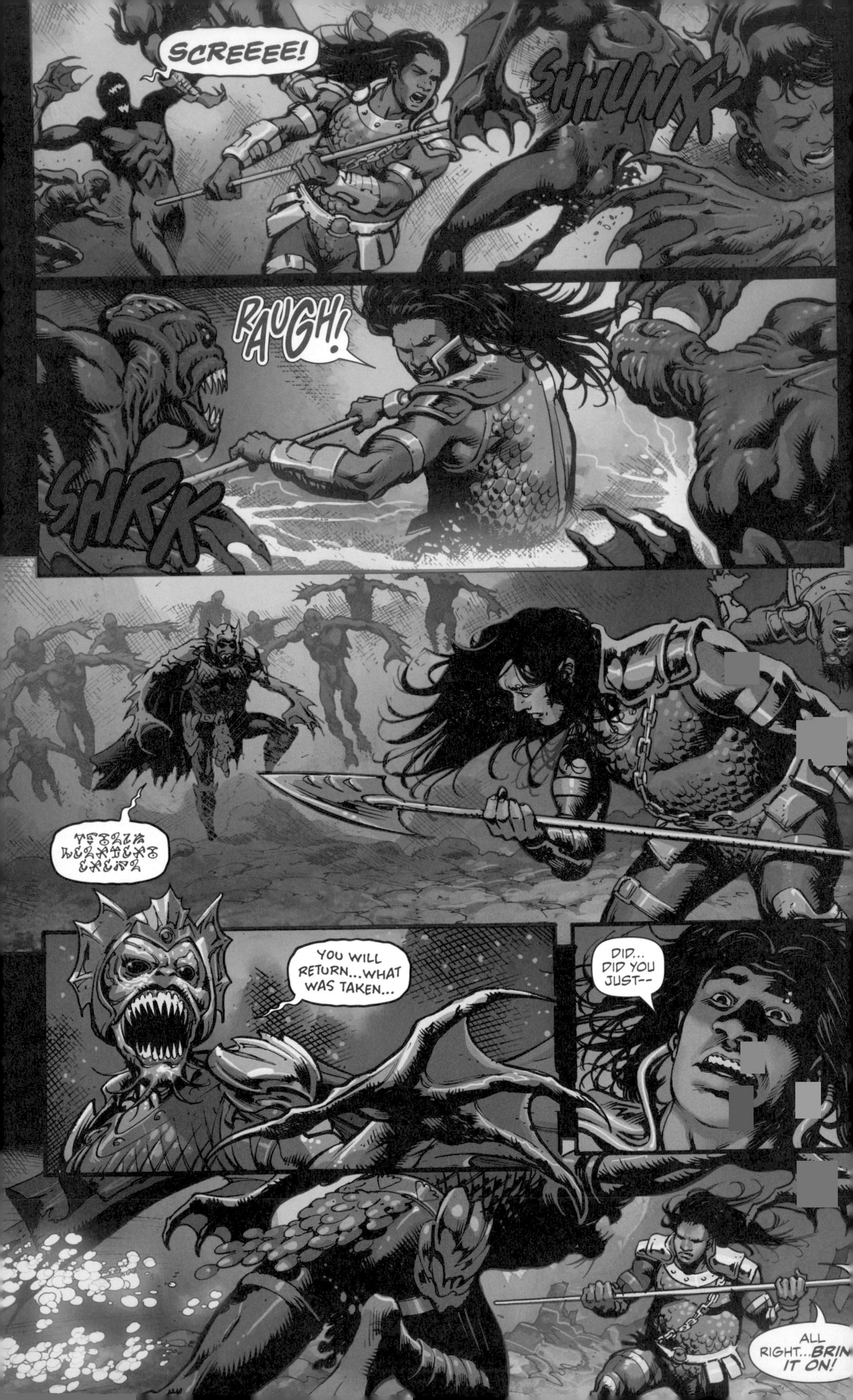
SCREEEE!
SHHUNKK
RAUGH!
SHRK
YOU WILL RETURN...WHAT WAS TAKEN...
DID... DID YOU JUST--
ALL RIGHT...BRING IT ON!

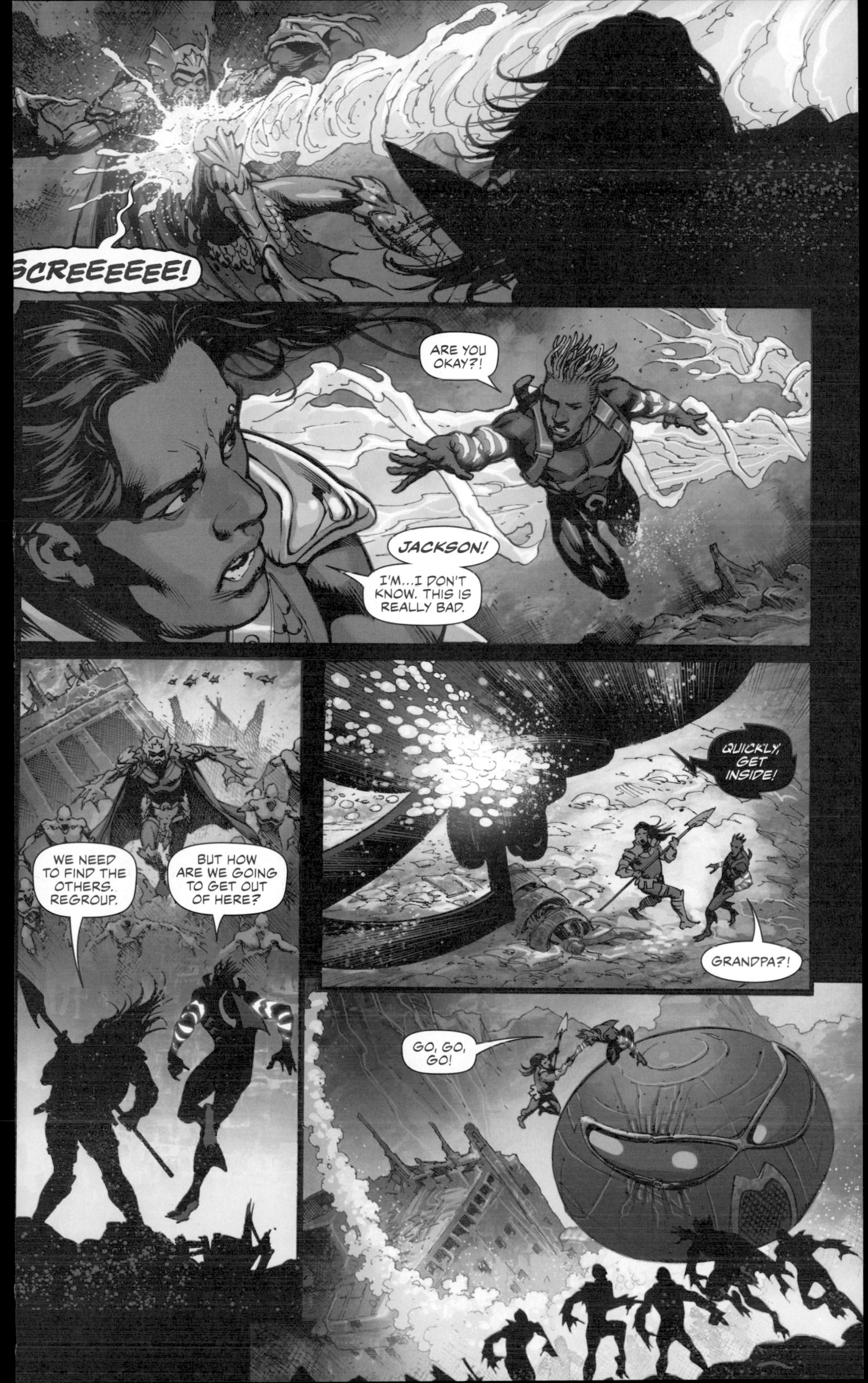
SCREEEEEEE!
ARE YOU OKAY?!
JACKSON!
I'M...I DON'T KNOW. THIS IS REALLY BAD.
WE NEED TO FIND THE OTHERS. REGROUP.
BUT HOW ARE WE GOING TO GET OUT OF HERE?
QUICKLY, GET INSIDE!
GRANDPA?!
GO, GO, GO!

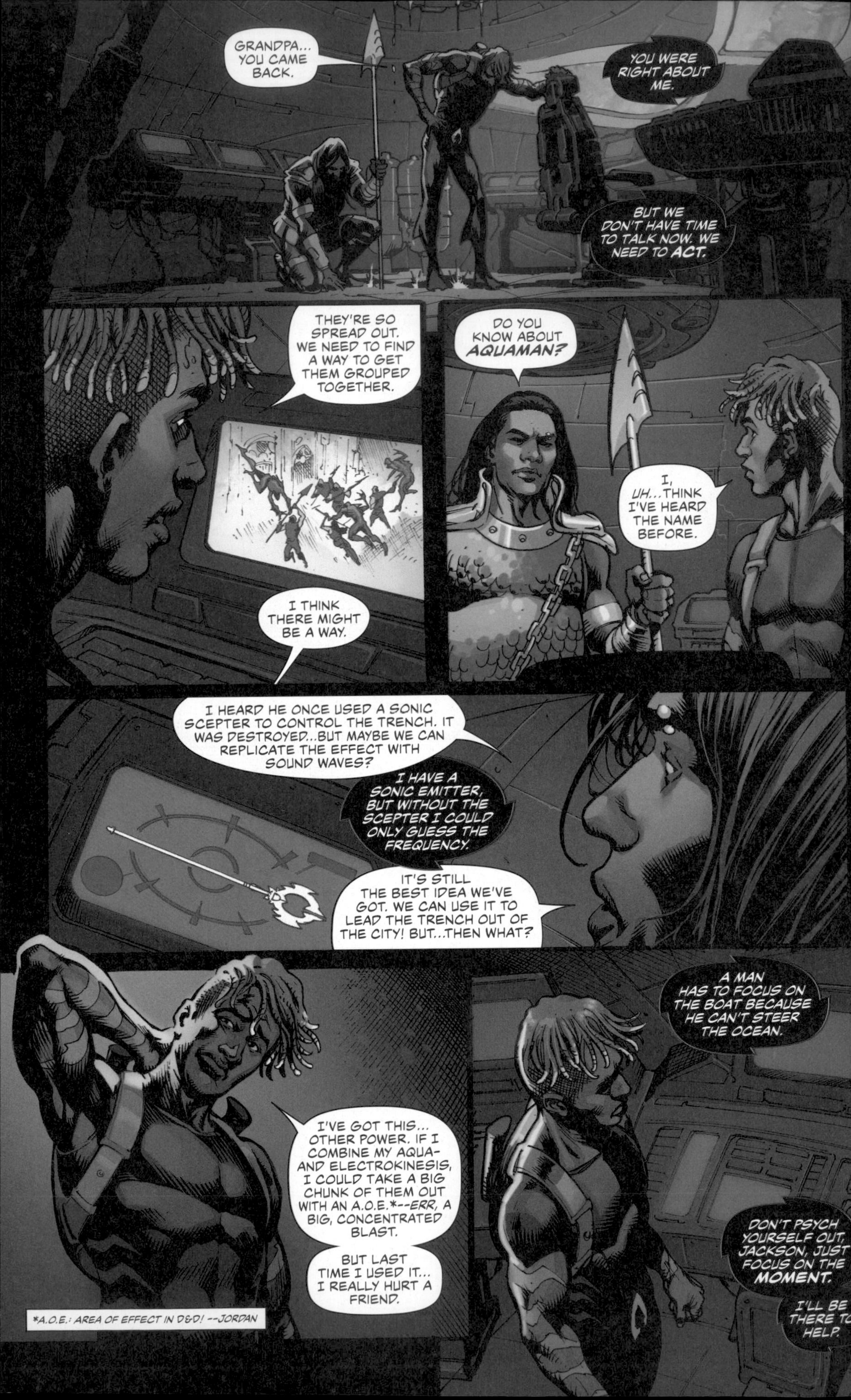

GRANDPA... YOU CAME BACK.
YOU WERE RIGHT ABOUT ME.
BUT WE DON'T HAVE TIME TO TALK NOW. WE NEED TO ACT.
THEY'RE SO SPREAD OUT. WE NEED TO FIND A WAY TO GET THEM GROUPED TOGETHER.
I THINK THERE MIGHT BE A WAY.
DO YOU KNOW ABOUT AQUAMAN?
I, UH... THINK I'VE HEARD THE NAME BEFORE.
I HEARD HE ONCE USED A SONIC SCEPTER TO CONTROL THE TRENCH. IT WAS DESTROYED...BUT MAYBE WE CAN REPLICATE THE EFFECT WITH SOUND WAVES?
I HAVE A SONIC EMITTER, BUT WITHOUT THE SCEPTER I COULD ONLY GUESS THE FREQUENCY.
IT'S STILL THE BEST IDEA WE'VE GOT. WE CAN USE IT TO LEAD THE TRENCH OUT OF THE CITY! BUT...THEN WHAT?
I'VE GOT THIS... OTHER POWER. IF I COMBINE MY AQUA- AND ELECTROKINESIS, I COULD TAKE A BIG CHUNK OF THEM OUT WITH AN A.O.E.*--ERR, A BIG, CONCENTRATED BLAST.
BUT LAST TIME I USED IT... I REALLY HURT A FRIEND.
*A.O.E.: AREA OF EFFECT IN D&D! --JORDAN
A MAN HAS TO FOCUS ON THE BOAT BECAUSE HE CAN'T STEER THE OCEAN.
DON'T PSYCH YOURSELF OUT, JACKSON, JUST FOCUS ON THE MOMENT.
I'LL BE THERE TO HELP.

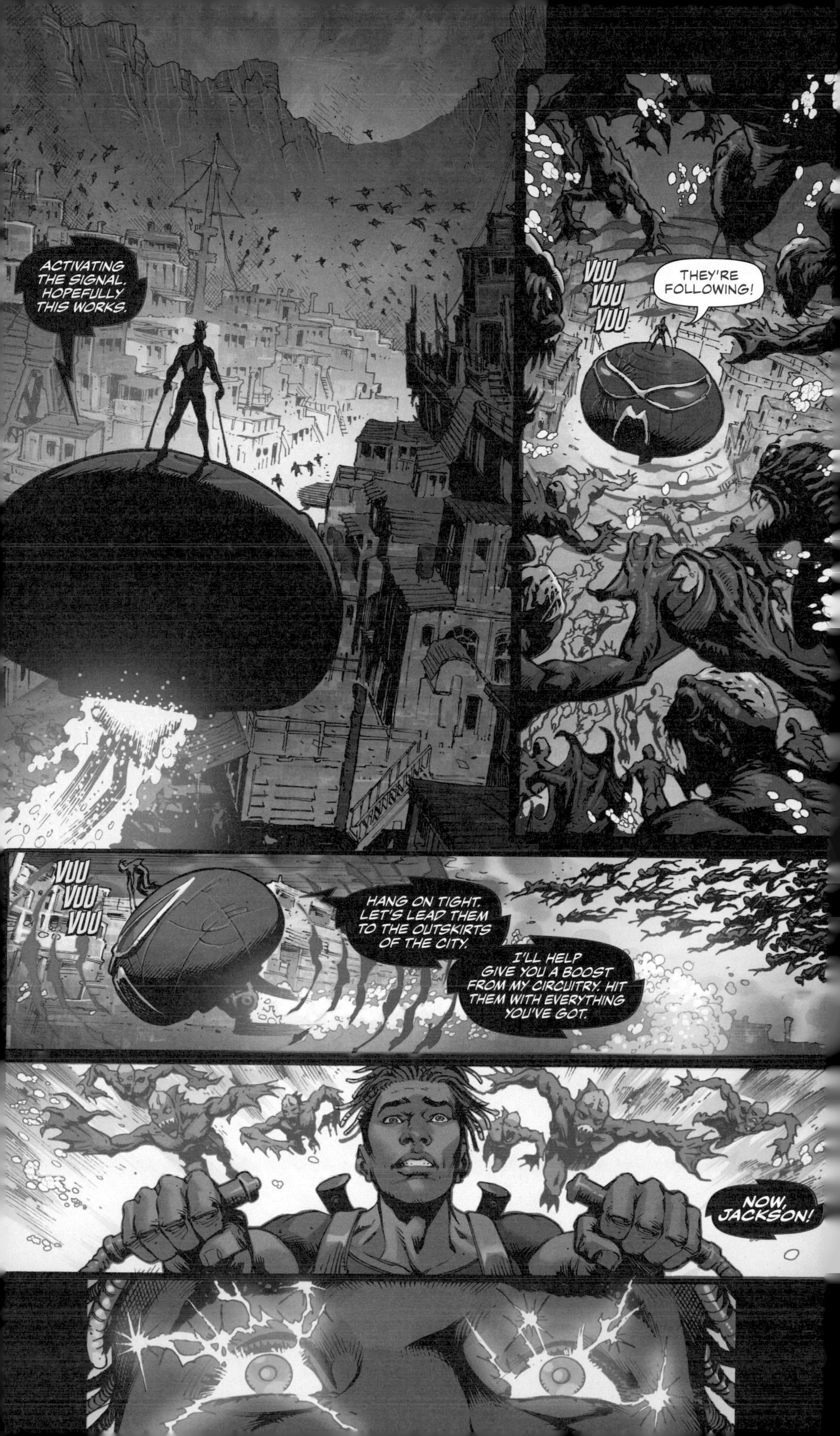

ACTIVATING THE SIGNAL. HOPEFULLY THIS WORKS.
VUU VUU VUU
THEY'RE FOLLOWING!
VUU VUU VUU
HANG ON TIGHT. LET'S LEAD THEM TO THE OUTSKIRTS OF THE CITY.
I'LL HELP GIVE YOU A BOOST FROM MY CIRCUITRY. HIT THEM WITH EVERYTHING YOU'VE GOT.
NOW, JACKSON!

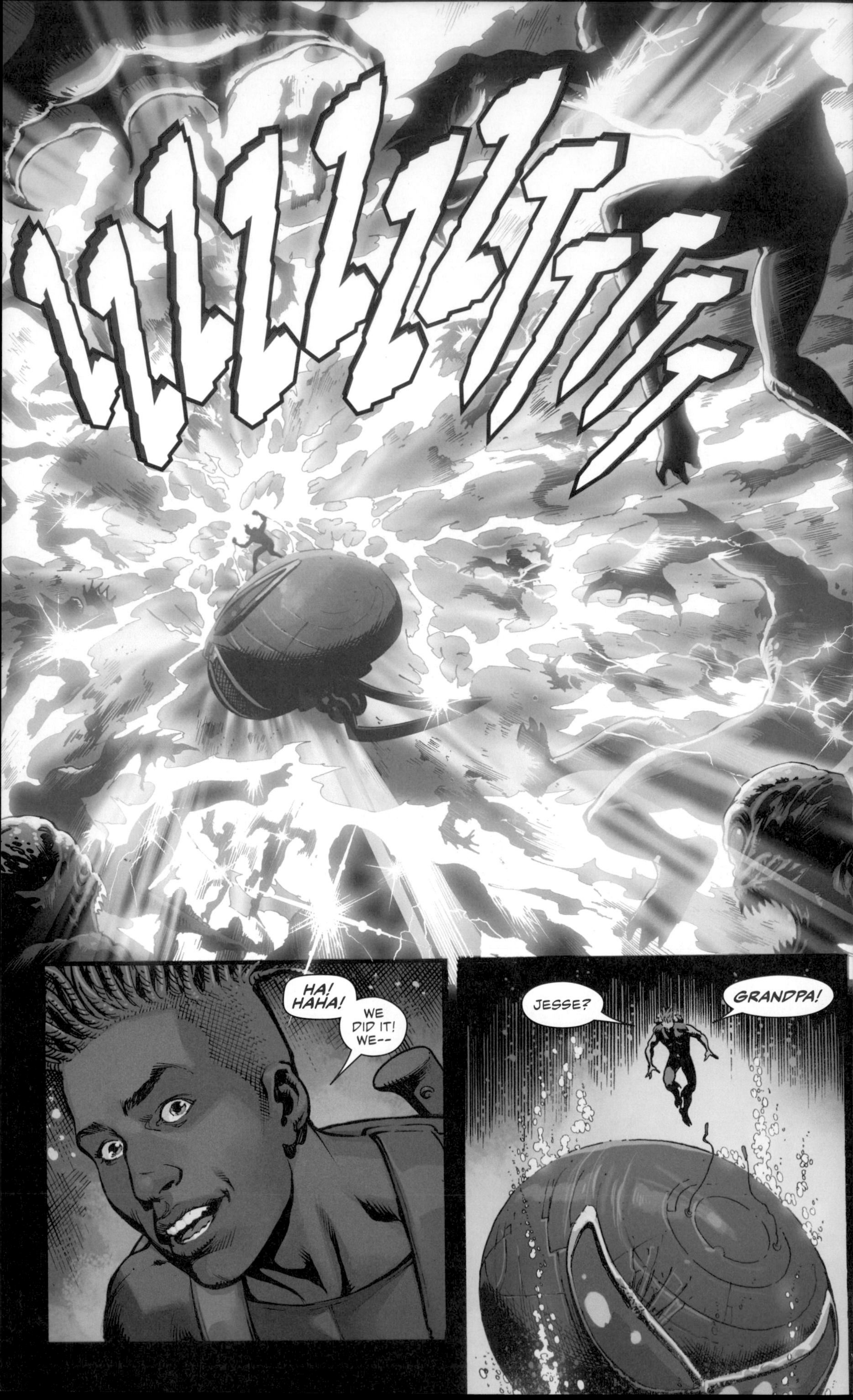
HA! HAHA!
WE DID IT! WE--
JESSE?
GRANDPA!

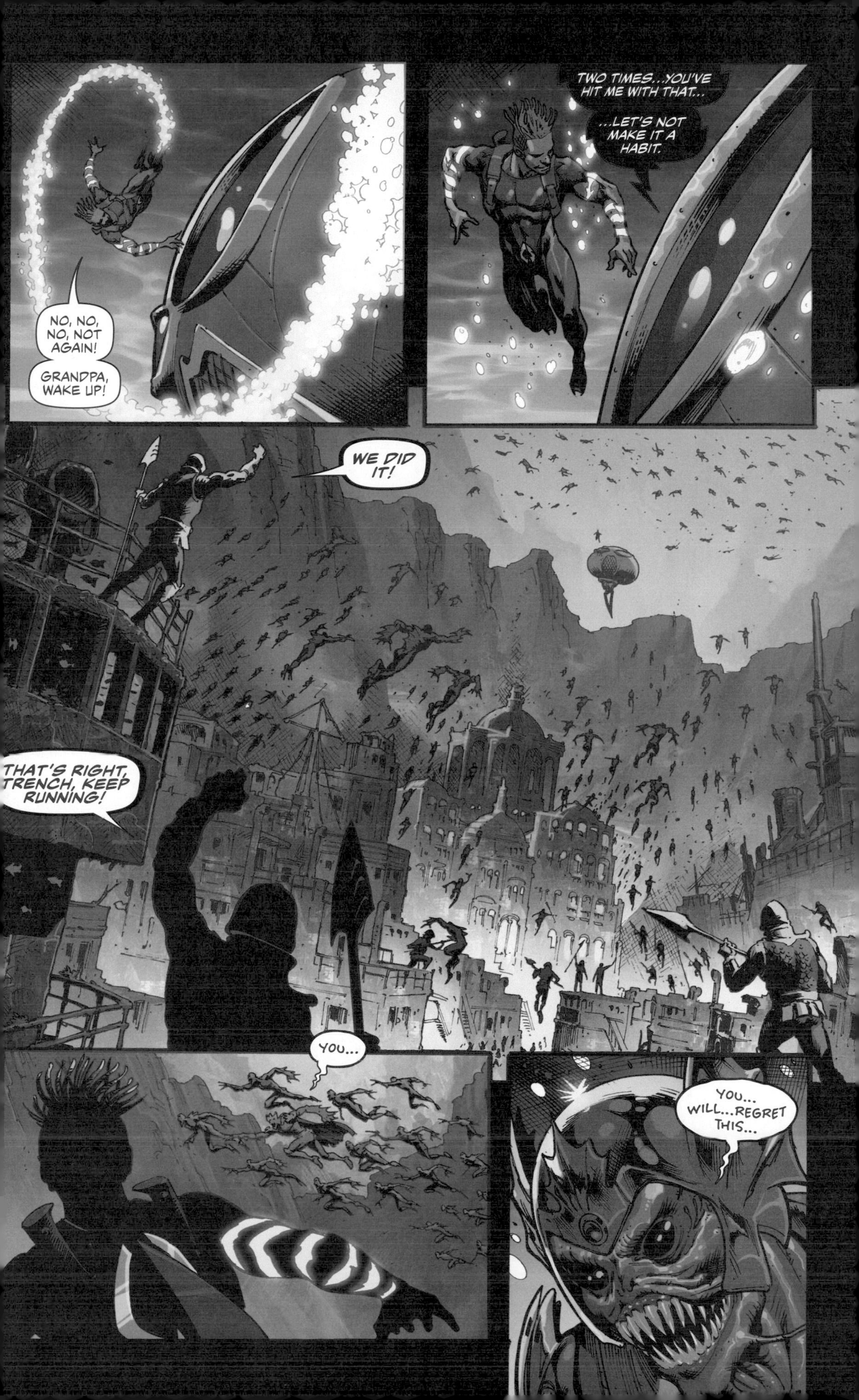

NO, NO, NO, NOT AGAIN!
GRANDPA, WAKE UP!
TWO TIMES...YOU'VE HIT ME WITH THAT...
...LET'S NOT MAKE IT A HABIT.
WE DID IT!
THAT'S RIGHT, TRENCH, KEEP RUNNING!
YOU...
YOU... WILL...REGRET THIS...

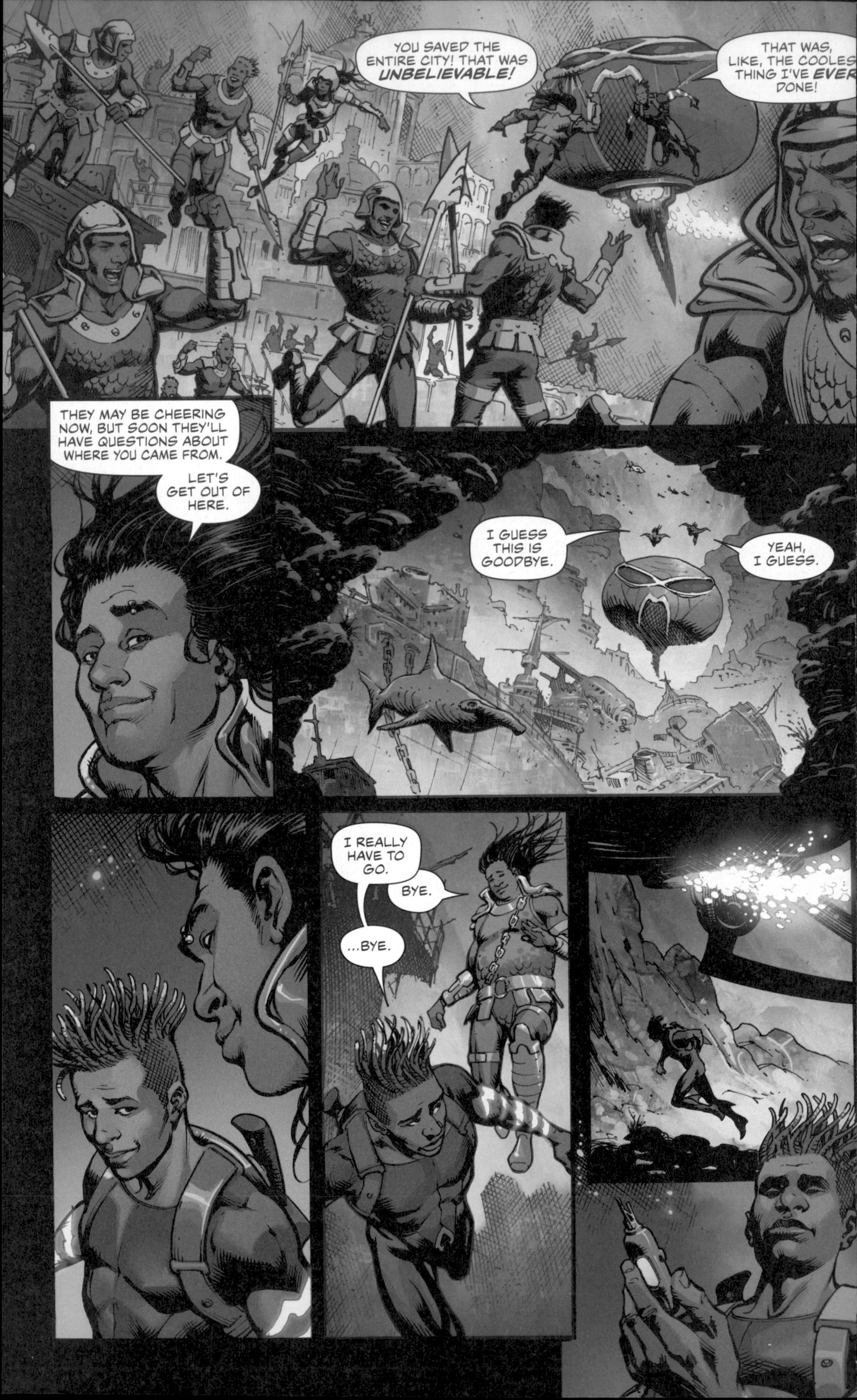
YOU SAVED THE ENTIRE CITY! THAT WAS *UNBELIEVABLE!*
THAT WAS, LIKE, THE COOLES THING I'VE *EVER* DONE!
THEY MAY BE CHEERING NOW, BUT SOON THEY'LL HAVE QUESTIONS ABOUT WHERE YOU CAME FROM.
LET'S GET OUT OF HERE.
I GUESS THIS IS GOODBYE.
YEAH, I GUESS.
I REALLY HAVE TO GO.
BYE.
...BYE.

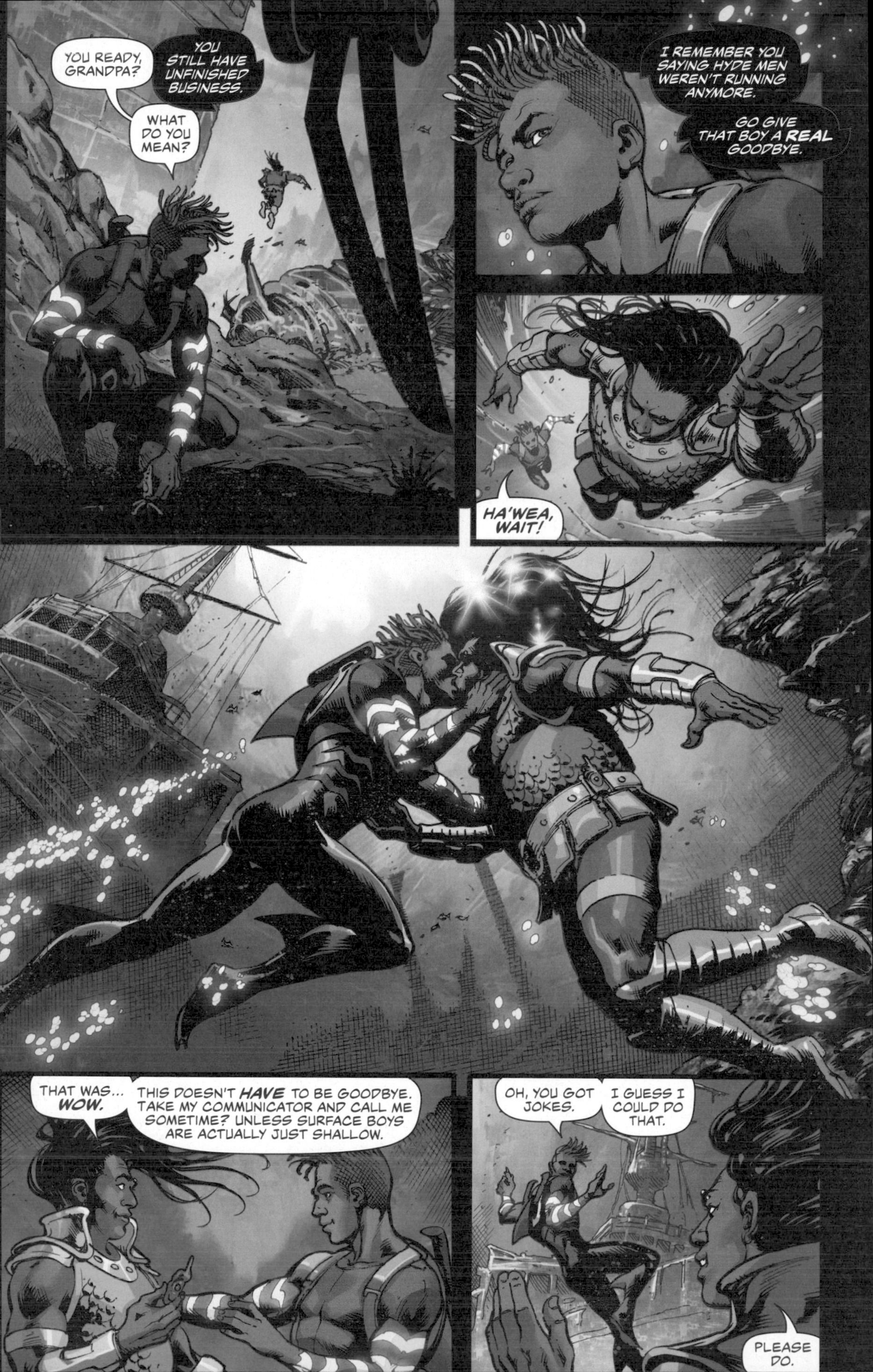
YOU READY, GRANDPA?
YOU STILL HAVE UNFINISHED BUSINESS.
WHAT DO YOU MEAN?
I REMEMBER YOU SAYING HYDE MEN WEREN'T RUNNING ANYMORE.
GO GIVE THAT BOY A **REAL** GOODBYE.
HA'WEA, WAIT!
THAT WAS... **WOW.**
THIS DOESN'T ***HAVE*** TO BE GOODBYE. TAKE MY COMMUNICATOR AND CALL ME SOMETIME? UNLESS SURFACE BOYS ARE ACTUALLY JUST SHALLOW.
OH, YOU GOT JOKES.
I GUESS I COULD DO THAT.
PLEASE DO.

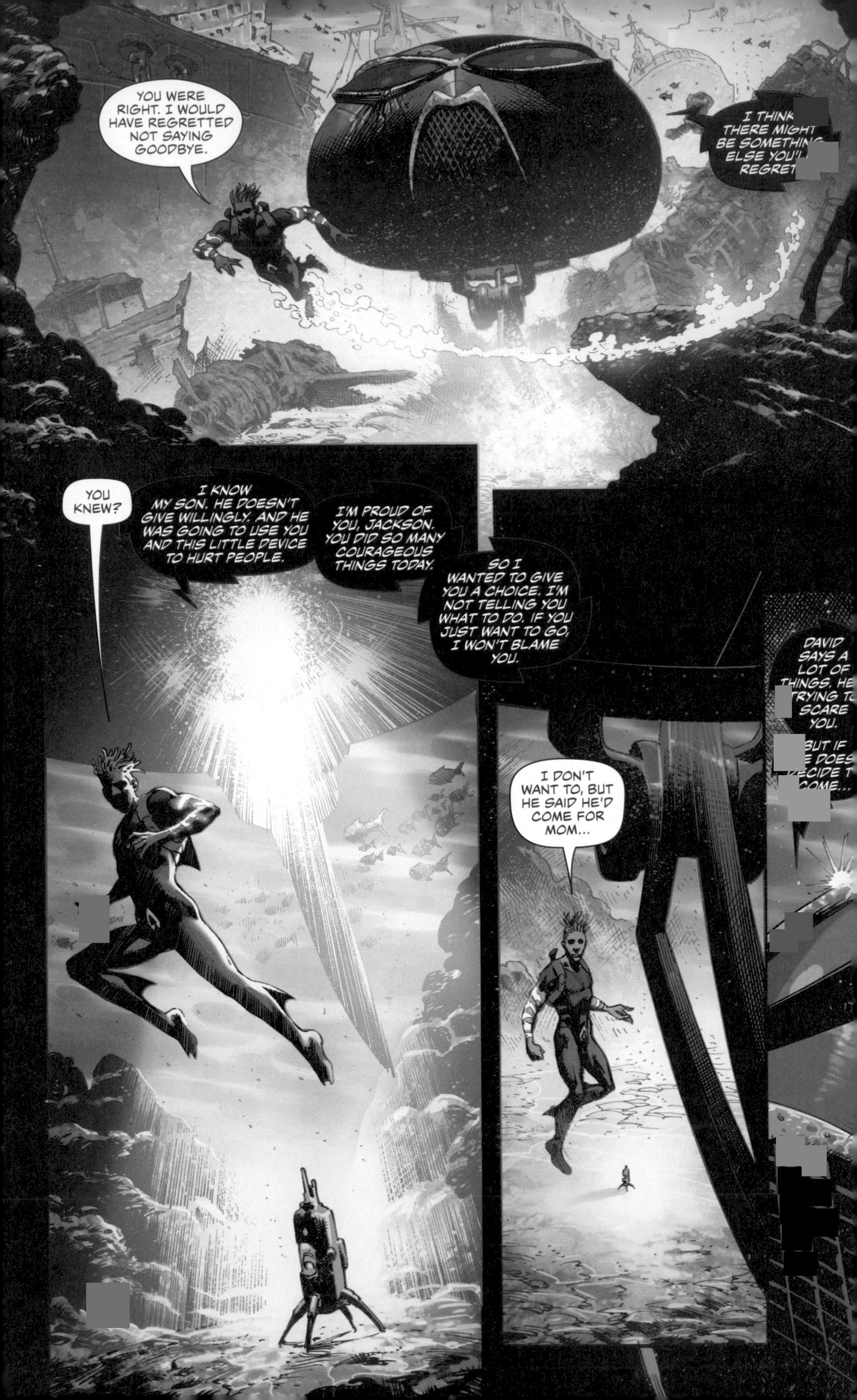
YOU WERE RIGHT. I WOULD HAVE REGRETTED NOT SAYING GOODBYE.
I THINK THERE MIGHT BE SOMETHIN ELSE YOU'L REGRET
YOU KNEW?
I KNOW MY SON. HE DOESN'T GIVE WILLINGLY. AND HE WAS GOING TO USE YOU AND THIS LITTLE DEVICE TO HURT PEOPLE.
I'M PROUD OF YOU, JACKSON. YOU DID SO MANY COURAGEOUS THINGS TODAY.
SO I WANTED TO GIVE YOU A CHOICE. I'M NOT TELLING YOU WHAT TO DO. IF YOU JUST WANT TO GO, I WON'T BLAME YOU.
I DON'T WANT TO, BUT HE SAID HE'D COME FOR MOM...
DAVID SAYS A LOT OF THINGS. HE TRYING T SCARE YOU.
BUT IF DOES ECIDE T COME...

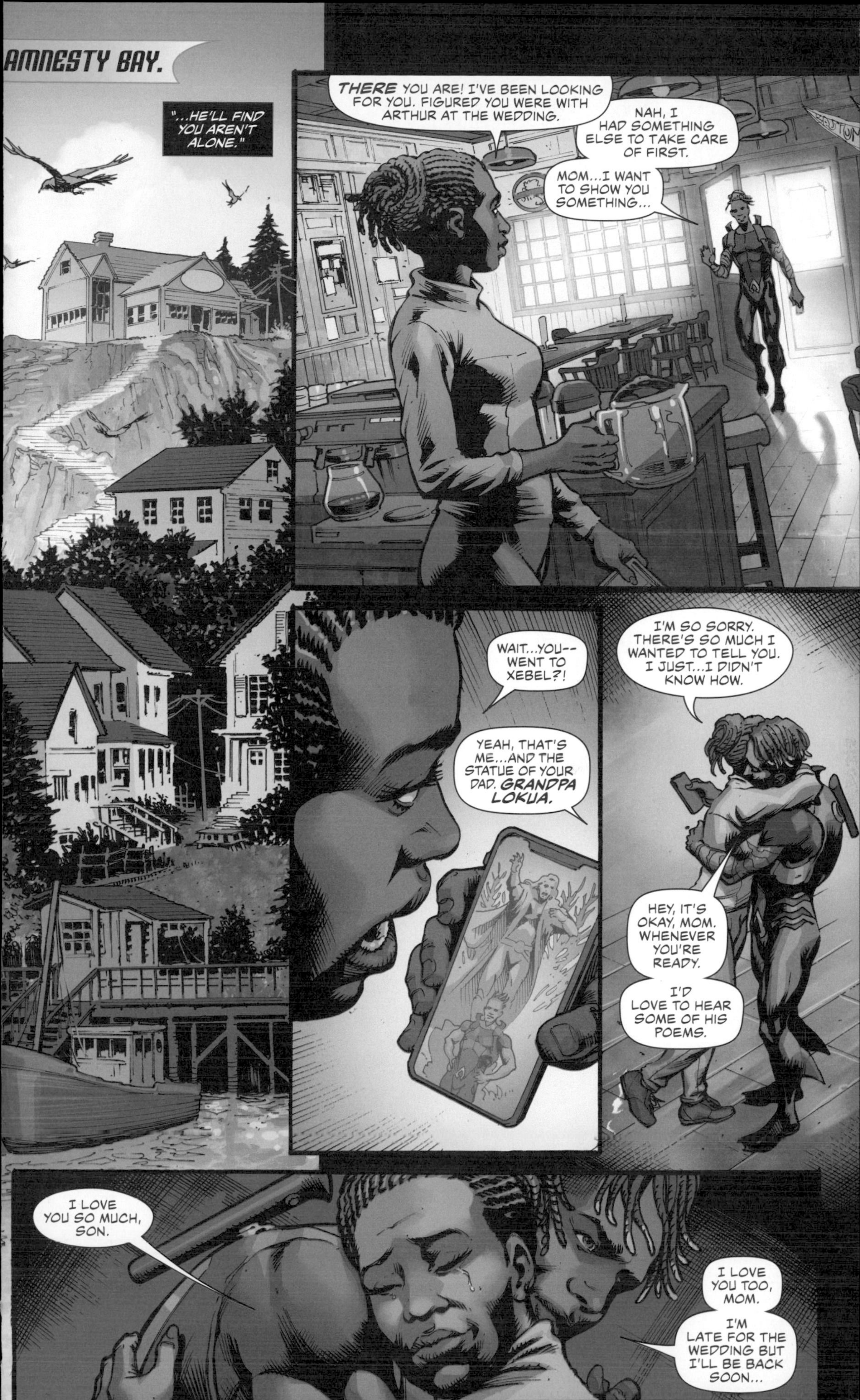
AMNESTY BAY.
"...HE'LL FIND YOU AREN'T ALONE."
THERE YOU ARE! I'VE BEEN LOOKING FOR YOU. FIGURED YOU WERE WITH ARTHUR AT THE WEDDING.
NAH, I HAD SOMETHING ELSE TO TAKE CARE OF FIRST.
MOM...I WANT TO SHOW YOU SOMETHING...
WAIT...YOU--WENT TO XEBEL?!
YEAH, THAT'S ME...AND THE STATUE OF YOUR DAD. GRANDPA LOKUA.
I'M SO SORRY. THERE'S SO MUCH I WANTED TO TELL YOU. I JUST...I DIDN'T KNOW HOW.
HEY, IT'S OKAY, MOM. WHENEVER YOU'RE READY.
I'D LOVE TO HEAR SOME OF HIS POEMS.
I LOVE YOU SO MUCH, SON.
I LOVE YOU TOO, MOM.
I'M LATE FOR THE WEDDING BUT I'LL BE BACK SOON...

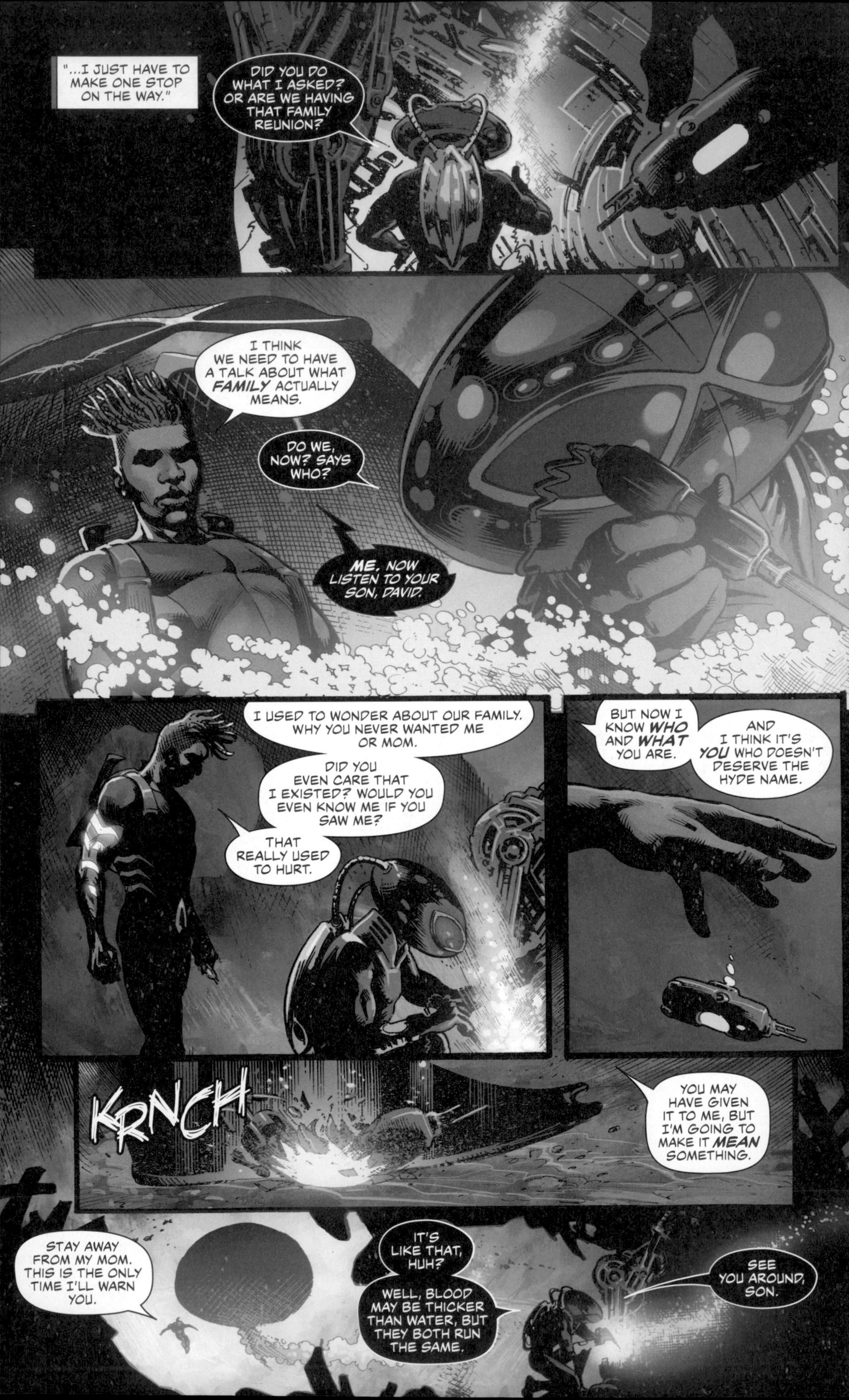
"...I JUST HAVE TO MAKE ONE STOP ON THE WAY."
DID YOU DO WHAT I ASKED? OR ARE WE HAVING THAT FAMILY REUNION?
I THINK WE NEED TO HAVE A TALK ABOUT WHAT FAMILY ACTUALLY MEANS.
DO WE, NOW? SAYS WHO?
ME. NOW LISTEN TO YOUR SON, DAVID.
I USED TO WONDER ABOUT OUR FAMILY. WHY YOU NEVER WANTED ME OR MOM.
DID YOU EVEN CARE THAT I EXISTED? WOULD YOU EVEN KNOW ME IF YOU SAW ME?
THAT REALLY USED TO HURT.
BUT NOW I KNOW WHO AND WHAT YOU ARE.
AND I THINK IT'S YOU WHO DOESN'T DESERVE THE HYDE NAME.
KRNCH
YOU MAY HAVE GIVEN IT TO ME, BUT I'M GOING TO MAKE IT MEAN SOMETHING.
STAY AWAY FROM MY MOM. THIS IS THE ONLY TIME I'LL WARN YOU.
IT'S LIKE THAT, HUH?
WELL, BLOOD MAY BE THICKER THAN WATER, BUT THEY BOTH RUN THE SAME.
SEE YOU AROUND, SON.

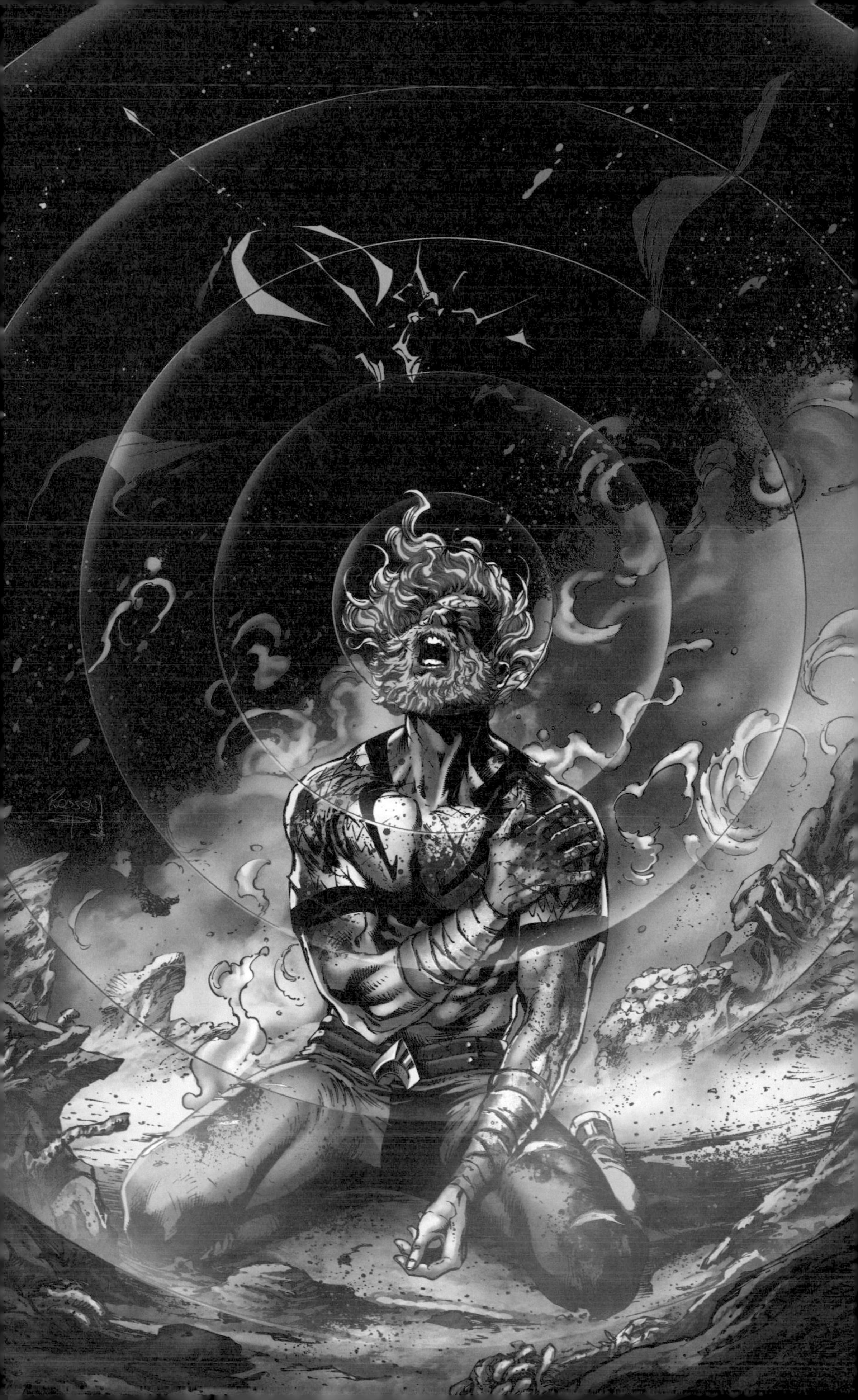

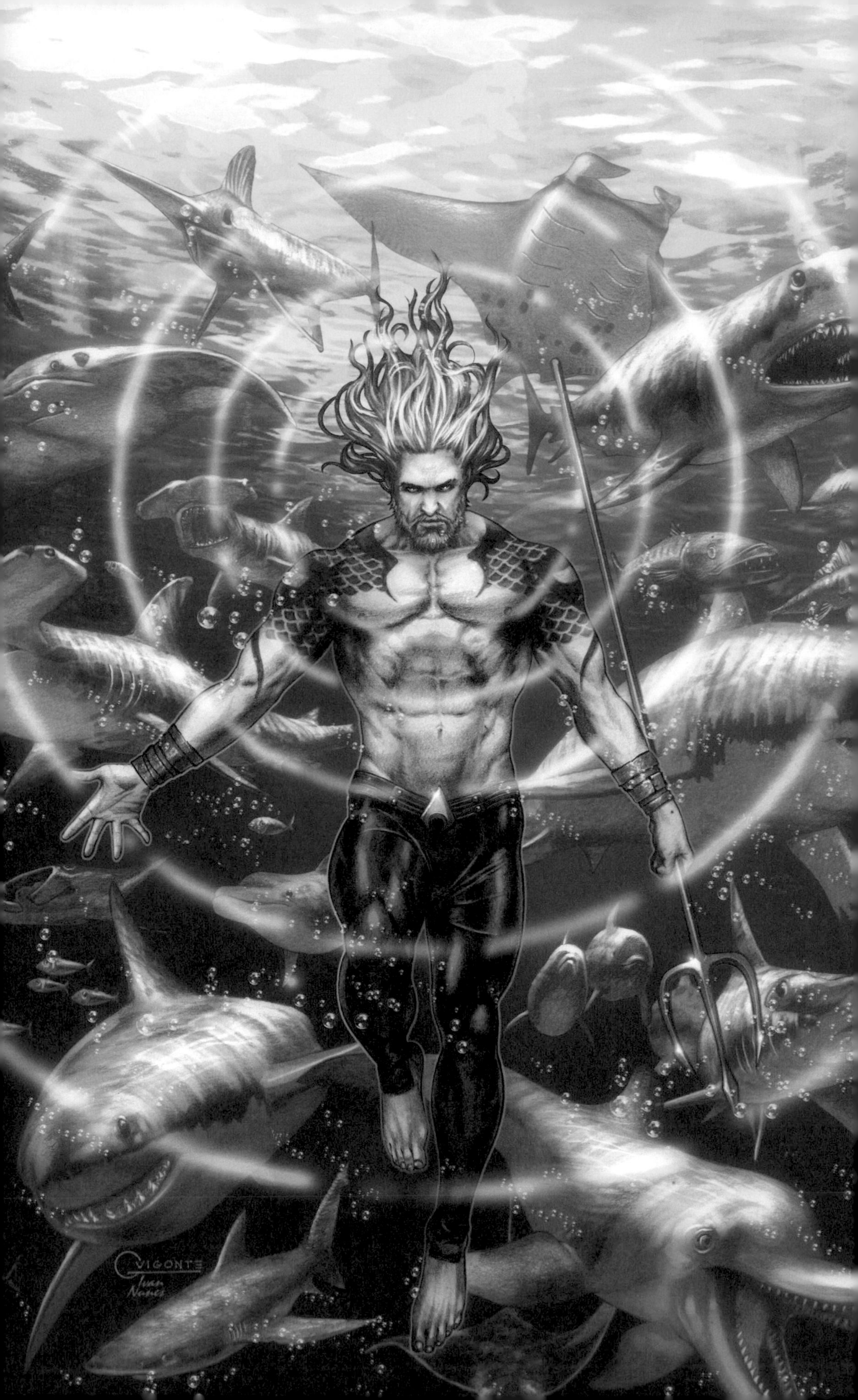
VIGONTE

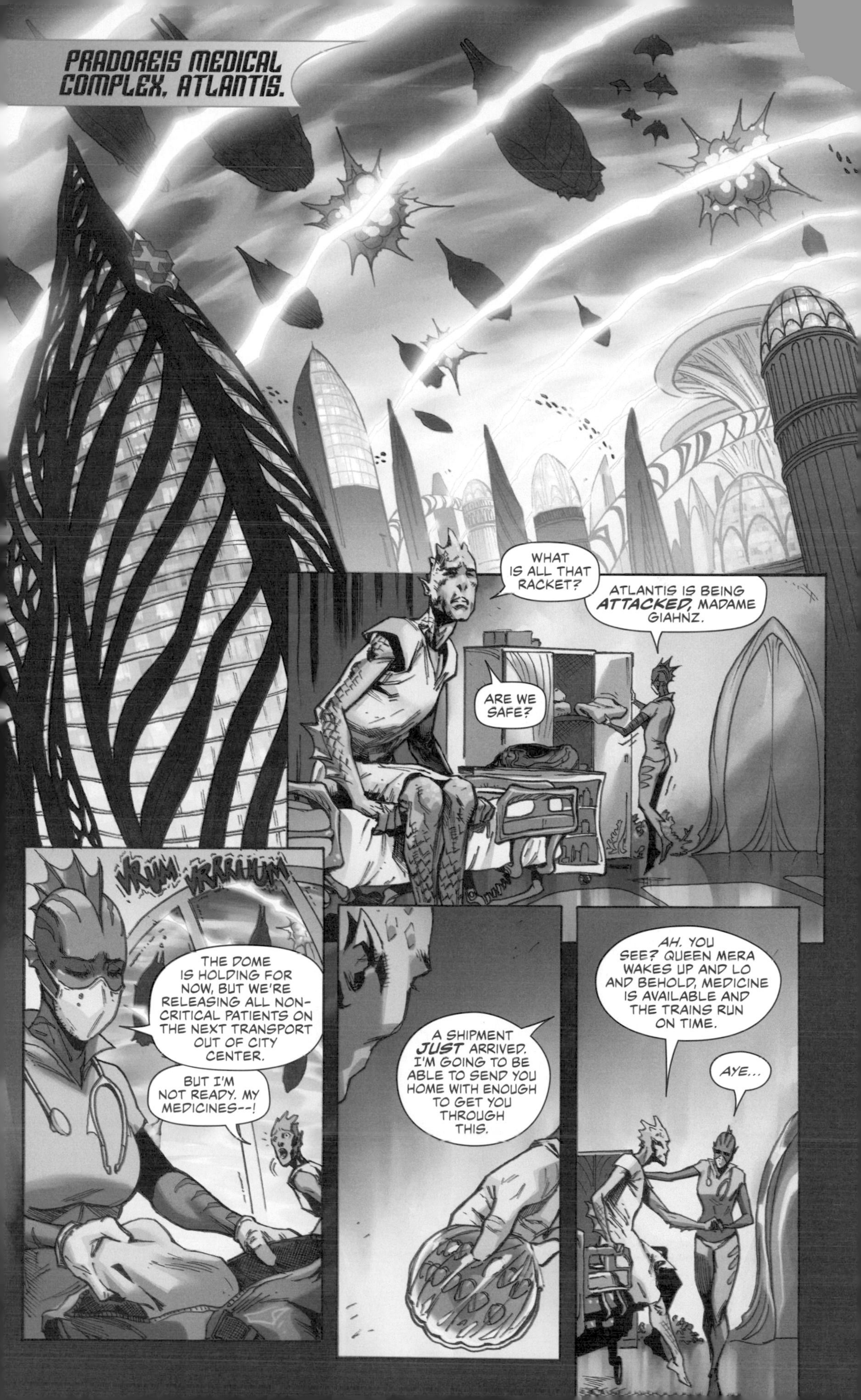
PRADOREIS MEDICAL COMPLEX, ATLANTIS.
WHAT IS ALL THAT RACKET?
ATLANTIS IS BEING ATTACKED, MADAME GIAHNZ.
ARE WE SAFE?
VRUM! VRRRUUM
THE DOME IS HOLDING FOR NOW, BUT WE'RE RELEASING ALL NON-CRITICAL PATIENTS ON THE NEXT TRANSPORT OUT OF CITY CENTER.
BUT I'M NOT READY. MY MEDICINES--!
A SHIPMENT JUST ARRIVED. I'M GOING TO BE ABLE TO SEND YOU HOME WITH ENOUGH TO GET YOU THROUGH THIS.
AH. YOU SEE? QUEEN MERA WAKES UP AND LO AND BEHOLD, MEDICINE IS AVAILABLE AND THE TRAINS RUN ON TIME.
AYE...

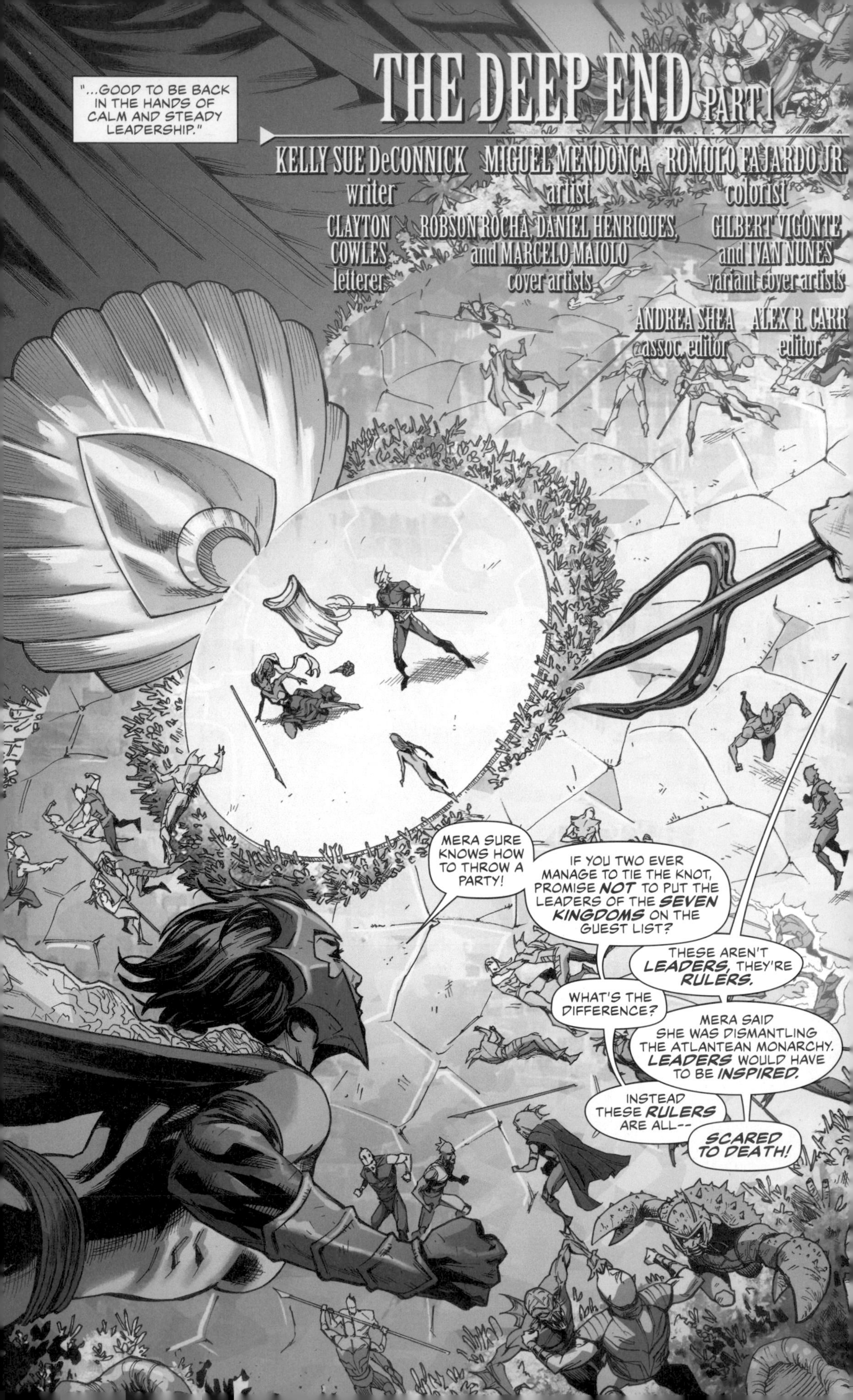
"...GOOD TO BE BACK IN THE HANDS OF CALM AND STEADY LEADERSHIP."
THE DEEP END PART 1
KELLY SUE DeCONNICK writer
MIGUEL MENDONÇA artist
ROMULO FAJARDO JR. colorist
CLAYTON COWLES letterer
ROBSON ROCHA, DANIEL HENRIQUES, and MARCELO MAIOLO cover artists
GILBERT VIGONTE and IVAN NUNES variant cover artists
ANDREA SHEA assoc. editor
ALEX R. CARR editor
MERA SURE KNOWS HOW TO THROW A PARTY!
IF YOU TWO EVER MANAGE TO TIE THE KNOT, PROMISE NOT TO PUT THE LEADERS OF THE SEVEN KINGDOMS ON THE GUEST LIST?
THESE AREN'T LEADERS, THEY'RE RULERS.
WHAT'S THE DIFFERENCE?
MERA SAID SHE WAS DISMANTLING THE ATLANTEAN MONARCHY. LEADERS WOULD HAVE TO BE INSPIRED.
INSTEAD THESE RULERS ARE ALL--
SCARED TO DEATH!

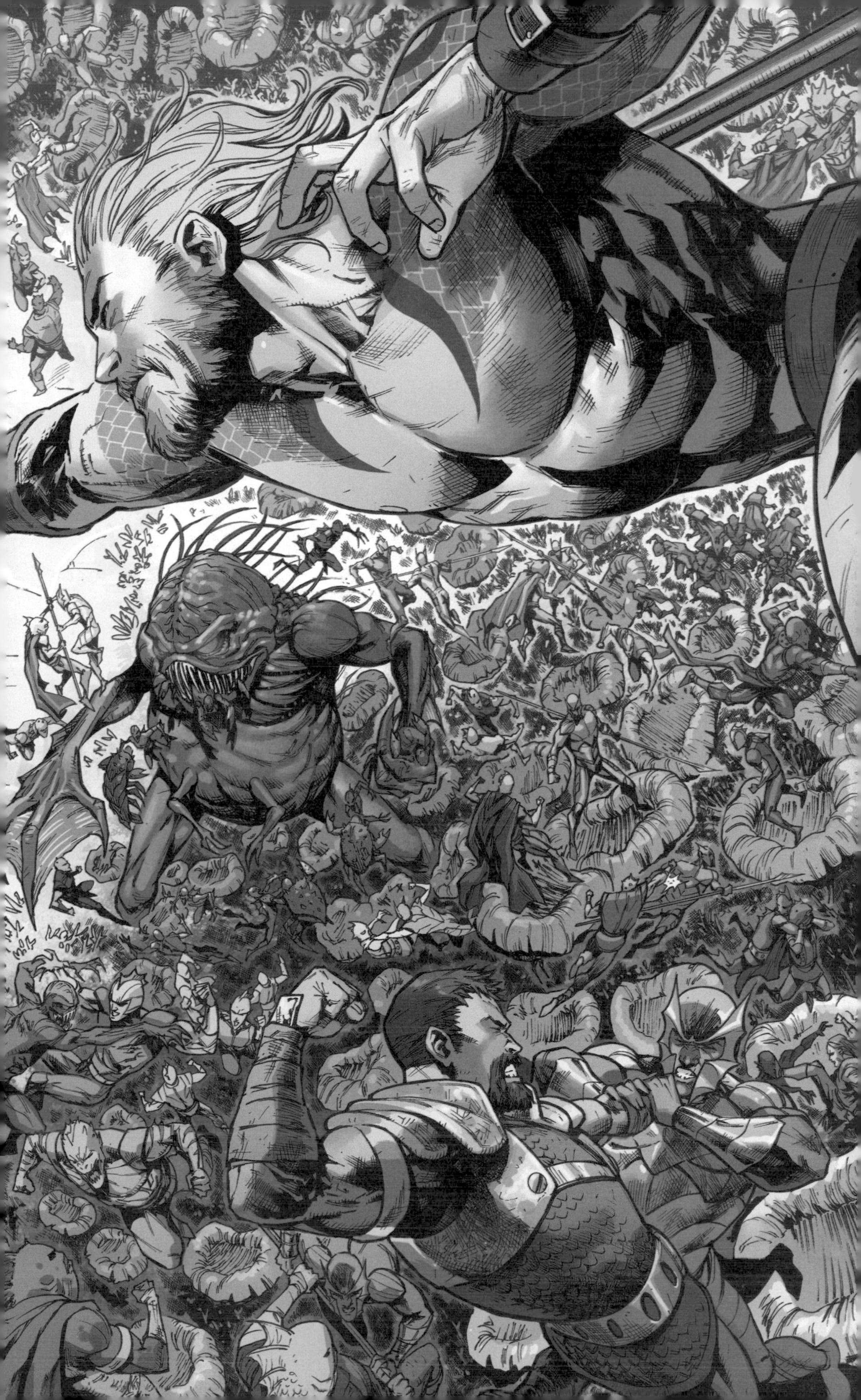

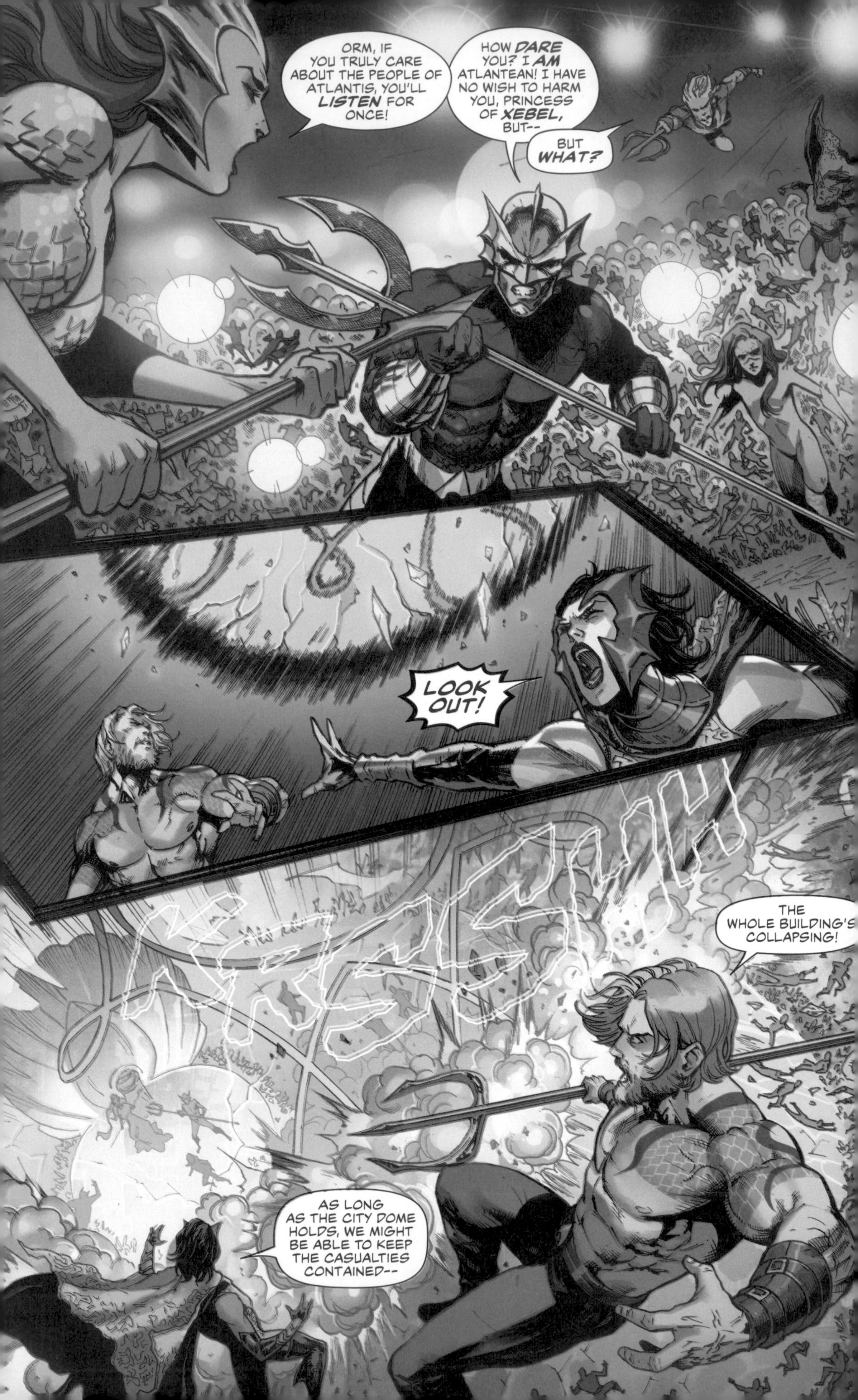
ORM, IF YOU TRULY CARE ABOUT THE PEOPLE OF ATLANTIS, YOU'LL LISTEN FOR ONCE!
HOW DARE YOU? I AM ATLANTEAN! I HAVE NO WISH TO HARM YOU, PRINCESS OF XEBEL, BUT--
BUT WHAT?
LOOK OUT!
KRASSH!
THE WHOLE BUILDING'S COLLAPSING!
AS LONG AS THE CITY DOME HOLDS, WE MIGHT BE ABLE TO KEEP THE CASUALTIES CONTAINED--

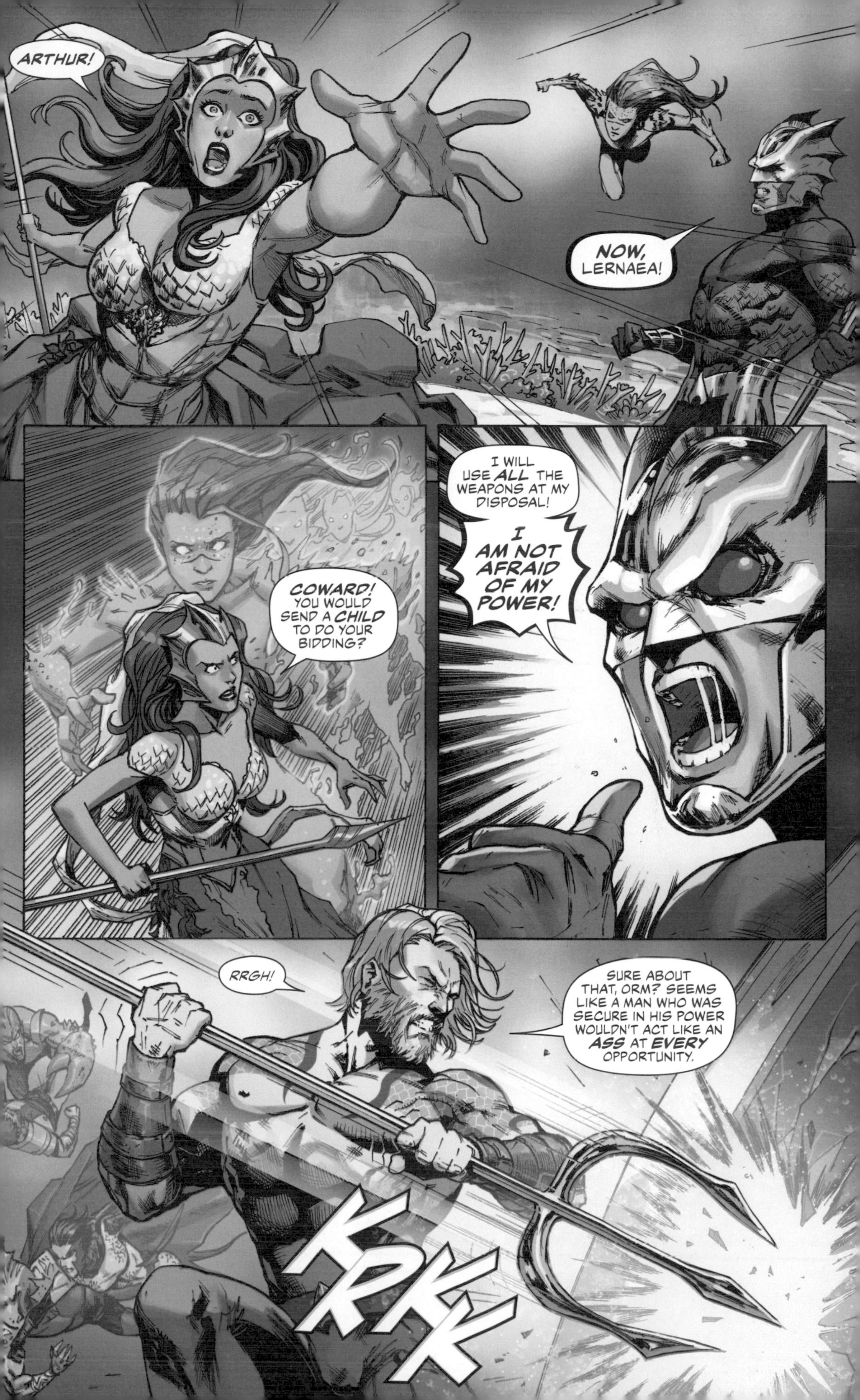
ARTHUR!
NOW, LERNAEA!
COWARD! YOU WOULD SEND A CHILD TO DO YOUR BIDDING?
I WILL USE ALL THE WEAPONS AT MY DISPOSAL!
I AM NOT AFRAID OF MY POWER!
RRGH!
SURE ABOUT THAT, ORM? SEEMS LIKE A MAN WHO WAS SECURE IN HIS POWER WOULDN'T ACT LIKE AN ASS AT EVERY OPPORTUNITY.
KRKK

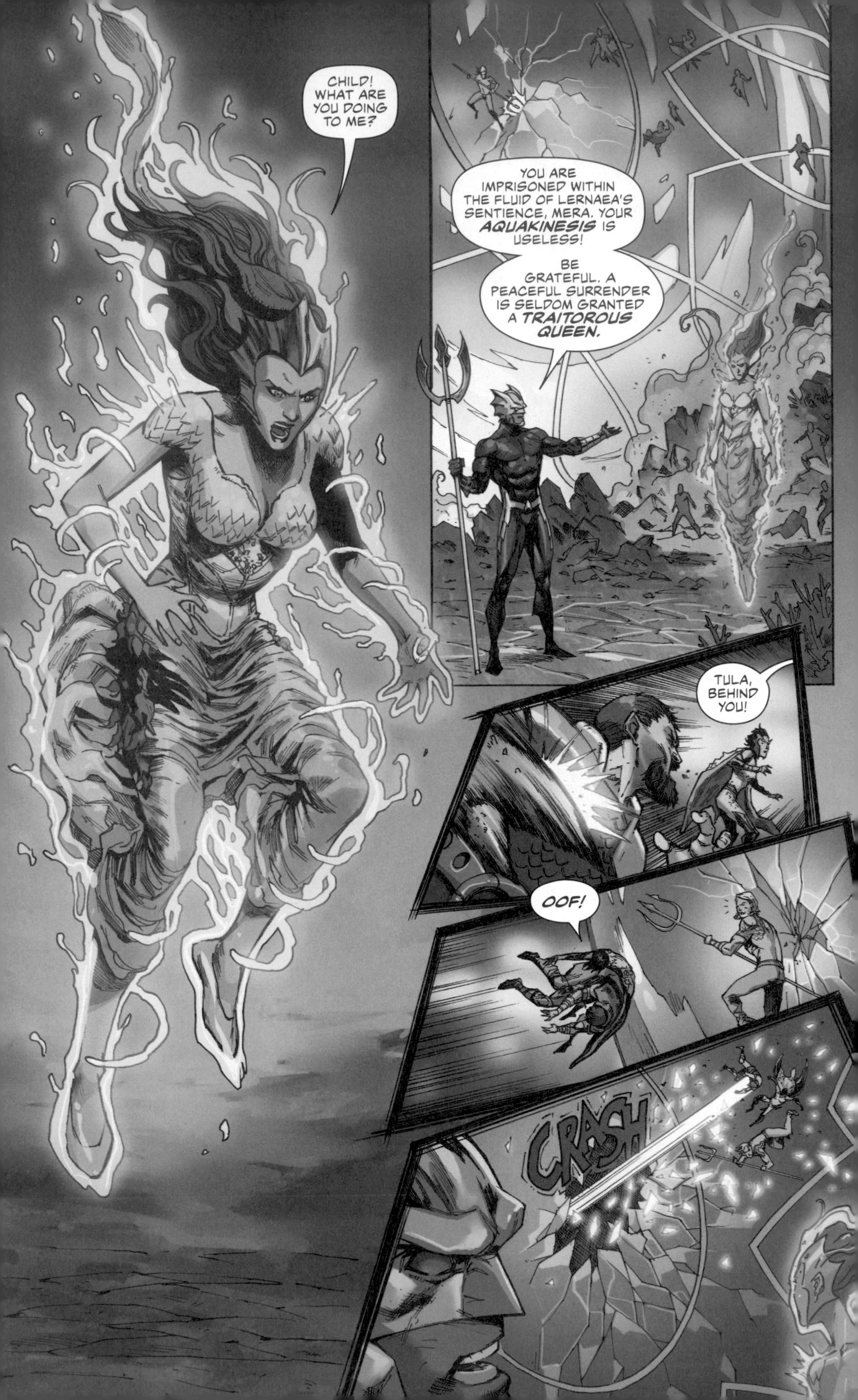
CHILD! WHAT ARE YOU DOING TO ME?
YOU ARE IMPRISONED WITHIN THE FLUID OF LERNAEA'S SENTIENCE, MERA. YOUR AQUAKINESIS IS USELESS!
BE GRATEFUL. A PEACEFUL SURRENDER IS SELDOM GRANTED A TRAITOROUS QUEEN.
TULA, BEHIND YOU!
OOF!
CRASH

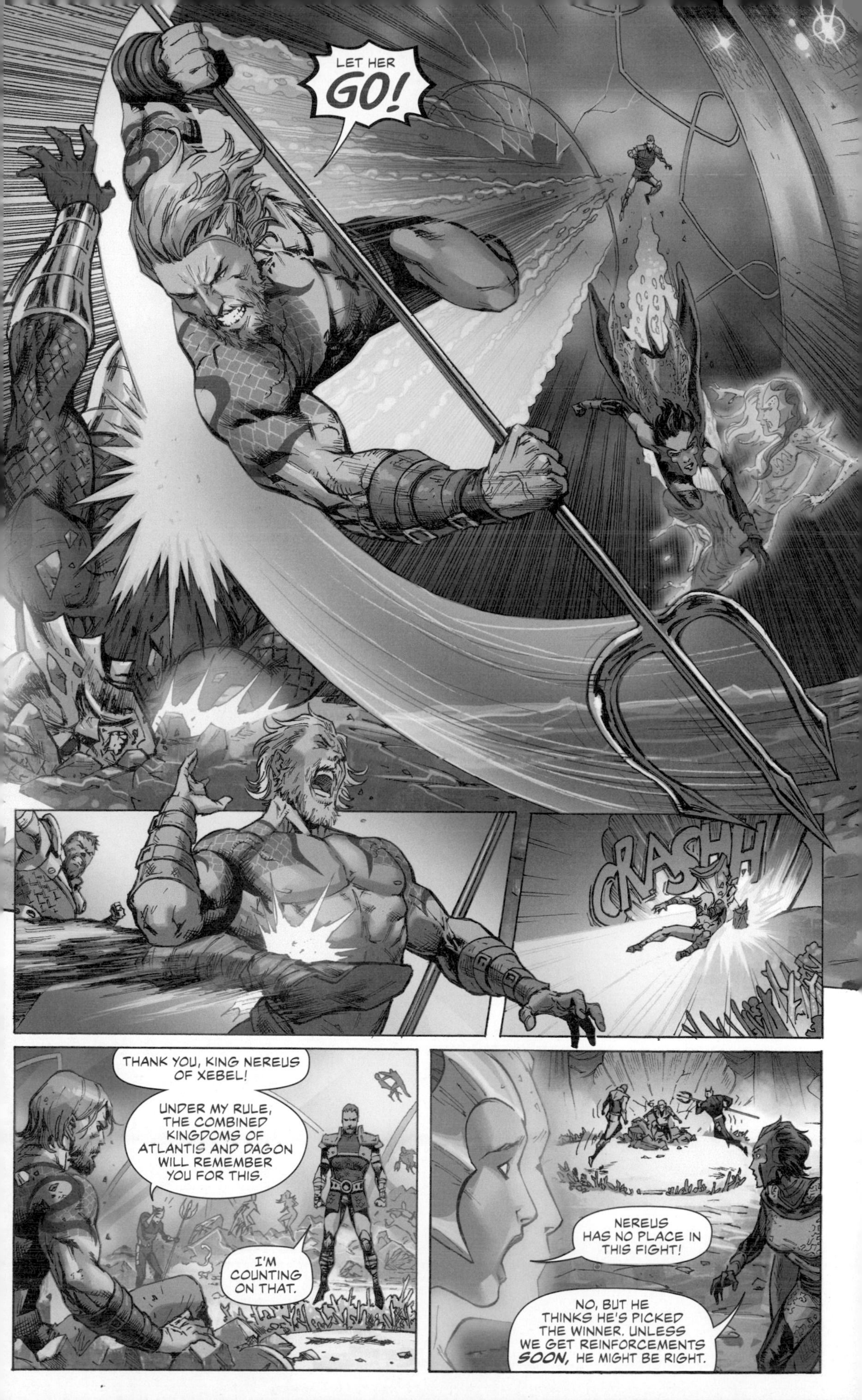
LET HER GO!
CRASHH
THANK YOU, KING NEREUS OF XEBEL!
UNDER MY RULE, THE COMBINED KINGDOMS OF ATLANTIS AND DAGON WILL REMEMBER YOU FOR THIS.
I'M COUNTING ON THAT.
NEREUS HAS NO PLACE IN THIS FIGHT!
NO, BUT HE THINKS HE'S PICKED THE WINNER. UNLESS WE GET REINFORCEMENTS SOON, HE MIGHT BE RIGHT.

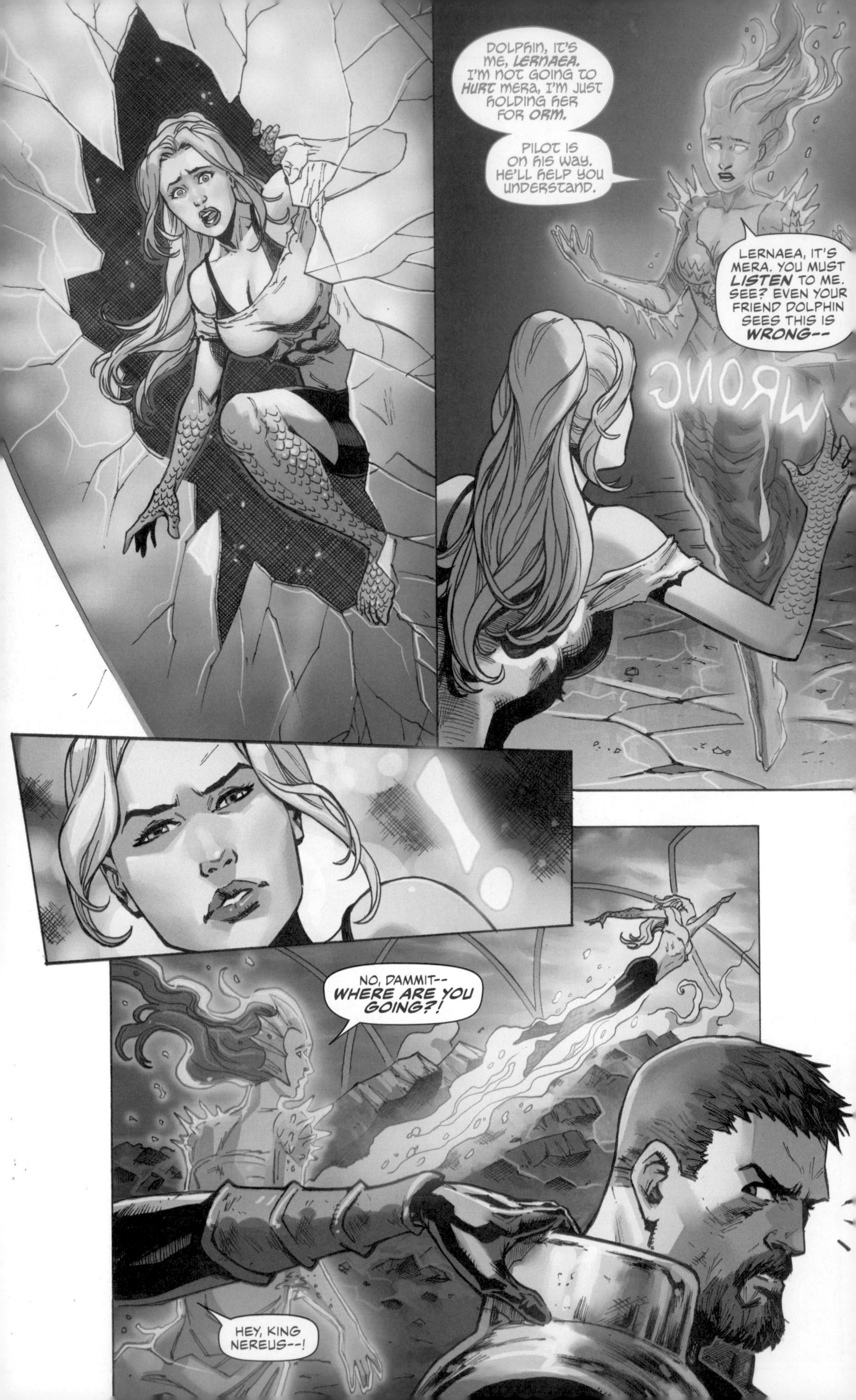
DOLPHIN, IT'S ME, LERNAEA. I'M NOT GOING TO HURT MERA, I'M JUST HOLDING HER FOR ORM.
PILOT IS ON HIS WAY. HE'LL HELP YOU UNDERSTAND.
LERNAEA, IT'S MERA. YOU MUST LISTEN TO ME. SEE? EVEN YOUR FRIEND DOLPHIN SEES THIS IS WRONG--
NO, DAMMIT-- WHERE ARE YOU GOING?!
HEY, KING NEREUS--!

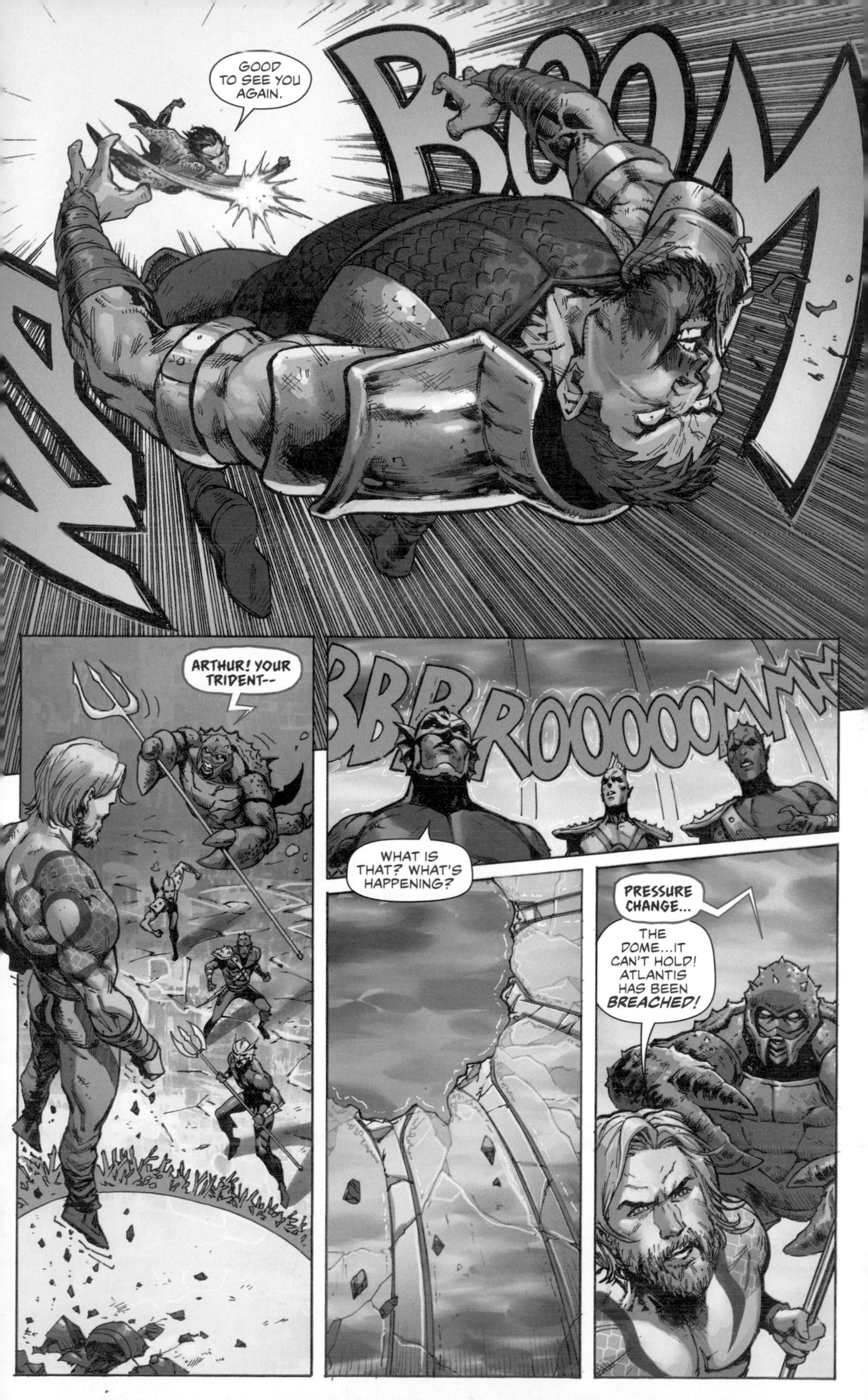
GOOD TO SEE YOU AGAIN.
BOOOM
ARTHUR! YOUR TRIDENT--
BBBROOOOOMM
WHAT IS THAT? WHAT'S HAPPENING?
PRESSURE CHANGE...
THE DOME...IT CAN'T HOLD! ATLANTIS HAS BEEN BREACHED!

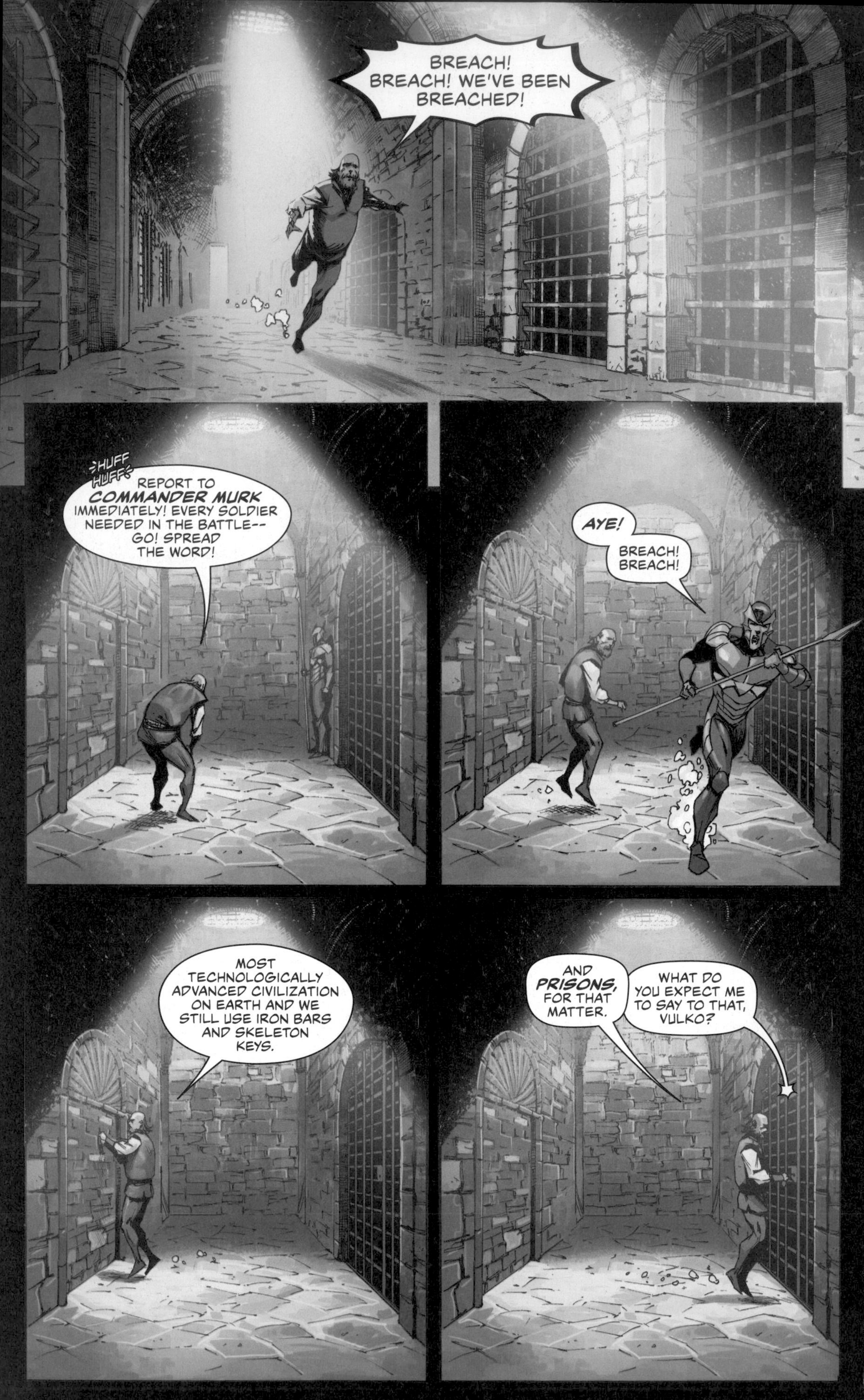
BREACH! BREACH! WE'VE BEEN BREACHED!
HUFF HUFF
REPORT TO COMMANDER MURK IMMEDIATELY! EVERY SOLDIER NEEDED IN THE BATTLE-- GO! SPREAD THE WORD!
AYE!
BREACH! BREACH!
MOST TECHNOLOGICALLY ADVANCED CIVILIZATION ON EARTH AND WE STILL USE IRON BARS AND SKELETON KEYS.
AND PRISONS, FOR THAT MATTER.
WHAT DO YOU EXPECT ME TO SAY TO THAT, VULKO?

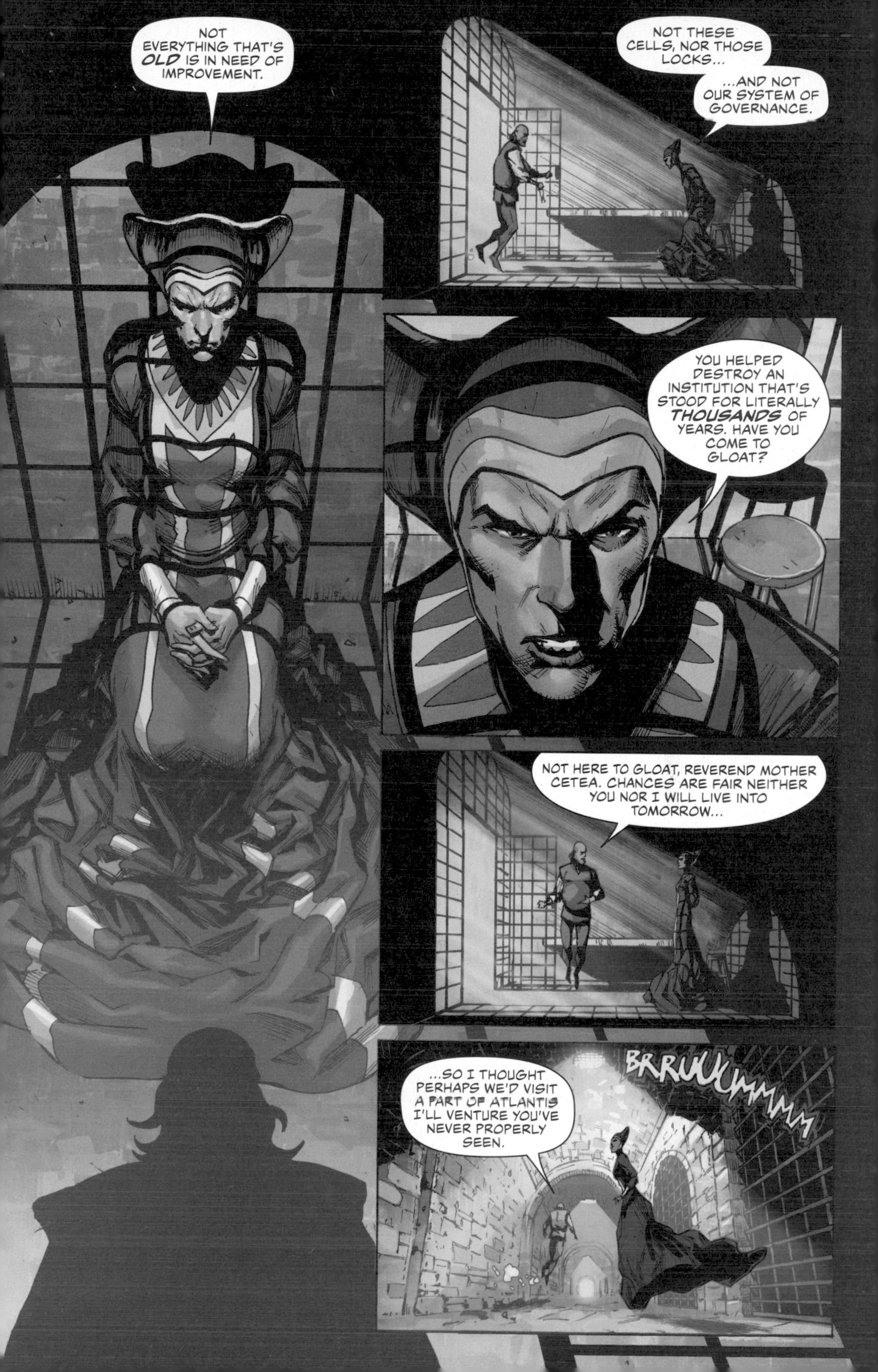
NOT EVERYTHING THAT'S OLD IS IN NEED OF IMPROVEMENT.
NOT THESE CELLS, NOR THOSE LOCKS...
...AND NOT OUR SYSTEM OF GOVERNANCE.
YOU HELPED DESTROY AN INSTITUTION THAT'S STOOD FOR LITERALLY THOUSANDS OF YEARS. HAVE YOU COME TO GLOAT?
NOT HERE TO GLOAT, REVEREND MOTHER CETEA. CHANCES ARE FAIR NEITHER YOU NOR I WILL LIVE INTO TOMORROW...
BRRUUUMMMM
...SO I THOUGHT PERHAPS WE'D VISIT A PART OF ATLANTIS I'LL VENTURE YOU'VE NEVER PROPERLY SEEN.

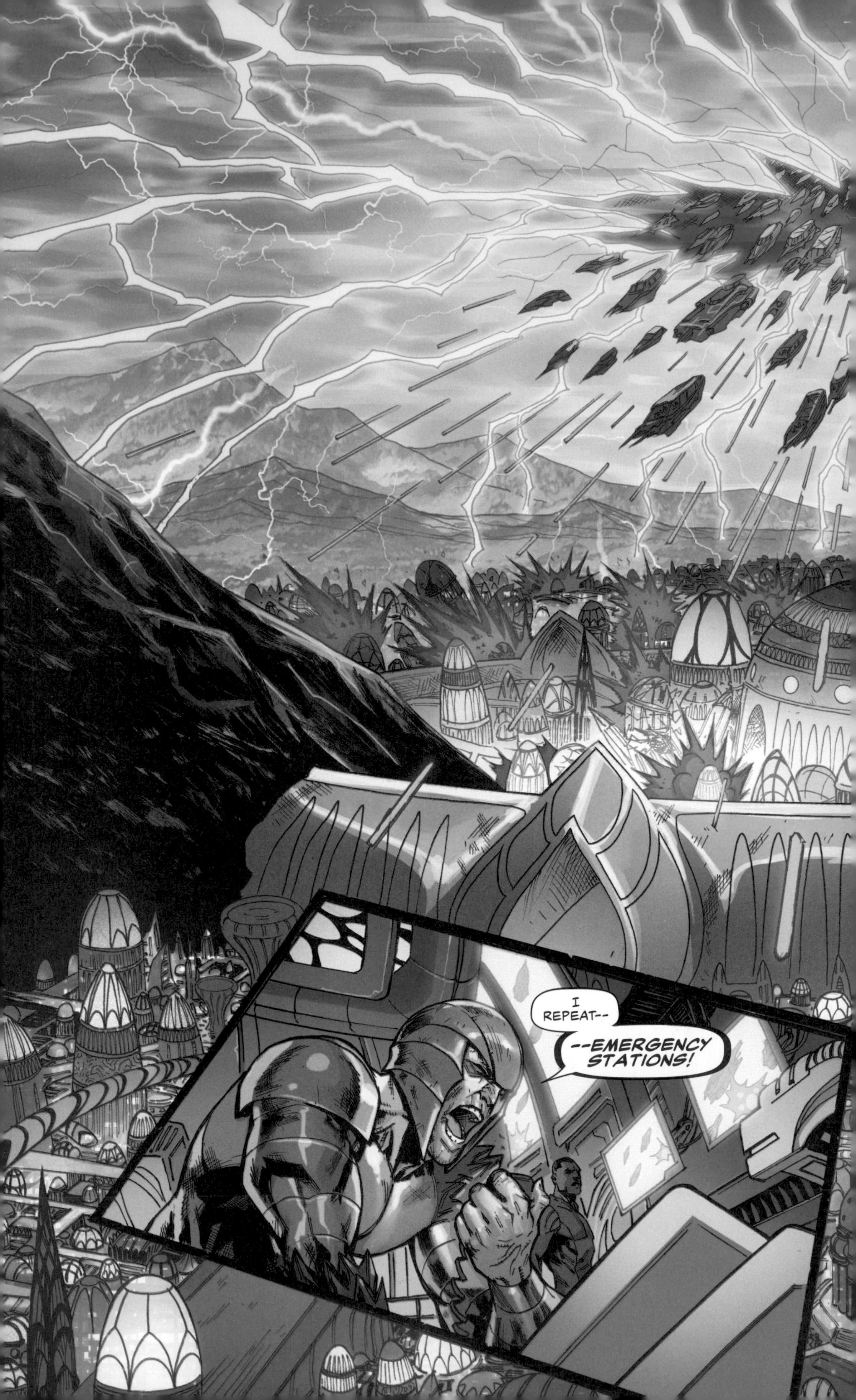
I REPEAT--
--EMERGENCY STATIONS!

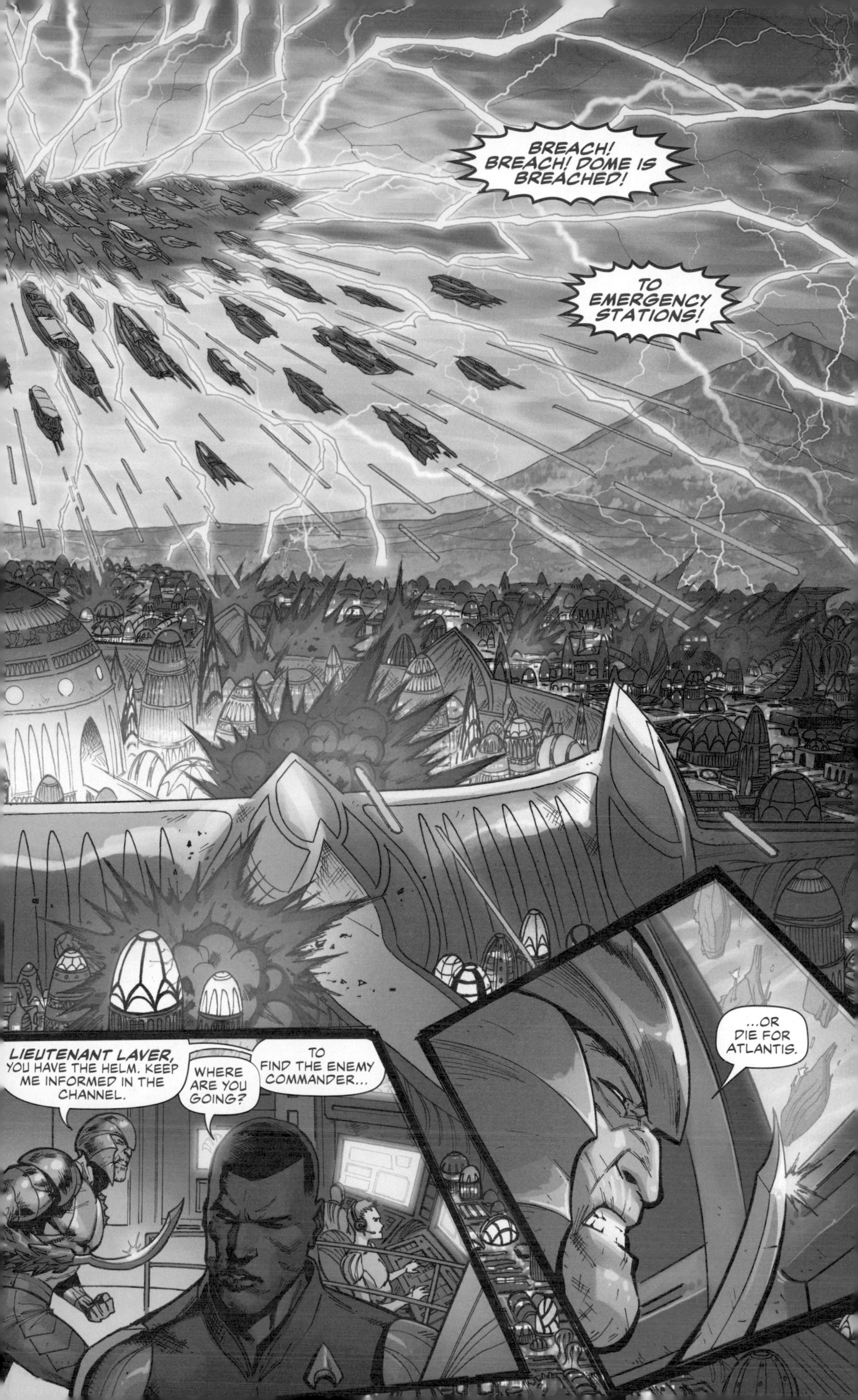
BREACH! BREACH! DOME IS BREACHED!
TO EMERGENCY STATIONS!
LIEUTENANT LAVER, YOU HAVE THE HELM. KEEP ME INFORMED IN THE CHANNEL.
WHERE ARE YOU GOING?
TO FIND THE ENEMY COMMANDER...
...OR DIE FOR ATLANTIS.

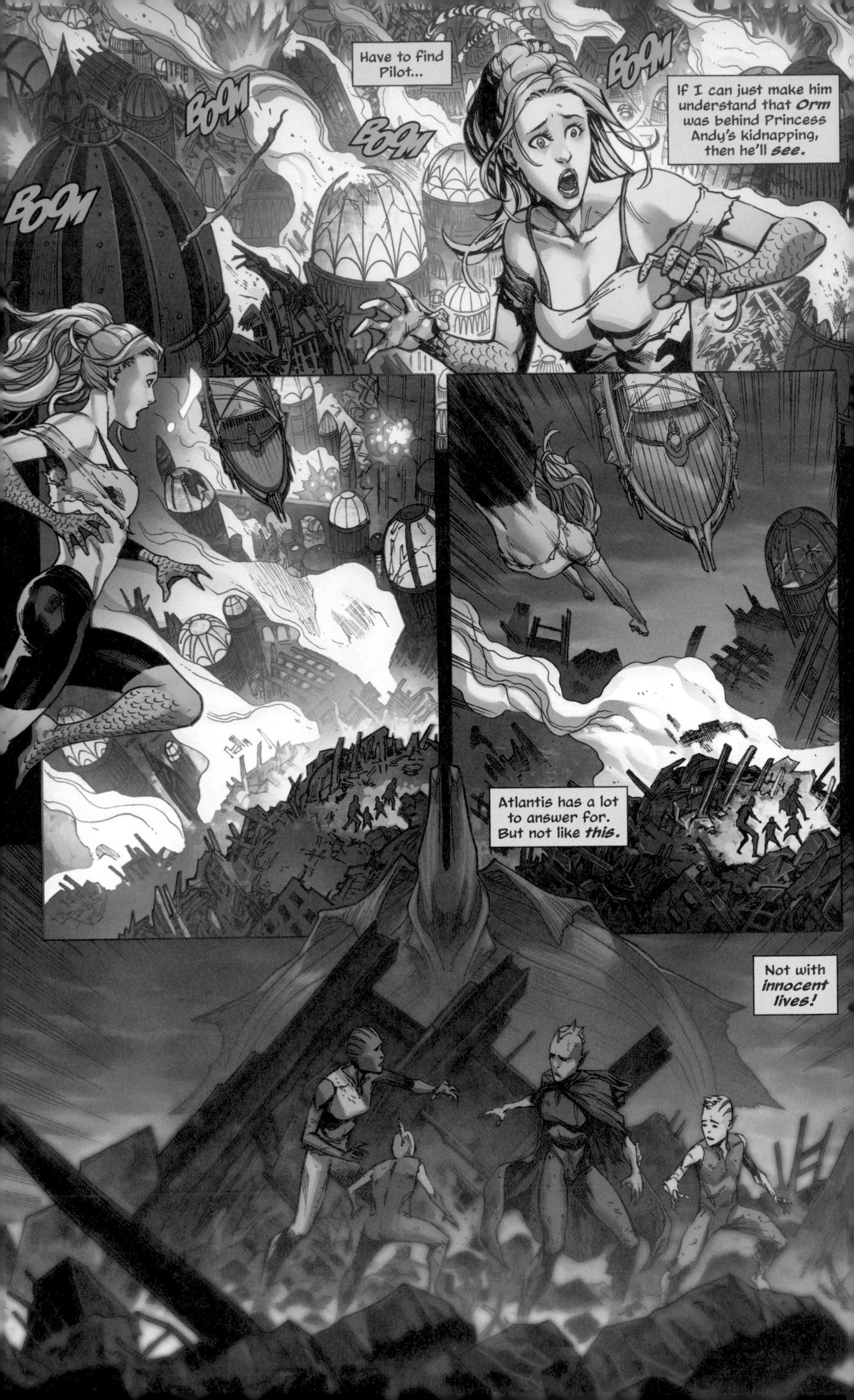
Have to find Pilot...
BOOM
BOOM
BOOM
BOOM
If I can just make him understand that Orm was behind Princess Andy's kidnapping, then he'll see.
Atlantis has a lot to answer for. But not like this.
Not with innocent lives!

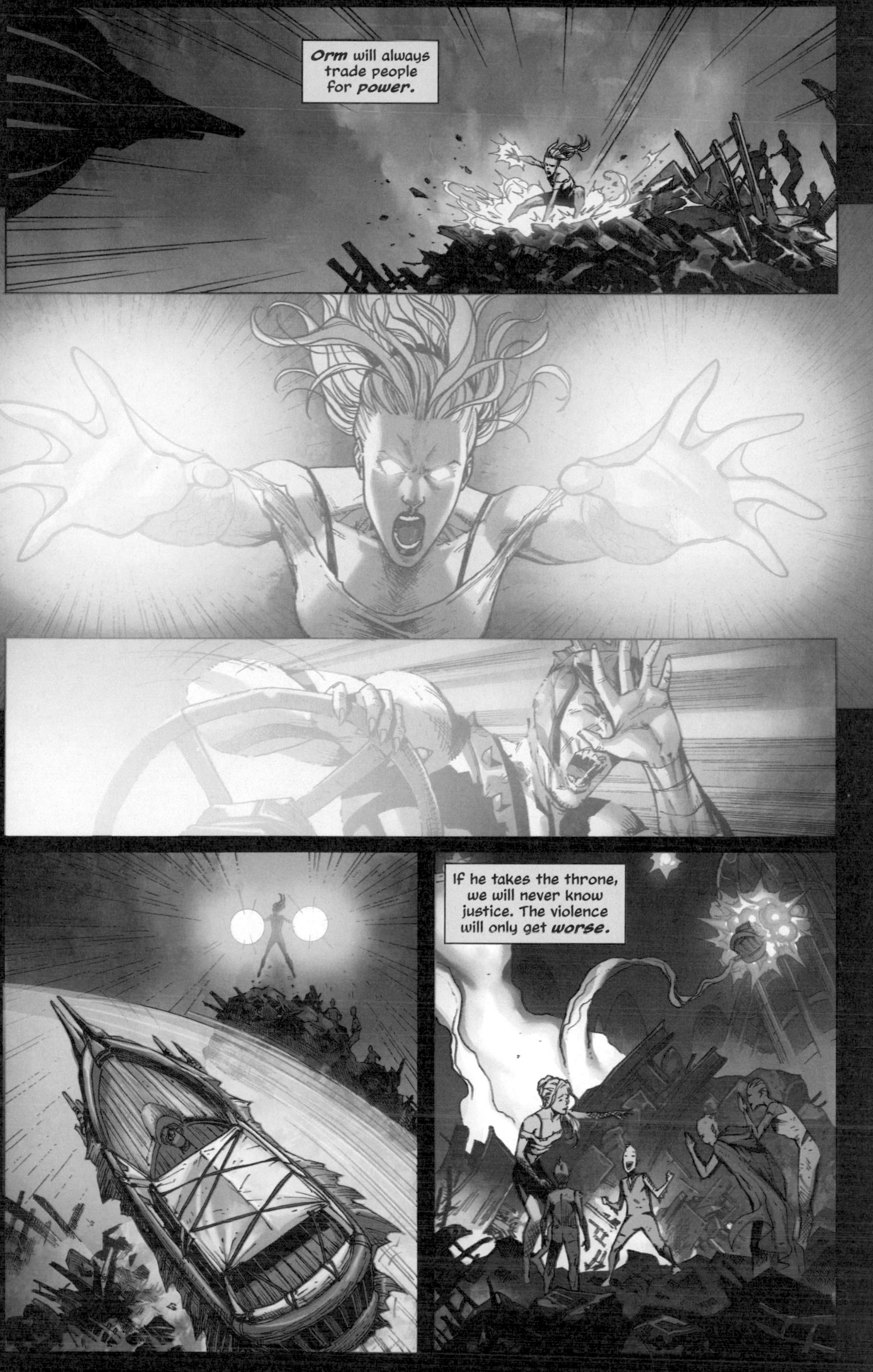
Orm will always trade people for power.
If he takes the throne, we will never know justice. The violence will only get worse.

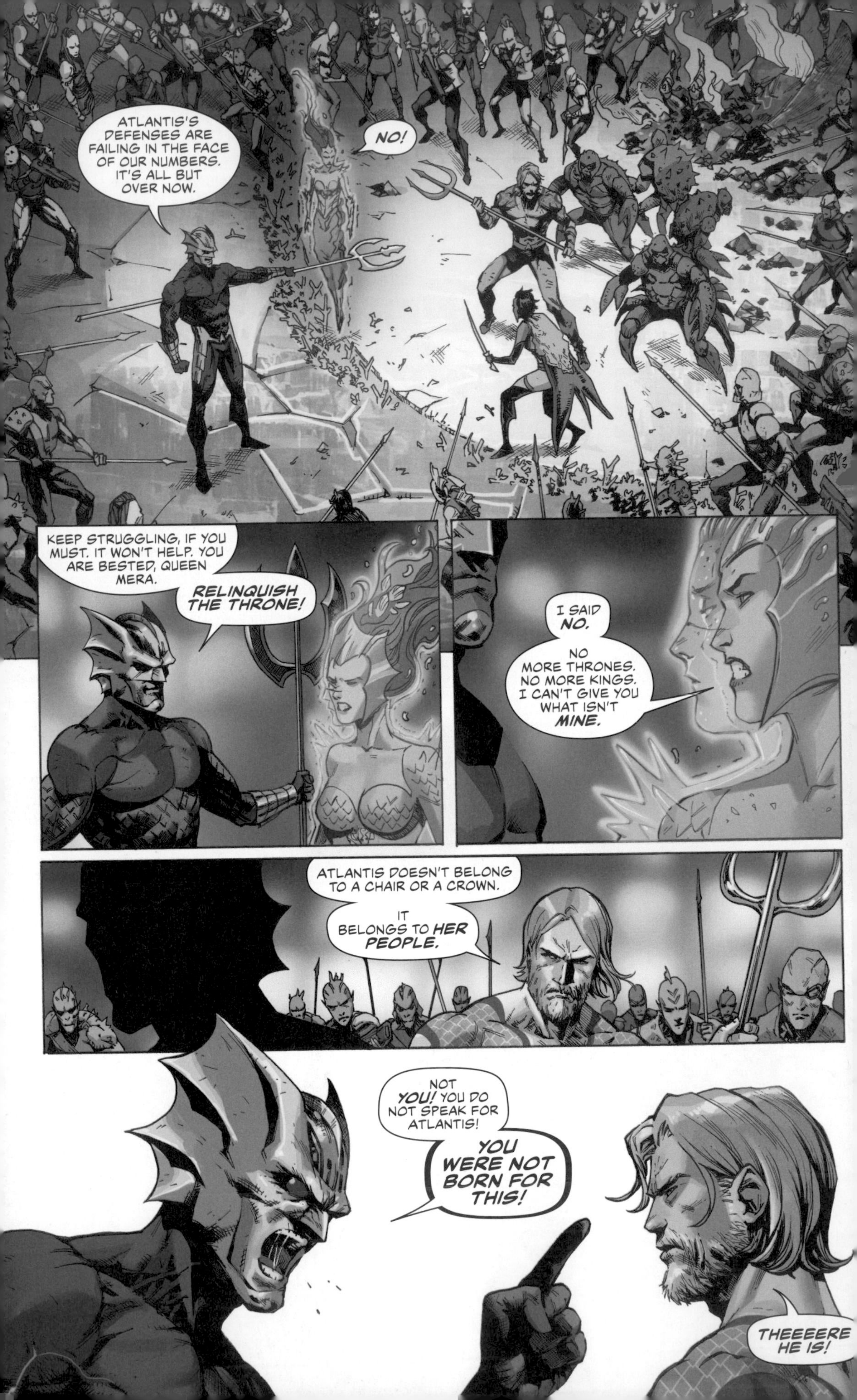
ATLANTIS'S DEFENSES ARE FAILING IN THE FACE OF OUR NUMBERS. IT'S ALL BUT OVER NOW.
NO!
KEEP STRUGGLING, IF YOU MUST. IT WON'T HELP. YOU ARE BESTED, QUEEN MERA.
RELINQUISH THE THRONE!
I SAID NO.
NO MORE THRONES. NO MORE KINGS. I CAN'T GIVE YOU WHAT ISN'T MINE.
ATLANTIS DOESN'T BELONG TO A CHAIR OR A CROWN.
IT BELONGS TO HER PEOPLE.
NOT YOU! YOU DO NOT SPEAK FOR ATLANTIS!
YOU WERE NOT BORN FOR THIS!
THEEEERE HE IS!

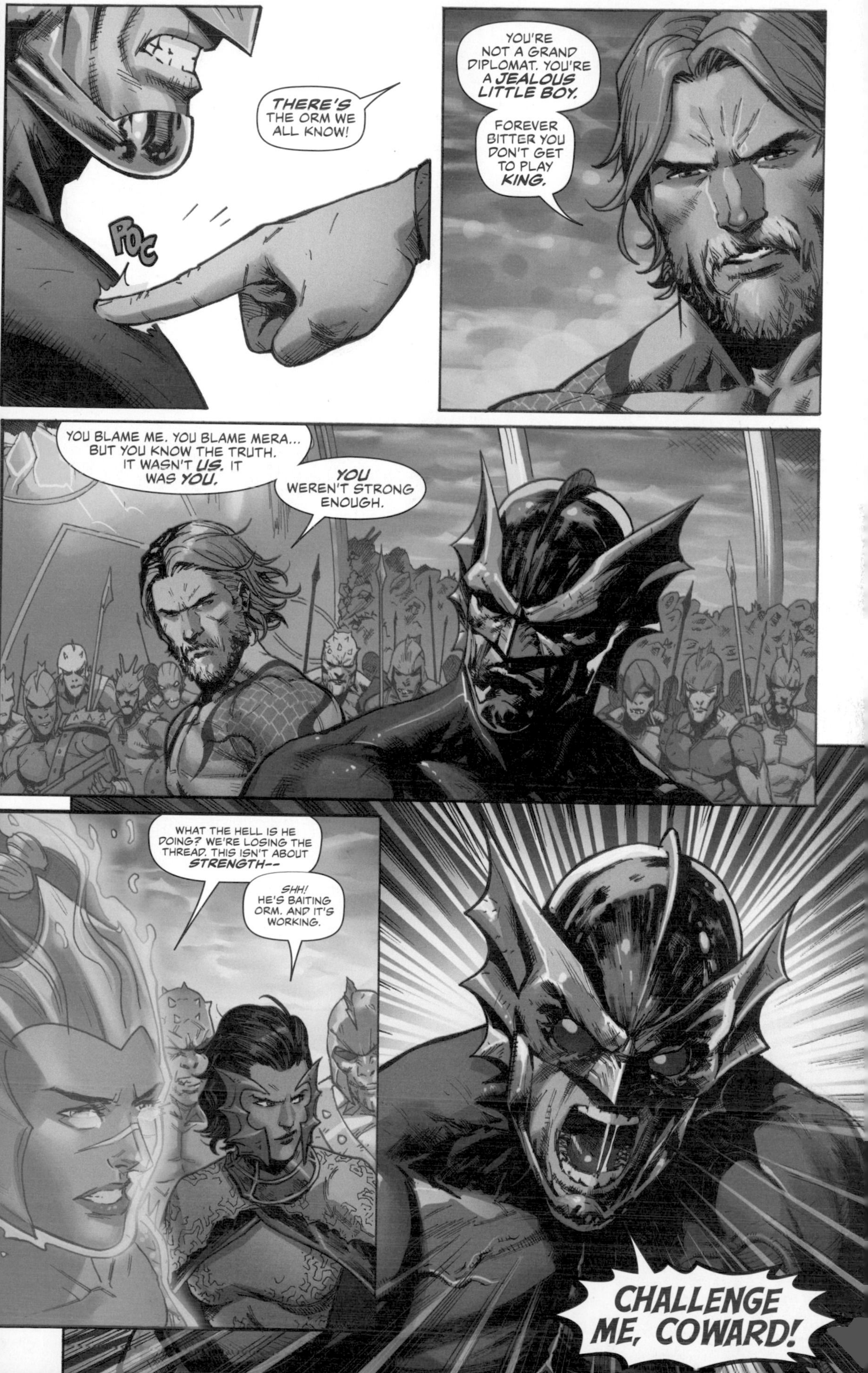
THERE'S THE ORM WE ALL KNOW!
POC
YOU'RE NOT A GRAND DIPLOMAT. YOU'RE A JEALOUS LITTLE BOY.
FOREVER BITTER YOU DON'T GET TO PLAY KING.
YOU BLAME ME. YOU BLAME MERA... BUT YOU KNOW THE TRUTH. IT WASN'T US. IT WAS YOU.
YOU WEREN'T STRONG ENOUGH.
WHAT THE HELL IS HE DOING? WE'RE LOSING THE THREAD. THIS ISN'T ABOUT STRENGTH--
SHH! HE'S BAITING ORM. AND IT'S WORKING.
CHALLENGE ME, COWARD!

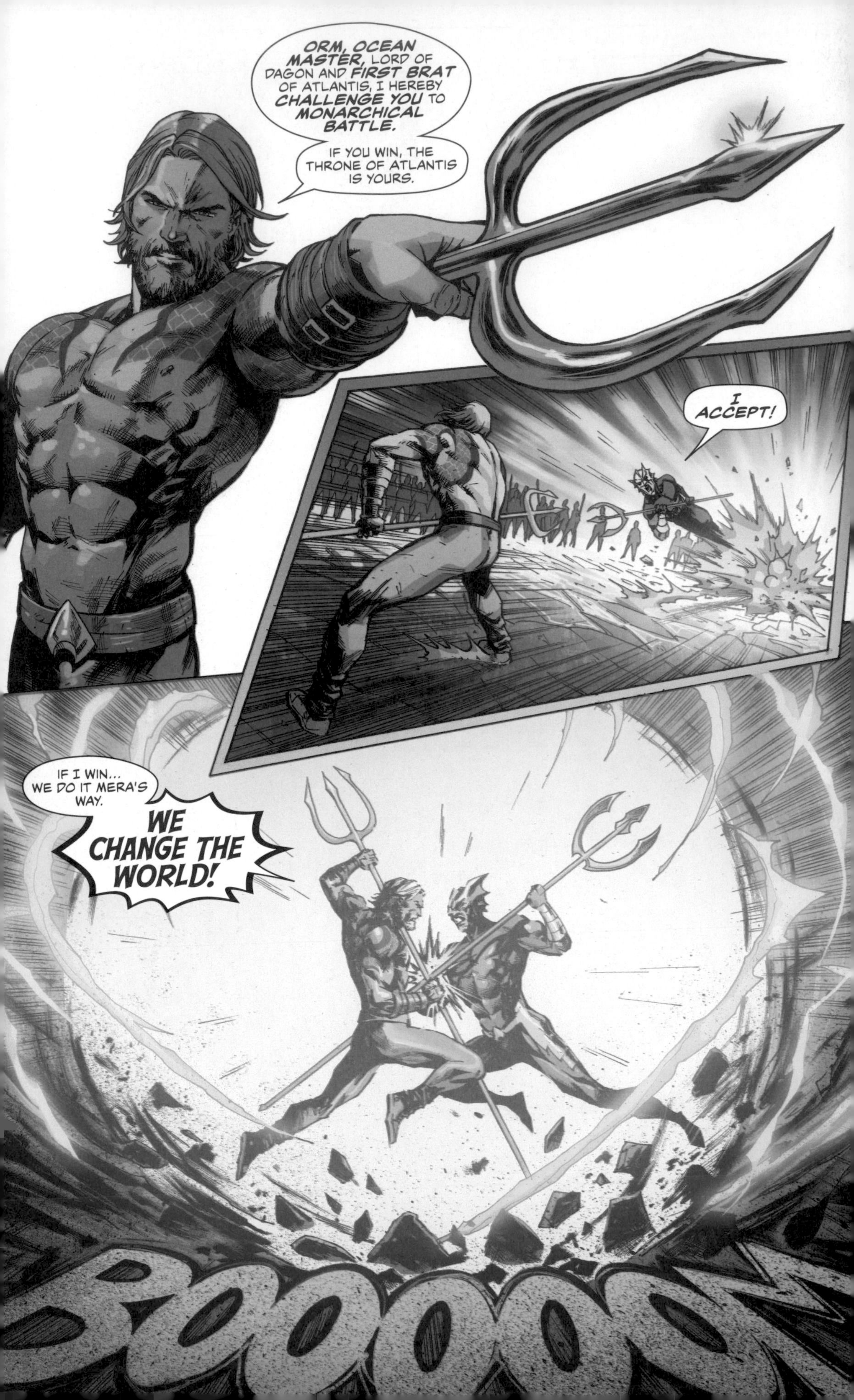
ORM, OCEAN MASTER, LORD OF DAGON AND FIRST BRAT OF ATLANTIS, I HEREBY CHALLENGE YOU TO MONARCHICAL BATTLE.
IF YOU WIN, THE THRONE OF ATLANTIS IS YOURS.
I ACCEPT!
IF I WIN... WE DO IT MERA'S WAY.
WE CHANGE THE WORLD!

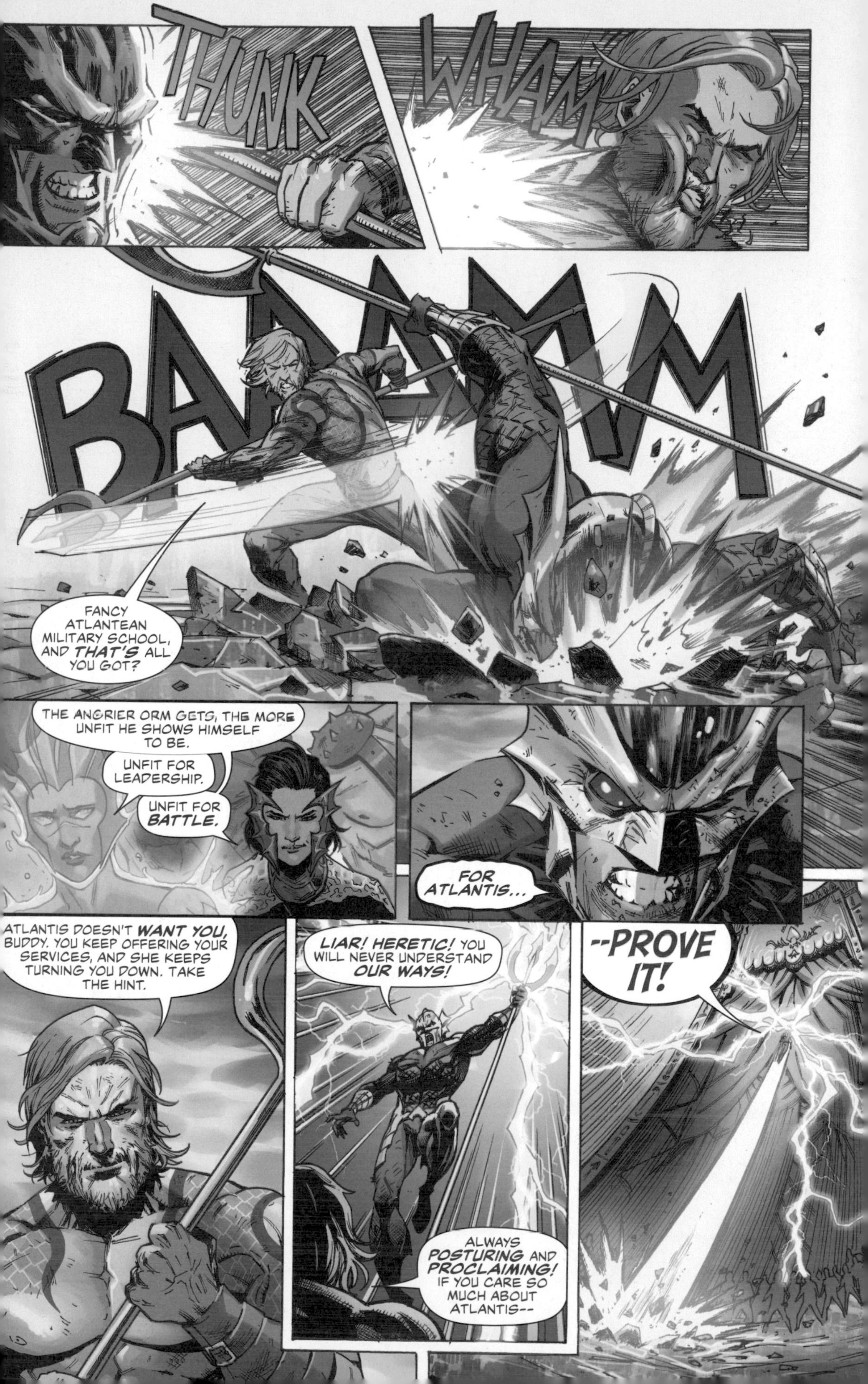
THUNK
WHAM
FANCY ATLANTEAN MILITARY SCHOOL, AND THAT'S ALL YOU GOT?
THE ANGRIER ORM GETS, THE MORE UNFIT HE SHOWS HIMSELF TO BE.
UNFIT FOR LEADERSHIP.
UNFIT FOR BATTLE.
FOR ATLANTIS...
ATLANTIS DOESN'T WANT YOU, BUDDY. YOU KEEP OFFERING YOUR SERVICES, AND SHE KEEPS TURNING YOU DOWN. TAKE THE HINT.
LIAR! HERETIC! YOU WILL NEVER UNDERSTAND OUR WAYS!
ALWAYS POSTURING AND PROCLAIMING! IF YOU CARE SO MUCH ABOUT ATLANTIS--
--PROVE IT!

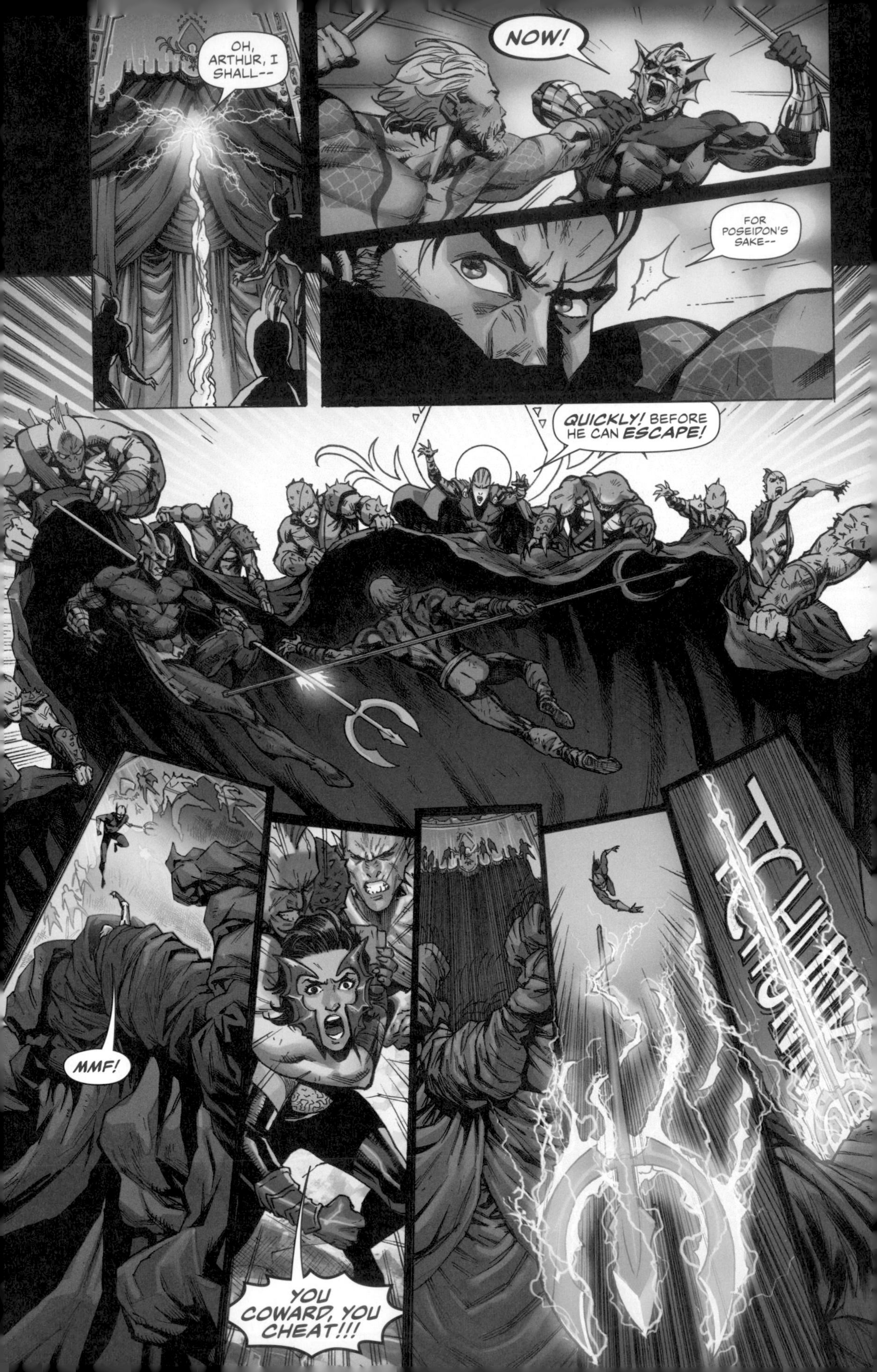
OH, ARTHUR, I SHALL--
NOW!
FOR POSEIDON'S SAKE--
QUICKLY! BEFORE HE CAN ESCAPE!
MMF!
YOU COWARD, YOU CHEAT!!!

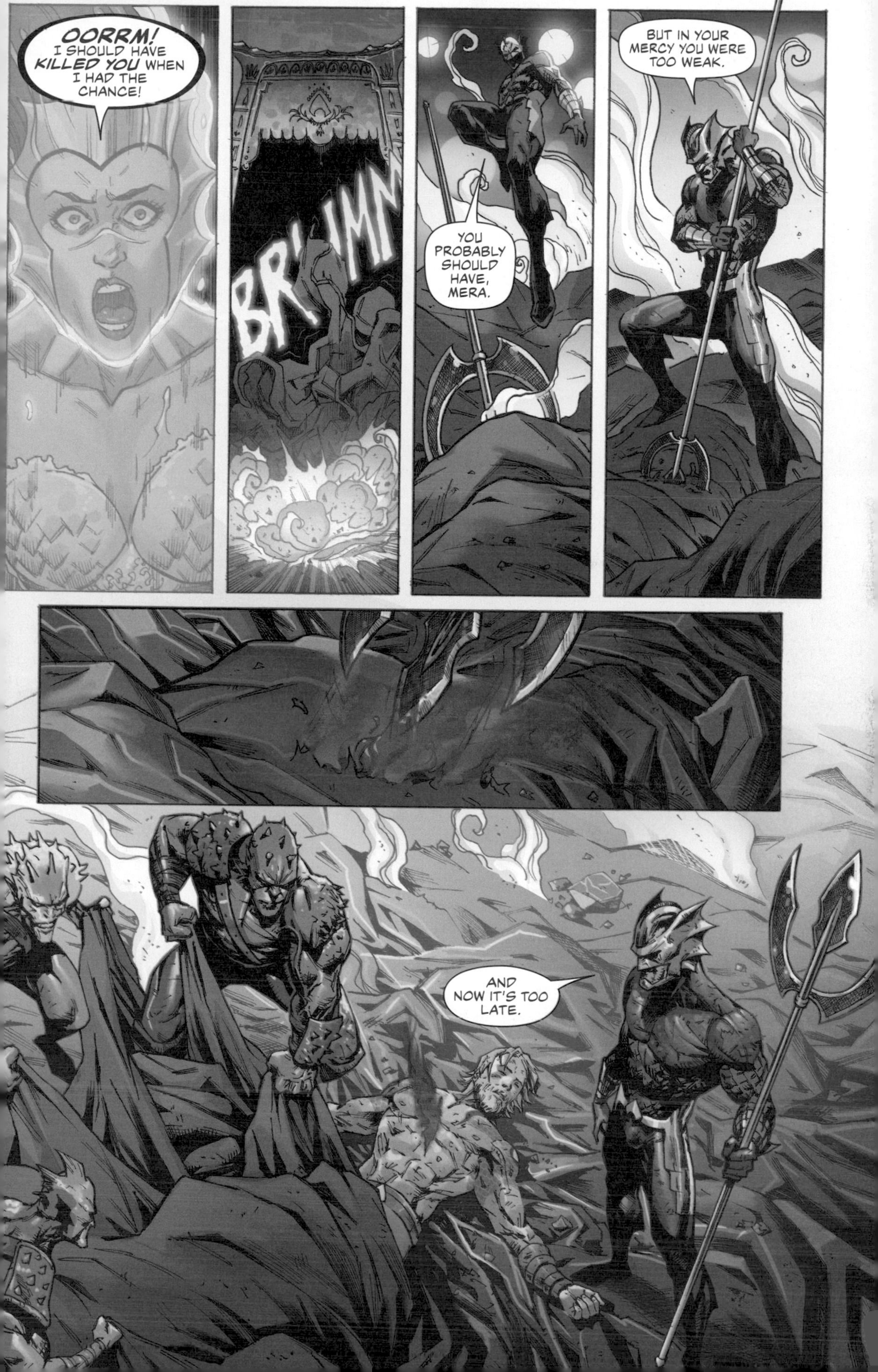
OORRM! I SHOULD HAVE KILLED YOU WHEN I HAD THE CHANCE!
BR'IMM
YOU PROBABLY SHOULD HAVE, MERA.
BUT IN YOUR MERCY YOU WERE TOO WEAK.
AND NOW IT'S TOO LATE.

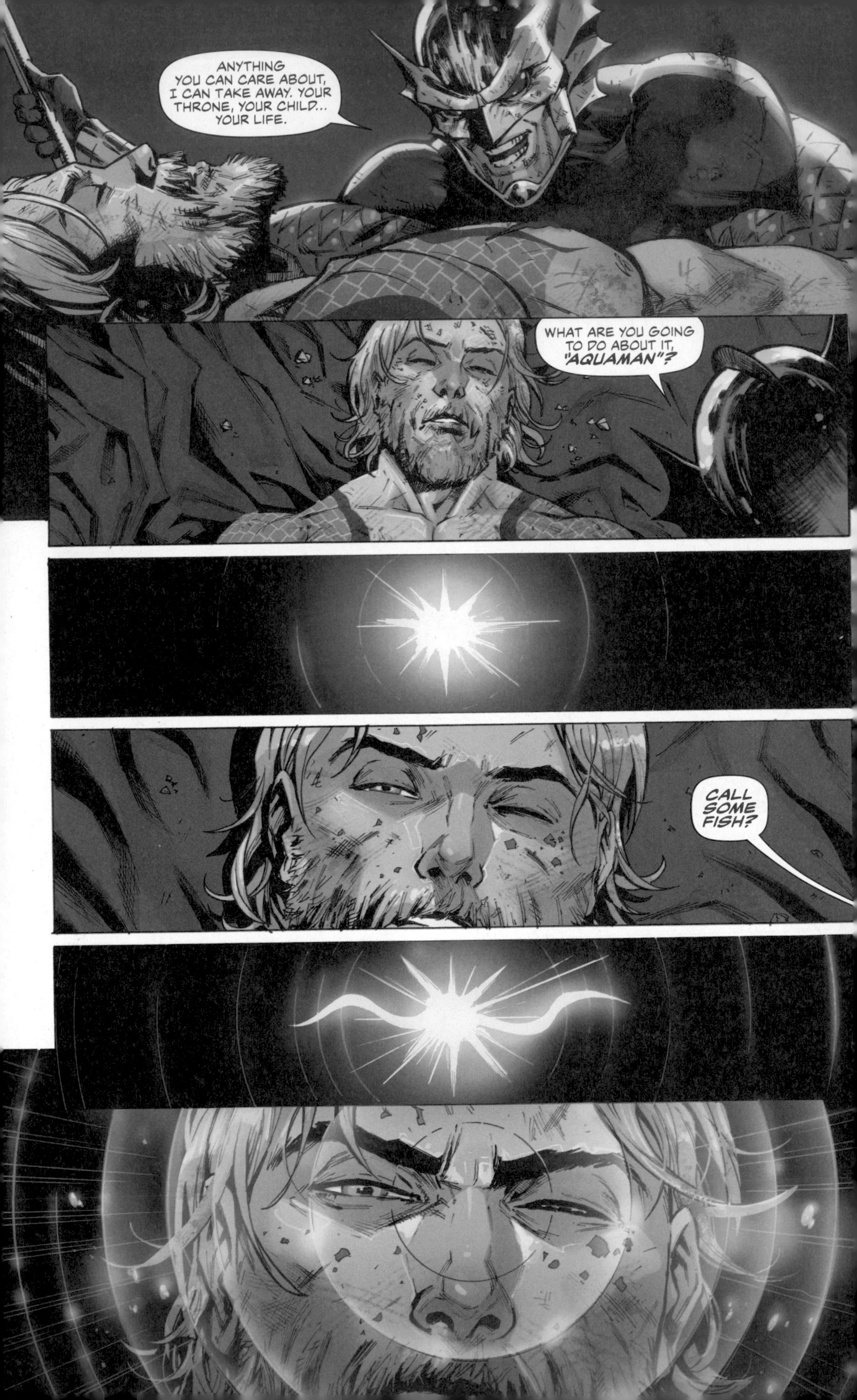
ANYTHING YOU CAN CARE ABOUT, I CAN TAKE AWAY. YOUR THRONE, YOUR CHILD... YOUR LIFE.
WHAT ARE YOU GOING TO DO ABOUT IT, "AQUAMAN"?
CALL SOME FISH?

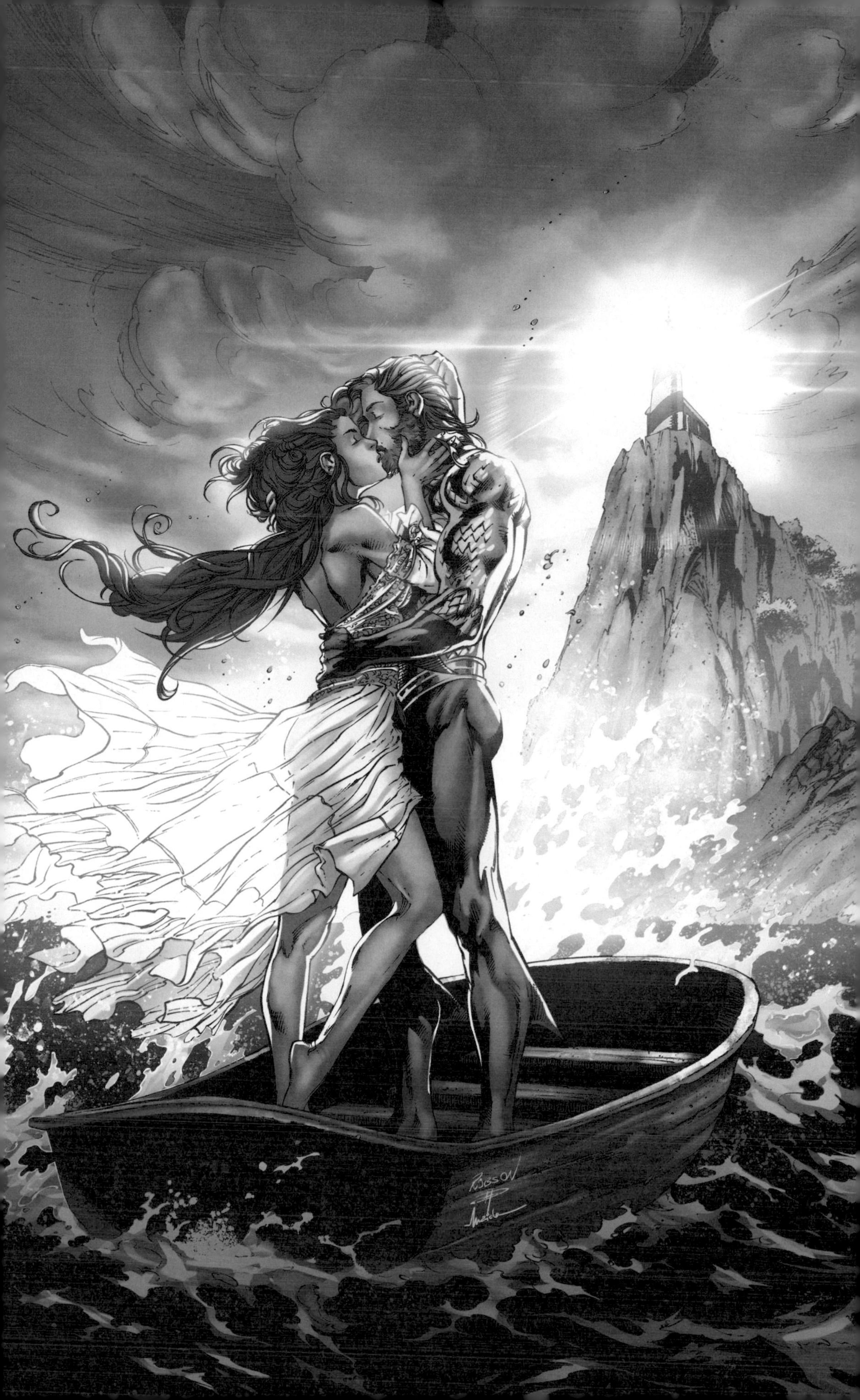

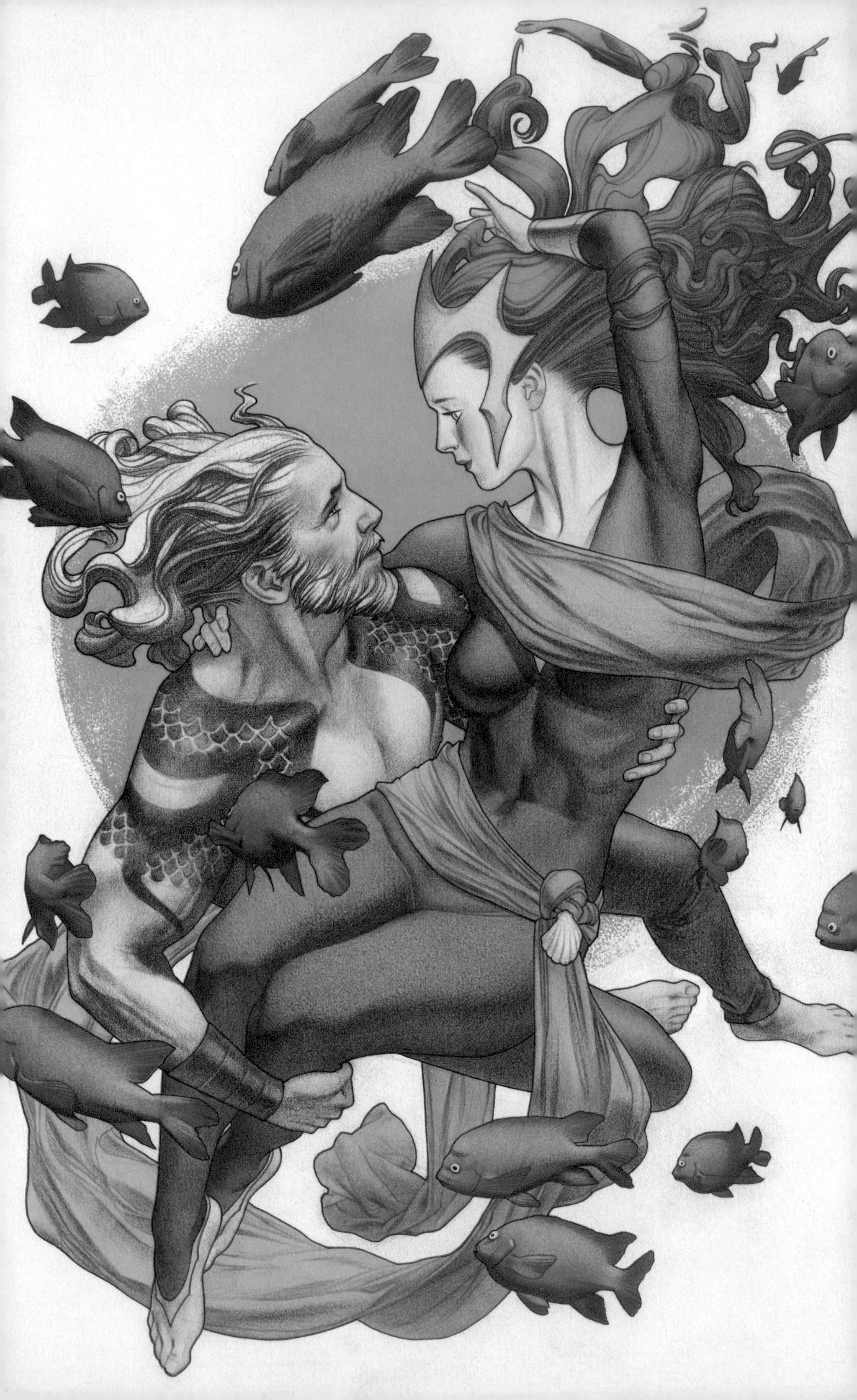

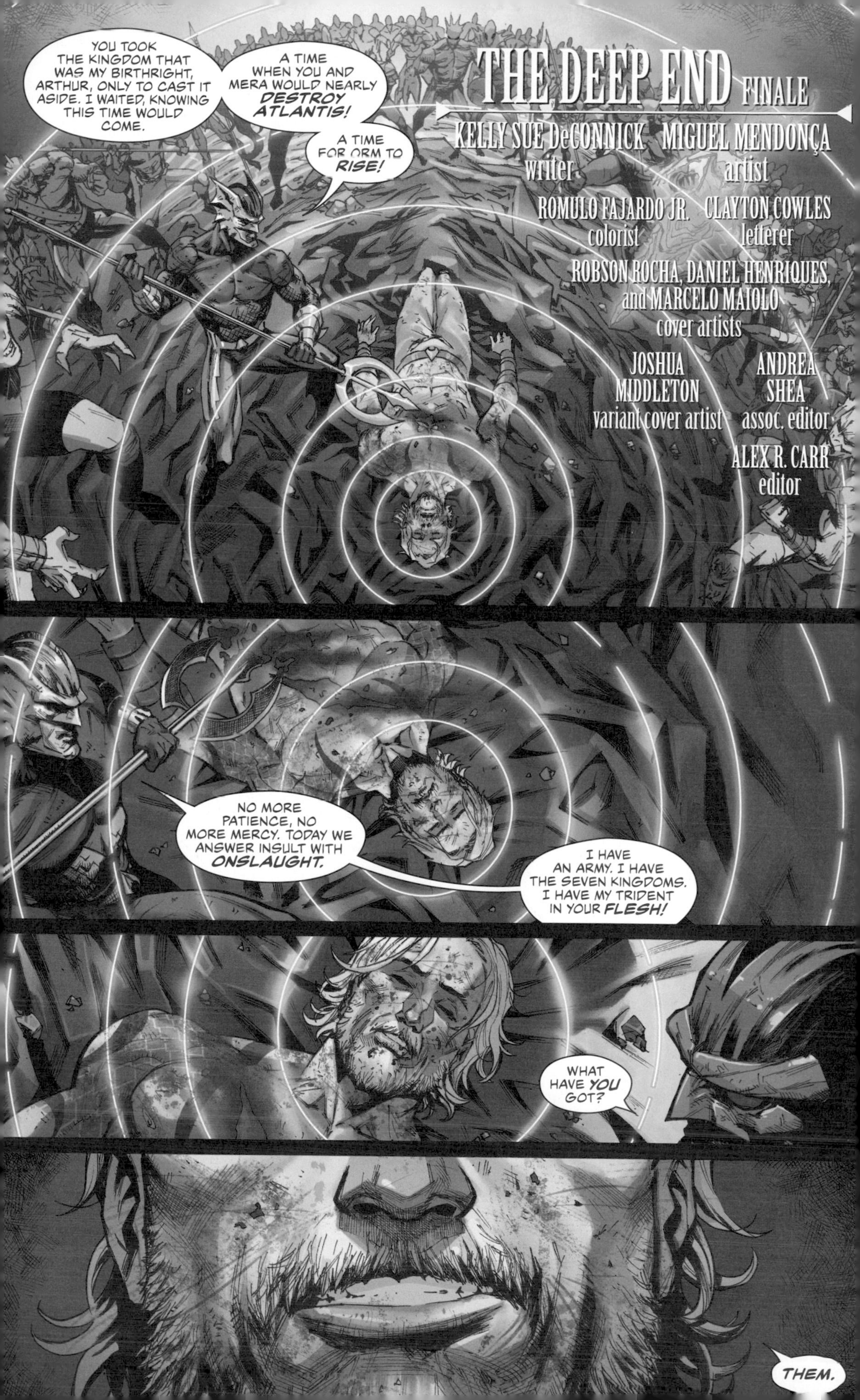

YOU TOOK THE KINGDOM THAT WAS MY BIRTHRIGHT, ARTHUR, ONLY TO CAST IT ASIDE. I WAITED, KNOWING THIS TIME WOULD COME.
A TIME WHEN YOU AND MERA WOULD NEARLY DESTROY ATLANTIS!
A TIME FOR ORM TO RISE!
THE DEEP END FINALE
KELLY SUE DeCONNICK writer
MIGUEL MENDONÇA artist
ROMULO FAJARDO JR. colorist
CLAYTON COWLES letterer
ROBSON ROCHA, DANIEL HENRIQUES, and MARCELO MAIOLO cover artists
JOSHUA MIDDLETON variant cover artist
ANDREA SHEA assoc. editor
ALEX R. CARR editor
NO MORE PATIENCE, NO MORE MERCY. TODAY WE ANSWER INSULT WITH ONSLAUGHT.
I HAVE AN ARMY. I HAVE THE SEVEN KINGDOMS. I HAVE MY TRIDENT IN YOUR FLESH!
WHAT HAVE YOU GOT?
THEM.

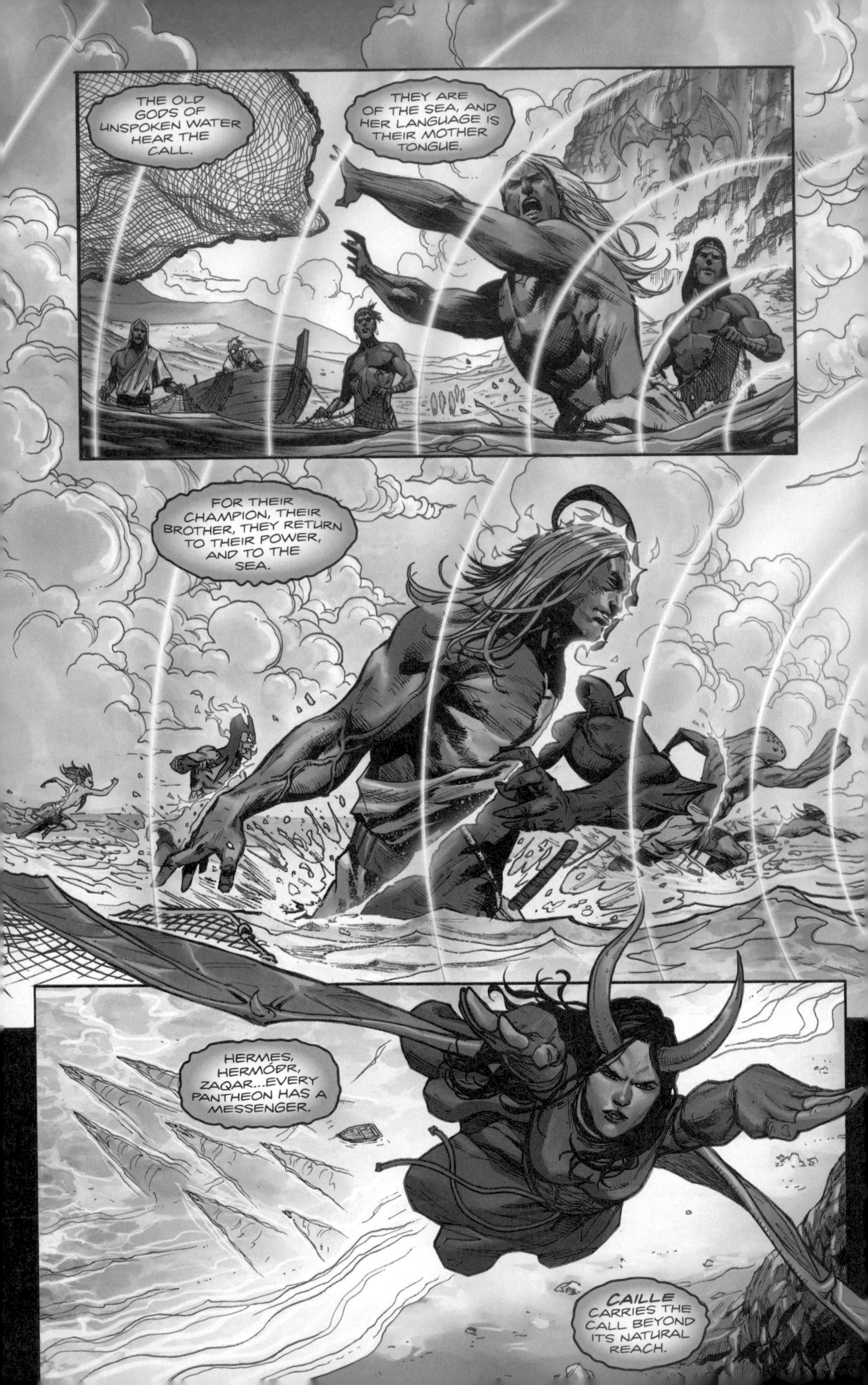
THE OLD GODS OF UNSPOKEN WATER HEAR THE CALL.
THEY ARE OF THE SEA, AND HER LANGUAGE IS THEIR MOTHER TONGUE.
FOR THEIR CHAMPION, THEIR BROTHER, THEY RETURN TO THEIR POWER, AND TO THE SEA.
HERMES, HERMÓÐR, ZAQAR...EVERY PANTHEON HAS A MESSENGER.
CAILLE CARRIES THE CALL BEYOND ITS NATURAL REACH.

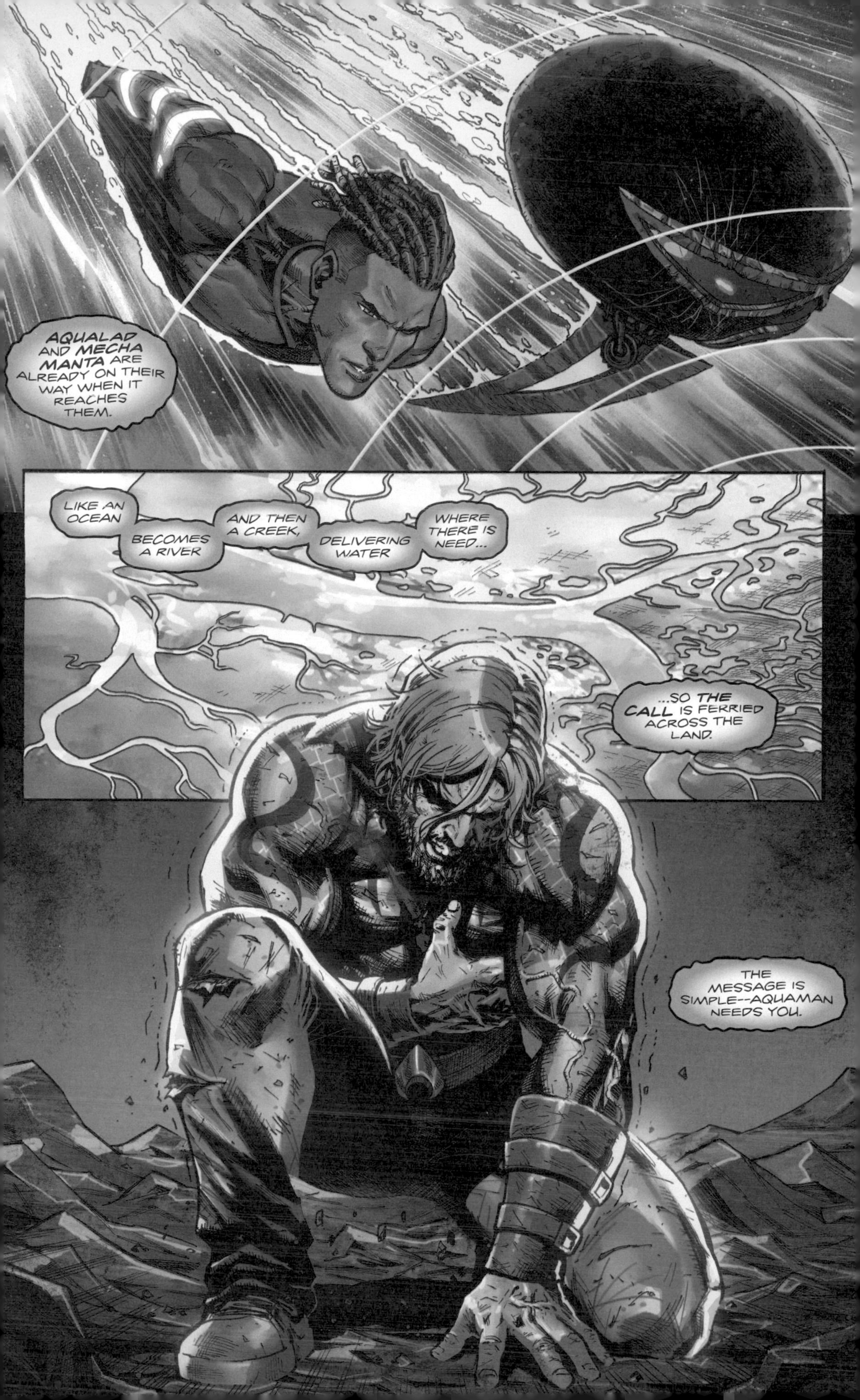
AQUALAD AND MECHA MANTA ARE ALREADY ON THEIR WAY WHEN IT REACHES THEM.
LIKE AN OCEAN
BECOMES A RIVER
AND THEN A CREEK,
DELIVERING WATER
WHERE THERE IS NEED...
...SO THE CALL IS FERRIED ACROSS THE LAND.
THE MESSAGE IS SIMPLE--AQUAMAN NEEDS YOU.

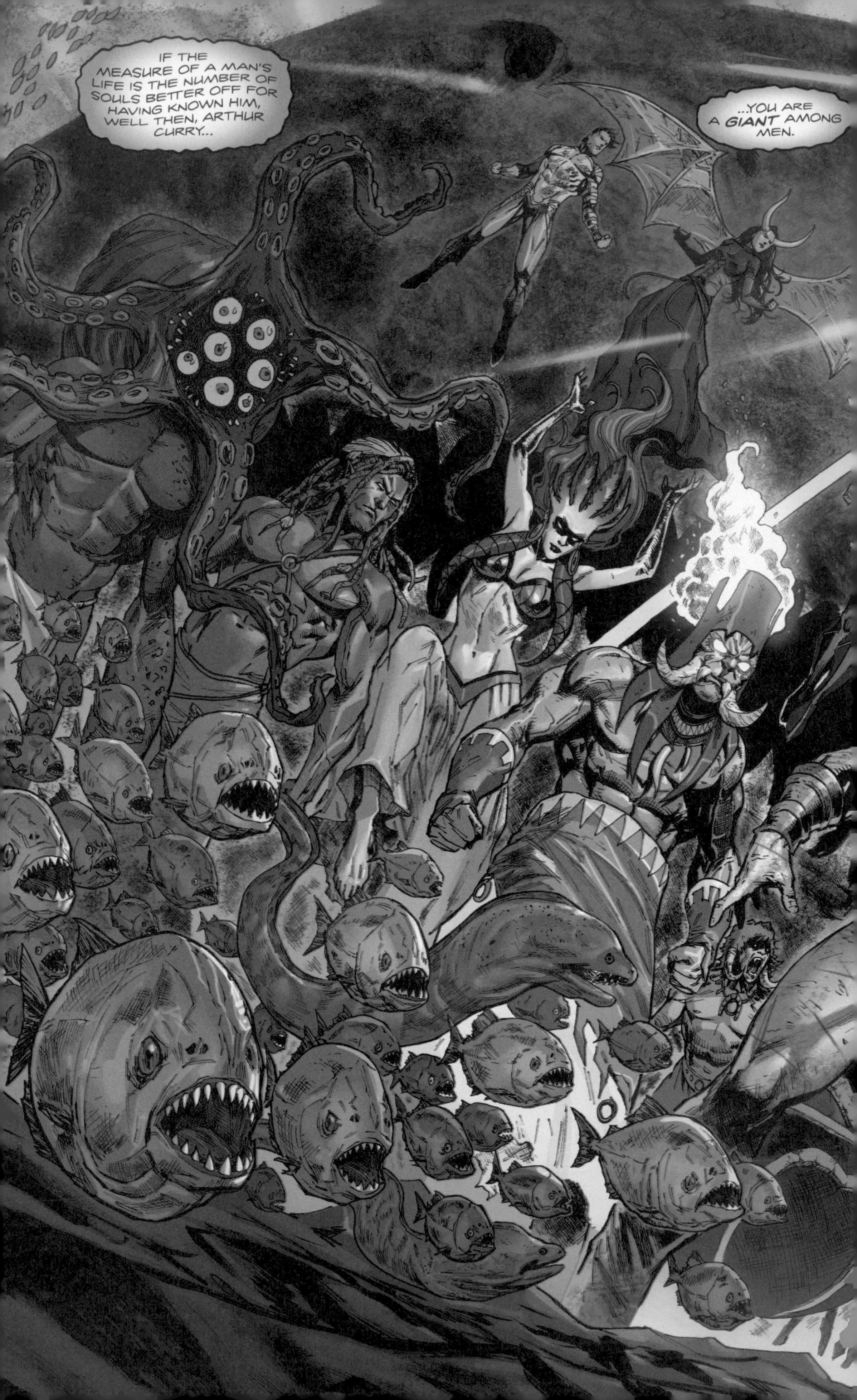
IF THE MEASURE OF A MAN'S LIFE IS THE NUMBER OF SOULS BETTER OFF FOR HAVING KNOWN HIM, WELL THEN, ARTHUR CURRY...
...YOU ARE A GIANT AMONG MEN.

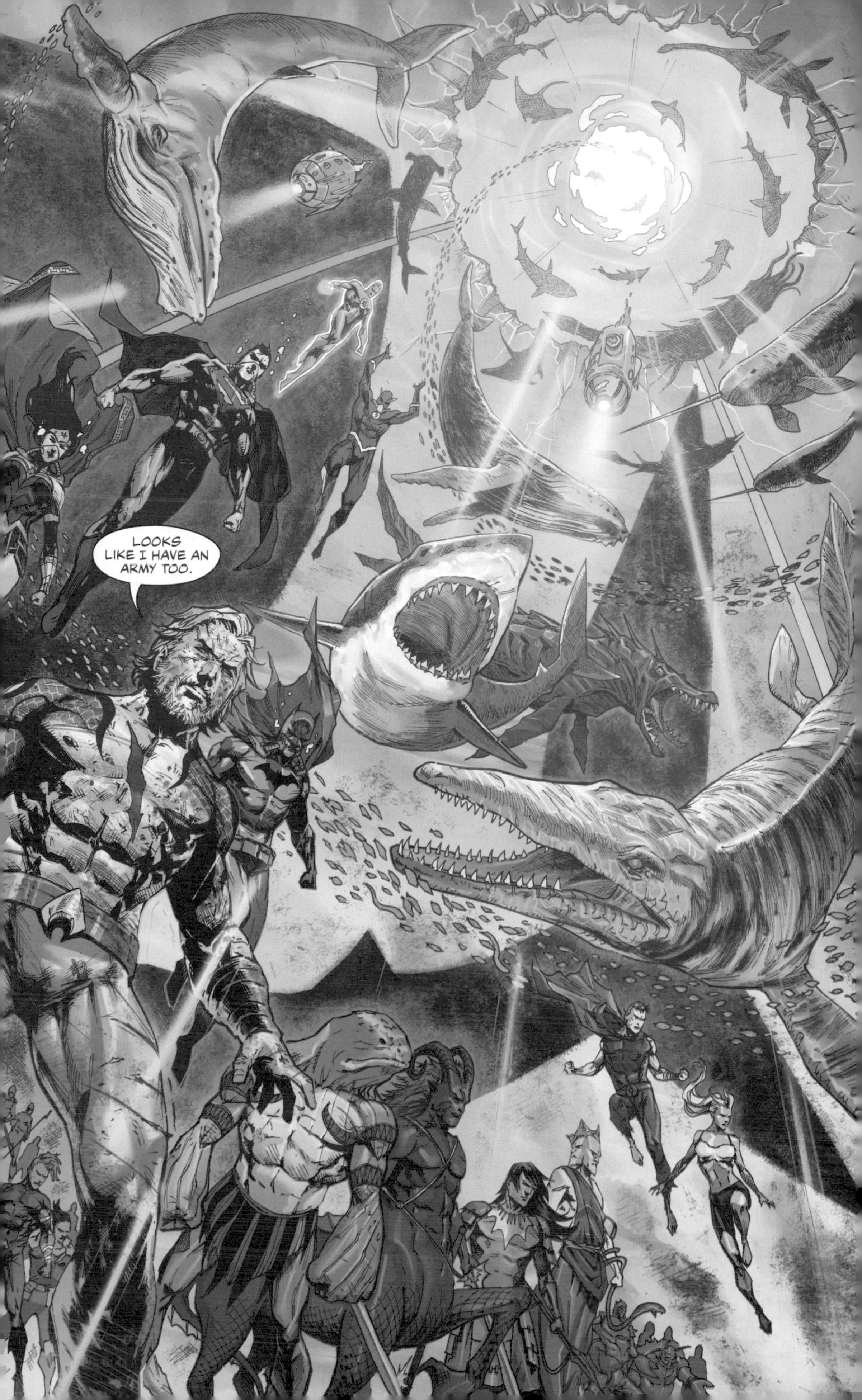
LOOKS LIKE I HAVE AN ARMY TOO.

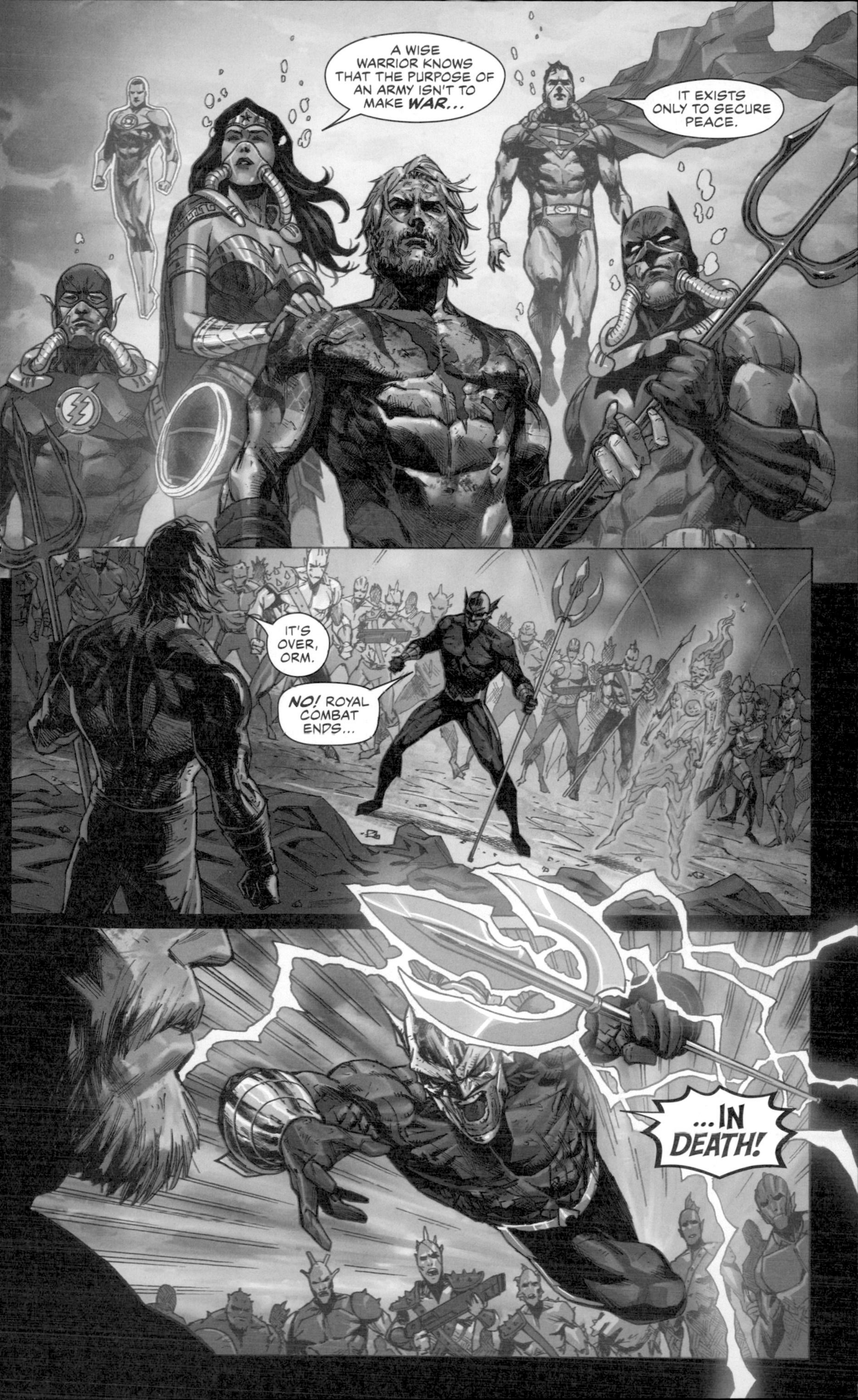
A WISE WARRIOR KNOWS THAT THE PURPOSE OF AN ARMY ISN'T TO MAKE **WAR...**
IT EXISTS ONLY TO SECURE PEACE.
IT'S OVER, ORM.
NO! ROYAL COMBAT ENDS...
...IN DEATH!

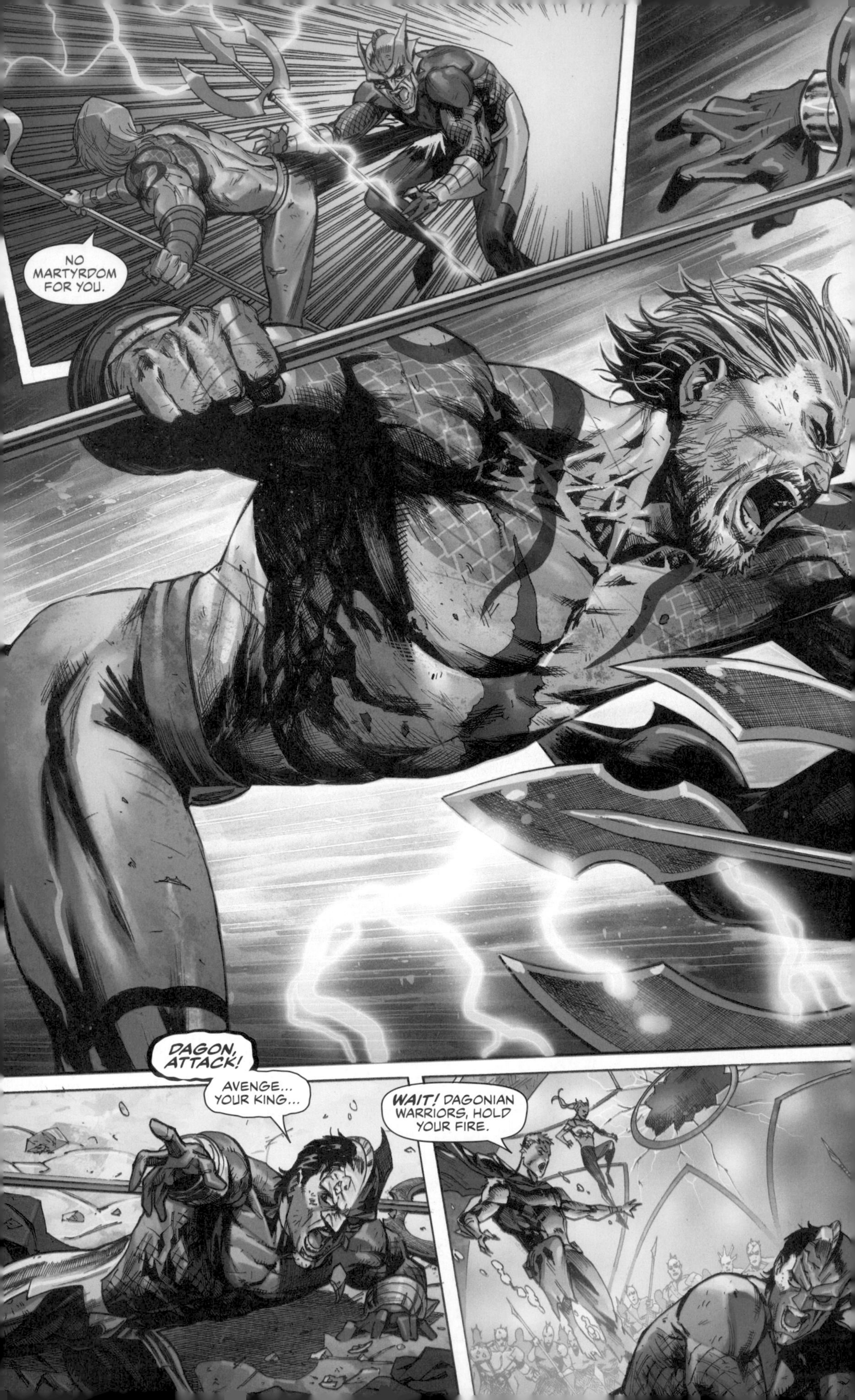
NO MARTYRDOM FOR YOU.
DAGON, ATTACK!
AVENGE... YOUR KING...
WAIT! DAGONIAN WARRIORS, HOLD YOUR FIRE.

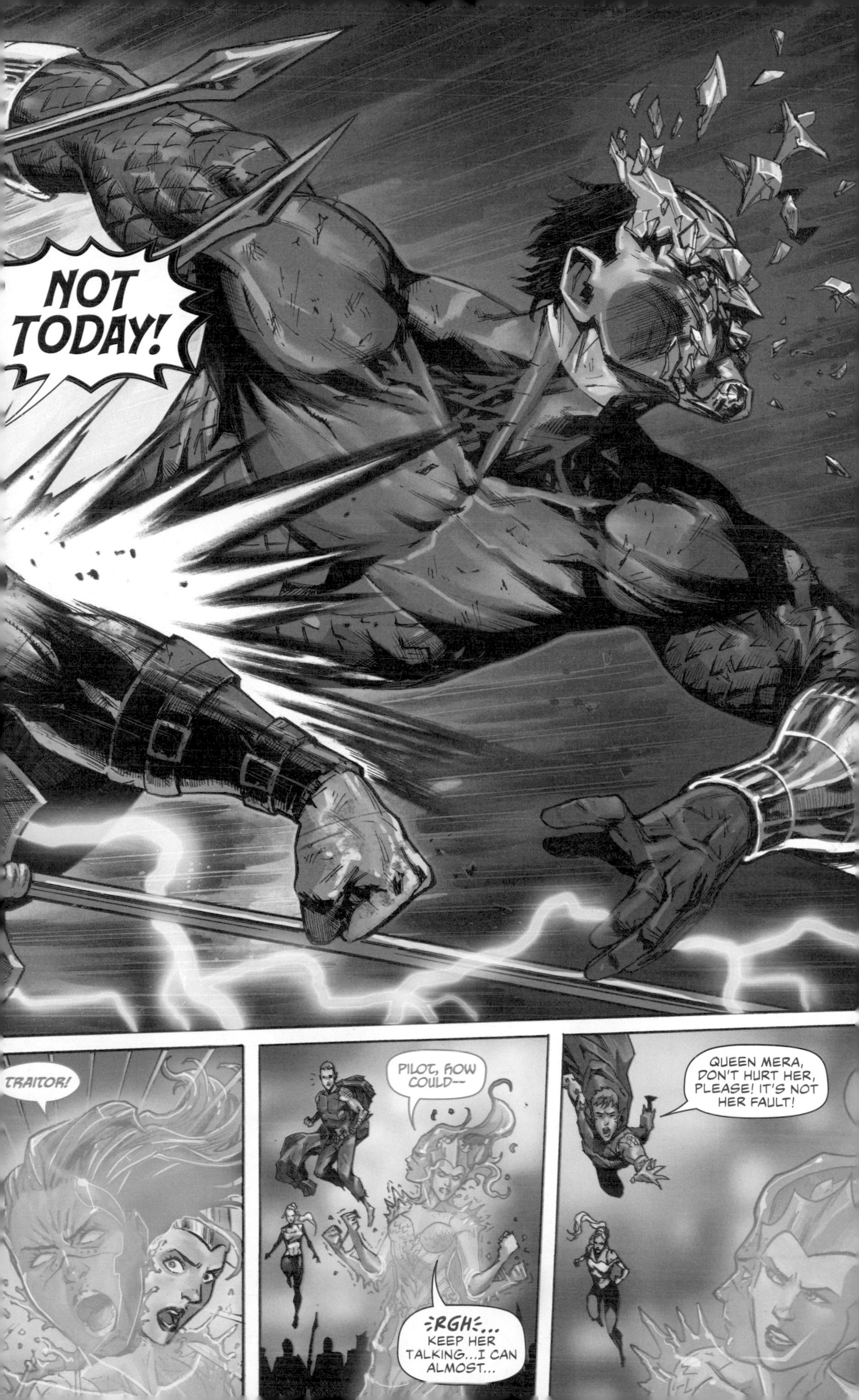
NOT TODAY!
TRAITOR!
PILOT, HOW COULD--
RGH... KEEP HER TALKING...I CAN ALMOST...
QUEEN MERA, DON'T HURT HER, PLEASE! IT'S NOT HER FAULT!

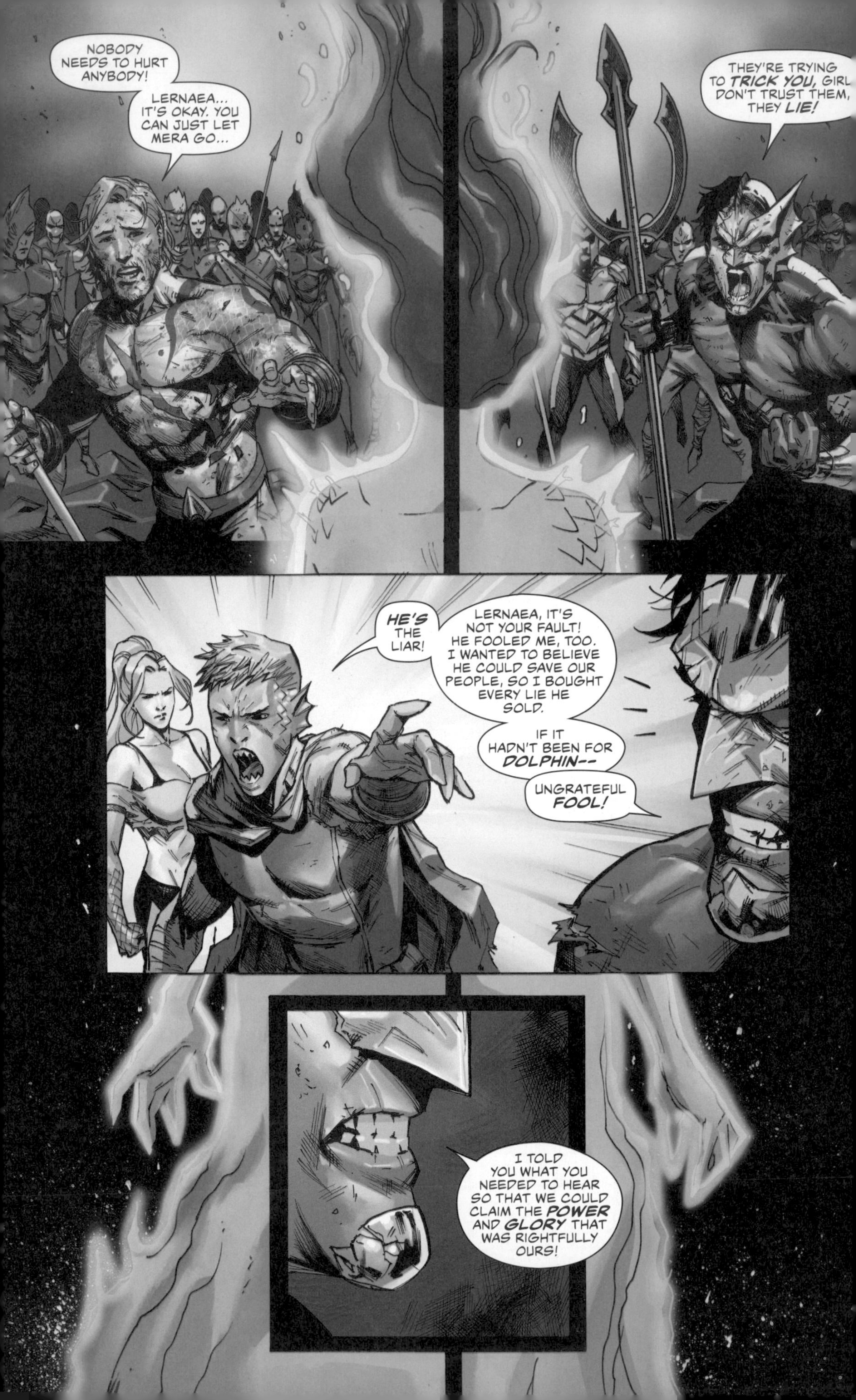
NOBODY NEEDS TO HURT ANYBODY!
LERNAEA... IT'S OKAY. YOU CAN JUST LET MERA GO...
THEY'RE TRYING TO TRICK YOU, GIRL. DON'T TRUST THEM, THEY LIE!
HE'S THE LIAR!
LERNAEA, IT'S NOT YOUR FAULT! HE FOOLED ME, TOO. I WANTED TO BELIEVE HE COULD SAVE OUR PEOPLE, SO I BOUGHT EVERY LIE HE SOLD.
IF IT HADN'T BEEN FOR DOLPHIN--
UNGRATEFUL FOOL!
I TOLD YOU WHAT YOU NEEDED TO HEAR SO THAT WE COULD CLAIM THE POWER AND GLORY THAT WAS RIGHTFULLY OURS!

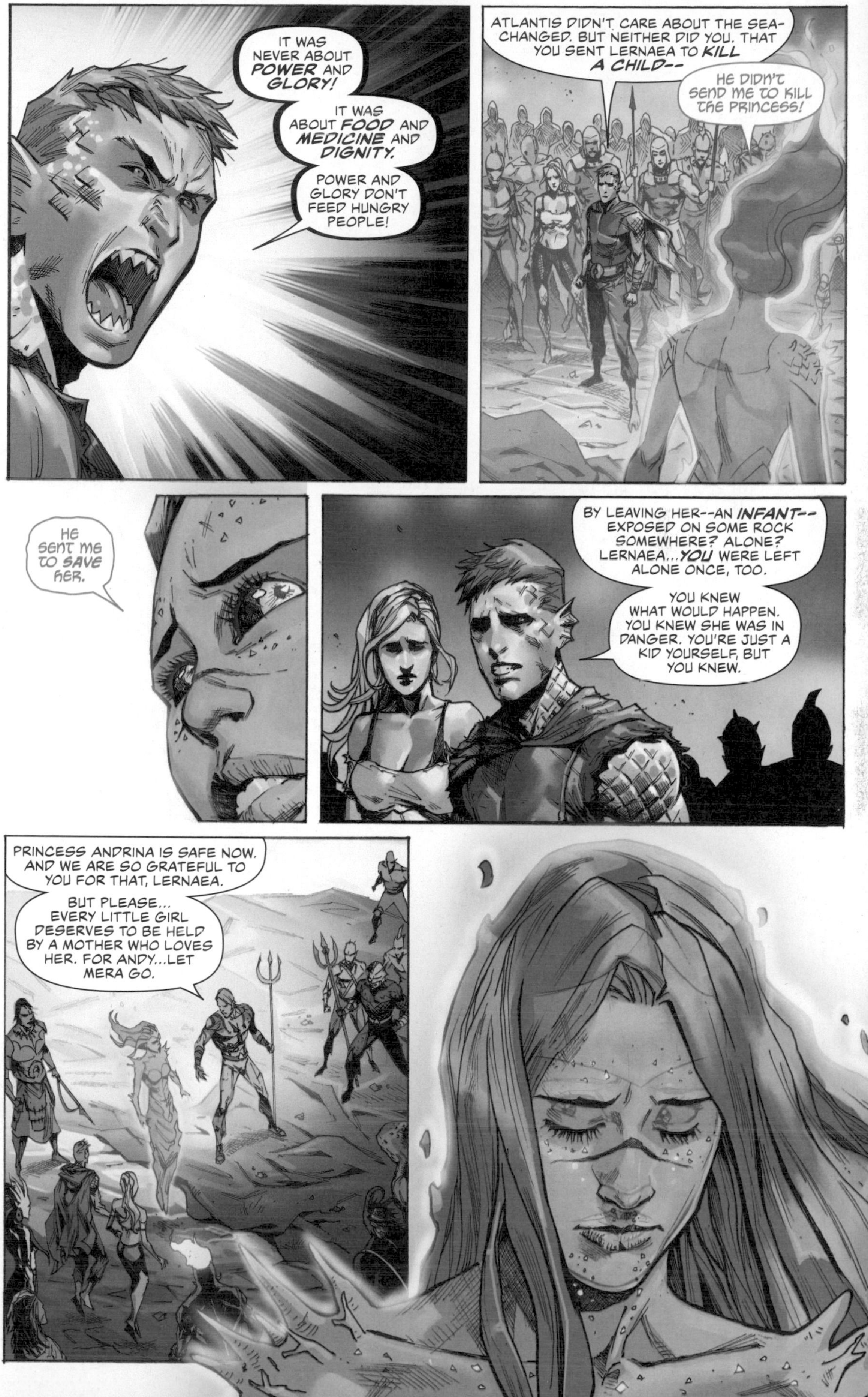

IT WAS NEVER ABOUT *POWER* AND *GLORY!*
IT WAS ABOUT *FOOD* AND *MEDICINE* AND *DIGNITY.*
POWER AND GLORY DON'T FEED HUNGRY PEOPLE!
ATLANTIS DIDN'T CARE ABOUT THE SEA-CHANGED. BUT NEITHER DID YOU. THAT YOU SENT LERNAEA TO *KILL A CHILD--*
HE DIDN'T SEND ME TO KILL THE PRINCESS!
HE SENT ME TO *SAVE* HER.
BY LEAVING HER--AN *INFANT--* EXPOSED ON SOME ROCK SOMEWHERE? ALONE? LERNAEA...*YOU* WERE LEFT ALONE ONCE, TOO.
YOU KNEW WHAT WOULD HAPPEN. YOU KNEW SHE WAS IN DANGER. YOU'RE JUST A KID YOURSELF, BUT YOU KNEW.
PRINCESS ANDRINA IS SAFE NOW. AND WE ARE SO GRATEFUL TO YOU FOR THAT, LERNAEA.
BUT PLEASE... EVERY LITTLE GIRL DESERVES TO BE HELD BY A MOTHER WHO LOVES HER. FOR ANDY...LET MERA GO.

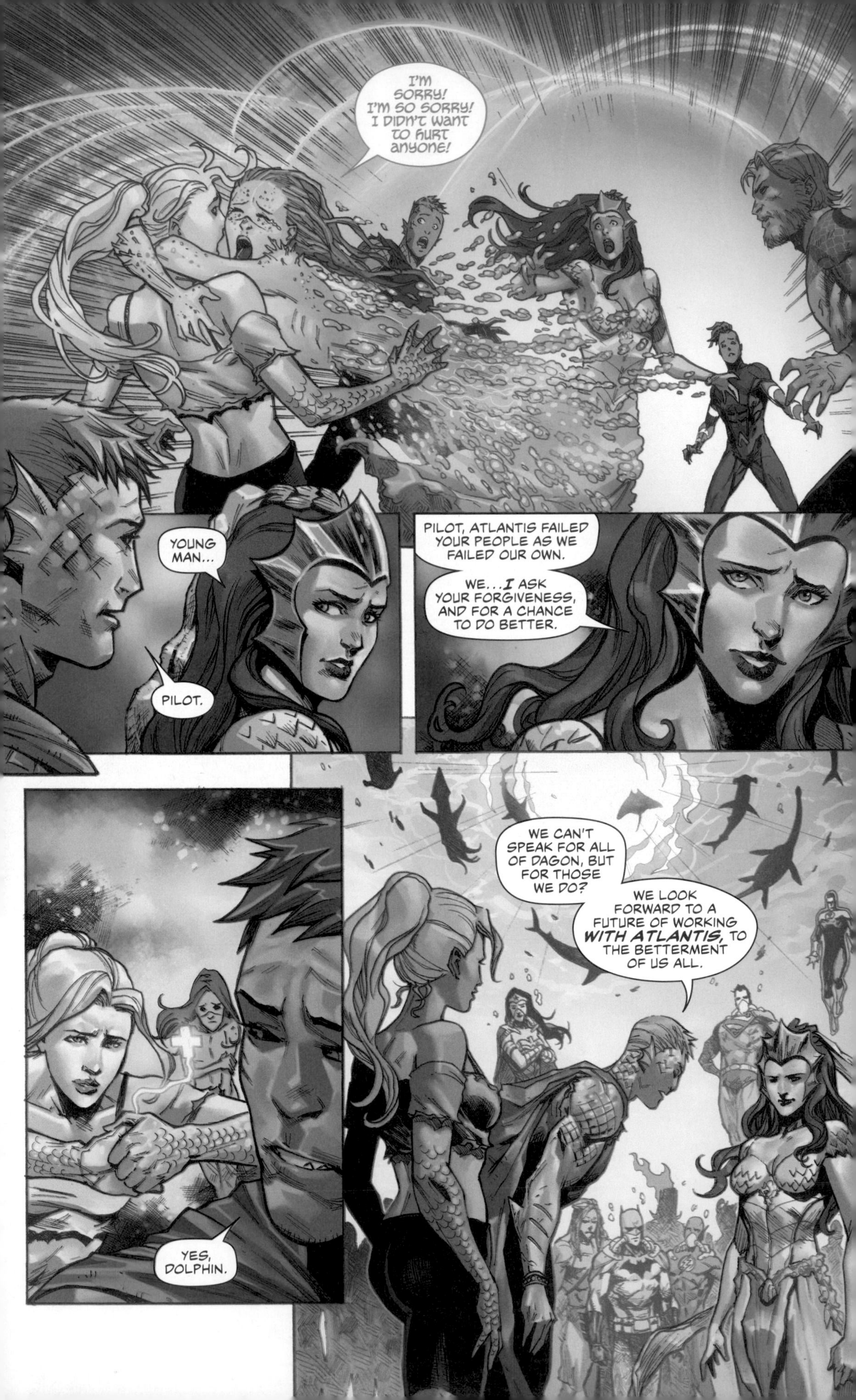
I'M SORRY! I'M SO SORRY! I DIDN'T WANT TO HURT ANYONE!
YOUNG MAN...
PILOT.
PILOT, ATLANTIS FAILED YOUR PEOPLE AS WE FAILED OUR OWN.
WE... I ASK YOUR FORGIVENESS, AND FOR A CHANCE TO DO BETTER.
YES, DOLPHIN.
WE CAN'T SPEAK FOR ALL OF DAGON, BUT FOR THOSE WE DO?
WE LOOK FORWARD TO A FUTURE OF WORKING WITH ATLANTIS, TO THE BETTERMENT OF US ALL.

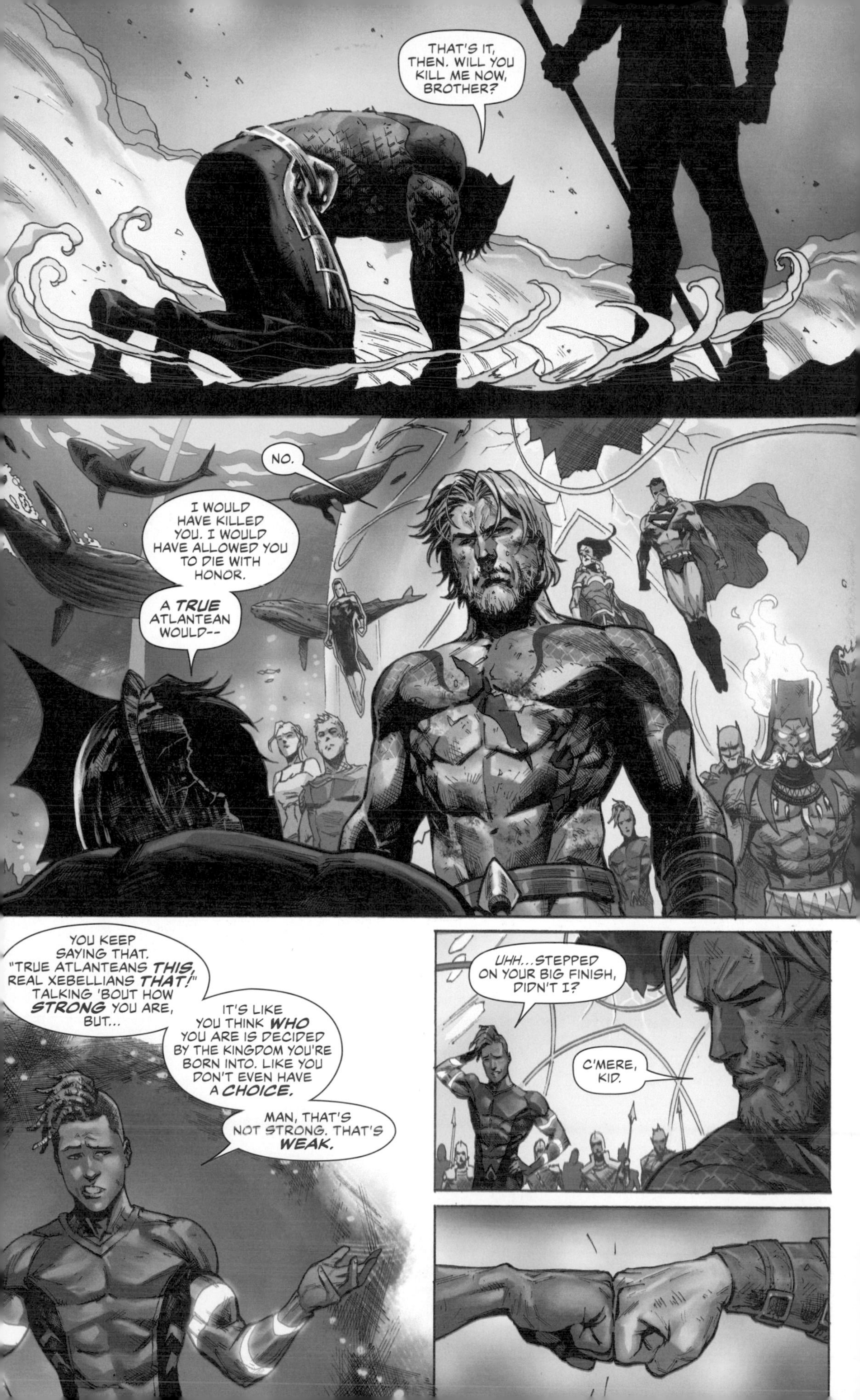
THAT'S IT, THEN. WILL YOU KILL ME NOW, BROTHER?
NO.
I WOULD HAVE KILLED YOU. I WOULD HAVE ALLOWED YOU TO DIE WITH HONOR.
A TRUE ATLANTEAN WOULD--
YOU KEEP SAYING THAT. "TRUE ATLANTEANS THIS, REAL XEBELLIANS THAT!" TALKING 'BOUT HOW STRONG YOU ARE, BUT...
IT'S LIKE YOU THINK WHO YOU ARE IS DECIDED BY THE KINGDOM YOU'RE BORN INTO. LIKE YOU DON'T EVEN HAVE A CHOICE.
MAN, THAT'S NOT STRONG. THAT'S WEAK.
UHH...STEPPED ON YOUR BIG FINISH, DIDN'T I?
C'MERE, KID.

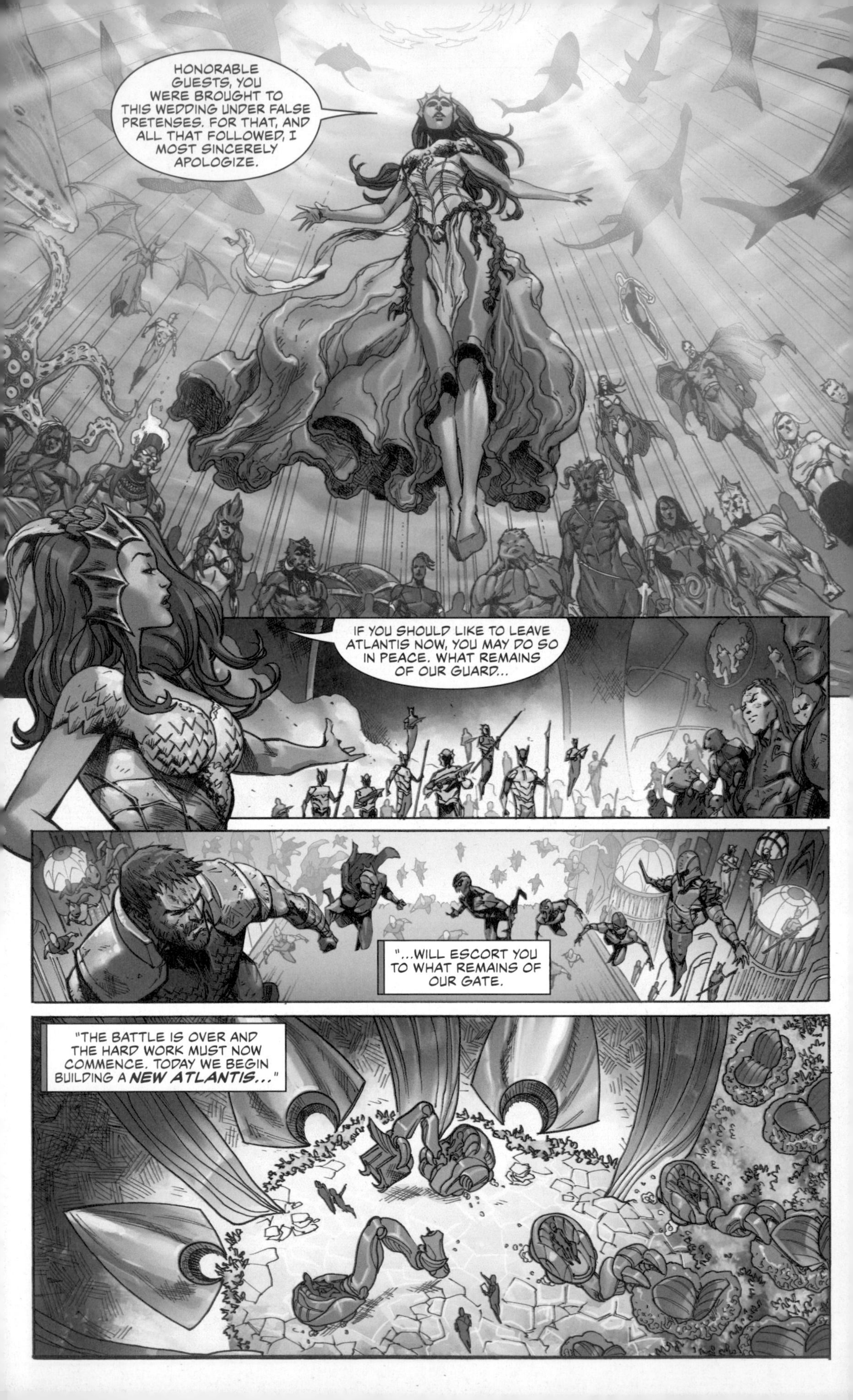
HONORABLE GUESTS, YOU WERE BROUGHT TO THIS WEDDING UNDER FALSE PRETENSES. FOR THAT, AND ALL THAT FOLLOWED, I MOST SINCERELY APOLOGIZE.
IF YOU SHOULD LIKE TO LEAVE ATLANTIS NOW, YOU MAY DO SO IN PEACE. WHAT REMAINS OF OUR GUARD...
"...WILL ESCORT YOU TO WHAT REMAINS OF OUR GATE.
"THE BATTLE IS OVER AND THE HARD WORK MUST NOW COMMENCE. TODAY WE BEGIN BUILDING A NEW ATLANTIS..."

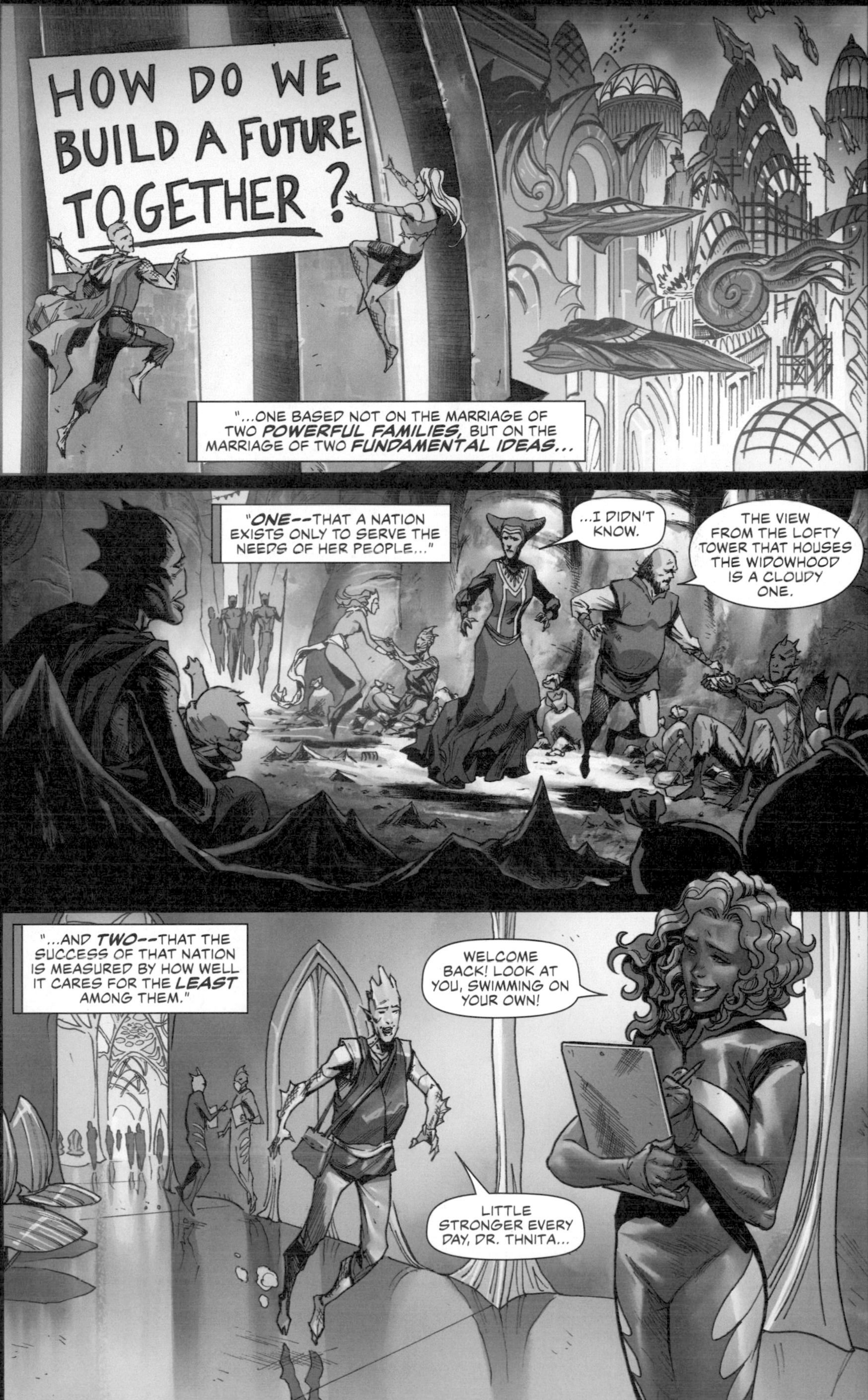
HOW DO WE BUILD A FUTURE TOGETHER ?
"...ONE BASED NOT ON THE MARRIAGE OF TWO POWERFUL FAMILIES, BUT ON THE MARRIAGE OF TWO FUNDAMENTAL IDEAS...
"ONE--THAT A NATION EXISTS ONLY TO SERVE THE NEEDS OF HER PEOPLE..."
...I DIDN'T KNOW.
THE VIEW FROM THE LOFTY TOWER THAT HOUSES THE WIDOWHOOD IS A CLOUDY ONE.
"...AND TWO--THAT THE SUCCESS OF THAT NATION IS MEASURED BY HOW WELL IT CARES FOR THE LEAST AMONG THEM."
WELCOME BACK! LOOK AT YOU, SWIMMING ON YOUR OWN!
LITTLE STRONGER EVERY DAY, DR. THNITA...

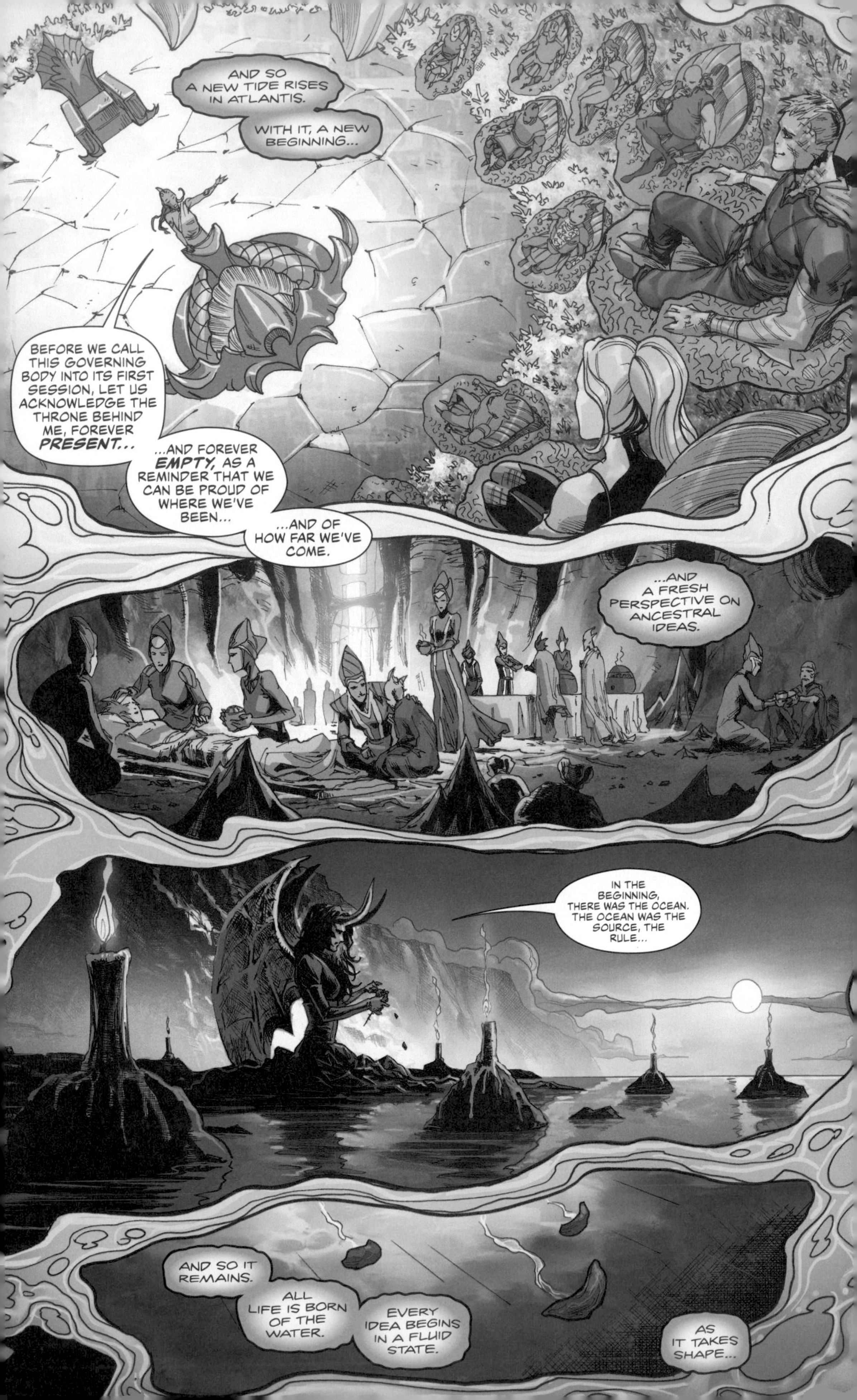
AND SO
A NEW TIDE RISES
IN ATLANTIS.
WITH IT, A NEW
BEGINNING...
BEFORE WE CALL THIS GOVERNING BODY INTO ITS FIRST SESSION, LET US ACKNOWLEDGE THE THRONE BEHIND ME, FOREVER PRESENT...
...AND FOREVER EMPTY, AS A REMINDER THAT WE CAN BE PROUD OF WHERE WE'VE BEEN...
...AND OF HOW FAR WE'VE COME.
...AND A FRESH PERSPECTIVE ON ANCESTRAL IDEAS.
IN THE BEGINNING, THERE WAS THE OCEAN. THE OCEAN WAS THE SOURCE, THE RULE...
AND SO IT REMAINS.
ALL LIFE IS BORN OF THE WATER.
EVERY IDEA BEGINS IN A FLUID STATE.
AS IT TAKES SHAPE...

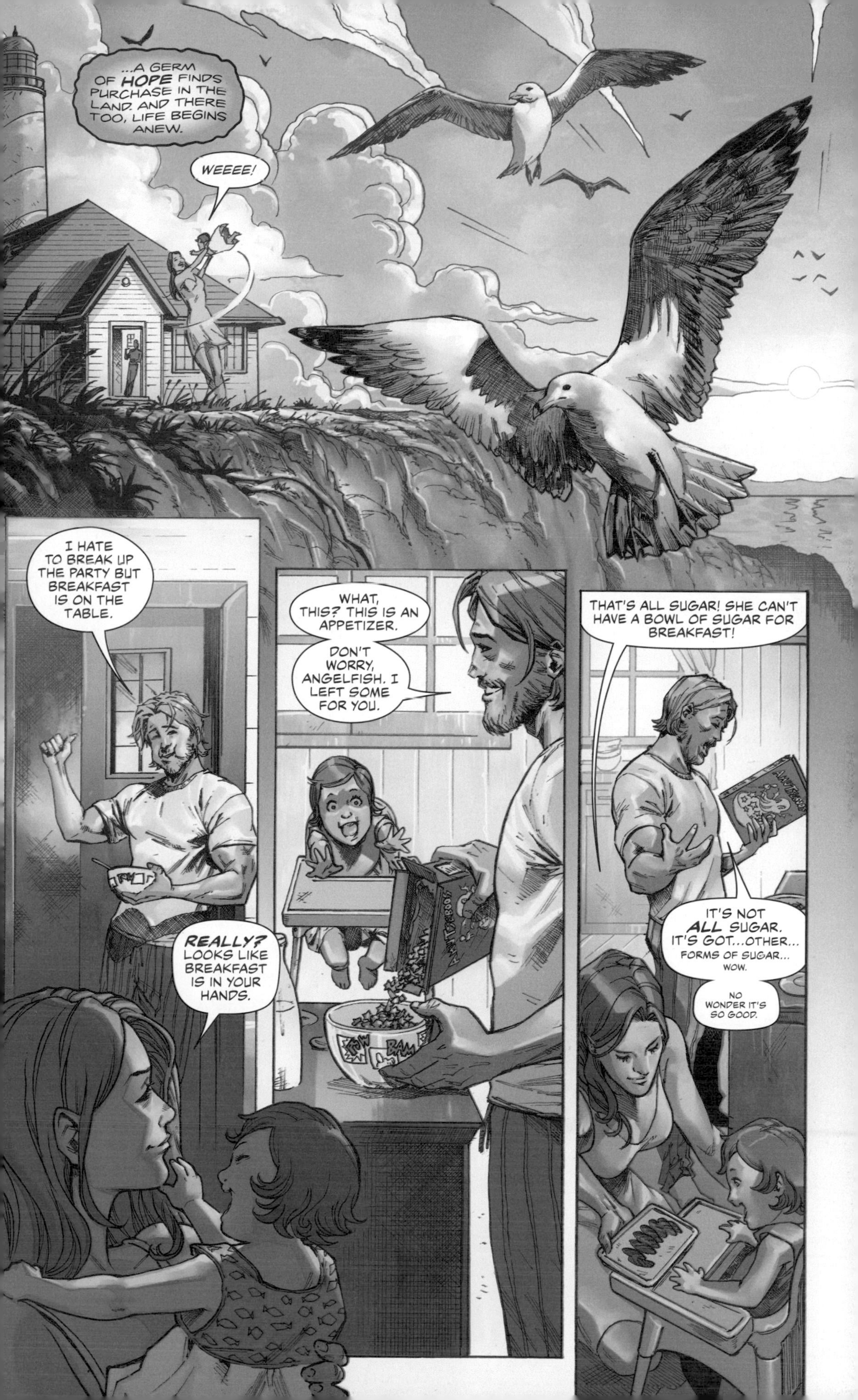
...A GERM OF HOPE FINDS PURCHASE IN THE LAND. AND THERE TOO, LIFE BEGINS ANEW.
WEEEE!
I HATE TO BREAK UP THE PARTY BUT BREAKFAST IS ON THE TABLE.
REALLY? LOOKS LIKE BREAKFAST IS IN YOUR HANDS.
WHAT, THIS? THIS IS AN APPETIZER.
DON'T WORRY, ANGELFISH. I LEFT SOME FOR YOU.
THAT'S ALL SUGAR! SHE CAN'T HAVE A BOWL OF SUGAR FOR BREAKFAST!
IT'S NOT ALL SUGAR. IT'S GOT...OTHER... FORMS OF SUGAR... WOW.
NO WONDER IT'S SO GOOD.

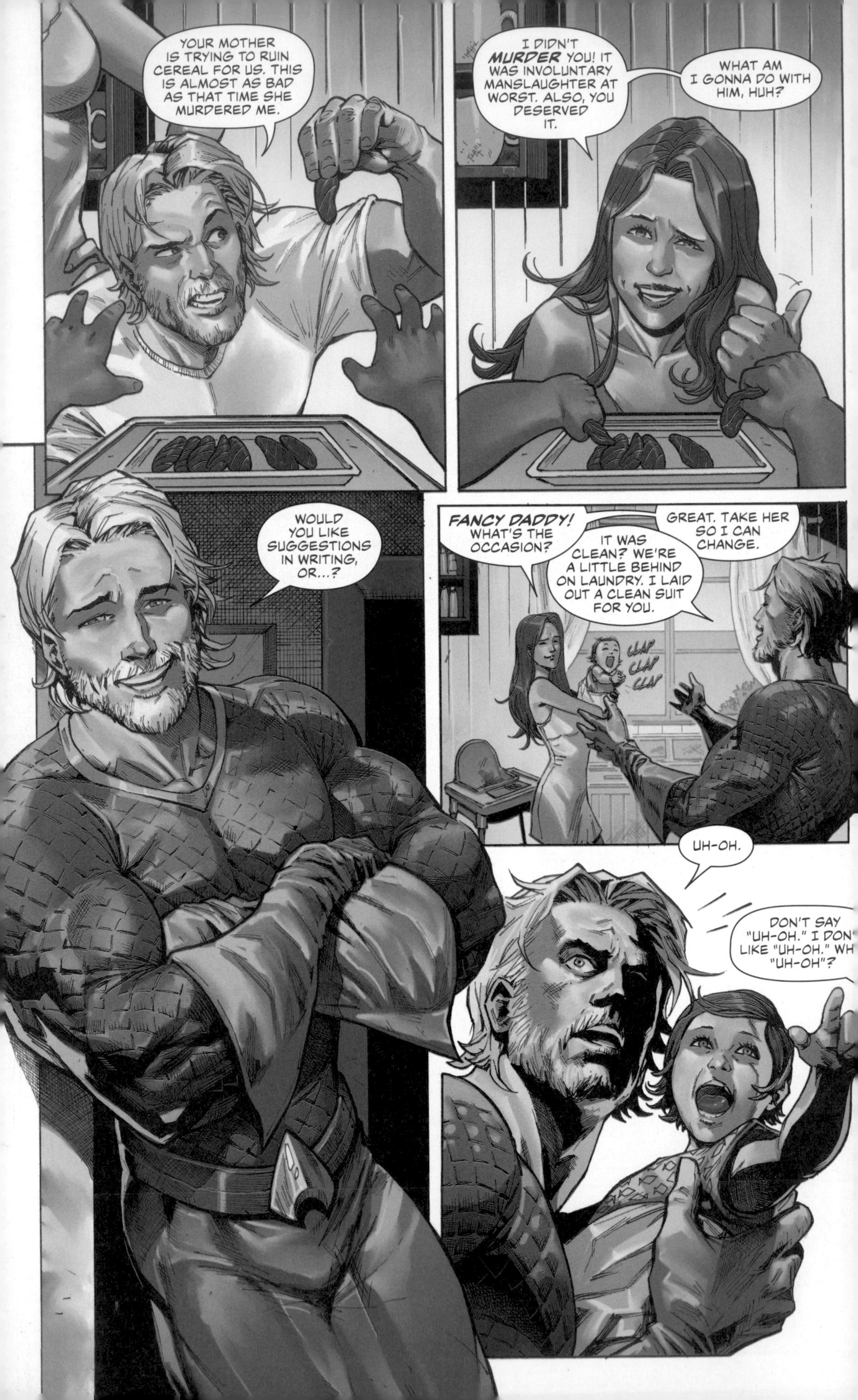
YOUR MOTHER IS TRYING TO RUIN CEREAL FOR US. THIS IS ALMOST AS BAD AS THAT TIME SHE MURDERED ME.
I DIDN'T MURDER YOU! IT WAS INVOLUNTARY MANSLAUGHTER AT WORST. ALSO, YOU DESERVED IT.
WHAT AM I GONNA DO WITH HIM, HUH?
WOULD YOU LIKE SUGGESTIONS IN WRITING, OR...?
FANCY DADDY! WHAT'S THE OCCASION?
IT WAS CLEAN? WE'RE A LITTLE BEHIND ON LAUNDRY. I LAID OUT A CLEAN SUIT FOR YOU.
GREAT. TAKE HER SO I CAN CHANGE.
CLAP CLAP CLAP
UH-OH.
DON'T SAY "UH-OH." I DON "UH-OH." WH "UH-OH"?

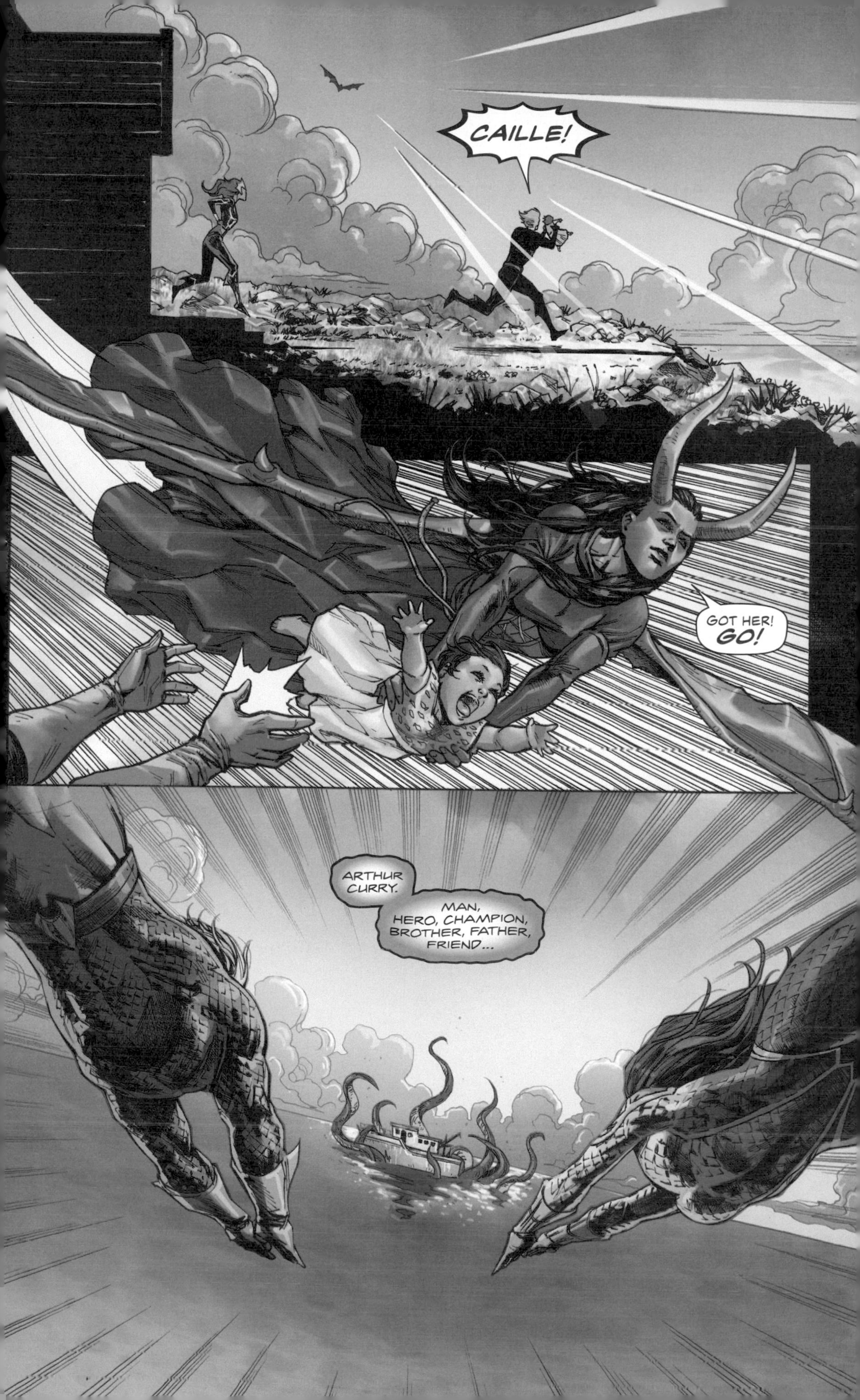
CAILLE!
GOT HER! GO!
ARTHUR CURRY.
MAN, HERO, CHAMPION, BROTHER, FATHER, FRIEND...

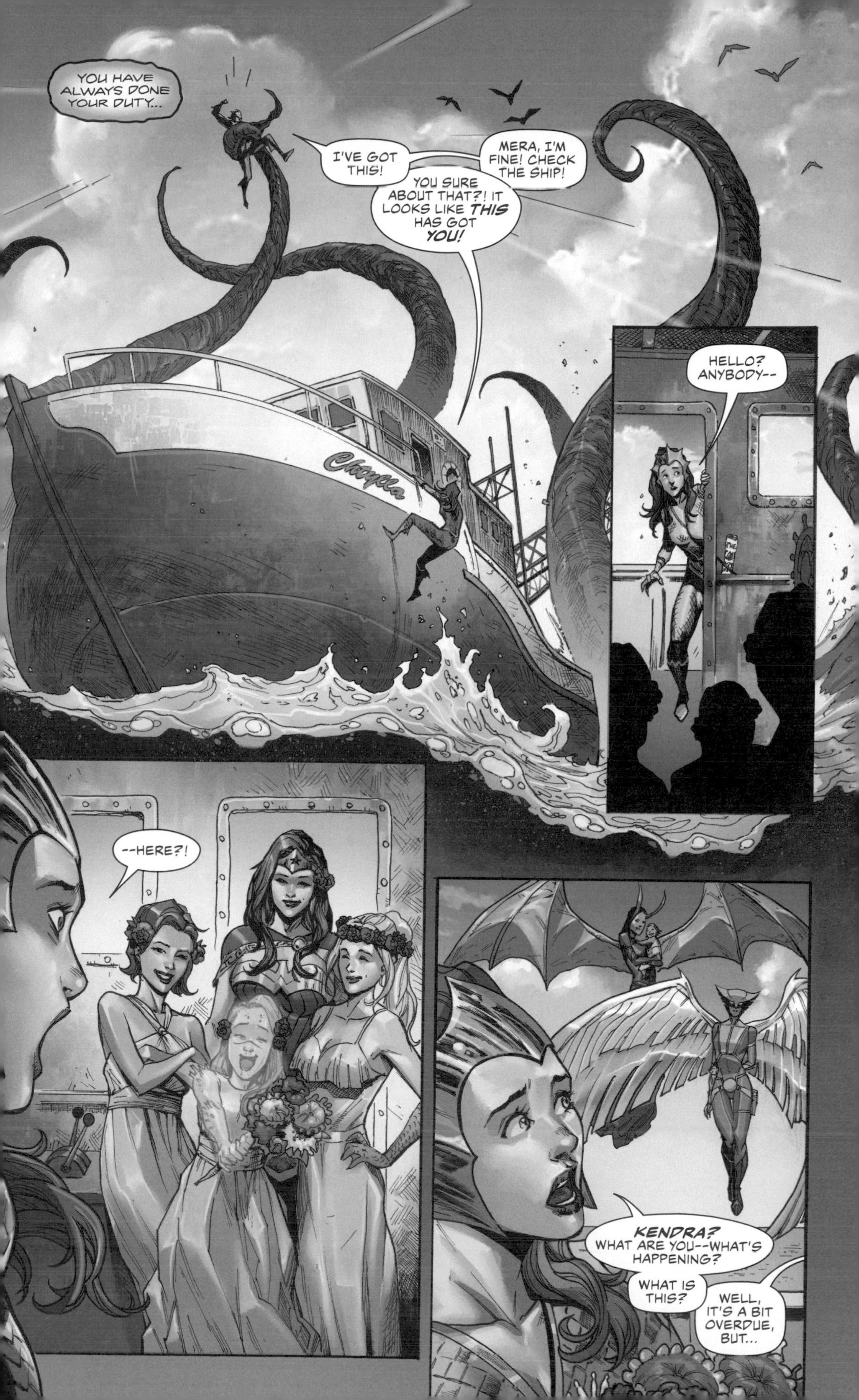

YOU HAVE ALWAYS DONE YOUR DUTY...
I'VE GOT THIS!
MERA, I'M FINE! CHECK THE SHIP!
YOU SURE ABOUT THAT?! IT LOOKS LIKE THIS HAS GOT YOU!
HELLO? ANYBODY--
--HERE?!
KENDRA? WHAT ARE YOU--WHAT'S HAPPENING?
WHAT IS THIS?
WELL, IT'S A BIT OVERDUE, BUT...

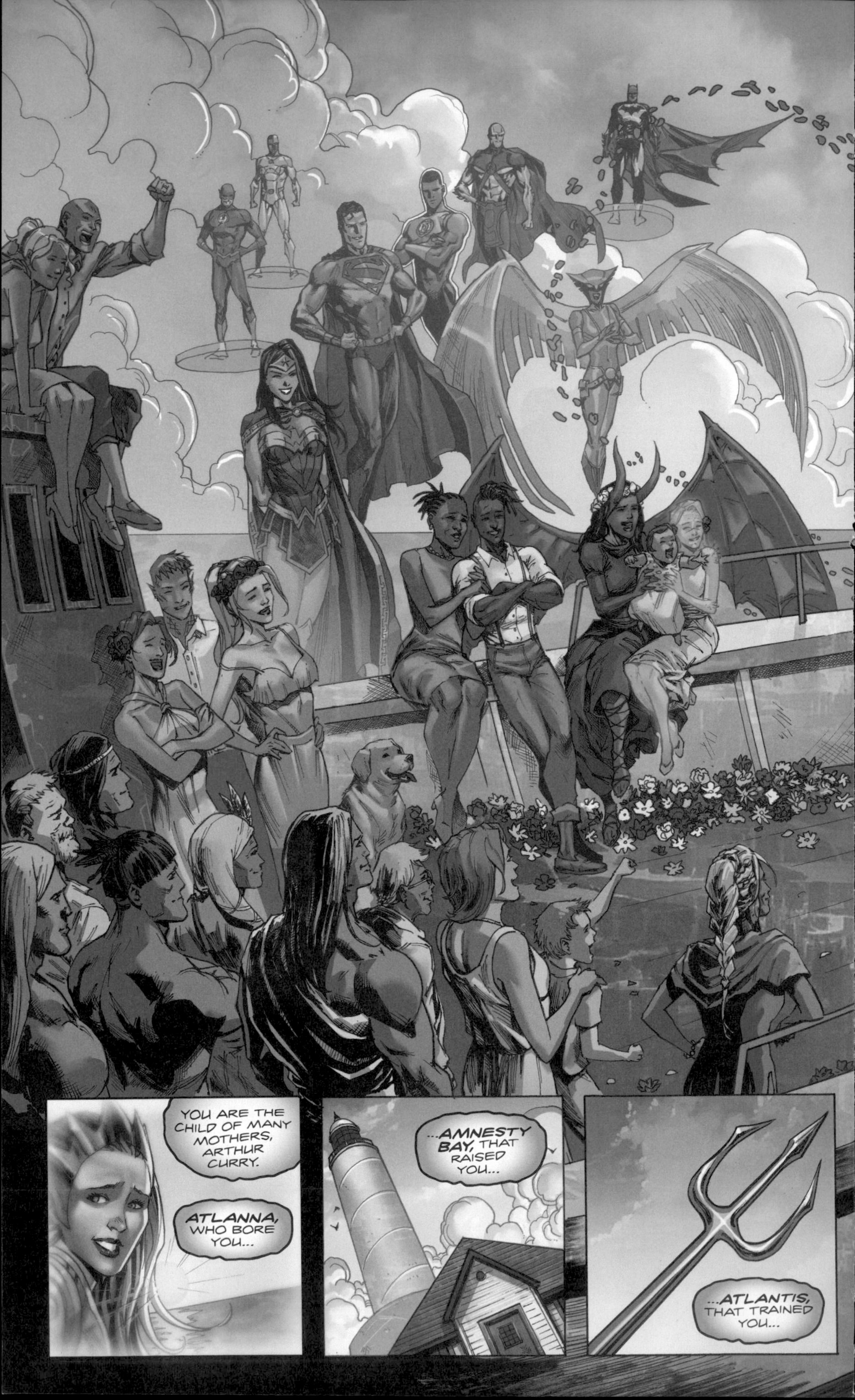
YOU ARE THE CHILD OF MANY MOTHERS, ARTHUR CURRY.
ATLANNA, WHO BORE YOU...
...AMNESTY BAY, THAT RAISED YOU...
...ATLANTIS, THAT TRAINED YOU...

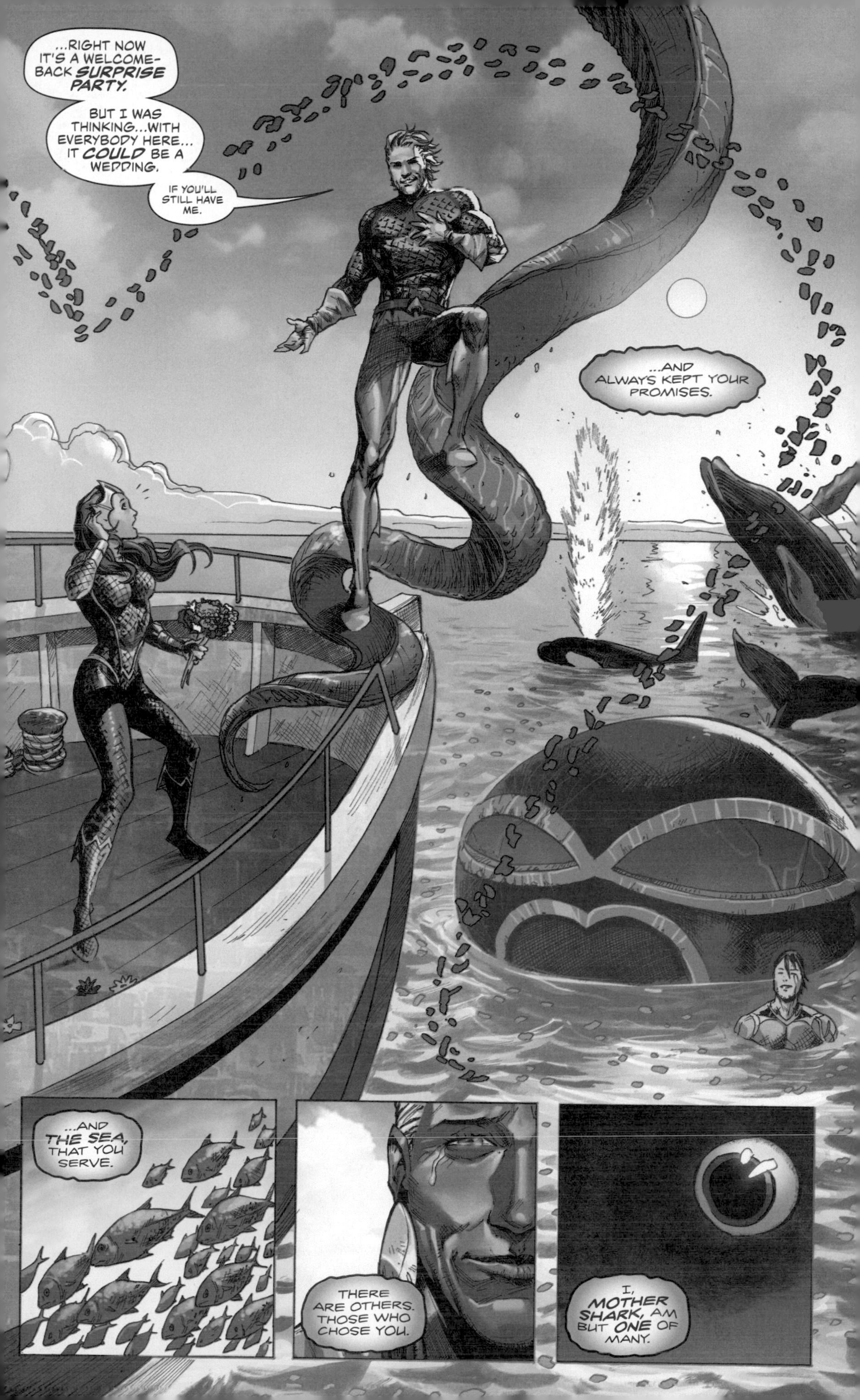
...RIGHT NOW IT'S A WELCOME-BACK SURPRISE PARTY.
BUT I WAS THINKING...WITH EVERYBODY HERE... IT COULD BE A WEDDING.
IF YOU'LL STILL HAVE ME.
...AND ALWAYS KEPT YOUR PROMISES.
...AND THE SEA, THAT YOU SERVE.
THERE ARE OTHERS. THOSE WHO CHOSE YOU.
I, MOTHER SHARK, AM BUT ONE OF MANY.

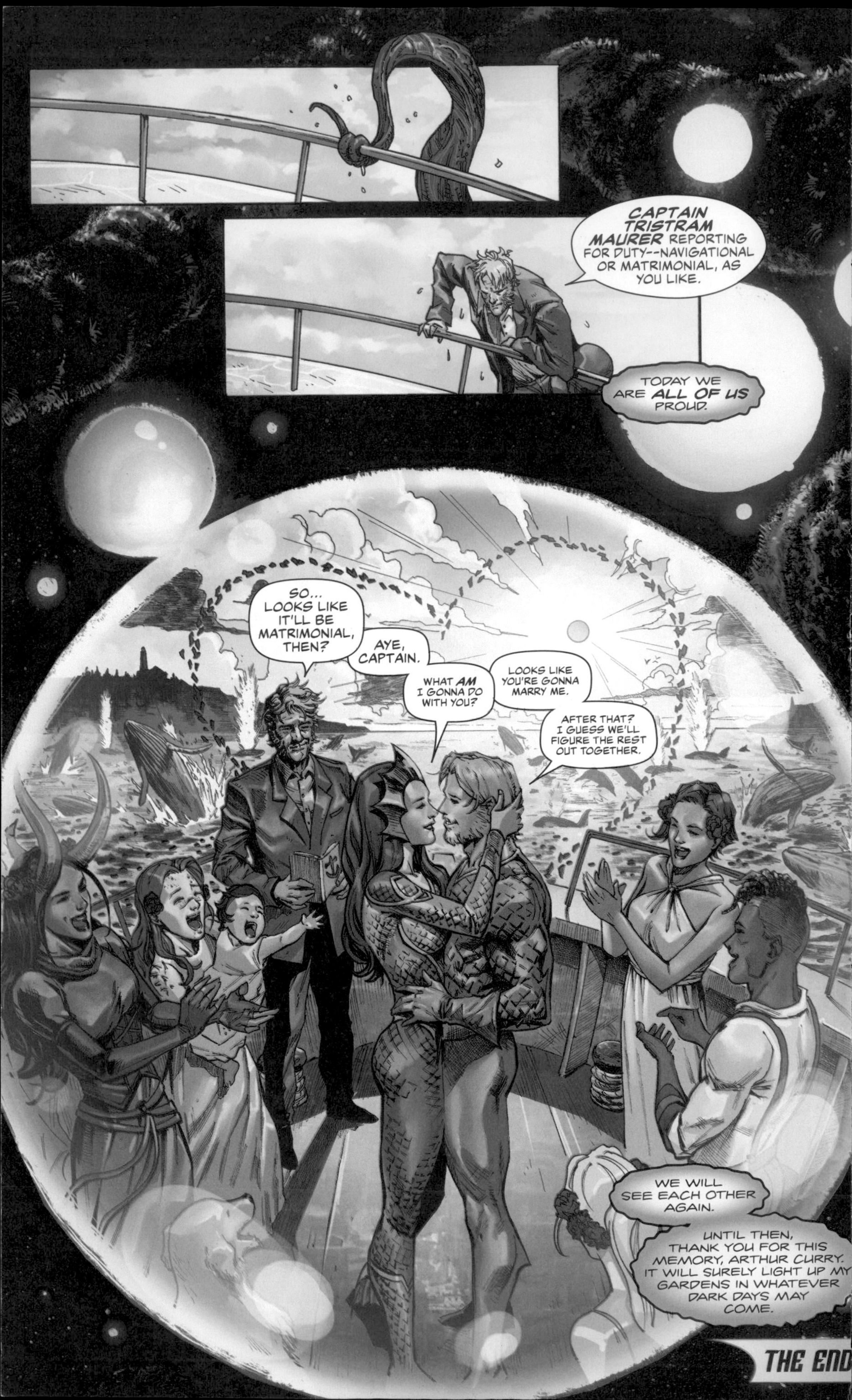
CAPTAIN TRISTRAM MAURER REPORTING FOR DUTY--NAVIGATIONAL OR MATRIMONIAL, AS YOU LIKE.
TODAY WE ARE ALL OF US PROUD.
SO... LOOKS LIKE IT'LL BE MATRIMONIAL, THEN?
AYE, CAPTAIN.
WHAT AM I GONNA DO WITH YOU?
LOOKS LIKE YOU'RE GONNA MARRY ME.
AFTER THAT? I GUESS WE'LL FIGURE THE REST OUT TOGETHER.
WE WILL SEE EACH OTHER AGAIN.
UNTIL THEN, THANK YOU FOR THIS MEMORY, ARTHUR CURRY. IT WILL SURELY LIGHT UP MY GARDENS IN WHATEVER DARK DAYS MAY COME.
THE END

PROCESS ART PAGES BY MIGUEL MENDONÇA

***AQUAMAN* #58 PAGE 3**

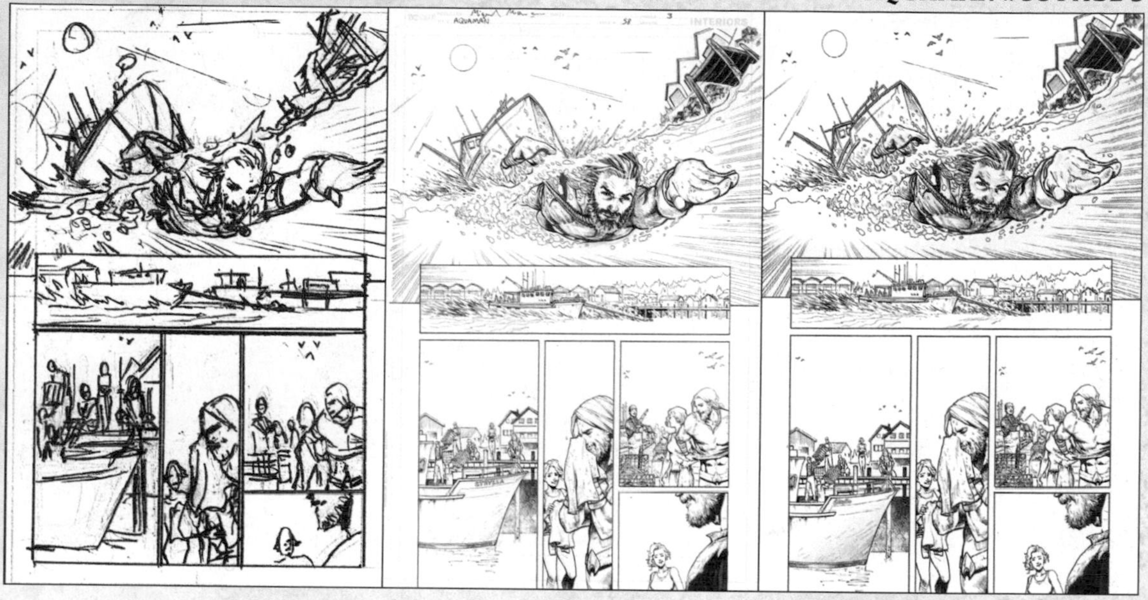

***AQUAMAN* #60 PAGE 1**

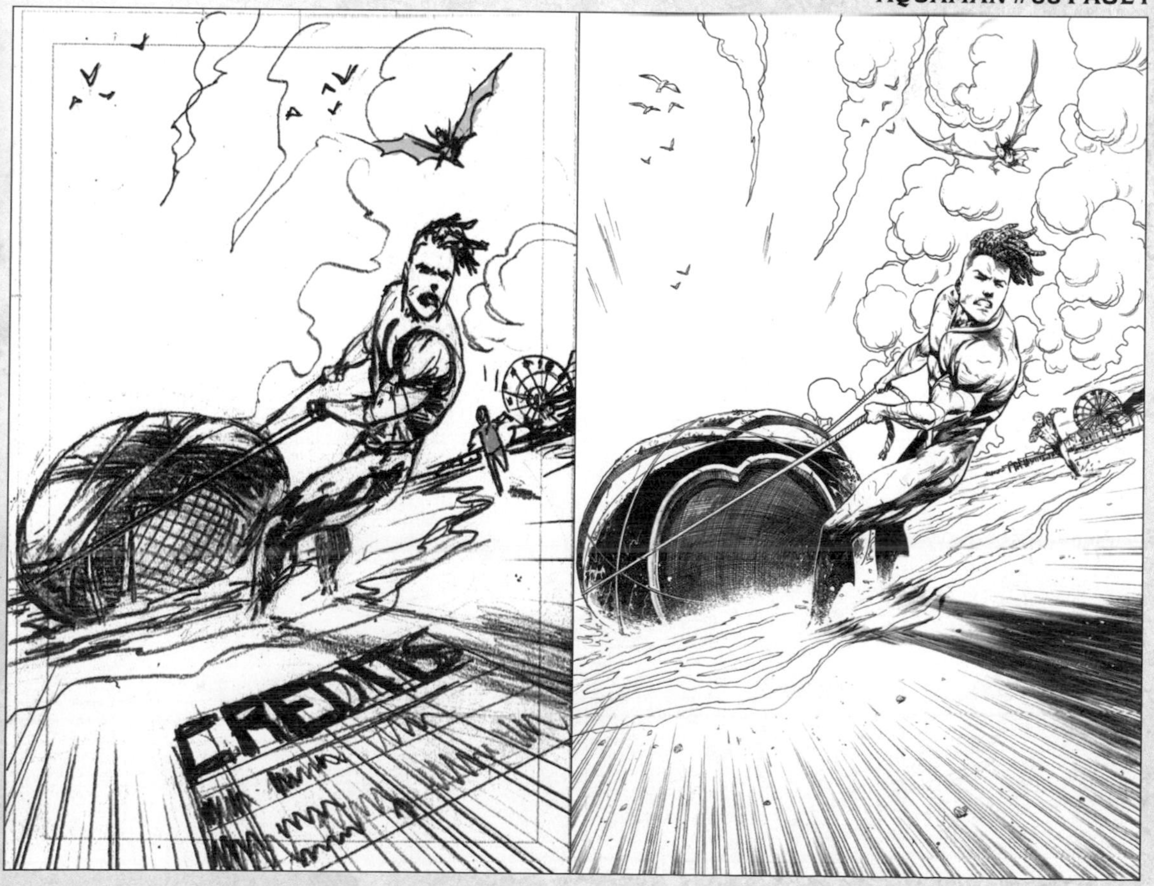
CREDITS

AQUAMAN #60 PAGES 18-19

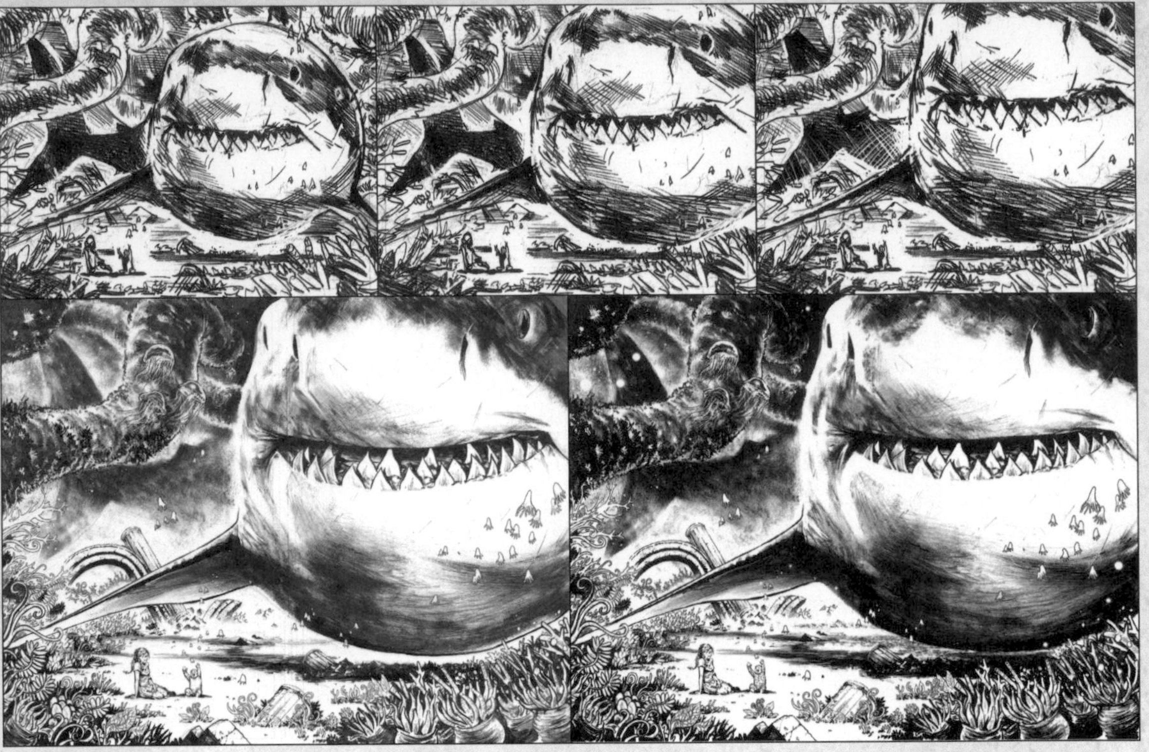

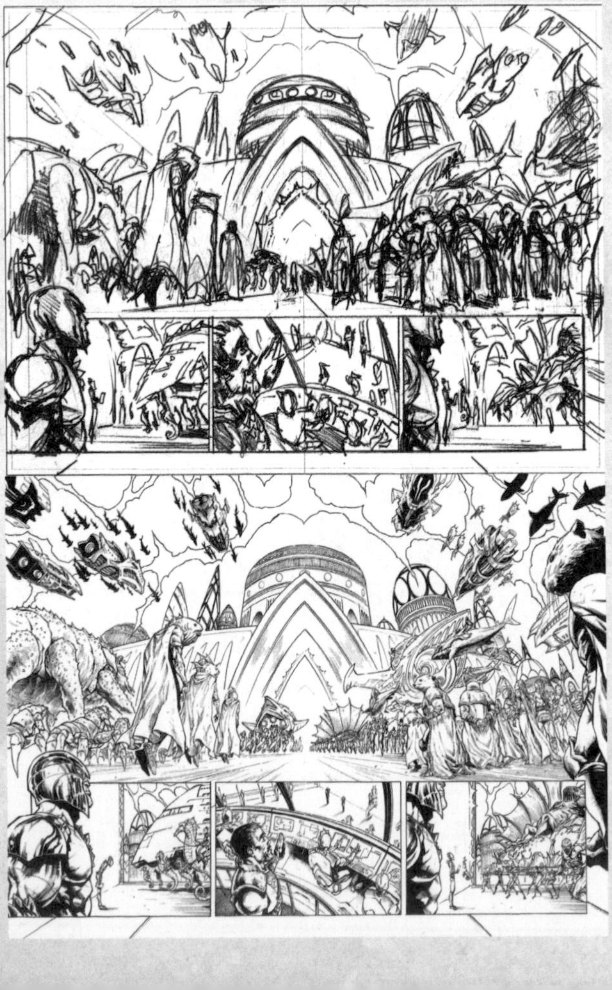

AQUAMAN #61 PAGES 4-5